Counter-Narratives

COUNTER-NARRATIVES

HISTORY, CONTEMPORARY SOCIETY, AND POLITICS IN SAUDI ARABIA AND YEMEN

EDITED BY

MADAWI AL-RASHEED AND
ROBERT VITALIS

COUNTER-NARRATIVES
© Madawi Al-Rasheed and Robert Vitalis, 2004

A version of chapter 6 first appeared in Karen Merrill, ed., *The Modern Worlds of Business and Industry: Cultures, Technology, Labor* (Brepols, 1999), and is reprinted with permission. Chapter 10 appeared in *Comparative Studies in Society and History*, Vol. 45, No. 4 (October 2003), and is reprinted with the permission of Cambridge University Press.

First published 2004 by
PALGRAVE MACMILLAN™
175 Fifth Avenue, New York, N.Y. 10010 and
Houndmills, Basingstoke, Hampshire, England RG21 6XS
Companies and representatives throughout the world

PALGRAVE MACMILLAN is the global academic imprint of the Palgrave Macmillan division of St. Martin's Press, LLC and of Palgrave Macmillan Ltd. Macmillan® is a registered trademark in the United States, United Kingdom and other countries. Palgrave is a registered trademark in the European Union and other countries.

ISBN 1–4039–6387–8 hardback

Library of Congress Cataloging-in-Publication Data
    Counter-narratives : history, contemporary society, and politics in Saudi Arabia and Yemen / edited by Madawi Al-Rasheed and Robert Vitalis.
        p. cm.
    Includes bibliographical references and index.
    ISBN 1–4039–6387–8
      1. Saudi Arabia—Social conditions. 2. Yemen—Social conditions. 3. Saudi Arabia—History. 4. Yemen—History. I. Al-Rasheed, Madawi. II. Vitalis, Robert, 1955–

HN663.A8C68 2003
306'.09533—dc22   2003058085

A catalogue record for this book is available from the British Library.

Design by Newgen Imaging Systems (P) Ltd., Chennai, India.

First edition: February 2004
10 9 8 7 6 5 4 3 2 1

Printed in the United States of America.

CONTENTS

List of Maps

Acknowledgments

There is a short but vital list of people we have to thank for help with this project. Imco Brouwer and Lotta Svantesson, our hosts and facilitators in Florence in March 2001. Ellis Goldberg, Halah Fattah, and Ibrahim al-Marashi, who also took part in the Florence workshop. David Faris and Ed Webb, of the political science department at the University of Pennsylvania, who have assembled and edited the final manuscript for publication. And we are grateful for the support of David Pervin, our editor at Palgrave.

NOTES ON CONTRIBUTORS

Isa Blumi has earned an M.A. in Political Theory from the New School for Social Research and is a Ph.D. candidate at the Joint History and Middle Eastern Studies program at New York University, where he is completing his dissertation on late Ottoman Yemen and Albania.

Gabriele vom Bruck is an independent scholar. She has taught at the London School of Economics and the School of Oriental and African Studies and writes on issues of gender, religious conflict, and elite transformation in the Yemen.

Sheila Carapico is Professor of Political Science at the University of Richmond, where she teaches courses in international political economy and Middle East politics. Author of *Civil Society in Yemen: The Political Economy of Activism in Modern Arabia* (London: Cambridge University Press, 1998) and numerous articles on Yemen, she is currently researching Western and international efforts to promote democracy in some Arab countries.

Abdulaziz H. Al-Fahad has a B.A. from Michigan State University (1979); an M.A., from the School of Advanced International Studies, Johns Hopkins University (1980); and a J.D., Yale Law School (1984). Mr. Fahad is a practising attorney in Riyadh, Saudi Arabia.

Gwenn Okruhlik is a Visiting Scholar at the University of Texas at Austin and a recent Fulbright Scholar in Saudi Arabia. Her recent publications include "Making Conversation Permissible; Islamism in Saudi Arabia" (in *Islam and Politics: A Social Movement Theory Approach*, Indiana University Press, forthcoming); "Networks of Dissent: Islamism and Reform in Saudi Arabia" in *Current History* (January 2002); and "Rentier Wealth, Unruly Law and the Rise of Opposition: The Political Economy of Oil States," *Comparative Politics* (April 1999). Her online essay on "Understanding Political Dissent in Saudi Arabia" (October 2001 at www.merip.org) has been widely disseminated.

Madawi Al-Rasheed is Senior Lecturer in Social Anthropology at King's College, University of London. She is specialist on Saudi Arabia, history, politics, and society. She has written *Iraqi Assyrian Christians in London: The Construction of Ethnicity* (The Edwin Mellen Press, 1998), *History of Saudi Arabia* (Cambridge University Press, 2002), and several articles in academic journals. She is currently working on Gulf transnational connections.

Guido Steinberg is a D.Phil., historian, and islamicist. An author of several publications on Saudi Arabian social and cultural history and politics, he is currently working on merchants and businessmen in the Arab East (nineteenth–twentieth centuries).

Robert Vitalis is Associate Professor of Political Science and the Director of the Middle East Center at the University of Pennsylvania. He is completing his second book, *America's Kingdom*, on the origins of the United States–Saudi Arabia special relationship.

Lisa Wedeen is Assistant Professor of Political Science at the University of Chicago. Among her publications are *Ambiguities of Domination: Politics, Rhetoric, and Symbols in Contemporary Syria* (University of Chicago, 1999) and "Conceptualizing Culture: Possibilities for Political Science" (*American Political Science Review*, December 2002). She is currently working on a book about political identifications in unified Yemen.

John M. Willis is a Ph.D. candidate in the departments of History and Middle Eastern Studies at New York University. His dissertation deals with the relationship between state rule and the geographical imagination in North and South Yemen.

Introduction

Madawi Al-Rasheed and Robert Vitalis

Images of Saudi Arabia and Yemen come into view in the capital cities of the West, in the commentaries of pundits, on the pages of newspapers, and most of all, on television screens, and then dissolve into the ether. Faint shadows of these images may remain for a while—outlines of oil wells and skyscrapers, of foreign ministers and intrepid travelers, of military bases and *madrasas*—until the next war or uprising or bombing refreshes them. Then our students, colleagues, and neighbors might glance at the maps that show up with breakfast, on the weekend, to look for Khobar, Riyadh, Dhahran, Aden, Hodeidah, Jibla, Hadhramaut, and Sanaa.

For teachers, such moments represent opportunities to provide context, give images depth, make places and people understandable, and move the discussion in a different direction. We do this, in large part, by introducing the latest scholarship, showing students what is at stake in the arguments among intellectuals, working through the logic of a piece of analysis and identifying its position in the lineage of research and writing on history, society, and politics. Yet, over the past decade or more there has been little to read and assign to our students. We need texts that challenge the myths that states tell about themselves, and commentaries that give voice to the vibrant communities of argument that animate political life.

Counter-Narratives offers a set of self-conscious and compelling revisionist accounts of life in two countries of the Arabian Peninsula, Saudi Arabia and Yemen. Our colleagues are self-conscious above all about moving research agendas in new directions, venturing into analytical *terra incognita*. They do so inspired in part by scholars of the region, Paul Dresch, Greg Gause, and John Peterson, and in part by students of other places and times, Patty Limerick, Jean and John Comaroff and Hanna Pitkin. What one will not find here is a recycling of the myths of Philby, the Arabian American Oil Company (Aramco), and their progeny. All of the authors believe there is indeed much to argue about these two places, not least, the grounds for bringing them together in a single volume. An ancient civilization with a well-established national identity, a unified Yemen came into being only in 1990. Saudi Arabia is a recent creation based on the unification of four distinct regions, Hijaz, Najd, Hasa, and Asir in 1932. In both countries, political culture and the evolution of the state had roots in theological interpretations derived from Islam. Wahhabism in Saudi Arabia and the Zaydi tradition in North Yemen combined with strong tribal loyalties and identities have shaped the character of the two societies. This has not been the full story, however. Historians who have written about the two countries remain preoccupied with a narrow range of phenomena—rulers and tribes—that are believed to continue to shape contemporary society and politics. Our authors widen the scope of historical analysis and give fuller play to the complexity of past and present. Identity and nation building, the multiplicity of historical agencies, and the ruptures of the past are some of the ways that complexity is wrestled with here.

A second means of engaging with complexity is through dialogue with scholars and others involved in the production of knowledge within the Arabian Gulf. This dialogue is important now, a moment when Western academic constructs have become part of a global language appropriated by both states and citizens. Combining our reading of well-known historical records with locally produced knowledge enriches this work and deepens intellectual engagement with indigenous actors and forces. Doing so is more of a necessity than a choice at this juncture in light of the proliferation of indigenously produced historical works that differ from the older conventional chronicles, which were never in short supply either in Yemen or Saudi Arabia. By the 1970s, both countries were home to their own historians and social scientists, trained in modern methods, engaged in studying manuscripts, archival records, and oral traditions.

Saudi Arabia and Yemen

The history of Saudi Arabian–Yemeni relations for many is a chronicle of antagonism, conflicts, and border disputes. Political scientists and specialists in international relations have charted the long conflict between the two countries in the twentieth century, from the first war of 1934 to the settlement of the border disputes in 2000.[1] This preferential option for conflict unfortunately steered analysis away from a longer and more complex history of the intertwining of peoples that needs to be recovered. As Detalle argues, "understanding the issues involved in the Saudi–Yemeni conflict also means taking into account the non-conflictual and less-conflictual elements of the relationship, i.e. those that involve state machinery, groups and individuals at the cultural, social, economic, and political levels."[2]

Intense social, economic, and political interactions have been a constant feature of relations between the two countries, even before the creation of the modern states. Yemeni and Hadrami merchants had long been established in the Hijaz before the oil era. A Yemeni by origin and Saudi by nationality until 1994, Usama bin Laden is certainly the most famous, but he is one personality among a circle of prosperous and successful merchants and businessmen who had been economically integrated in Saudi Arabia. The Yemeni Imams, descendants of the Hashemites trace their ancestry to Quraysh, the Prophet Mohammad's tribe in the heart of the Hijaz. Zaydi and Wahhabi *ulama* engaged in heated theological debates since the eighteenth century. More recently Wahhabi interpretations challenge the Zaydi tradition.[3] While the plans for greater Ottoman control over Yemen began in Istanbul, the Hashemite rulers of Hijaz were crucial for extending this control into Yemen. Yemeni immigrant workers were among the first to work in the oil fields and construction industry in Saudi Arabia. They were also among the first casualties of war after Saddam Hussein's invasion of Kuwait in 1990. Their remittances changed the landscape and lives of villages in the remote highlands of Yemen.

Mythologies of most tribes in Saudi Arabia emphasize descent from Qahtan, an epical ancestor whose homeland was nowhere but Yemen. The same place had always been a source of authenticity conjuring images of chivalry, authenticity, and Arab ancestry. Several descendants of Ibn Saud, the founder of the Kingdom, often had Yemeni mothers kidnapped in the 1930s and presented to him as concubines.[4] Their alleged beauty lured the monarch to seek wives amongst them. Yet, from the eighteenth century on, Yemen had also represented a frontier barrier to Saudi religious, political, and military expansion. Geography mattered, but so did social and cultural differences that were not easily overcome by early Saudi-Wahhabi adventurers. More recently, Yemen has been represented as a 'security threat' as a result of its 1962 revolution, with its mixture of nationalist and leftist rhetoric, which represented real challenges to the Saudi monarchy. The socialist regime in Aden did little to reduce the Kingdom's fears.[5]

Throughout the second half of the twentieth century, Saudi rulers poured huge sums of money into Yemen in an attempt to lure tribal sheikhs and revolutionary leaders to accept their hegemony. In the early 1960s, the Kingdom welcomed the deposed Imams of North Yemen and supported Yemeni royalists against Nasserite revolutionaries. During the 1970s and 1980s, Saudi Arabian leaders continued to involve themselves in Yemeni domestic politics. The perception of Yemen as a "source of trouble" has dominated policy toward this southern neighboring state. This tendency has been strengthened by recent political events. Since the Gulf War of 1990, a Saudi Islamist opposition has gathered momentum in the country.[6] Dissidents have found in Yemen a safe haven from which to launch attacks on the Kingdom.[7] And since September 2001, journalists have sought to tie the two places more tightly still, hunting for evidence of transnational terror networks.

With the exception of work on international relations and border disputes, the two countries have never inspired comparative study. This is perhaps due to the apparent and obvious differences that on the surface seem to deter any attempt at comparison. Saudi Arabia has evolved into a monarchy inspired by a religious interpretation far removed from Zaydi interpretations, while Yemen moved from Imamate to Republic, followed by political upheavals, civil wars, and finally unification. A mixture of pastoral nomadic tradition, oasis agriculture, and trade, Saudi society seemed far removed from Yemeni society whose livelihood depended more than anything else on agriculture. Tribalism could have been grounds for comparison and contrast given that this mode of social and political organization had been dominant in both countries since time immemorial. Scholars have highlighted the salience of tribal identity and politics in the region.[8] Yet this common denominator has failed to inspire a comparative research program. Such work became even more an unlikely endeavor for academic research agendas as the Saudi economy and society were transformed with the discovery of oil. Although Yemen does have a modest share of this natural resource, the impact of oil on the country's infrastructure could hardly be compared with that in Saudi Arabia. Under the rubric of the "rentier state," scholars have found grounds for comparing Saudi Arabia with other oil-producing countries in the Gulf, but not with Yemen.[9] Kiren Chaudhry is the great exception.[10] Otherwise, scholars have resisted the temptation to venture into a difficult and rugged terrain.

While acknowledging obvious contrasts in history, religious tradition, culture, and society, there are good grounds for bringing studies of the two countries together in a single volume. *Counter-Narratives* explores parallels and common themes in history and contemporary society that underlie the overwhelming differences between the two countries. Ten historians, political scientists, political economists, and social anthropologists offer new readings of the historical record and new interpretations of contemporary society and politics. While acknowledging the prevalence of different historical trajectories and sharp social distinctions, there remains a vast scope for discerning underlying forces, actors, and social and political themes that necessitate revision and reassessment.

New Historical Research and Agendas

In the twentieth century the dominant historical narrative in Saudi Arabia and Yemen has been the story of state formation. Yemen is distinguished by its ancient history, well-established identity, and Imamate tradition. Its long-standing proto-state distinguished the country from the majority of its neighbors. In contrast Saudi Arabia is a recent creation. Both countries, however, became the focus of increased interest by scholars in the 1970s, as a result of the rising importance of oil resources, especially those of Saudi Arabia. In Saudi Arabia the story of Ibn Saud's legendary unification of the country and the revival of the eighteenth-century reformist Wahhabi movement have been told countless times, using archival sources in London, accounts by diplomats and foreign officials stationed in the region, and the reports of travelers fascinated by the exotic. The writing of the history of Saudi Arabia could not be understood without reference to the historical context of its production, a context in which foreign actors and interests played an important role.[11] In a recent review of the literature of the history of the Arabian Peninsula, Peterson rightly points our attention to the shortcomings of previous historical accounts. "All too often, new writings consists of a rehash of stories already told, frequently relying on the same secondary sources, or of superficial country surveys prompted by the region's high profile over the last decade or two."[12]

In Yemen, the writing of history seems to be dominated by sources rooted in sectarian difference and outside views that do not correspond to what Yemenis thought and did. According to Dresch, "For the North [Yemen] we have predominantly Zaydi sources, which obscure much of Shafii life: for the South we have British views and local views that obscure what ordinary people thought: for Hadramawt a literature of learning and politics. Modern works, worst of all, work in modern terms . . . but there are no central archives from which to recover past forms of life save those of the British, whose views were a small part of what affects Yemenis." [13]

The prospect of writing a comprehensive history is rendered more difficult given that most local sources, archives, and chronicles are beyond the reach of both outside and indigenous scholars. The oil boom of the 1970s allowed states in the region to invest heavily in "capturing the past" by encouraging the printing of local manuscripts and publications. While states have their own political agendas guiding their efforts in what is often coined the "heritage industry" or the "invention of tradition," a positive outcome of the process has been the increased availability of at least some new sources. Today a history of the Arabian Peninsula based only on sources gathered in Istanbul, London, or Washington is work that other historians would recognize as flawed according to prevailing professional norms. It is now becoming common practice to combine the Western archive with local manuscripts and oral histories collected by scholars in the field. Indeed, the richest historical accounts of the past ten years are those that have drawn on a widened record set and that have made use of the rich oral tradition of the region, for example, oral poetry, narratives, and accounts of the past, often told in the context of remembering a bygone era. The value of doing so is demonstrated by our colleagues in *Counter-Narratives* who offer nuanced readings based not only on their explorations of the Western archive, but on their familiarity with the region, its local tradition, society, and culture.

In the opening chapter, Carapico invites scholars to reflect on the Arabian Peninsula as a whole and move away from research based on the assumptions of *realpolitik*. She rightly draws attention to the importance of investigating transnational phenomena that link the Peninsula, Africa, and the Indian subcontinent. She urges scholars to consider the ethnic and multicultural diversity of the Peninsula, which suggests a complex social history. Furthermore, she calls for a reconsideration of political contentiousness and opposition movements in the 1970s. Participation in these groups crossed national boundaries, drawing people from Yemen, Saudi Arabia, and Oman. While states in the region continue to patrol boundaries and apply strict definitions of citizenship to guard against "infiltration" and dispersal of national wealth, the interconnections between citizens of these states could not be overlooked by scholars or masked by beliefs about the uniqueness of one or another society, by separate historical trajectories, or by state rhetoric about authenticity. The interconnections between Saudi Arabia and Yemen involve more than border disputes and the clash of armies.

Two pieces on Saudi history follow, by Al-Fahad and Steinberg, that move away from the grand narrative of state formation to explore new topics drawn from their concern with local social and economic history. Al-Fahad challenges one of the most dominant narratives in the literature on the Saudi state, namely its description as the archetype of a desert-based Kingdom founded on tribal solidarity and *bedu* heritage. While he explains why the myth persists, he also lays out an alternative interpretation of state formation based on a close and expert reading of local archives and chronicles recently made available. He argues that the sedentary communities (*hadar*) of Najd, the central province of Saudi Arabia, were active agents in state formation, with the bedouin providing auxiliary military support. The demise of the *Ikhwan* in the 1930s, the truly bedouin element in the state, attests to the marginality of the tribal and bedouin dimension. Neither the Al Saud leadership nor the state envisaged by this leadership corresponded to bedouin aspirations. Steinberg draws attention to agents often displaced from historical accounts, namely the merchants and *ulama*, religious scholars of Najd, who can be fairly described as an ancient transnational elite with commercial transactions and religious knowledge bringing them into contact with societies as far as the Indian subcontinent and the Far East. Notwithstanding the material and intellectual deprivation dominant in the interior of Arabia throughout the nineteenth century, the *ulama* and merchants were the first intellectual–religious–commercial elite to have risen in Arabia. A congruence of culture and economy has shaped the intellectual history of Saudi Arabia until the present day. Like Al-Fahad, Steinberg shifts analysis away from the mighty and noble bedouins and tribes to the sedentary communities of the Arabian Peninsula, whose contribution to state formation, culture, and society has been overlooked for far too long.

Blumi and Willis both turn to Yemen and, like Al-Fahad, revisit the concept of the tribe, the analytical tool that has focused the minds of generations of social scientists and historians not only of Yemen but also of the region. Both scholars question the dominant narrative of tribe and tribalism as useful analytical tools and categories to explain the history of Yemen. Blumi proposes that the study of Ottoman North Yemen is a valuable exercise for investigating the process of identity formation, political and commercial networks, state-building, and nationalism. He argues against the application of tribal and sectarian models, as these would obscure diverse social relations. Willis traces the genesis of the "tribe" in British colonial discourse in the context of the Aden Protectorate. He offers a "historicized" account of the concept and shows how Aden was "made tribal" in British colonial discourse. Based on his reading of Imamic and colonial texts, he highlights the importance of the interaction between local practice and regimes of knowledge and power.

Vitalis shifts analysis to a corner of Saudi Arabia famous for its wealth, namely the Eastern Province where most of the oil fields are situated. He revisits the moment when Saudi Arabia was discovered by Aramco. While this moment was crucial for the transformation of Saudi Arabia, little has been written on the early years of the encounter between Arabian society and the foreign, mainly American managers and skilled employees. The existing canon provides abundant details on the oil concession, oil production, and the American "pioneers" but the economic and social history of Aramco's Saudi and other Arab workers is a history yet to be written, a project that needs to be tackled to understand not only early labor history in the main industry of the country, but also the nature of Saudi–American relations. Vitalis situates this vital relationship not only in the corridors of power and diplomacy, but also locates it on the ground, mainly in Aramco's reservations or camps, as they were known. More importantly, he dismantles the argument for Arabia's exceptionalism and documents the colonial-like turn in the 1940s and 1950s.

Contemporary Society and Politics

While previous historical research on the Arabian Peninsula has been preoccupied with the question of state formation, access to Arabian society has been a problem for the majority of social scientists working on contemporary Issues.[14] Yemen has allowed a substantial number of foreign fieldworkers and ethnographers to conduct grass-root research, but Saudi Arabia has been all but inaccessible for foreigners, especially social anthropologists. Over the last decade, this has been slowly changing, partly because Arabian societies have been drawn into globalization and partly because of economic imperatives necessitating greater openness. States in the region are under scrutiny by the international community in an age of increased communication and contact. One effect of the Gulf War of 1990–91 was the acceleration of the process. Understanding contemporary Peninsula societies is now an agenda of the states, citizens, and outside observers. While Yemen had a long history of attracting foreign tourists to its ancient treasures, it came as a surprise when in 2000 Saudi Arabia initiated a program to encourage tourism in a country not used to an open door policy.

Al-Rasheed and Okruhlik highlight the importance of historical narratives initiated by the Saudi state in its quest for legitimacy, nation-building, and consolidation of identity and heritage. In a society unknown for elaborate festivities and spectacle, the centennial celebrations in 1999, marking 100 years of Saudi rule, were staged to impress not only Saudi citizens but also the international community. The state mobilized its resources in an attempt to consolidate a unity between rulers and subjects, to glorify its pioneering role in modernization, and renew allegiance to the leadership (Al-Rasheed). Similarly, opening the country for a limited number of tourists is part of Saudi Arabia's attempt to accommodate global capitalism with forging a national identity (Okruhlik). Both chapters argue that the process of fixing national identity and allegiance by controlling imagination, representation, and experience does not proceed without challenges, contradictions, and contestation. Saudi Arabia's attempt to control the symbolic representations of the nation, its past, and heritage is bound to generate counter-narratives, challenging voices, and dissent. Thanks to increased literacy, education, and exposure to sources of knowledge beyond state control, Saudis are no longer passive recipients of official narratives. They are more experienced and articulate in producing their own versions of "being Saudi."

The question of identity is taken up in vom Bruck's chapter on the *Sadah*, the deposed religious and political elite of North Yemen. The introduction of the notion of citizenship by the Republican regime in Yemen after 1962 was meant to transcend identities based on descent, kinship, and prestige of birth. Faced with a systematic onslaught on their heritage, past privileges, and particularistic history, the Sadah responded by mobilizing their memory, redefining their position in society, and adapting to new circumstances, a process with its own cycle of trauma, alienation, and healing. The Sadah's biographies not only shed light on this Yemeni elite but can also offer ample comparative perspective on other deposed groups in the region where similar political changes, purges, and upheavals have been recurrent themes.

Wedeen concludes the book with a close and counterintuitive reading of three events in the aftermath of Yemeni unification in 1990. Her work suggests that democratic practices may exist because a state is weak and effective connection to nationness only mildly constraining. Experiences of moral panic may be just as effective as, or even more effective than, spectacles in generating a sense of being a part of Yemen. Experiences of national belonging may actually be shared at those moments when people seek the state's authority and protection.

One of the commonalities that emerge in these studies is the concern of both Saudi Arabia and Yemen with questions of identity, belonging, and nation-building. These concerns seem to draw increased attention today. Saudi Arabia is constantly struggling with accommodating its allegiance to a particularistic version of Islam with rapid modernization and the forces of globalization. Accommodation, however, is bound to present challenges, ruptures, and uneasy social and political relations. Consolidating old identities with new ones produced under the influence of rapid change is bound to be an ongoing process, which draws on the past with the objective of "fixing" present loyalties and allegiances. Yemen faced serious historical challenges to its unified identity. Its old Zaydi heritage was denounced in the process of creating allegiances to the new nation-state. The recent unification of the country poses yet another challenge in a country that has been politically divided and fragmented.

We hope this volume clears some space in the future for explicit comparative study of Saudi Arabia and Yemen, taking us beyond the history of boundary conflicts and armed intervention. Our analytical maps from the oil era create a "Gulf": one set of "rentier" states and societies linked by production of a commodity for the world market, and, beyond its borders, an outland called Yemen, which, in reality, is deeply entangled in the processes of economic and social transformation.

Notes

1. Saeed M. Badeeb, *The Saudi-Egyptian Conflict over North Yemen 1962–1970* (Boulder, CO: Westview Press, 1986); F. Gregory Gause, *Saudi-Yemeni Relations. Domestic Structures and Foreign Influence* (New York: Columbia University Press, 1990).

2. Renaud Detalle, ed., *Tensions in Arabia: The Saudi-Yemeni Fault Line* (Baden-Baden: Nomos Verlagsgesellschaft, 2000), 52.

3. Sheila Weir, "A Clash of Fundamentalisms: Wahhabism in Yemen," *Middle East Report* 204 (1997), 22–6.

4. Joseph Kechichian, *Succession in Saudi Arabia* (New York: Palgrave, 2001).

5. Fred Halliday, *Arabia Without Sultans* (London: Penguin, 1974); Paul Dresch, *A History of Yemen* (Cambridge: Cambridge University Press, 2000).

6. Madawi Al-Rasheed, "Saudi Arabia's Islamic Opposition," *Current History* 95 (1996), 16–22.

7. Mamoun Fandy, *Saudi Arabia and the Politics of Dissent* (Houndmills: Macmillan Press, 1999).

8. Paul Dresch, *Tribes, Government and History in Yemen* (Oxford: Clarendon, 1989); Donald Cole, *Nomads of the Nomads: The Al Murrah Bedouin of the Empty Quarter* (AHM Publishing, 1975); Lancaster, *The Rwala Bedouin Today* (Cambridge: Cambridge University Press, 1981); Steve Caton, *Peaks of Yemen I Summon: Poetry as Cultural Practice in a Yemeni Tribe* (Berkeley: University of California Press, 1990).

9. F. Gregory Gause, *Oil Monarchies: Domestic and Security Challenges in the Arab Gulf States* (New York: Council of Foreign Relations, 1994); Michael Herb, *All in the Family: Absolutism, Revolution, and Democracy in the Middle Eastern Monarchies* (New York: State University of New York Press, 1999).

10. Kiren Chaudhry, *The Price of Wealth: Economies and Institutions in the Middle East* (Ithaca: Cornell University Press, 1997).

11. J. Kelly, *Arabia, the Gulf, and the West* (New York: Basic Books, 1980).

12. J.E. Peterson, "The Arabian Peninsula in Modern Times: A Historiographical Survey," *American Historical Review* 96 (1991), 1435–49, esp. 1436.

13. Dresch, *History in Yemen*, xiii.

14. Gwenn Okruhlik, "From Imagined Scholarship to Gendered Discourse: Bringing the Peninsula in from the Periphery," *Middle East Report* 204 (1997), 36–7; Dresch, *History in Yemen*.

Chapter 1

Arabia Incognita: An Invitation to Arabian Peninsula Studies

Sheila Carapico

Between Africa and Asia lies a subcontinent that appears clearly on maps but only indistinctly in Western journalism and scholarship about the Middle East. Known to earlier orientalists and modern cinema fans as "Arabia," the land of sand and shrine, the Peninsula is nowadays often erroneously referred to as "the Gulf," the sea of oil. A vast land area is thereby reduced to a narrow slice of the Gulf coast, a rather curious place where according to most representations atavistic tribalism and Islamic conservativism thrive alongside ultramodern globalism. Only rarely do we step back to look at the whole of the Arabian Peninsula.

This chapter explores the contours of the Arabian Peninsula at the turn of the millennium, which turned out to be on September 11, 2001. I attempt to look beyond the oil wells and shopping malls of the Gulf, on the one hand, and the mythic figure of the desert tribesman, on the other, to see the whole Peninsula, from the Persian Gulf to the Red Sea and the Indian Ocean—in its commonalities, its dualism, its diversity, and its contradictions. My purpose is to invite scholars to recognize the Peninsula as a subregion of the Arab world, comparable to North Africa (the *Maghrib*), the Nile Valley, and the Arab East (the *Mashriq*), a large area with a significant population and distinctive, shared, yet varied cultural and historical experiences. This means, among other things, bridging the gap between Gulf Studies and Yemeni Studies in the hopes of finding in the whole something missing from separate examination of its parts; and getting past the myth of Arabian isolationism especially by looking at deep and abiding connections to Asia and Africa. Perhaps by considering the Arabian

Peninsula in terms unfettered from standard nation-building narratives and exclusivist citizenship criteria we can gain new insights into the political economy and culture of twentieth and twenty-first century Arabia, and perhaps by recognizing the Peninsula as an Arab subculture with often overlooked Indian Ocean and Red Sea connections we can understand more about the "Middle" East and its position in the world. But this chapter has much more modest, descriptive ambitions to map out some general parameters.

The Peninsula

As the maps in this chapter illustrate, Arabia is almost an island, surrounded by water and sand. Egypt, Sudan, and the Horn of Africa lie to the west across the narrow Red Sea. Arabia's southwestern tip, the Bab al-Mandab, almost touches the Horn of Africa. Southern Arabia faces the Gulf of Aden, the Arabian Sea, and the Indian Ocean, only a short sail to Pakistan and India or Zanzibar and Kenya. To the east it overlooks the Persian Gulf and the Gulf of Oman. Its easternmost point at the Straight of Hormuz is very near historical Persia, now Iran. To the north, across a desert renowned since Roman times for its trade caravans, Arabia meets Mesopotamia and historic Palestine, with the Mediterranean and Europe beyond. Like any island, and throughout recorded history, Arabia was both cut off from and connected to the rest of the world by sand and water. Its position at the intersection of the European, Asian, and African continents made it a natural crossroad already in antiquity. The spread of Islam from Mecca and Medina across the Peninsula and thence to large parts of Africa, Asia, and southern Europe was the single greatest moment of Arabian influence on the rest of the world, but not an isolated instance.

In times past, as maps 1.1 and 1.2 reproduced here indicate, most of the population clustered along the western edge of the Peninsula, between the mountains and the Red Sea. South of the Tropic of Cancer (which cuts the Peninsula almost in half) mountain-trapped Indian Ocean breezes created Arabia's most hospitable environment for crops, livestock, and people. Fabled home of the Queen of Sheba and the Maji, famed for its frankincense and later its coffee, this zone was known to the Romans and later to European cartographers as *Arabia Felix*, in contrast to the *Arabia Deserta* of the north and east (see map 1.1). Several ancient cities flourished and died in this once-verdant region, their remains subsequently covered by sand. Other towns endured over the centuries, or emerged in modern times, as centers of religious scholarship or of trade.

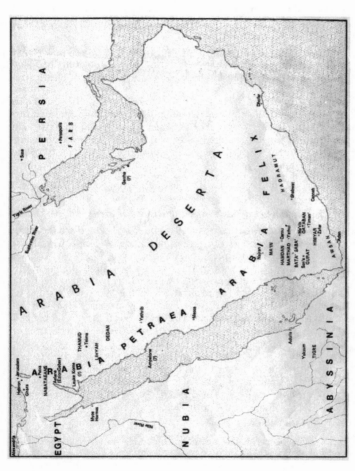

Map 1.1 Ancient Arabia

Source: Kamal Salibi, *A History of Arabia* (Delmar, N.Y.: Caravan Books, 1980), p. 42.

Map 1.2, drawn by Herman Moll in 1712, depicts "desert" and "happy" Arabia. Moll's rendering clearly indicates the higher density of named settlements in the west–southwest reaches of the Peninsula, especially the temperate mountainous regions overlooking the Red Sea down near the Indian Ocean. Also clearly visible is the north–south dotted line of towns that links Jerusalem with south Arabian ports facing the Arabian Sea and the Indian Ocean, a long string of trading posts down the western side of the Peninsula. Note also the seafront location of the more widely spaced towns of eastern Arabia, all facing outward.

Arabian urban development paled in comparison with that of grand imperial cities like Istanbul, Cairo, and Baghdad; or cosmopolitan Mediterranean towns like Beirut or Alexandria; or Jerusalem, the intersection of Arabia and Europe. According to population estimates on a detailed, full-color Century Atlas of 1897 map (not reproduced here) entitled "Part of Turkey in Asia, Arabia, Oman and Aden," the Arab capitals of Cairo, Damascus, Beirut, and Baghdad had populations of over 100,000. In the Peninsula, by contrast, only Mecca, the nearby Red Sea port of Jiddah, and Basra on the Persian Gulf coast had over half that many inhabitants. Sana'a, Aden, and Muscat were all towns with about 25,000–50,000 people each. So there were two Gulf cities, Basra and Muscat; two on the Red Sea, Jiddah and Aden; and two religious centers, Mecca and Sana'a, inland from the Red Sea. With four cities, dozens of smaller named towns, and unmarked thousands of villages, the west–southwest region, especially the highlands, sustained the highest population densities. All settlements were discernibly connected into intercontinental oceanic and/or caravan trade.

National boundaries had not appeared by the end of the eighteenth century, but neither were colonial borders drawn. In 1897 the whole Peninsula was marked ARABIA in large caps: regions identified in smaller type were the Hijaz stretching from the Sinai Peninsula to Jiddah and Mecca, Asir south of that, and then Yemen; Hadramawt in the south-central part of the Peninsula; OMAN and al-Hasa in the east along the Persian Gulf, and the Najd in central Arabia. Of these, only Oman was marked in large letters as a nation on this particular late-eighteenth-century rendering. Different cartographers varied the identification, typeface differentiations, and placement of these regional labels; there was great variation in the spelling of the names of towns and localities.

Arabia has its own vernaculars, traditions, and traits. Arabian Arabic is distinguished from Levantine and African dialects by pronunciation of all the consonants and a tendency toward classical constructions as in *Li madha* and *ghadan*. These permeate both everyday speech and characteristic poetic forms. Among the obvious still-thriving customs of the Peninsula are the *majlis*, where men sit on cushions in a rectangular room

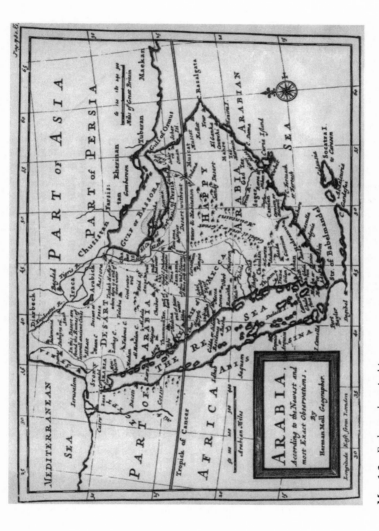

Map 1.2 Early modern Arabia

Original source: Moll, H., *Arabia* (1712). Copied from: G.R. Tibbetts, *Arabia in Early Maps, a Bibliography of Maps Covering the Peninsula of Arabia Printed in Western Europe from the Invention of Printing to the Year 1751* (Naples, New York, and Cambridge: Falcon–Oleander, 1978), p. 130.

or tent to counsel the host on business or politics. Virtually all Arabian men wear moustaches if not beards; for reasons ecological as well as religious, women (and men too) have almost always covered their heads outdoors. Until quite recently, caravans connected weekly markets throughout the Peninsula in a concentric network of interlocking circles. Tribal organization, values of honor, and the concept of "protected" holy sites are more or less shared throughout Arabia. In many ways, then, the people of the Peninsula "speak the same language." Shared ecology, history, and even identity are part of an Arabian commons. Contemporary border guards, passport authorities, and national icons notwithstanding, state-centered definitions of who is Saudi, Omani, Yemeni, or Sharjahi are of only shallow lineage.

In terms of religion the Peninsula is both unified by Islam and divided along sectarian lines. With only handfuls of Jews remaining in a few villages and towns since the founding of the state of Israel, and no indigenous Christian minority, Arabia is Muslim: it is the birthplace of Islam, home to its holy cities of Mecca and Medina. Such homogeneity notwithstanding, the Peninsula also hosts considerable doctrinal diversity in the form of several distinct schools of thought whose philosophies of governance differ from one another and from the great Islamic empires centered in Damascus, Baghdad, and Cairo. Both Shi'a and Sunni schools of Islam are represented. Several Arabian denominations each put forward a unique, plausible historical and doctrinal claim to authenticity based on propinquity and/or ancestry to the Prophet, his family, or his disciples. Their interpretations of law, history, and governance vary considerably. The Bahraini and Hasawi Shi'a of the Gulf Coast, for geo-historical reasons, shared many ideas and religious customs with the Persian Twelvers whose practices are anathema to some other Arabian sects. Khawarij Ibadis established one sort of imamate in what is now Oman. Zaydi Shi'as, who appear to many observers as much like Sunnis as they are like Twelvers, instituted a different kind of imamate in northern Yemen. Yet like the Hijaz, both Oman and Yemen had large Sunni populations. Innumerable Shaf'ai Sunni sultans built palaces along the Gulf of Aden, in Hadramawt, Abyan, and Lahij; saints' tombs dotted the landscape. Always a minority sect, Isma'ilis inhabited ghetto enclaves in the mountains of Najran and Yemen, internally isolated perhaps but not quite cut off from the Agha Khan's transnational establishment. Wahhabis displaced some but not all customary religious ideas and practices when they mastered the vast, unevenly populated landmass that is now the Kingdom of Saudi Arabia including the holy city of Mecca. But considerable diversity in doctrine and ritual persists.

The Peninsula's experience with European imperialism was very different from the Arab Mediterranean encounter, much less the conquest of

Africa and India. Whereas North Africa, the Nile Valley, and the Mashriq experienced firsthand Ottoman, British, and French imperialism, only a few coastal districts of Arabia were subject to direct foreign domination for very long. Whereas cityscapes and legal systems were redrawn and rewritten by outsiders in the Arab north, in Arabia this was not the case. Whereas European wars spilled over into North Africa and the Holy Land repeatedly throughout history, for Arabians the Crusades and two world wars were distant battles that tended, if anything, to boost trade. Seaside Portuguese forts and trading stations were short-lived. Ottoman influences on law, governance, and architecture in the Arab Mediterranean drifted south from historic Palestine along the Red Sea coast into the Hijaz, Asir, and Yemen, and from Basra along the upper Persian Gulf coastal region of al-Hasa. But the Turkish legacy was marginal in comparison with Syria or Egypt. Istanbul's Hejaz railroad project was never completed. When the Ottoman Empire was carved up after World War I, the League of Nations mandate system authorized France and Britain to administer the Fertile Crescent region where they helped establish contemporary Syria, Lebanon, Israel/ Palestine, Jordan, and Iraq. But the Peninsula, never thoroughly Ottomanized, and thus not among the spoils of its defeat, escaped the mandate system.

This is not to say that Arabia escaped the effects of Western imperialism entirely (see map 1.3). Great Britain established a post at Aden, a small town astride a natural harbor overlooking the mouth of the Red Sea, in 1839. During the next several decades Ottoman influence in North Yemen, the opening of the Suez Canal in 1869, the politics of British rule in India, and London's interests in the Persian Gulf all increased Aden's strategic value. Eventually the port city became the only full-fledged British Crown Colony in the whole Arab world, gaining independence only in 1967. Elsewhere in Arabia, the British Empire exercised indirect influence through treaties and arrangements that helped solidify the powers of local shaykhs, sultans, and amirs along the Arabian Sea and Persian Gulf coasts. Although Britain played a probably crucial role in the formation and boundary-ing of states of the twentieth century, its arrangements were indirect, limited to foreign and military affairs, and administered partly via India. London exercised military hegemony vis à vis other world powers until the 1960s when its forces withdrew from Kuwait and then Aden, intervening as kingmaker now and then, policing "pirates" of the Trucial Coast that resisted the Royal Navy. In the petroleum era, Britain and America have shared military protection of Arabian oil monarchies, with the United States taking the lead since the oil price crisis of the 1970s prompted the Carter Doctrine.

Notwithstanding the role of Anglo-American oil companies and armed forces in the international relations of the subregion, then, historically the

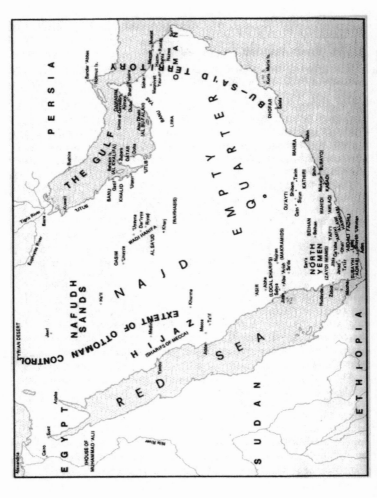

Map 1.3 Early twentieth-century Arabia, "Arabia on the Eve of the Ottoman–British Partition" (ca. 1903)

Source: Kamal Salibi, *A History of Arabia* (Delmar, N.Y.: Caravan Books, 1980), p. 186.

Arabian Peninsula absorbed fewer European languages, ideas, and elements of material culture than most of its Arab, African, and Asian neighbors. Apart from often lonely individual Agents or Residents, and again unlike the Arab north, India, or coastal Africa, few Westerners made homes anywhere in Arabia. No city had a real European quarter. Even in colonial Aden, a major port and naval installation, there were hardly any actual settlers; it was no grand colonial city for English families but rather a barren collection of Arab, African, and South Asian communities clustered around the harbor and the military base. Only later did oil companies set up exclusive suburban-style camps off in the erstwhile Empty Quarter to give foreign oil workers an extraterritorial lifestyle apart from Arabian society. Officer training and petroleum business surely required English as a second language in the Gulf, but on the whole colonial education scarcely took root. Foreign missionaries were medical practices that did not run Christian schools, proselytize, or win more than a few converts. So Arabic and Islam remained unsullied. The term "post-colonial" as applied to Africa and Asia had little resonance in Arabia beyond the polyglot immigrant workforce of Aden harbor who momentarily embraced Marxist (or Maoist) ideas about revolution.

Eventually the petroleum industry would transform eastern Arabia in many ways, bringing unimagined wealth especially to royal families, drawing immigrants from abroad, and revolutionizing consumption patterns. But because companies utilized imported labor, capital, and technology to pump oil onto ocean-bound tankers, and because Arabian oil fields were mostly desert or offshore sites remote from population centers, the industry did not disrupt underlying property, labor, and social relations in the way that plantation farming, diamond mining, or urban planning schemes remade colonial societies elsewhere.

In terms of Western knowledge, too, whereas the Mediterranean region and the Tigris–Euphrates basin had been thoroughly surveyed, mapped, and excavated, Arabia was, in clichéd terms, veiled against the Western gaze. Much of what we know about Arabia through the middle of the twentieth century still comes from personal diaries of intrepid travelers like Gertrude Bell, St. John Philby, Wilfred Thesiger, Sir Richard Burton, Freya Stark, and Amin Rihani. Their diaries and pictures depict a primitive and exotic land, untamed.

Limited direct European cultural penetration should not be confused with detachment from the rest of the world, however. Throughout its history Arabia was a hub of international travel and visitation, with pilgrims and migrants and immigrants from and to Asia and Africa. Persians and East Africans always crossed over, as did Arabs in the other direction. Arabian merchants traded northward to Iraq and Palestine, westward across

Map 1.4 The Arabian Sea

Original source: Langren, H. *Orae maritimae Abexiae* (1596). Copied from: G.R. Tibbetts, *Arabia in Early Maps, a Bibliography of Maps Covering the Peninsula of Arabia Printed in Western Europe from the Invention of Printing to the Year 1751* (Naples, New York, and Cambridge: Falcon–Oleander, 1978), p. 55.

the Red Sea, eastward with Persia and Asia Minor, and seaward with India and Southeast Asia.

Some travelers were not merely adventurers and traders but colonists and missionaries "in their own right." Omani princes and princesses commanded palaces and slaves in Zanzibar, Lamu, and elsewhere along the East African coast. Hejazi, Asiri, and Yemeni entrepreneurs founded companies in Asmara and Port Sudan. Ordinary Arabian migrants intermarried and intermingled all along the Swahili coast, contributing much to its linguistic, genetic, and material character. Sufi orders as far away as Senegal and Mali trace their roots to Arabia. In the other direction there were Hadrami administrators in the Nizam of Hyderabad, on the Indian subcontinent, and preachers elsewhere. Hadrami missionaries settled extensively in what is now Indonesia, where their descendents remain prominent in modern political, economic, and cultural life. Arabian investments and newspapers appeared in Singapore, Jakarta, and South Africa. A great deal of social, political, religious, intellectual, and legal history remains to be written on these overseas activities, including but also beyond their slave trading. But we already know that families from the Peninsula established themselves abroad as rulers, teachers, missionaries, and merchants, diffusing Arabic words, concepts, and customs along with Islam throughout the vast Indian Ocean basin. In some parts of Africa and Asia, colonization is said to have begun with the Arabs.

Cultural and even political influences also flowed inward from abroad. Many of the traces of Arabian transnationalism are physical, linguistic, or material. The Red Sea coast or Tihama shares many features with the Swahili coast, among them conical mud-and-thatch huts arranged in outdoor corrals; colloquial use of a *mim* instead of a *lam* (as in *am-bab*); Abyssinian breeds of goats, cattle, and poultry; feminine dress featuring long colorful skirts and halter tops; and male apparel including a white wraparound skirt, white coat, and straw skullcap. Tihami people physically resemble East Africans. By the same token, along the southeast-facing coast there are many traces of Asia, from the human faces to the flight patterns of migratory birds to elements of material culture. Along the southern coast and indeed throughout southern Arabia many men wear a *futa*, a colorful Indonesian sarong. My Omani cookbook offers little in common with standard Mediterranean Arab fare, but instead describes foods from the Indian Ocean basin, rich with fish and flavored with curry; lentils are called *dal* (the Indian menu term) not *adas* (as in northern Arabic cuisine). Carved wooden doors and other embellishments reminiscent of the Indian subcontinent and Swahili Africa typify Arabian port cities. While compared with Mediterranean dialects Arabian Arabic remained relatively unsullied by European neologisms, loanwords and constructions were exchanged among Arabic, Persian, Pashtu, Urdu, Somali, and Swahili.

There must have been many political crosscurrents as well as material, genetic, and linguistic cross-fertilization. Aden's colonial government was administered via India and later from East Africa, thus filtering its colonial experience through other parts of the empire and facilitating the flow of people and ideas. Independently of any European intervention, Arabian travelers and settlers in the greater Indian Ocean region infused local politics in myriad ways yet to be systematically investigated. But there is ample anecdotal evidence. For instance, in the late 1870s, Dhufaris rallied around a religious leader from the mixed Arab community in India, and a nineteenth-century Ibadi revival in Oman derived much of its inspiration and intellectual leadership from Zanzibar. A politically significant Islamic League—cousin to a movement still active in Pakistani politics today—was founded in Aden in the 1940s by a subcontinent Muslim businessman. Some Aden revolutionaries adopted the Gandhi-esque hunger strike. A kind of Islamic identity connected to the Hadramawt was central to the Indonesian independence movement and still stirs loyalties and passions in contemporary Indonesia. A separatist identity rooted partly in ethno-religious, cultural, and economic ties to western Arabia stirred anti-Ethiopian passions in Eritrea; moreover the Eritrean Liberation Front found campsites in Yemen and cash subsidies in Saudi Arabia. And so forth. Apart from South Yemen, men and some women from the Peninsula experienced anticolonial, "third world" style politics not as a movement in their homelands but from their positions as landowners, merchants, and students in places like Singapore, Bandung, Cairo, Hyderabad, and Asmara.

The Gulf

American research agendas in the Arabian Peninsula have been so shaped by *realpolitik* and oil that instead of thinking in terms of the whole Peninsula, we typically refer to "the Gulf" (see map 1.5). The Gulf for the Persian Gulf can refer to the larger region including now-hostile Iran and Iraq, but also is often shorthand for the countries whose governments have joined the Gulf Cooperation Council (GCC), a pro-American political, economic, cultural, and security alliance comprised of Saudi Arabia, Kuwait, Oman, Bahrain, Qatar, and the United Arab Emirates. The Gulf is where American interests lie. The Gulf also refers to what Gause called the oil monarchies, and, by logical extension, to the citizen-subjects of those kingdoms. Within the territory governed by GCC governments— one of which, Saudi Arabia, covers well over half the Peninsula's land mass—the Gulf refers specifically to that part of eastern Arabia from which most Arabian crude is pumped and shipped. This Gulf has brand-new cities built and maintained by a large cadre of international labor migrants. Home to the U.S. Central Command, the Gulf is the zone whose stability the 1991 Kuwait War dubbed Desert Storm was fought to protect. And within the Arab world, the Gulf is indeed a zone of tranquility, order, and cleanliness. Even the searing heat and bitter dryness are mitigated by profligate air conditioning and green-gardening.

The Gulf has been constructed, in both image and concrete, by the GCC governments and their external clients. The GCC monarchies on the western edge of the Persian Gulf define themselves as a unique cultural subregion within the larger Arab and Islamic context. Their exceptionally strong cultural traditions are, according to the various official myths of the Gulf's dynasties, the values of the desert and of the Qu'ran, rendered icono-graphically in items such as the immaculate off-white *dishdasha*, stylized camel racing, miniature coffee cups, opulent gold jewelry, aqua-blue prayer rugs, and garish modernistic public art. Each GCC administration defines its own people and national character in special ways that verify the privi-leges conveyed via patrimonial lineage to ruling families and male citizens. So the people of the Gulf are the descendants of the Arabian founders of the modern Saudi and Kuwaiti and emirate states, including sons and daughters who may be part Asian or African; but not the "immigrants" whose numbers would otherwise overwhelm the "indigenous" population.

Imported or "alien" labor was indispensable to the physical fabrication of the Gulf. During the oil boom, veritable armies of Arabs, Asians, and Westerners flocked to the Gulf to share, as wage earners, as entrepreneurs, and as subcontractors, in its heretofore unimaginable wealth. Individual sojourners are temporary workers remitting their earnings to families in the countries to which they will eventually return. But defining them simply as temporary foreign migrants, as the Gulf governments must to insulate their national self-definitions, is also sociologically misleading on several counts. First, the purely endogenous view ignores the long-standing connections of Indian, Pakistani, Indonesian, Malaysian, and Philippine Muslims to the Peninsula—through Arabian ancestors, family names, and relatives; in the local histories of their communities; or in contemporary business connec-tions, labor contracts, and religious institutions. Second, the myth of Arabian endogamy renders the working class, who are the numerical major-ity in the Gulf cities and oil fields, politically irrelevant. Finally, the myth of exclusive descent from founding fathers of the GCC states fails to take into account the naturalization of scores of thousands of Yemeni entrepre-neurs and politicians who are immigrants, not migrants. From the 1960s through the 1990s Yemeni dissidents of various stripe—from sultans to socialists—have found political refuge in Saudi Arabia, Kuwait, Oman, or the Emirates. Whether for historical, political, or economic reasons, many individuals hold dual citizenship; many if not most Gulf families trace their lineage to Yemen; and many Yemeni families have Gulf kinfolk.

As scholars we are influenced by our own countries' economic and strategic interests in the Gulf and by the self-characterizations of the Gulf states to describe stability, predictability, and prosperity. Anglo-American governmental and corporate funding is available for academic centers, programs, conferences, and publications on the Gulf. If GCC states have tolerated, or even funded, Anglo-American scholarship, it has been under the rubric of "Gulf Studies," preferably economic and strategic studies utilizing aggregate data. Research and journalism are proscribed in various ways to inhibit the production of knowledge that might lead to questioning of the national myths or legitimizing narratives of contemporary governments. For all these reasons, too many scholars, both Western and Arab, accept at face value the notion that the Gulf, so utterly modern in many respects, is governed by "traditional" values of the "pure" desert-born Islamic and tribal culture embodied in the ruling dynasties of the Persian Gulf coast. In this Arabia, the players are merchants, kings, and bedouin. This sets the stage for the passage quoted by Al-Rasheed and Vitalis from Peterson's 1991 article: "All too often, new writing consists of a rehash of stories already told" . . . and fails to "move beyond the comfortable horizons of country studies and political analysis." Al-Rasheed and Vitalis add: "the basic narrative of state formation itself was not questioned."

Searching for a collection of Arabian Peninsula maps to study for this chapter, I came across a wonderfully produced full-color compendium of maps, cited earlier, entitled *The Gulf in Historic Maps 1493–1931*.[1] The editor, Sultan Bin Muhammad al-Qasimi, arranged chronologically a couple of hundred maps from his own collection featuring the Gulf. The original maps are cartographic masterpieces. Most were originally Arabian Peninsula maps; others depicted Persia, Asia, Asia Minor, or the Near East. On each extra large page is reproduced a miniature of the original map alongside an enlargement of the Gulf—from what is now Kuwait to what is now Oman, the body of water, and part of Iran. This rendering literally crops, squares, and enlarges the Gulf from the larger Peninsula, setting it apart, and situating it in the foreground. Few of the original European maps isolated or identified the Gulf as it is now known, so it is not simply a close-up. Whereas the cartographers drew the Peninsula, or Arabia, the modern map collector, identified as "the ruler of Shariqah," consciously chose to de-emphasize the original renderings in favor of a sharp-edged rectangular zone. Little more than a maritime subculture until the advent of the modern oil industry, this rectangular place has been depicted in countless maps published in newspapers, magazines, and books in the past several decades.

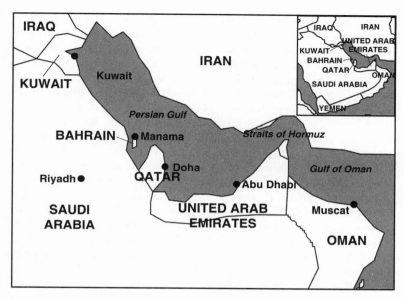

Map 1.5   The Gulf

Source: Raad Alkadiri, PFC.

Map 1.5 is an example of the latter, with the larger Peninsula shown as an inset. Depicting lower Iraq including the port city of Basra, the part of Saudi Arabia that includes Riyadh, northeast Oman, and more settlements in the Emirates and Qatar than in Iran, it enlarges the smallest city-states by blocking out most of Iran, Iraq, and Saudi Arabia. The repetition of this representation reinforces the separate identity of the Gulf states from the larger Peninsula or still larger Asia Minor.

Dualism

There is a reason why the Gulf is depicted separately, of course. Above and beyond the diversity of the Peninsula, the oil industry has shaped the Gulf as a global substation where international banks, five-star hotels, Ruby Tuesday's, and the Dubai Airport animate the local version of international capitalism. For the economy of the Gulf is highly extroverted. Little endures of a local economy once comprised of pearls, fish, lamb, leather, wool, ships, crafts, mud architecture, and weekly markets. What remains is mostly being reproduced offshore: for instance, "traditional" silver jewelry on sale in Oman consists largely of Indian knockoffs. Yet (and efforts at import substitution notwithstanding) actual consumption in the Gulf is comprised heavily of imported commodities: Indian hennas, Pacific foodstuffs, Japanese and Korean electronics, European leatherwear, American name-brands. Cities have sprung up where none existed before, while existing villages and markets were deserted, repositioned, and rebuilt from scratch. Some features of these newly assembled environments, like wide motorroads, huge parking lots, strip-mall commercial development, pansy gardens in traffic medians, all geared toward an oil-driven car culture, look a lot like Arizona or Florida. Other typical features of the Gulf, such as grandiose mosques, kitschy road-art, and fields of curiously camel-like oil pumps, apply exogenous materials and labor to the local culture and ecology. One striking feature of the Gulf is its multilingualism—Arabic is the language of the sociopolitical elite, but the streets are a polyglot of Urdu and other languages, and the *lingua franca*, needed even for ordinary shopping, is English.

The rest of the Peninsula is not like that. Whereas Gulf men uniformly wear each country's subtly distinguished *dishdasha* in shades of white unless the occasion calls for business suits, south of the Tropic of Cancer men don individualized, rough-and-ready outfits variously combining white robes, plaid futas, fatigues, sports jackets, assorted headgear, and side arms. In the Gulf the Arabian curved dagger is a public art icon, frequently cast larger-than-life; in Yemen the actual dagger is an item of everyday sartorial expression for many men. Whereas Gulf architecture is sleek and linear, Yemeni buildings are crooked and organic. Even new Yemeni construction features indigenous flourishes such as arched stained glass windows. Whereas Gulf streets are lined with lawns kept trim by Asian gardeners, Yemeni streets are strewn with garbage. What was once the coast of Desert Arabia is luxurious; Happy Arabia is now squalid. The Gulf imports labor from Yemen and other parts of the Third World; Yemen receives Horn of Africa refugees. Southern Arabians throng to the Gulf; few Gulf Arabs set foot in Yemen. The GCC states are aid donors, funding humanitarian relief and development projects in the poorer Arab countries, Africa, and Asia; Yemen begs for foreign aid.

Whereas the Gulf has traffic circles, Yemen has traffic jams. Gulf police direct cars; in Yemen they man checkpoints. In striking contrast to the Gulf, Yemen's popular markets are filthy, chaotic, bumpy, and tangled. Yemen is kaleidoscopic; the Gulf is monochrome. If Oman, with its gentility and its unmarried, English-educated sultan, is "queer," Yemen, with its polygamous military leader and gun-toting tribesmen, is "macho." The GCC and its member states have been remarkable for their internal political order and stability, whereas from the 1950s through the 1990s South Arabian politics were convulsed by coups, assassinations, and civil wars.

The Gulf is silent, the un-Gulf is noisy. The Gulf's domestic politics are domesticated, whereas Yemen's are feral. The Gulf is pacified; the periphery is raucous. The Gulf is a vital American interest; Yemen is a backwater. The Gulf is good for business; Yemen is good for ethnography.

Both underdevelopment theory and postmodern cultural studies tell us that wealth and impoverishment, orderliness and chaos are not two different conditions of separate places but two parts of one condition. This was the lesson of neo-Marxism and it is the lesson of postmodernism as well—dualism is their common thread or insight. Within the Peninsula, the Gulf is cosmopolitan core, while the Arabia Felix of old is the periphery. While by now even Dhufar and Asir, the parts of Oman and Saudi Arabia furthest from the Gulf, have been Gulf-ized to some degree, Yemen, with half the citizen population of the Peninsula, is increasingly underdeveloped economically and politically. If the Gulf is a world unto itself, Yemen is very much part of what we used to call the Third World. Yet whereas a dependency model assumes Third World nations are linked to a western or northern cosmopole, Yemen's fate has been tied to a Saudi star. Viewed differently, the rich, ultramodern Gulf is a sub-core with its own south Arabian and Indian Ocean periphery.

This is not the place to recount every intrigue, rumor, and conspiracy theory blaming turmoil in republican Yemen on the machinations of Saudi Arabia, much less to also consider the flow of funds from other Gulf monarchs and erstwhile alternative sources of support from the Iraqi, Libyan, or Soviet governments. One might venture to speculate nonetheless that the intensity and persistence of Saudi interference attest to a strong abiding interest in Yemeni affairs by the Saudi state as such and by individuals within and outside the Saudi government. Surely the Kingdom looked askance at the Zaydi imams but feared the officers who declared a Yemen Arab Republic in 1962 and hated the leftist People's Democratic Republic of Yemen. Yemeni unity and democratization in 1990 provoked threat perceptions as well. But the level and complexity of Saudi involvement in Yemeni domestic politics goes beyond pure self-preservation. At times it seems that Saudi princes and politicians are playing out their own internal power struggles by factional proxy in Yemen, and probably elsewhere.

One vehicle for influence in lower Arabia and abroad was the public and private charitable financing of Islamic institutions. Saudi Arabia financed Yemeni public and private education on a massive scale from the 1960s through the 1980s, in the hopes of cultivating conservative public opinion amenable to Saudi interests. Schools and mosques were endowed in many parts of Africa and Asia, too, and supplied with Arabic-speaking teachers and preachers from Egypt, Sudan, Palestine, Yemen, and elsewhere. During the seventies, at the height of the Cold War, Islamic education served as the vehicle for an explicitly anticommunist agenda in Yemen, Pakistan, Afghanistan, Sudan, Palestinian refugee communities, Egypt, Algeria, Somalia, Senegal, Indonesia, and elsewhere. Even before the Soviet intervention in Afghanistan intensified the militancy of this movement, a new brand of puritanical piety was preached to poor communities in Yemen and the Third World. Full veils, full beards, and fire-and-brimstone sermons on cassette tape became all the rage in Yemen and abroad in the 1980s. In some respects this was a new Arabian Islamic missionary movement, financed through a combination of foreign aid and private philanthropy. In Afghanistan it became an outright *jihad*, financed and conceived by the Saudi government in conjunction with the American Central Intelligence Agency, to drive Soviet forces from Afghanistan. Young men recruited in migrant or immigrant communities in the Gulf and from a wide network of Islamic schools volunteered for guerrilla warfare against the communist infidels. Their victory over the Soviet forces and their eventual repatriation to their homelands in victory further glamorized Islamic fundamentalism and militancy. The repercussions of this romanticized *jihad* have been felt from Algeria to Aceh.

As the only Gulf state whose territory stretches the full breadth of the Peninsula, Saudi Arabia is ambivalent regarding its Gulf and Arabian identities. On the one hand, it is very much a Gulf Kingdom, and a proponent of a separate Gulf identity emphasizing monarchy, royal privilege, and a combination of pro-American foreign policies with deeply conservative domestic policies. On the other hand as its name indicates the Kingdom identifies itself with all of Arabia, and is viewed by all its neighbors as having hegemonic designs over the entire Peninsula. Many in the Saudi opposition in exile, writing from England, Egypt, or Pakistan, now routinely refer to the Arabian Peninsula as a single political unit. Then again, others speak of the Peninsula as comprised of "greater Hijaz" and "greater Yemen." Although the Saudi government sometimes appropriates all of Arabia in its self-exposition through films, maps, exhibitions, and photo-books, then, along with its GCC allies the House of Saud also insists that Gulf politics are uniquely if not xenophobically insular. Where Yemen deviates from these "pure" and "traditional" politics it becomes foreign. So, for instance, whereas Saudi dissidents abroad praised female participation in Yemen's historic 1993 elections, calling them an example for the entire Peninsula, Riyadh dismissed the whole exercise—the parliamentary elections as such, and especially women's registration as voters, candidates, and parliamentarians—as "un-Islamic." Notwithstanding the globalization of the material culture and workforce of the Gulf monarchies, according to the official line "un-Islamic" foreign political influences should not muddy the purity of Arabian culture. Kuwait, Bahrain and the other Gulf monarchs have tested a more liberal approach on elections and women's participation, but very cautiously and with great emphasis on the continuity of political values rooted in local culture.

Devotion to carefully chosen traditions defines a political culture deliberately defended against exogenous movements, practices, and ideas. Leaders practice consultation and seek consent. Continuity is a paramount virtue. In this milieu dissent, disarray, and discontent by definition reside and should remain abroad, or be expelled. Elites display the hegemonic view that their way of life is a model for others, and a sense of noblesse oblige toward less fortunate Muslims overseas. But alien politics are embargoed.

Yet social movements cultivated for export have come back to haunt the Gulf's ruling elite. Dissenters challenge princes to practice the asceticism, puritanism, and Islamic xenophobia preached for the Afghanistan *jihad* against the Soviet Union. Not long ago Usama bin Laden was but one among a number of maverick *mujahideen* commanders ensconced, like the Marlon Brando figure in the *Heart of Darkness* film rendition *Apocalypse Now*, in camps in Afghanistan, Yemen, Sudan, and other chaotic regions of the Indian Ocean basin. A series of attacks on American targets—Khobar, Aden, Nairobi, Dar es-Salam, and New York—have been launched under the slogan of removing foreign troops from the Arabian Peninsula. This is not just about protecting Mecca and Medina from infidels; it is about resisting foreign domination and toppling great powers. The guerrilla methods, the fundamentalist discourses, and the hubris of this resistance movement were inspired by the anti-Soviet crusade.

Currently the single most salient, this particular Frankenstein's monster or Pandora's box, the new Islamic *jihad*, is not the sole product of policies and conditions that export politics. The flow of petrocurrencies to Zaydi royalists, some Yemeni nationalists, selected Nasirists, certain Socialists, die-hard tribalists, Islamists of various stripe, and avid red-baiters revealed both the extent of engagement in internal Yemeni politics and the range of political sympathies among wealthy Gulf donors. Philanthropy, charity, foreign aid, and outright patronage became vehicles of influence and outlets for political energies, a proxy politics channeled outside the Gulf states' narrow political confines. In this manner overt politics suppressed in the Gulf leaked into Yemen, often like oil on smoldering embers. As the twentieth century closed, even while negotiating a boundary that might insulate the Kingdom from the Brandos and Bin Ladens in its unruly populous periphery, Riyadh was also offering Saudi citizenship to thousands of Yemenis in the Hadramawt, Shabwa, Sa'da, and other border areas. Subsidies continued to flow to selected tribal, religious, and military leaders, although most official government assistance was suspended on account of Yemen's recalcitrant position on the 1990/91 Gulf War. Dubai, Oman, and other parts of the Gulf, meanwhile, absorbed the left-leaning,

Socialist-led segment of the Yemeni political elite exiled after 1994. So there is also, again, a backward leakage, or political reabsorption. Political and religious tendencies suppressed in the Gulf—including traditions associated with Sufism, the Isma'ili sect, Shi'a and Sunni folk Islam, and militant salafism as well as modern ideologies like feminism or Ba'thism—find open expression in Yemen. In 2000 the Saudi government executed several individuals whom Najran prosecutors said were Yemeni "sorcerers" but local Isma'ilis said were mosque preachers. The government blamed the ensuing public protests on the Yemeni leaders of the trans-border Yam tribe.

Besides mutual absorption along a porous frontier and engagement in neighborhood affairs, the "politics of the outside" has another dimension. Enabled by wealth and motivated by hellish summer weather, the Gulf elite holds dual residence in the posher districts of London, Washington, Cairo, Beirut, Rome, and other cosmopolitan cities. So much that is forbidden in the Gulf—politics, publications, alcohol, strip-shows, cocktail dresses—is available in the home-away-from-home. The Gulf elite also enjoy an intellectual escape when they study abroad in England, America, or Egypt. These outlets then serve as a shock absorber for the Gulf itself, effectively sanitized from either debauchery or dissonant information.

In short, the Gulf is neither an island, nor, as its name literally implies, an empty space. All geo-cultural markers—the West, the Middle East, and black Africa, and for that matter so too Saudi Arabia and Canada—are human constructs. But the Gulf is of more recent coinage and cynical device than most. As Western, especially American, scholars, I think we have been missing something by habitually separating Yemen from the Gulf and rarely looking at the Peninsula as a whole. The relatively recent works that do so are amazingly few, and focused largely on military or security issues, migration, boundary disputes, and other bilateral issues, with some recent attention to comparisons of state or economic systems. Histories of Arabia and studies of its dialects remain to be written. There seems not to be any solid English-language historical or ethno-religious account of medieval and/or modern Islam specifically in Arabia. Edited collections other than several issues of *Arabian Studies* have been few and far between. The paucity of scholarly work on the Peninsula is being rectified especially by F. Gregory Gause and J.E. Peterson, and chapters in this volume show that promising discoveries are being made by younger scholars. Moreover, some of the gaps I identified in 2000 when I first drafted this chapter have begun to be addressed three years later. Still, the increased urgency of understanding the Arabian Peninsula has vastly outpaced academic research.

What then might be the agenda for Arabian studies? The standard Gulf or Saudi history has a tranquility that might be fruitfully complicated by an updated account that includes peasant politics as well as the political engagements of Arabians (Omanis and Yemenis in particular) in movements that swept the whole Afro-Asian region, with notable connections to Zanzibar/Tanzania, Pakistan, and Indonesia in mid-century, and to Afghanistan, Indonesia, Somalia, Sudan, and Senegal today. A new social history might call more attention to certain kinds of "racial" (by American categories) diversity and multiculturalism that are buried under the GCC states' narrow definitions of citizenship. If there is an Arabia, one might ask, then who are the Arabians, or perhaps the Arabian peoples—in the Peninsula, and in the diaspora?

A second question is whether there were political trends across the Peninsula in the twentieth century that can be written about cogently. In addition to tribalism and political Islam, there may be parallels to the processes some of us have studied in Yemen, including both customary and novel activities in the sphere beyond any state, above the family, and outside the business sector: participation in formal organizations, material contributions to social services, intellectual production, and organizing or attending special events. Such activities are not constant but sporadic, responsive, and opportunistic, depending on broader circumstances.

In the absence of central states until well into the twentieth century, the institutions of the civic realm provided basic services to urban and rural communities through religious, trade, municipal, and tribal mechanisms. Such mechanisms, including *waqf*, tribal subscriptions, municipal and market taxes, and other forms of philanthropy and communal action functioned in Arabian cities and towns at least until oil-enriched governments began constructing welfare states that displaced, nationalized, and upgraded primitive services. There are also modern *waqf* endowments, foundations, and charities that play an important private sector role today in Kuwait and elsewhere. Distinctly modern sorts of civic activism gained momentum in Aden during the anticolonial movement, when labor unions and political parties galvanized public involvement among a mixed Arab, Asian, and African population. Workers also staged strikes and labor actions in the emerging oil economies, notably Bahrain, in the 1950s, 1960s, and early 1970s. Self-help provided basic services in republican North Yemen at a time when government, lacking either a tax base or rents, was hardly capable of building roads, schools, water projects, or other infrastructure. Even if the rest of the Peninsula has been spared the need for auto-taxation and the monarchies have successfully restricted the parameters of political and civic space, surely not all politics are as bland and centralized as they have been portrayed.

While restricting internal activism the monarchies seem to have produced special kinds of civic activism for export, such as expatriate presses, investments in overseas *waqf*, patronage of political and religious institutions abroad, and so forth. More research is needed to understand the channels whereby contributions from governments, businesses, and families in the richest part of the Arab world reached needy Palestinians during the current *intifada*, for instance. Connections—institutional, political, financial—between the *jama`iyya khayriyya al-islah* in Kuwait and Yemen and perhaps elsewhere are yet to be documented. It is a pity that the vast grant-making networks of private petrodollar foundations to Islamic causes in many Afro-Asian communities had hardly been recognized by scholars when they came under U.S. intelligence scrutiny. Such channels, some of them generations old, can't be understood simply under the rubric of terrorism, which are the radical fringe not the waft and web. In the aggregate, perhaps, inconspicuous threads may be illuminated as conduits of political electricity.

Some movements inside the GCC states—the Dhufar rebellion backed by then-revolutionary South Yemen, and more recent Isma'ili activism in Najran said to originate inside northern Yemen, to cite just two examples— are so subaltern that it is easy to see them as marginal to Omani or Saudi national politics. Nonetheless, in a larger context we might see a version of political pluralism/cultural diversity that disappears beneath the monotone merchants-and-princes view of the Gulf. Political Islam itself, in the varying conceptions of regimes, counter-elites, exiles, and radical militants, is hardly monolithic; it has its own kind of pluralism and diversity, with sectarian and political divisions crosscutting current boundaries and political arrangements. Ignoring these evidently led the American Central Command to overlook potential resistance to its presence in the region coming not from Iran or Iraq but from within Arabia itself—or, rather, from its politics of the outside. Even as scholars and policy analysts attempt to understand this particular threat to American interests, neither local affinities nor potential pan-Arab, pan-Islamic, or pan-Arabian movements are too far-fetched for scholars to think about. Politics itself is not necessarily bound by the statist bias that marks official, journalistic, and scholarly commentary.

The notion—one might say, the identity—of *al-Jazira* or "the Peninsula" is gaining renewed currency within the region itself. This seems partly, perhaps, a quest to define a media market for publications and broadcasts, as in the popular new satellite broadcast network from Qatar called *al-Jazira*. Indeed there is anecdotal evidence that the wide popularity of *al-Khalij* or *Khaliji* as commercial and brand names, which probably reached a saturation point, has given way to *al-Jazira*. The opposition has also appropriated the notion of the Peninsula, as in the short-lived publication by the London-based Committee for the Defense of Legitimate Rights called *al-Jazira al-`Arabiyya*. Within the Peninsula, the notion of *al-Jazira* can have both hegemonic and subversive implications. Arabian Studies is not necessarily either one or the other. Nor is it by definition an orientalist inquiry, although it may seem so because so little work has been done since the heyday of Orientalism. Instead, looking across the Peninsula may help us to unearth the territory that has remained for too long *Arabia Incognita*.

Note

1. Sultan bin Muhammad Al-Qasimi, *The Gulf in Historic Maps*. Leicester: Thinkprint Ltd., 1996.

Chapter 2

The `Imama vs. the `Iqal: Hadari–Bedouin Conflict and the Formation of the Saudi State

Abdulaziz H. Al-Fahad

At the height of the Ikhwan's power in the 1910s and 1920s, a ranking Wahhabi Shaykh, Sulayman ibn Sihman (d. A.H. 1349/1930–31), was observed in Riyadh wearing an `iqal on top of his headdress, contrary to the customary attire of the Najdi *ulama* who until this day eschewed donning this piece, which to them symbolized worldly concerns.[1] The pious scholar was led to this action by the confluence of some extraordinary events that were threatening to unravel the long-fought-for achievement of imposing central authority in Arabia and the application of the *shari`a*. Among these was the notion held by the Ikhwan that those Bedouins who wore the `iqal instead of the newly fashioned `imama (a thin white turban) were not real Muslims and could be fought. This shaykh not only wore the piece to demonstrate its permissibility and that such customary dress had no legal or theological significance, but authored at least two legal/polemical tracts against this belief[2] in addition to joining in a number of *fatwas* disapproving of the practice.[3]

By investigating this and related controversies, this chapter aims to examine the nature of the Saudi state and the relationship between its two main social components, namely the *Hadar*, or settled communities, and the Bedouins, or nomadic tribes. For in writings about the country, the Saudi state is typically identified with the Bedouin, the tribe or nomads, and "tribal values" are supposed to suffuse the state, at least at its inception. Such identification is difficult to sustain notwithstanding its prevalence, for this state had been (and continues to some extent to be) an exclusively *Hadari* endeavor with profound anti-tribal and anti-Bedouin tendencies, and circumscribed roles for the Bedouins and their tribes.[4]

The origin of the Saudi state has been seriously characterized as an "act of God," presumably implying that there are no readily discernible or rationally analyzable causes.[5] We need not succumb to this modern Ash`arism (or question divine omnipotence) to be able to identify a number of factors that led to its formation and eventual consolidation. First and foremost, the Saudi state is a *Hadari* project that aimed, among other things, to end Bedouin historical hegemony throughout pre-modern Arabia. The Wahhabi revivalist movement, and the state that emerged therefrom, had been conceived, spearheaded, and manned by the *Hadari* communities, especially those of the southern areas of Najd, through a long and arduous process of coalition building by the founders of the movement/state.[6]

Wahhabism was the response to the profound crisis that Najdi society had been experiencing in the eighteenth century, a crisis rooted in two prominent characteristics of the society at the time. First, the Najdi *Hadari* population, especially in its southern areas, where the Wahhabi movement originated, had lost its tribal organization and suffered from political instability.[7] Second, and this concerns the Bedouin communities, Najdi pastoral nomadism had been characterized by a high degree of flux resulting in instability in inter- and intra-tribal as well as Bedouin–*Hadari* relations.

The earliest known political formations, which could be loosely described as "states" in Najd, were very limited and either depended on tribal support or inherited religious charisma, that is, `Alawi descent. The Kinda of southern Najd, which flourished a few centuries before Islam, was a tribally based polity, followed by the hegemony of the Banu Hanifa who were one of the last tribes to accept Islam and who were later to contribute significantly to the *ridda* wars and Khariji rebellions.[8] The Umayyads exercised a degree of control, which the Abassids were unable to maintain for long. The Banu al-'Ukhaydir emerged in the ninth century in the Khidhrima (today's Kharj, south of Riyadh) and were the closest thing to an indigenous dynasty, relying for their power on their legitimist pretensions as descendants of the Prophet with a Zaydi creed.

After the collapse of the Banu al-'Ukhaydir (mid-eleventh century) very little is known about the history of the area.[9] There are no known local Najdi sources and precious few references to the region in other Islamic chronicles until about the seventeenth century when some rather primitive local recording of events starts. This "black hole" (C.E. eleventh–sixteenth centuries) in Najdi historical narrative makes it difficult to paint an accurate picture of the society during those long centuries. Even after that period, and until the advent of Wahhabism, the little that actually survived is of limited value. Nevertheless, it appears that Najd, or parts of it, was subject to periodic invasions/raids by the neighboring powers; the Sharifis in Hijaz made occasional forays but the succession of the tribally based polities in the east appear to have had closer ties. The objective of such raids seems to be mainly the pacification of the various nomadic tribes and protection of trade/pilgrim routes as well as collection of tribute.[10] It does not appear that any direct control was imposed.

On the basis of rudimentary, pre-Wahhabi written records, al-Juhany suggests that population growth was significant after the fifteenth century and contributed to the emergence of the Wahhabi movement. While this suggestion has been challenged by Cook, detribalization, which is not necessarily inconsistent with al-Juhany's demographic explanation, has been proposed as the main social process that led to the emergence of Wahhabism.[11] Starting with the destruction of the Banu Hanifa in the early Islamic centuries, the *Hadari* population of Najd gradually lost any meaningful tribal organization. By the eighteenth century, the *Hadaris* were reduced to a melange of small communities, where every town boasted a number of large families, often of differing genealogical origins. Moreover, the redoubtable Banu Hanifa were on the verge of extinction and only small remnants survived in a few towns, especially in Dir`iyya. The other well-known Najdi tribe, Tamim, fared much better and had somehow managed to preserve its identity despite its complete sedentarization and total loss of any nomadic component. Still, Tamim was never able to recover its pre- and early Islamic dominance, although a number of its leading families were able to maintain some tenuous "rule" over a few villages in Najd.

Chronicles are replete with references to the crises these towns were facing. None of the towns had any stable rule and many were split into a number of antagonistic neighborhoods and warring chiefs; violence was endemic.[12] Indeed, a striking characteristic of *Hadari* society had been its utter failure to develop any reliable mechanism for effective rule and orderly succession. In many cases, more than one family had been vying for dominance, sometimes from differing genealogical backgrounds and succession was more often effected through murder. The history of pre-Wahhabi Najd is in many respects a chronicle of these events, a relentless trail of blood-soaked struggle and political intrigue at a localized level.[13]

The history of the Bedouins and their tribes is even less understood than that of the settled communities although we know enough general events to be able to venture a few generalizations. Perhaps the most impressive feature of Najdi nomadism is its relative instability in comparison with other tribal systems in the area. In North Yemen, for example, Dresch draws a portrait of Yemeni tribes that had managed to maintain themselves more or less intact over the same territory from pre-Islamic times until the present. Similarly, the tribes of southwest Saudi Arabia in the `Asir and southern mountains of Hijaz have maintained their territorial and genealogical continuity over many centuries.[14] The tribes of those mountainous areas, unlike Najdi Bedouins, are mostly sedentary. This phenomenon is not replicated in Najd where there has been high turnover in tribal formations through both immigration into Najd from the south and southwestern areas and migration out of Najd into the Fertile Crescent.[15] The seemingly constant movement into and out of Najd created a complex process of fission and fusion among the nomadic tribes (and to a lesser extent, the *Hadar* communities), where today it is practically impossible to trace, with any degree of confidence, the original roots of most surviving clans and lineages.[16]

The persistent state of flux that characterized Najdi nomadic tribes is readily identifiable and is repeated many times over. At any given time, a tribe would move from the south or southwest into upper Najd, presumably because of population pressures or droughts in its original home, seeking access to pasture lands and watering places of the area either peacefully or by force.[17] Defeated tribes would move east and north, causing further displacement, and a ripple effect would reach as far as al-Jazira in northern Mesopotamia, the northern-most ecological frontier of Arabian nomadism. As a result of this incessant process, genealogies become hopelessly intertwined, further complicating the political situation. But Bedouin political culture readily accommodates this instability by means of alliance building, where the newly-emerging sections are quickly accepted and eventually taken for granted to be part of the tribe's genealogy.[18] This process is not as readily available to the *Hadar* since genealogy (and tribalism in particular) plays a considerably less prominent role in their social and political life.[19]

In this landscape, like many others, dominance is dependent on military prowess with profound consequences to Bedouin (and to a lesser extent, *Hadari*) political culture and social structure. Because of their dependence on the use and threat of force to ensure survival in the desert, those Bedouins who fail to maintain their military strength are gradually reduced to an inferior status.[20] By failing to maintain independence vis-à-vis others, a nomadic tribe could only survive economically by paying tribute to the stronger, dominant tribe in order to maintain access to pasturages, losing in the process its *asil* ("pure") Arabian genealogy. Through such a process, many tribes became "outcasts" and the *asil* tribes would cease intermarriage with them. This "caste" formation emerged as an effective way to maintain the stronger tribes' monopoly of resources and as a means of collecting tribute from the inferior ones.[21] Being a function of military strength, the process is reversible if and when the requisite power is demonstrated.[22]

Curiously enough, the *Hadar* who historically paid tribute to their neighboring tribes did not suffer the same fate and the *asil* elements of the *Hadar* maintained their "pure" genealogies, including the ability to inter-marry with the *asil* Bedouins. Nonetheless, *Hadari* society exhibited the same attitudes as the Bedouins toward their *Hadari* non-*asil* groups, called Banu Khadir, and the *asil Hadari*s would not intermarry with them.[23] Unlike the case of the Bedouins, however, it is difficult to see any obvious economic function for this "caste" system within *Hadari* society, and it may be nothing more than a holdover from Bedouin attitudes, or perhaps a way for the dominant *Hadari asil* groups to establish, when available, alliances with neighboring *asil* tribes.[24] The *Hadari* non-*asil* social group has been the most overlooked element within the Wahhabi/Saudi coalition despite its critical contributions to the process of state formation and consolidation, where they were major beneficiaries.

Bedouin society has been defined according to an ideology based on kinship where patrilineal descent operates as the overriding organizing principle. *Hadari* identity, on the other hand, is far less dependent on kinship and is markedly territorial and more defined by common residence. Towns were typically composed of a number of families or lineages claiming descent from differing tribes, some of which survived only as *Hadar*. The towns of `Arid were very mixed, with Tamim, Banu Hanifa, Subai`, `A'idh, Lam, Dawasir, `Anaza, and many others living together.[25] Despite these apparent genealogical distinctions and the constant internal conflict in the towns that had characterized the life of the *Hadar*, it is clear that by the eighteenth century a territory-based definition of the inhabitants had taken hold, the most important manifestation of which is dialect. Although there have been a few studies of Najdi dialects, they tend to be more concerned with "tribal" rather than the *Hadari* inhabitants. Yet, as recently as a generation ago, it was possible to identify any individual simply by the way he spoke. While these dialects are mutually intelligible, enough differences exist in pronunciation, intonation, and lexicon to be *easily* identifiable along Bedouin–*Hadari* and regional lines. An aspect of dialect in Najdi society is the possibility of identifying a speaker as Bedouin or *Hadari* through dialect, though for both communities there exist marked differences among their constituent groups dialects. For the *Hadar*, each of the "regions" into which Najd is traditionally divided has a uniform dialect. From region to region, dialects gradually but perceptibly change and are distinctly identifiable: thus, from south to north, there are dialects for Wadi al-Dawasir, Aflaj, Fura`, `Arid, Sha`ib, Mihmal, Sudayr, Washm, Zilfi, Qasim, Jabal Shammar; and in `Alyat Najd, al-`Ird and Dawadimi.[26]

While dialect is probably the most prominent feature of territorial identity among the *Hadar*, other manifestations of this identity may be found in two other common Najdi practices, `*uzwa or nakhwa*, best translated as war cry, and *wasm*, the system of symbols used to brand animals.[27] It appears that every Najdi town or group of settlements (or even a whole region) typically employs one standard *nakhwa*, which is derived from some physical features of the area or invoking a person's name or a noble deed as with tribal customs.[28] Perhaps the most famous is that of `Arid, *ahl al-`awja*, of uncertain origin, but used by inhabitants of the territory regardless of tribal (or Khadiri) affiliation.[29] Even within `Arid there are various local *nakhwa*s, for example, Muzahimmiyya/Durama (*ahl al-hamad*, a reference to the plains they inhabit) and Riyadh (*ahl al-dirayn*, a reference to two local hills).[30] Another well-known *nakhwa* is that of the whole of Qasim, *awlad `Ali*, which connotes no particular ancestor and is used by all groups within the area.[31] The *nakhwa* of Zilfi is `*yal al-Juraysi*.[32] `Usahqir, the stronghold of many of the modern Tamimi clans uses as its *nakhwa* `*ukl*, the old name of the town, derived from the name of an ancient tribe.[33]

Branding (*wasm*) is one of the most widely used practices in pre-modern Arabia by both Bedouin and *Hadar*.[34] Typically, a clan would brand its camels in a standard way to facilitate the immediate identification of the owners. On occasion various groups within a clan would seek to distinguish their property by employing an auxiliary *wasm*, called *shahid*, which it would affix in addition to the standard *wasm*. A raiding party would therefore be able to avoid those camels that belong to its co-tribesmen or allied clans. This practice is widespread within the *Hadari* communities as well, although it appears that *Hadari wasm*s are determined not along the lines of clans or lineages but according to a territorial identity. Thus, the inhabitants of Qasim typically use as their common *wasm* the *hayya* ("serpent") with the various towns employing different *shahid*s. In Zilfi, the region with which I am most familiar, the *wasm* is presumably that of the dominant `Utaybi clan, the *halqa* (or "circle," much like the letter O) and all residents, regardless of tribal or Khadiri background, would so brand their camels. The northern settlements in Zilfi use a *shahid* to further distinguish their camels in the shape of a *mish`ab*[35] (or "stick," much like the letter T with only the right part of the cross).[36]

Situated in marginal lands with scarce vegetation and water, Najd could offer its inhabitants only a precarious existence and surplus was limited.

Economic relations among the various social groups in pre-modern Arabia are nevertheless complex with the *asil* nomadic tribes the clear winners. There is of course peaceful, non-coercive, and reciprocal economic exchange of goods between the "desert and the sown," where the *Hadar* and Bedouin would transact goods and obtain their value in return. But the pre-modern system has significant coercive aspects that ensure the transfer of resources within the Bedouin economy from non-*asil* to *asil* tribes and from *Hadari* communities and individuals to the same nomadic tribes. The effective vehicle for ensuring this economic dominance is military superiority institutionalized in the venerable Bedouin tradition of raiding (*ghazw*), the major occupation of Bedouin men.[37] While seemingly of uniform nature, the *ghazw* in fact performs differing functions within the pre-modern Arabian economy. Within *asil* nomadic groups, this practice is reciprocal and no more than a sporting event, where small raids are organized and death is minimized; it serves to ensure a general balance in the distribution of resources, principally camels. Through this type of *ghazw*, resources are simply circulated among the nomads and no net gain to the *asil* nomadic economy is realized. A less common but more lethal form of *ghazw*, called *manakh*, usually embracing large sections of a tribe(s) and lasting sometimes for months at higher toll in human life, is periodically engaged in by the Bedouins for control over pasture lands and watering places.[38] The winner of these battles obtains exclusive possession of pasturages and associated water wells, while the loser is reduced to a tributary of the winner or ends up departing to other areas.

While both types of *ghazw*, from the perspective of the *asil* Bedouin economy taken as a whole, are economically neutral, this cannot be said of the tributes, *khuwa*, collected from the inferior tribes and the *Hadari* populations which represent net gains in the "balance of payment" of the *asil* tribes.[39] Again, military power, as reflected in the *ghazw*, is the mechanism through which this transfer is effected. The *Hadari* communities could always protect their livestock, agriculture produce, and trade routes from nomadic predations if they are able to muster enough military resources; this would require the existence of larger political units, something the *Hadar* were unable to achieve prior to Wahhabism. Failing such effective organization, the *Hadar* were reduced to tributaries of the more powerful nomadic tribes and regular payments had to be maintained. Those payments were typically made by a town, village, or settlement to one of the chiefs of the tribe or clan within whose territory (*dira*) it is located. Though difficult to document, most Najdi towns had to pay tributes to the surrounding Bedouins or risk loss of property.[40] Another mechanism for collection of tribute is the custom of the *rafiq* in which a person, group, or caravan, in order to pass through a tribal *dira* without fear of harm and expropriation of property, must purchase protection through retaining one or more members of this tribe. Unlike the *khuwa* paid by towns, this practice is more readily documented in the literature with prices varying according to circumstances. This institution must have been lucrative for the Bedouins, as any (capable) member of the tribe could extend this protection and collect the *khuwa* for himself.[41]

The security cost shouldered by the *Hadari* economy is made all the more onerous by the high "turnover" within the Najdi tribal system. In areas with stable tribal formations, most inhabitants of the towns would be co-tribesmen of the dominant group and, relying on genealogical politics, would be exempt from payment of *khuwa*. This case is illustrated, for example, by Jabal Shammar (Ha'il) and its dominant tribe of the same name.[42] However, in most other areas of Najd, towns and villages were too genealogically mixed to benefit from this tribally-based exemption, and security had to be purchased, apparently at considerable cost. Relative to other areas, they were at a distinct disadvantage, which contributed to their attempt (and eventual success) at overturning Bedouin hegemony.

It is under these conditions that Wahhabism appeared. Its founder, a *Hadari* Najdi Shaykh, Muhammad ibn `Abd al-Wahhab, envisaged nothing short of a radical transformation of the moral, political, economic, and social landscape of Najd. Expressed through the vehicle of revivalist Islam of the *mujaddid* tradition, ibn `Abd al-Wahhab effectively utilized Hanbali ideas and doctrines that first emerged in Baghdad (C.E. ninth-eleventh centuries) and were elaborated in Damascus two centuries later.[43] Through this *da`wa*, he sought to unify the warring towns and bring the Arabian Bedouin to the fold of Islam. His views required the destruction of old patterns, of superstitions, Sufism (perhaps it was antinomian and particularistic), raiding, and not least extra-*shar`i* taxes. He was not to die (1792) until he saw the success of the movement he had launched.

When embarking on his reforms, ibn `Abd al-Wahhab did not seek the support of the Bedouin tribes, all of whom he held in deep contempt.[44] Instead, he began his preaching among the *Hadar* of `Arid who were ideally suited for his cause as that area at the time had the largest concentration of *Hadar*, and relatively minor Bedouin elements.[45] In `Uyayna, the largest town in Najd and ruled by Ibn Mu`ammar, a Tamimi like the Shaykh himself, the reformer targeted some common practices that were held to be inadmissible and met with initial successes. His activities attracted the attention of the hegemonic power at the time, the Humaydi rulers of the Banu Khalid tribe who held sway over al-Hasa and extended their suzerainty to some Najdi towns. Because of `Uyayna's economic dependence on the Humaydis, the chief of the town had to withdraw his support and the Shaykh was obliged to leave.[46] He took refuge in Dir`iyya, a smaller town with a chief by the name of Muhammad ibn Sa`ud (r. 1139–79/1726–65), the founder of the Saudi dynasty.[47] The deal that was struck reflects that the two parties, the Shaykh and the *Amir*, clearly understood the political goal they sought, the establishment of a single polity in the area that would unite the warring towns, villages, and tribes into a realm with one imam and where the *shari`a* would reign supreme.[48]

It is common to ascribe to the Saudi family a genealogy and an affiliation that would ensure its strong tribal/Bedouin identity. The lineage of the family is reckoned by some authorities to come from the Masalikh of the `Anaza tribe, despite the fact that the Wahhabi sources are unanimous that it belonged to the remnants of Banu Hanifa.[49] It appears that this ascription solves the puzzle of the prominence of the family and the success of Wahhabism, which perhaps could be conceived only through the Khaldunian model of tribal `asabiya. Yet, it is indeed the relative *insignificance* of the Saudi family at that time that allowed it the success it gradually achieved.[50] For it was that characteristic of the family above all else, of being neither Bedouin nor affiliated with a large tribe, that allowed it to build the effective *Hadari* coalition which eventually defeated its many opponents, the most serious of whom had considerable Bedouin and tribal backing. While the Bedouins did contribute to the process, their role, on the whole, had been opportunistic and subsidiary to that of those detribalized *Hadaris*.

Using Dir`iyya as its base, the Wahhabi *da`wa* was initially conducted by peaceful means that eventually had to give way to military *jihad*. In a process that would last close to half a century, the Wahhabis slowly defeated their opponents both ideologically and militarily. The pace of the expansion of the realm was by no means spectacular but it was steady, not least because the Wahhabis had to rely on ideological subversion more than physical force, which they did not manage to deploy effectively until later in their history. Never able to muster a large standing army, the Wahhabis depended heavily on the *Hadar* to man their armies, with Bedouins only serving more or less opportunistically.[51] The chronicles suggest that, at least initially, most of the warfare had been directed against other towns, but in due course even the Bedouins were subdued. For the *Hadari* communities, incorporation within the Wahhabi state resulted in several changes. First, the Saudi Imams would maintain their *Hadari* coalition by appointing local *amirs* to the conquered towns and would rarely replace them with outsiders.[52] The tax system would also change as *zakat* would be collected and any extra-*shar`i* levies would be abolished. A *shari`a* expert would be appointed as judge to administer the law, and to the extent that non-*shar`i* customs were enforced, that too would be eliminated. Less-learned individuals, the *matawi`a*, were also dispatched to the various communities to proselytize; occasionally they had to forfeit their lives when towns rebelled against Wahhabi rule.

The changes brought by Wahhabism to Bedouin society were just as drastic. The Bedouins were instructed in the principles of the faith, and ritual observance was enforced.[53] More profoundly, not only were old Bedouin privileges of raiding and collection of tributes from other Bedouins, *Hadari* towns and travelers abolished, but the tribes had to pay *zakat* to the *Hadari* treasury, a reversal of the pre-Wahhabi regime. Ibn Bishr unfailingly highlights these achievements. Writing during the period of the Saudi civil war, following the death of Imam Faysal in 1865 when the Saudi state disintegrated and insecurity was rampant, the author appears to be acutely aware of the Bedouins' power, and his unqualified contempt for and hostility to them are palpable. For example, in a section devoted to the *manaqib* of the second Saudi Imam, `Abd al-`Aziz (killed 1218/1803), he devotes several pages to his success at curbing Bedouin hegemony and imposing security throughout the realm.[54] His diagnosis of the Bedouin problem is typical of the general *Hadari* view. In a sort of eternal, binary opposition, the hostility between the *Hadar* and the Bedouins is perceived as natural and the Bedouins could be tempered only by the "sword".[55] The Wahhabi Imam was ruthless with the Bedouins and employed several strategies to deal with them. For their transgressions, he would impose heavy fines and put their shaykhs in jail; in one instance, for maximum humiliation, the chief of `Anaza, al-Humaydi ibn Haththal, was jailed, shackled with a non-*asil* Hutaymi Bedouin.[56]

To bring the Bedouin "problem" under control, the Wahhabis deployed legal concepts that exploited the nomads' own social system in order to provide the means for ensuring security and compliance with the law. A fascinating passage written by an eminent Wahhabi scholar, shaykh `Abd al-Latif Al al-Shaykh (d. 1293/1876), relates the response to a question he had addressed to his father, `Abd al-Rahman (d. 1285/1868–69).[57] His father was another eminent scholar, and the question concerned the legality of the practice of the Najdi *amirs* of holding men responsible for the transgressions of their kin. In his long response, the father recalls the conditions of Najd before the *da`wa* where nomads oppressed the *Hadar*, hardly observed any *shar`i* rules, and were engaged in constant strife. When the Wahhabi reformers launched the *da`wa* the Bedouins were hostile to it but the reformers pressed the fight; when one tribe would "obey God and adhere to the *shari`a*" they would use it to fight those still in error. But even after they had accepted Islam, the stronger tribes would continue to oppress weaker Bedouins and *Hadar*. So a Bedouin would steal or commit highway robbery and then take refuge with his strong tribe that would offer him its protection. If the tribe is left alone and only the person who had committed the crime is held responsible and who is protected by the tribe, all rights, life, and property would be lost and the *shari'a* would be abandoned. Collective responsibility would be the only way to ensure the application of the law through which security could be achieved, and it is thus legal for those administering justice to hold tribal relatives responsible until they deliver the accused.[58] This opinion is qualified only to the extent that those held responsible for the crimes of their kin must be of stature and influence and are able to deliver, and not just simply kinsmen who are of no consequence.[59]

The first Saudi state was highly successful at the twin tasks of forging *Hadari* unity and Bedouin pacification. Perhaps its constant, successful wars with its many opponents ensured that parties, especially the Bedouins, had plenty of resources to compensate for losses stemming from the overthrow of the old order. But despite the incorporation and pacification of the nomadic tribes in the Wahhabi realm, it is difficult to see any role for them besides their opportunistic participation in the wars of conquests whose core forces were always the *Hadar*. As indicated above, the Saudi Imams followed a conscious policy of coalition building among the *Hadar* and, after the conquest, typically left the ruling chiefs (or their relatives) in charge of the towns and settlements. When they occasionally needed to post an outsider, he was always *Hadari*, and no Bedouin would ever be appointed *amir* over a *Hadari* settlement, a practice that survives to this day.[60] Indeed, it was possible for the Saudi Imams to employ *Shi'i amirs* for the Qatif region, but no nomads could achieve this post. In fact, the only direct employment I can find for nomads is in a limited number of military commands.[61]

The expansion of the Saudi state was ended by the superior power of Egyptian arms and by 1818, Dir'iyya was in ruins. With such crushing defeat, the old ways quickly reasserted themselves. Towns became independent again and the nomads merrily reverted to their old pre-occupations. Wahhabi historians freely hurl accusations of treachery at the tribes for their cooperation with the Egyptians, but the *Hadar* do not escape unscathed either. The upshot is a marked decline in order which the Saudi Imams along with their Wahhabi *ulama* tried to restore, a task at which they were partially successful. The post-invasion reigns of Imam Turki (r. 1236/1820–1246/1830) and his son, Faysal (r. 1246/1830–1254/1838 and 1258/1843–1282/1865), are characterized by constant conflict within Najdi society, with a tendency for the Bedouins to figure more prominently in their campaigns than had been the case with the first state. Chronicles show a picture of a society rent by centrifugal forces on several fronts. The realm had substantially shrunk in both size and power with the Saudi writ confined to Najd and areas of the eastern coast. There were efforts to expel the remnants of the invading Egyptians and restore Najdi independence and unity. The nomadic tribes appeared again as a major obstacle to unity and a menace threatening *Hadar* settlements, and frequent expeditions were launched against the disobedient Bedouins. An example of the length to which the Imams had to go to restore peace is the decapitation of the leader of the `Ijman tribe in al-Hasa in 1262/1846 after he had plundered a caravan of pilgrims, apparently the first time the Saudis went to that extreme with the Bedouins.[62]

The first Saudi state that was vanquished by the Egyptians was remarkable for its stability. In pre-Wahhabi Najd, all settlements lacked a system of orderly succession and internecine wars were frequently the result. The Wahhabis successfully introduced the tradition of primogeniture that had not been practiced in the past either by Bedouins or *Hadar*. This stability gradually eroded during the hapless second Saudi state, first by the murder of Turki by his nephew, who was in turn killed by Turki's son, Faysal, and later by the outright rebellion of Saud against his older brother, `Abd Allah, shortly after the death of Faysal, their father. This era between the destruction of Dir`iyya and the Saudi civil war witnessed further transformation in the political life of Najd. On the nomadic front, two major, new tribes made their presence felt, the `Ijman in the east and `Utabya in upper Najd.[63] The annals are full of stories of their deeds and misdeeds along with those of their protagonists, both nomadic and settled. The Saudi Imams seem to have spent much of their energies in battles with the two tribes as well as others. For the *Hadar*, the most striking development had been the gradual emergence to prominence of the northern regions of Najd, specifically, Qasim and Ha'il.[64] Over the following several decades, both regions were to offer serious alternatives to the Saudi/Wahhabi coalition, but neither ultimately succeeded at supplanting the Saudi state.

The history of the Rashidi *amirate* in Ha'il starts with the appointment of its founder, `Abd Allah ibn `Ali ibn Rashid (d. 1847), to be the *amir* of the region by Imam Faysal in gratitude for the former's services to the Saudis, fulfilling ibn Rashid's lifelong ambitions. With the ascendance of ibn Rashid, we are able to identify a distinct shift in Najdi politics from a clearly and exclusively (hybrid) *Hadari* governance to a reliance on tribal affiliation as the basis of power. Arguably, for the first time in the history of Najd since the early Islamic centuries, an aspiring family pursued power on the strength of its nomadic tribal affiliation.[65] It must have been a conscious decision by the founders, for it is related that one of the earliest causes of friction between ibn Rashid and his predecessor, ibn ʿAli, who belonged to the same Shammari clan, was the accusation by ibn Rashid that the *amir* was not doing enough to support the nomadic Shammar in their battles with their ʿAnaza enemies.[66] Disobeying the *amir*'s instructions, ʿAbd Allah and his brother, ʿUbayd, took it upon themselves to organize military support and come to the aid of their Bedouin Shammar kinsmen.[67] This shift in the region's politics was to prove a critical factor both in the success and eventual failure of that Haʾil/Shammar hegemony.[68]

At the same time of Rashidi ascendancy, Qasim was developing its own local identity and striving for independence, including collection of *zakat* from neighboring tribes.[69] Known as the most enterprising merchants in Najd, the Qasimis developed extensive trading relations with the outside world, especially the export of camels to the Fertile Crescent and Egypt.[70] Heavily dependent on this trade with the north, Qasim was acutely interested in securing its caravan routes to the Levantine and Egyptian markets, which frequently brought it into conflict with the Rashidis. In this struggle (and the later conflict with the resurgent Saudis), the Qasimis suffered from several disadvantages. Being a thoroughly *Hadari* society, it was no match for the Rashidi *amirate* with its loyal Shammari tribesmen. In order to counter the Rashidis' tribal advantage, Qasim made common cause with the ʿAnaza Bedouins, the historical foes of the Shammar, but their alliance proved inadequate to overcome the Shammaris, both settled and nomadic.[71] A further disadvantage was the Qasimis' chronic inability to achieve unity, the bane of *Hadari* politics. The two major towns, Burayda and ʿUnayza, were ruled independently, and Burayda's attempt to control the region always stumbled on ʿUnayza's obstinacy. A further limitation on Qasim's bid for its own independence came from the profound Wahhabi penetration of its society, rendering it susceptible to Saudi influence, and the local Wahhabi *ulama* had a major role in advancing the Saudi cause against both the quest for independence and Rashidi designs. Other members of the Qasimi elite, especially the ʿuqayli merchants, were aware of the Rashidis' ability to block their trade routes, and influential segments advocated an alliance with Haʾil.[72]

Relying on the combined powers of their *Hadar* and Shammari supporters, the Rashidis gradually displaced their competitors, and by 1889 their realm extended throughout Najd after expelling the last Saudi *amirs* from Riyadh. Although the Rashidis attained and maintained their rule on the basis of a specific tribal Bedouin *ʿasabiya*, it is clear that their more astute leaders always recognized that unless the chronic Bedouin–*Hadari* problem was dealt with properly their dominion would be shaky.[73] The great Rashidi *amir*, Muhammad ibn ʿAbd Allah (r. 1869–97) appears to have been aware of the need to curb Bedouin hegemony in order to prop up the dynasty's rule; he reportedly vowed that were he to live long enough he would abrogate all Bedouin *khuwa* on the *Hadar*.[74]

Even foes of the Rashidi dynasty give him credit for his political acumen. In the aftermath of the Sarif debacle (1318/1901) in which his successor, `Abd al-`Aziz ibn Mut`ib (r. 1897–1906), routed his many opponents, Saudis and others, near Qasim, al-`Ubayyid reports that Imam `Abd al-Rahman (King `Abd al-`Aziz's father) was asked whether there was any hope left for the Saudis to recover their rule in Najd. His answer is indicative of the profound awareness of the problematic issue of Bedouin–*Hadari* relations. `Abd al-Rahman's response starts with charting the possible reactions now open to the Rashidi victor. One possibility, which would preclude a Saudi recovery, would be for `Abd al-`Aziz ibn Rashid to emulate the conduct of Muhammad ibn Rashid, his predecessor, after the latter's own triumph at Mulayda (1308/1890). "Listen people of Najd," the chronicle reports Muhammad declaring,

> the transgressor, the victim, the good and the bad: Today we start with a clean slate in Najd; it is in my protection (*wajh*) and the security of God, from Wadi al-Dawasir [in the extreme south] to Jauf al-`Amr [in the extreme north]. As to you Bedouins, listen [carefully]: by God, if [a Bedouin] deprives a *Hadari* of a *mahashsh* [a small scythe], I shall deprive him of his head. Listen to me again, oh Bedouins, do not say that Muhammad ibn Rashid has deceived us, [by God] . . . I shall raid you [in early morning for] a *mahashsh* you take from a *garrash* [typically a *Hadari* collector of desert grass and wood]; so be quiet and obey me and I shall protect you from all dangers.[75]

Unfortunately for the Rashidi House, his successor was long on bravery and short on diplomacy and never followed the example of his able predecessor. Relying on his solid support among the Shammar, he embarked on a policy of confrontation with all surrounding powers (with the exception of the Ottomans). In his relentless military expeditions against his foes, both *Hadar* and Bedouins, he succeeded only in forcing his adversaries to overcome their differences (at least temporarily) and unite against him. The major battle of Sarif, alluded to above, was a watershed in the history of the area. Responding to Rashidi provocations, the *amir* of Kuwait organized a large army composed of many Kuwaiti and Najdi *Hadari*s (including the exiled Saudi and Qasimi *amir*s) as well as a number of Bedouin groups. After routing the invaders, `Abd al-`Aziz ibn Rashid exacted terrible vengeance, in money and lives, against the defeated forces, further alienating the *Hadar* of the area, especially those of Qasim. The Rashidi/Shammar hegemony was proving to be too oppressive for the Najdi *Hadar*, thus giving an opening to a resourceful and determined young Saudi leader, `Abd al-`Aziz ibn Saud, who launched his successful attack to recover Riyadh and expel the Rashidis the following year.

The task facing ibn Saud was daunting. He had to unify the historical Saudi power base in `Arid, deal with Qasim, overcome Rashidi substantial power, and somehow confront the perennial Bedouin problem. Since the Wahhabi *ulama* had considerable influence and other local elites enjoyed close relations with the Saudis, the recovery of `Arid was accomplished with relative ease. His conquests of the areas further north and south were more difficult since the local elites either enjoyed running their affairs independently or were allied with the Rashidis, and in this respect, Qasim proved to be the most intractable. With its own elite split, a plurality wished to maintain its independence (or even accept Ottoman tutelage), with another faction convinced that an alliance with the Rashidis was best in order to protect the region's mercantile interests.[76] The pro-Saudi faction, represented mostly by the Wahhabi *ulama* and to a lesser extent by some of the `uqayl, was not strong enough to overcome the opposition immediately. By 1908, and after many broken promises and much treachery, the pro-Saudi faction finally gathered enough support to open the gates of Burayda in the middle of the night and admit in Saudi forces; Burayda's ambitious *amir* was immediately banished to Iraq.

The annexation of Qasim proved to be far easier than the destruction of the Rashidi *amirate*. With a loyal local *Hadar* population in alliance with the equally loyal Shammar Bedouins, the Rashidis were able to offer stiff resistance and the Saudis were unable to defeat the dynasty until 1921. With the fall of this dynasty, the Saudi model, basing its power on a heterogeneous *Hadari* coalition, proved its superiority over the tribally based polity of Ha'il. While the tribal nature of the Rashidi House has been correctly identified by many scholars, the critical *Hadari* character of the Saudi State has often been overlooked. Al-Rasheed, in describing the essential differences between the two dynasties, characterizes the Saudi polity as based on religion.[77] This is correct of course but it happens to be equally valid for the Rashidis who enjoyed their own authentic Wahhabi qualifications.[78] The key difference between the Saudi and Rashidi houses actually lies in the antithetical nature of their power bases. Relying on the Shammar as the main prop for their realm, the Rashidis offered other Najdis, both *Hadar* and nomads, no choice but to submit to the supremacy of that tribe, which the majority found threatening. The Saudi polity, on the other hand, had neither Bedouin nor tribal identity and was open to all social groups on (theoretically) equal footing. It was therefore inevitable that in due course the Saudi resurgence would triumph with relative ease.[79]

Defeating the Rashidis, difficult as it was, was a relatively easier challenge for the Saudis than finding a solution for the perennial Najdi problem, the nomadic tribes. Used to essentially unfettered freedoms, the Bedouins understandably view *Hadari* conflicts through the prism of their own immediate interests, namely plunder, freedom from payment of *zakat*, and the pursuit of *ghazw*. In practical terms, this meant a minimum of ideological loyalty and a readiness to join the winning side and enjoy the spoils of victory. The portrait of the Bedouin given by local historians (and preserved by collective memory) is clearly of a fickle group with no loyalty to anyone or anything except sharing in the loot of campaigns, for which end, if given the opportunity, they would even rob their own allies.[80] During the early Wahhabi battles, the Bedouins played supporting roles for the *Hadari* forces and few examples are given of typical Bedouin "treachery." Starting with the Egyptian invasion, Bedouins are frequently encountered in the traditional plundering role. Even the great Sarif defeat is partially attributable to Bedouin flight.[81] King `Abd al-`Aziz, perhaps the foremost expert on Bedouins, would employ Bedouins in *Hadari* campaigns by putting them in front and having the *Hadar* behind them to ensure that they did not flee so readily.[82]

Faced with the Bedouin problem, the Wahhabis employed a long-term strategy of proselytization as the best way to curb the violent practices of the nomads.[83] Indeed, as early as the original Wahhabi campaigns, we are able to discern a new trend toward a change in the moral outlook of the Bedouins, starting with the observance of rituals, especially the daily congregational prayers. Muhammad ibn Hadi ibn Qarmalah, the chief of Qahtan (the strongest tribe in Najd at the time) in late eighteenth/early nineteenth century, is reported to have had his own prayer *imam*.[84] The great `Utaybi chief, Turki ibn Humayd (d. 1280/1863–64) had a manumitted *Hadari* slave as his *imam* who was always in his company; his elegant poetry is a testimony to a surprisingly refined religious sensibility.[85] With this emerging religiosity, the transition toward delegitimation of raiding and *khuwa* becomes considerably less difficult. In fact, by the end of the nineteenth century, we find the chief of the Shayabin clan of `Utayba, Hadhdhal ibn Fuhayd, not only retaining his own *imam* (at one time, none other than al-`Ubayyid) and ensuring that all those around him observed prayer (and were punished if they failed to), but he would boast that he would never raid a *Hadari*; he confined his *ghazw* to Bedouins like himself.[86] He also returned 4,000 riyals (Maria Theresa thalers), a huge sum by the standards of the time, that were taken from a Mutayri Bedouin once its *Hadari* owners (the famous Bassams of `Unayza) were conclusively identified. This (new) moral vulnerability led him in one instance to accept the "brotherhood in Islam" as sufficient ground to return the donkey of a *Hadari* lifted by his tribesmen though by the customs of the desert he was under no obligation to do so.[87]

The Ikhwan movement should, therefore, be viewed as the logical culmination of a long, if unsystematic, process of *Hadari* proselytism that had its natural conclusion in the attempt to settle the nomads and fully induct them into the *Hadari's* moral outlook, that of Wahhabism.[88] The earliest reports we have of the *systematic* attempt to transform the nomads into reliable and peaceful *Hadar* concerns a Harbi Bedouin, ibn Fa'iz, at the head of a group of the Banu `Ali clan, who chose Artawiyya as the first *hijra*, a settlement that later became an important center of Ikhwan activity after the wholesale settlement of Mutayr there and elsewhere. By the 1920s, a large number of *hijar* (pl. of *hijra*) of varying tribes, size, and importance had proliferated in Najd. Through these *hijar* and its Ikhwan, the Bedouins would play a stronger role in Saudi affairs than had hitherto been the case.[89] By the time of attack on Ha'il, we see Ikhwan contingents fully participating in the Saudi conquest of the town and the overthrow of the Rashidi dynasty. The Ikhwan's role was to become more pronounced during the campaigns against the Sharifis of Hijaz where their fierce reputation preceded them and may have been a major cause of their easy victories.[90] After the annexation of Hijaz in 1926, most of the territorial expansion of the Saudi state had been accomplished and, not surprisingly, the Ikhwan emerged as the next front facing the *Hadari* State.

Local history (or at least what is accessible of it) is not very helpful in allowing us to determine the exact role played by the *Hadari* preachers, the *matawi`a*, who more than anyone else were responsible for this systematic transformation in Bedouin beliefs and life style; they were later to be accused of being behind their excesses.[91] For the Ikhwan quickly metamorphosed into a danger much worse than that of the early Bedouins, as this time it was armed with a righteousness that deprived it of its former sporting quality and traditional restraint, turning it into a deadly affair.[92] The new moral certainty inculcated into much of the Ikhwan provided them with a justification to commit horrible massacres and to terrorize the rest of the population, both *Hadar* and Bedouin. To the extent that Moore's equation between monotheistic belief and bloody fanaticism is correct, the Ikhwan provide an excellent case in point.[93] To this day, their antics are told and retold. Al-`Ubayyid, who experienced their tyranny first hand, writes (in the 1950s) about the Ikhwan with palpable horror and a good dose of contempt, not least because much of the Ikhwan religious views had simply no valid religious or legal basis; to him (and to much of the *Hadar*) they were ignoramuses masquerading as guardians of Islamic morality.[94]

The Ikhwan settlement, accordingly, has simply transformed the Bedouin menace to a more lethal form. While in the past a Bedouin expressed no interest in *Hadar*'s morality and confined his attention to looting, now a member of the Ikhwan was dangerously obsessed with *both*.[95] Formerly, the Bedouin would rob and avoid murder; now he feels obligated to do both with striking moral certitude.[96]

Following the conquest of Ha'il, and after much friction and conflict between the Saudis and the Sharifis, the Ikhwan were given the green light to attack and conquer Hijaz. They accomplished the first task, the fall of Ta'if, with maximum surprise and some losses in civilian lives.[97] The news of the Ikhwan's conduct in Ta'if preceded them and had the effect of delivering Mecca without a fight. Jidda was to succumb only after a long siege. The defenders of Medina, apparently fearful of the Ikhwan's lack of discipline, insisted that their surrender be made to one of the King's sons, for which task Muhammad ibn `Abd al-`Aziz was dispatched, and the famous Ikhwan chief of Mutayr, Faysal al-Duwish, was instructed to leave the area. This deprivation of glory was to add to his already considerable pique.

In the next few years, 1926–29, this great Bedouin chief, along with the chiefs of the Barqa clan of `Utayba and the `Ijman and a number of lesser sections of other tribes, entered into more or less open conflict with the Riyadh government.[98] Once conquests and spoils of war were no longer available, the chiefs and some of their tribesmen were practically disoriented. Settled after disposing of their livestock, spending much time in religious "learning", and having no productive pursuits, they really knew nothing except how to fight and enrich themselves in the process. If raiding is banned against local Bedouins because all had become *zakat*-paying Muslims, and if war against outsider infidels is prohibited by the encroachment of modern borders and international treaties, they are simply going to be reduced to second-rate *Hadar*, unable to compete with them in most economic pursuits.[99] The battle lines were being drawn in technical, legal, and theological terms, reflecting at their core much of the Bedouins sense of loss and a crumbling social and economic order.[100]

The signs of an impending crisis appeared much earlier. Ibn Sihman's tracts were both published in 1340/1921 in Egypt at Ibn Saud's own expense (and rank as one of the earliest publications of the Saudis), and at least the first was written in 1335/1916–17. In these polemics, as well as in the *fatwa*s issued by the *ulama*, a number of questions are discussed, all betraying an unusual degree of fanaticism and exclusivism, even by Wahhabi standards.[101] The Ikhwan held to certain beliefs that the *ulama*, including ibn Sihman, found no support for in the *shari`a*. The Ikhwan's attitude toward other nomads was chief among them, for they accuse anyone not settling and making the *hijra* to be a non-Muslim; even a Bedouin of the Ikhwan who went to areas of better pasturage with the intention of returning was so accused.[102] They wished to practice *hajr*, a sort of social boycott, for the slightest imperfection, and would use force to bring those not conforming to their ideal to correct their ways. For all their odd and problematic perspectives, however, nothing seems to match their position on the wearing of `*imama*, for the Ikhwan held that not to wear this headgear and instead adopt the `*iqal* would render one suspect of unbelief.[103]

There is very little in the *shari`a* about a proper Muslim vestimentary code.[104] In certain chapters in legal treatises, for example, prayer, one can find reference to the required cover for the body, occasionally certain material is prohibited (e.g., pure silk for men), and there is a general command not to emulate the unbelievers. Besides these standard references, the *shari`a* regards dress as a matter governed by custom and not an issue of worship.[105] There is no ground to believe that a Muslim needed to use a specific "sign" in his clothing and actually "standing out" is something the jurists would frown upon as a sign of immodesty. It is true that the Prophet wore the `*imama*, but so did the pagans of his time. Moreover, to the extent that the Ikhwan were trying to follow the *sunna*, the Prophet's example, they were wearing the wrong `*imama*, for the Prophet's was worn over a *qulunsuwa* (a head cap) and covered most of the head, came under the chin (*muhannaka*), and its end was left dangling on the back. The Ikhwan's `*imama* had none of these qualities, which is certainly permissible, according to the *ulama*, but it hardly amounts to emulation of the Prophet.[106] *Fatwa*s and polemics apparently did not put an end to the matter, as it would surface again until the final defeat of the Ikhwan.

The Ikhwan's alienation under the new order was becoming evident. Even during the conquest of Hijaz, signs of discontent were conspicuous. As related by al-`Ubayyid on the authority of al-Duwish's *imam*, Ibn Saud had instructed the chief to go to Yanbu` to support the troops besieging the town, but midway decided to go to Medina to make up for the missed opportunity in Ta'if where he did not participate. After he was dispatched away from Medina, his opposition to the Riyadh government took a more threatening tone. Nor was he alone, for both the chief of `Utayba, Sultan ibn Bijad, and the chief of `Ijman, Daydan ibn Hithlayn, were of similar opinion. In contrast with the other two, the `Utaybi chief was believed to have been inspired by a deep, albeit misguided, sense of religiosity. The ostensible causes for the escalating conflict were discussed in a public assembly (with 800 persons in attendance) that Ibn Saud gathered in Riyadh in 1346/1928. Not surprisingly, none of the three leaders attended. The matters discussed indicate a shift in the struggle for supremacy in Arabia; with the other nomads characterized as Muslims and *Hadar* out of reach, the Ikhwan had to look for other grounds to pursue their objectives.

As discussed in the assembly and as contained in the various contemporaneous *fatwa*s, the Ikhwan now wanted to ban the use of the telegraph on the theory that it was forbidden magic.[107] They were also finding objectionable Ibn Saud's inability to stop the British infidels from erecting fortifications on the Iraqi borders and his willingness to enter into friendly relations with them; they wanted permission to wage *jihad* against the Iraqi tribes and government.[108] With respect to British actions on the Iraqi borders, the consensus of the gathering was that they were provocative and considered the fortifications legitimate targets of attack, but acknowledged that, in matters of war, it was only the imam (i.e., Ibn Saud) who had the exclusive authority to declare it.[109] This assembly, in retrospect, was a last-ditch attempt to persuade the Ikhwan to stop their challenge to the government without resort to force, but it was not successful. By outlawing raiding of other Saudi-controlled Bedouins and forbidding *jihad* against the non-Muslim Iraqi government and tribes, the Ikhwan were asked to live in peace and enjoy the (probably meager) fruits of settled life and forgo their age-old occupation, constant war. And that they were not willing to do without a fight.

The Ikhwan did not spend their time idly. Their forces partook in raids and counter raids against the northern tribes and had their deadly encounters with British air power.[110] They also extended their wrath against "infidel" *Hadar*, especially those who happened to be in possession of potential loot. The old restraint was of course gone; when the Ikhwan raided Saudi Shammar, they found some men from Qasim whom they executed by smashing their heads with axes.[111] They organized a meeting near Qasim to invade ʿUnayza but their plans were prematurely leaked and thwarted. The leaders' ambitions took a new turn with a meeting they held in Artawiyya; according to al-ʿUbayyid, the major shaykhs made a pact, once the *Hadari* government was defeated, to divide Saudi-controlled territory among themselves.[112]

On several occasions, Ibn Saud dispatched a number of respected *ulama* to dissuade the rebels, but they found themselves accused of complacency in return for material gains.[113] By March 1929, all attempts at peaceful containment of the Ikhwan's rebellion came to naught and the competing camps organized for battle. The two armies met on the plains of Sabala in that month. On Ibn Saud's side were all the major *Hadar* forces and the loyal Ikhwan; the rebels were mostly Mutayr and ʿUtayba.[114] Ostensibly making a last-minute bid to avoid bloodshed, Al-Duwish visited the Saudi camp for negotiations, which led nowhere.[115] And again, the Bedouins, Ikhwan or otherwise, were no match for a determined *Hadari* army and the battle that ensued was short and dealt the rebels a lasting defeat. None of the leaders was killed though; Ibn Bijad, the ʿUtaybi chief, surrendered shortly afterward, was jailed until his death, and his *hijra* was emptied and razed to the ground. Al-Duwish, on the other hand, returned to his ways and engaged the government in skirmishes that ultimately forced him to take refuge with the main infidel force in the area, the British authorities in Iraq and Kuwait, all compunction about treating with unbelievers gone. He was turned over to Ibn Saud and thrown in jail until his death also.[116]

By the 1930s, the defeat of the Bedouins was probably inevitable. The telltale signs of the impending change in the balance of power between the Bedouins and *Hadari* control had already been witnessed in Iraq with the introduction of modern technology. In Najd, the Wahhabi ideological subversion of the nomads had been at work for close to two centuries; with the addition of modern technological innovations—the telegraph, the automobile, heavy weaponry—the odds against continued Bedouin independence became insurmountable. Henceforth, the Bedouins would unquestionably submit to *Hadari* authority, give up *ghazw*, *talio* and any kind of self-help, exclusive control over pasturages, submit to the *shari`a* and abandon anything "Bedouin" or "tribal" that was in conflict with the new triumphant order, *Pax Hadariana*.[117]

The Saudi state, for more than 200 years, was never a friendly place for the nomads and its only restraint in confronting the Bedouin tribes had been the practical limits on its power. While on occasion a Bedouin would be employed as military leader, no man of nomadic background would be entrusted with a significant function of the government. Administration of government would be exclusively vested in the *Hadari* community; all regional and town governors were of *Hadari* origin, as were the judges. Even to this day in the military, no Bedouin has been appointed as chief of staff.[118] Moreover, in the bastion of tribal and nomadic privilege, the National Guard, the erstwhile *asil* Bedouins have to share political and social space as well as resources with the non-*asil*, both *Hadar* and nomads, who maintain their own brigades. Not only would the Bedouins be excluded from much of the apparatus of the modern state, but even their traditional nomadic *hima*, the exclusive dominion a tribe enjoyed over its *dira*, would also be abolished while that of the *Hadari* villages and towns preserved.[119]

With such unqualified antipathy characterizing the Saudi state from its early history until the present, it is naturally surprising to see the Bedouins and the tribes accorded the prominent position they enjoy in much of the literature on the Saudi state. It is perhaps understandable; after all, the Bedouin cuts an impressive image. For the western travelers (who probably set the tone for subsequent scholarship), the appeal of the Bedouin was irresistible.[120] He had very little in common with the hated Turk, he was humanist in the richest sense, not prone to religious prejudice, and willing to judge a man by his own qualities.[121] The Najdi *Hadar*, in contrast, possessed none of these qualities, and were simply a more uncouth version of the Levantines made all the more unsympathetic by the excessive Wahhabi xenophobia. The Bedouins were equally impressive for other Arab and Muslim observers, but in a negative way, for they represented a perennial threat. Their frequent forays into the Levant were a menace to the inhabitants. The regularity of their pillaging of the pilgrimage caravans was both a memory and a living reality to most who would write about them.[122] For Arab writers, there were no redeeming qualities in the nomads, and Najd to them was nothing more than an incubator of Bedouins, and the *Hadar* hardly registered.[123] Whatever the reasons, the (reductionist?) preoccupation with the Bedouin and the tribe results in a serious misunderstanding of the Saudi state. The *Hadar*, unromantic and non-menacing as they may be, should be recognized for their role and the accomplishments they have made for a better understanding of the Saudi state, then and now.

Notes

1. For his biography, see `Abd Allah ibn `Abd al-Rahman al-Bassam, `*Ulama najd khilal thamaniyat qurun*, 2nd edtion, 6 vols. (Riyadh: Dar al-`Asimah, 1419/1998).
2. Sulayman ibn Sihman, *Irshad al-talib ila ahamm al-matalib* (Cairo: Mitba`at al-Manar, A. H. 1340), and *Minhaj ahl al-haqq wa al-`itidal fi mukhalaft ahl al-jahl wa al-ibtida* (Cairo: Mitba`at al-Manar, A. H. 1340). Abu `Abd al-Rahman ibn `Aqil suggests there is a third printed book, *al-Jawab al-fariq bayn al-`imama wa al-`as'ib*, which I have been unable to locate. See *Masa'il min tarikh al-jazira al-`arabiyya* (Riyadh: Mu'assasat Dar al-Asala, 1994).
3. See, e.g., `Abd al-Rahman ibn Muhammad ibn Qasim, ed., *al-Durar al-saniyya fi al-ajwiba al-najdiyya*, 16 vols. (N.p., 1935), 4: 258; and Hafiz Wahba, *Jazirat al-`arab fi al-qarn al-`ashrin* (Cairo: Matfa`at Lajna al-Talif wa al-Tarjawa al-Nauhr, 1956), 292.
4. The theme is pervasive. Joseph Kostiner's writings are thoroughly tribe- and Bedouin-centric. See for example *The Making of Saudi Arabia: 1916–1936* (Oxford: Oxford University Press, 1993). Stephen Duguid, "A Biographical Approach to the Study of Social Change in the Middle East: Abdullah Tariki as a New Man," *International Journal of Middle Eastern Studies* 1 (1970): 193–220, 199, notes "[T]he key to political power in Saudi Arabia is the tribal structure" where the royal family is the "dominant tribe." For Gary Troeller, *The Birth of Saudi Arabia: Britain and the Rise of the House of Saud* (London: Frank Cass, 1976), xz, xzii, 38, 102, King `Abd al-`Aziz was an "obscure tribal chief," Arabian society was "tribal in structure," and Troeller elevates a handful of King `Abd al-`Aziz's cousins, the `Ara'if, to the status of full tribe. Michael Cook,

"The Expansion of the First Saudi State: The Case of Washm," in *The Islamic World: Essays in Honor of Bernard Lewis*, C.E. Bosworth, Charles Issawi, Roger Savory and A. L. Udovitch, eds. (Princeton: The Darwin Press, 1989), 661, writes that "one modelizes a tribal population." Aziz al-Azmeh, *Islamic Modernities* (London: Verso, 1996), 105, 111, says that tribal `asabiya* is the linchpin of Wahhabite ideology, and he calls the state a "tribal polity," imputing a strength to the Saudi "clan" that is quite impressive if ahistorical. Azmeh in part bases his analysis on Waddah Sharara, *al-'Ahl wa al-ghanima* (Beirut: n.p., 1981), whose ideas are centered on "clans." J. E. Peterson, "The Arabian Peninsula in Modern Times: A Historiographical Survey," *American Historical Review* 96 (1991): 1435–49, 1437, lumps the Saudi polity with "tribal states" where the state "evolved out of tribal leadership," only to puzzle later over the success of a "minor family" and emphasizes King `Abd al-`Aziz heavy dependence on the Ikhwan. John B. Glubb, *War in the Desert* (London: Hodder and Stoughton, 1960), 161, calls `Abd al-`Aziz a "Bedouin." Iliya Harik, "The Origins of the Arab State System," in *The Foundations of the Arab State*, Ghassan Salame, ed. (London: Croom Helm, 1987), 24, in his typology of Arab states, finds Saudi Arabia a good example of a polity in which "authority is vested in a tribal chief. "Ghassan Salame, 'Strong' and 'Weak' States, a Qualified Return to the *Muqadimmah*," in Salame ed., *Foundations of the Arab State*, 213, imposing the Khaldunian model, argues that the success of Wahhabism (and the Saudi state) was the result of Wahhabis' attachment to "a strong tribal `asabiyya*, that of the Sa`ud family." Interestingly, but perhaps not surprisingly, practically no author names this impressive tribe of which Al Sa`ud are the presumed chiefs. For more on the same theme, see Donald Cole and Soraya Altorki, "Was Arabia tribal? A Reinterpretation of the Pre-Oil Society," *Journal of South Asian and Middle Eastern Studies* 15 (1992): 71–87.

5. Cook, "Expansion of the First Saudi State," 679. In the following pages, all factors and processes suggested as contributing to the emergence of the Saudi state are endogenous. This by no means implies that there were no exogenous elements, but our knowledge is so far insufficient to support more than speculations. Be that as it may, the rise of the state came on the heel of interesting changes internationally and regionally. Perhaps the presence of the Portuguese and other European powers in the Gulf could have altered trade and caravan patterns. The same may be said for the rise of *Shi`ism* in Safavid Iran and the later fall of the dynasty; one wonders about that conversion from *Sunnism* and its effects on pilgrimage routes which used to go through Hasa and Najd. In addition, the 1720s and 1730s witnessed intensive conflict between Iran and the Ottomans centered in Iraq, which may have disrupted certain trade patterns.

6. Najd here is defined as the areas bordered from the south by the Empty Quarter, the east by the Dahna sand belt, the north by the Nafud and the west by the Hijaz mountains. Geographically, it is divided into two parts, the western, `Alyat (Upper) and eastern, Safilat (Lower) Najd. `Alyat Najd geomorphology and soil conditions make it ideal as pasture for nomads when rain falls, but water is limited and only few permanent settlements can survive.

Conversely, the younger geological sedimentary formations of Safilat Najd with their extensive wadi systems, superior soil, and relatively abundant groundwater is where the *Hadar* are concentrated. For a competent summary of the geography and ecology of the area, see Uwaidah al- Juhany, "The History of Najd Prior to the Wahhabis: A Study of Social, Political and Religious Conditions in Najd During the Centuries Preceding the Wahhabi Reform Movement," Ph.D. diss., University of Washington, 1983, 44–71.

7. *Hadari* society is composed of two distinct groups, the *asil* families who are of "pure" Arabian descent and the non-*asil*, or Khadiri community (see later). That the *asil* groups maintain genealogies should not be confused with a tribal structure similar to the Bedouins. The loss of tribal organization is further exacerbated by the fact that most towns were of mixed population, and regions are even more mixed in terms of genealogies so that no contiguity is maintained to allow the rudiments of a tribal organization to exist in any given territory. Many tribes from which the *Hadar* claim descent are either extinct or have migrated to the Levant, and the surrounding tribes usually have no genealogical connections with much of the *Hadari* core areas. The great Tamimi groups are so dispersed throughout Najd as to render any *tribal* structure or control meaningless. They spread from Ha'il in the north down to Hawtat Bani Tamim in the south. The same is true about the other Wa'ili groups who are just as widely spread. For the latter and their dispersion, see `Abd Allah ibn Muhammad al-Bassam, *Tuhfat al-mushtaq min akhbar najd wa al-hijaz wa al-`iraq*, 99–102 [Transcription of original manuscript by Nur al-Din Shurayba, 1956.]

8. The process of detribalization may have begun as early as the seventh century. Dale F. Eickleman, "Musaylima: An Approach to the Social Anthropology of Seventh Century Arabia," *Journal of the Economic and Social History of the Orient* 10 (1967): 17–56, 28.

9. Hamad al-Jasir, *Madinat al-riyadh `abr atwar al-tarikh*, (Riyadh: Dar al-Yamama lil Tiba`a wa al-Nashr, A.H. 1386) is a short history of the region from earliest times down to the twentieth century.

10. Al-Juhany, "History of Najd," 266.

11. Al-Juhany, "History of Najd," 266; Cook, "Expansion of the First Saudi State," 677; and Khalid S. Dakhil, "The Social Origins of Wahhabism," Ph.D. diss., University of California at Los Angeles, 1998.

12. `Abd Allah ibn `Abd al-Rahman al-Bassam, *Khizanat al-tawarikh al-najdiyya*, 10 vols. (n.p., 1419/1999), 7: 74–5, 106. In this example, Tuwaym, a village in Sudayr, had four different chiefs assassinated in A.H. 1120/1708–9 and the solution to the problem was to divide the town into four independent quarters, the *marbu`a* (or quartet). Muqbil al-Dhukayr (d. 1363/1944), a foremost expert on Najdi history, concludes about the episode: "this is a microcosm of the prevalent conditions in Najd." `Ushayqir had two independent quarters.

13. The chronicles are rich in such news. One efficient way to appreciate the excessive instability within these towns and among them is to read the "*sawabiq*" section appended to `Uthman ibn Bishr, *`Unwan al-majd fi tarikh najd*, 2 vols. (Riyadh: Darat al-Malik `Abd al-`Aziz, 1982, 2: 295–377), which covers the

pre-Wahhabi period. Cook, "Expansion of the First Saudi State," offers a good picture of such politics in the Washm area, although his description of it as "tribal" misses the point, and if Qasab and Hurayyiq, which he excludes, are taken into account, the picture would be even bleaker. Saad Abdullah al-Sowayan, *al-Shi'r al-nabati* (Beirut: Dar al-Saqi, 2000), 403–96, touches on the politics of Sudayr settlements.

14. Paul Dresch, *Tribes, Government, and History in Yemen* (Oxford: Clarendon Press, 1993); Hamad al-Jasir, "Lamahat wa intiba'at 'an mushahadati fi al-sarawat," *al-Arab* 24 (1989): 58–71, and idem, "Harb qabilah qahtaniyya al-asl imtazajat biha furu' 'adnaniyya," *al-Arab* 25 (1990): 545–551.

15. The ecology of Najd is the most likely explanation of this phenomenon. A version of the biblical "seven-year" cycle has been documented, e.g., by al-Juhany, "History of Najd Prior to the Wahhabis," 108–14. Also see S. al-Barrak and G. Hussain, "A Study into the Agro-Climatic Conditions in the Central and Eastern Regions of Saudi Arabia," *Arabian Gulf Journal of Scientific Research* 1 (1983): 551–67. It seems that the nomads are the most vulnerable to droughts followed by the northern *Hadari* areas that depend on superficial (non-aquifer) groundwater for irrigation, especially Sudayr. Both communities regularly migrate in response to droughts, the Bedouins to the Levant and the *Hadar* to Iraq and Hasa.

16. Dominant tribes in early Islamic centuries (e.g., Asad, Bakr, Bahila) became weaker, merged into stronger groups or disappeared altogether. This process continued throughout the following centuries. By the seventh/thirteenth century, Lam was formed by the grouping of Tay and other clans, and it vied for supremacy in Najd with the other newly formed tribal federation, al-Dafir. By the tenth/sixteenth century, other tribes appeared including 'Anaza, which took over the pasture lands of upper Najd from al-Dafir. Perhaps due to climactic conditions, sections of 'Anaza and Shammar pushed northward into the Levant in the middle of the seventeenth century relieving the pressure on al-Dafir, which reasserted its dominance over Najd. See al-Juhany, "History of Najd Prior to the Wahhabis," 116. A century later Mutayr ascended and became the most powerful group. Qahtan and Dawasir emerged during the sixteenth century. By the nineteenth century, Qahtan had become the dominant tribe. New tribes still appeared in the nineteenth century: 'Utayba displaced Qahtan in Upper Najd and 'Ijman and Al Murrah pushed further eastward and displaced the Banu Khalid. For 'Utayba, see Muhammad 'Ali al-'Ubayyid, *al-Najm al-lami' lil nawadir jami'* (Manuscript, n.p., n.d.), 315 and *passim*, and Abu 'Abd al-Rahman ibn 'Aqil, *Diwan al-shi'r al-'ammi bi lahjat ahl najd*, 5 vols. (Riyadh: Dar al-'Ulum, 1982–86), *passim*. For 'Ijman, see Abu 'Abd al-Rahman ibn 'Aqil, *al-'Ijman wa za'imuhum rakan ibn hithlayn* (Riyadh: Dar al-Yamama lil Tiba'a wa al-Nashr, 1983).

17. See a discussion of this custom in ibn 'Aqil, *Diwan al-shi'r*, 1: 123.

18. Many of the well-known leading families and clans of the famous Arabian Bedouin tribes are acknowledged to have come from other tribes. The Al Humayd, chiefs of the Barqa section of 'Utayba, are reckoned to be from the Buqum; Duwish, the paramount chiefs of Mutayr, from Shahran; the

Dhuwaybi chiefs of Harb from `Utayba; the Jarba chiefs of the Jarba Shammar
are proud of their Sharifi descent and are considered fully Shammaris; the
Sa`dun of the Muntafiq in Iraq and the Tayyar of `Anaza are of Hashimi
origins. See al-`Ubayyid, *al-Najm al-lami`*, 262, 317–18, 321; and Abu `Abd
al-Rahman ibn `Aqil, *Al al-jarba fi al-tarikh wa-l-adab* (Riyadh: Dar al-
Yamama lil Tiba`a wa al-Nashr, 1983), 210.

19. There exists a tendency within *Hadari* society to identify with the dominant
    tribe that is closest in kin to them. But unlike the Bedouins, this process is less
    supple and of limited value since the *Hadar* are not participants in the life of
    the nomads and little benefit seems to accrue from such identification (other
    than the possibility to avoid payment of *khuwa*). Tribalism within *Hadari* soci-
    ety appears to mean nothing more than a recitation of genealogies as attested
    by the nasty disputes among the same lineages within each settlement.

20. Henry L. Rosenfeld, "A Military-Occupational Specialization of the Kin
    Among The Pastoral Bedouins: A Key to the Process of Caste Formation in the
    Arabian Desert," Ph.D. diss., Columbia University, 1951, 9, uses the term
    "caste" to designate this inferior position; within Arabian social structure this
    term is probably an exaggeration.

21. The non-*asil* tribes are collectively dubbed "Hutaym," a designation that many
    of its constituent groups reject. A typical classification would include Shararat,
    `Awazim, Banu Rashid, Huwaytat, and Banu `Atiyya. See al-`Ubayyid, *al-
    Najm al-lami`*, 372. The Salab were of even lower status.

22. In the early twentieth century, the non-*asil* Huwaytat, who had to pay tribute
    in the nineteenth century to the Shararat, another non-*asil* tribe, were essen-
    tially rehabilitated to a full *asil* status in recognition of their ascendant military
    prowess. See Alois Musil, *Northern Najd, a Topographical Itinerary* (New York:
    American Geographical Society, 1928), 8; Rosenfeld, "Military-Occupational
    Specialization," 45; and al-`Ubayyid, *al-Najm al-lami`*, 376. Note that the
    non-*asil* tribes are not equally non-*asil* in their own eyes; many would not
    intermarry with other, more inferior ones. The Banu Rashid trace their origins
    to ancient Arabian tribes and were on the ascendance when the modern Saudi
    state was consolidated in the 1930s. Professor Saad Abdallah Sowayan, who fol-
    lows tribal events in conjunction with his interest in *nabati* poetry, told me in
    a private conversation that if it had not been for the advent of the modern state,
    the Banu Rashid would have achieved full *asil* status in the twentieth century.

23. This is a large part of Najdi society, perhaps as much as a quarter of the popu-
    lation. It is not a "tribe" per se but a residual category in which any person with
    problematic (or no) genealogy would be classified. `Abd Allah ibn Muhammad
    ibn Khamis, *Tarikh al-yamama*, 7 vols. (Riyadh: Matabi` al-Farazdaq, 1987),
    4: 86, suggests that the name is a holdover from the Banu al-'Ukhaydir era
    when the dynasty attempted to stamp out tribalism in reaction to which some
    people had to abandon or hide their tribal identity. It is more likely that this
    term has an ethnic basis and is an expression of darker complexion. In north-
    ern parts of Najd, the term is not used and is replaced by derogatory epithets,
    such as *sunna`* (craftsmen) or `*abid*, i.e., slaves.

24. In *Hadari* society, Khadiris did not pay any special tribute to the *asil* groups
    and had wide latitude in terms of occupations; indeed *all* occupations were

open to them and it was only the *asil* ones who had restrictions. Only becoming chiefs of settlements seems to have eluded them. The one exception I can find is the assumption of power by a slave of the chief of Riyadh when his master died leaving minor children; he was expelled and the famous Diham ibn Dawas, the most energetic enemy of Wahhabism of his time, took over in A.H. 1151/1738–39. The other possible exception is the assumption of the amir/shaykh status by members of the non-*asil* Al Zuhayr family in al-Zubayr in southern Iraq. The town was, for all practical purposes, a natural extension of the Najdi social order. Even factions there were organized according to their original Najdi *towns* and not their tribe or genealogy. It is only after the advent of Wahhabism that we see the Khadiris assume prominent political and military positions. One of the earliest is the appointment of 'Ali al-Juraysi as *amir* of the town of Raghaba. See al-Bassam, *Tuḥfat al-mushtaq* 106; Barclay Raunkiaer, *Through Wahhabiland on Camelback* (New York: Frederick A. Praeger, 1969), 25; Abu 'Abd al-Rahman ibn 'Aqil, *Amir shu'ara al-nabat, muhammad ibn lu'bun* (Riyadh: Dar ibn Lu'bun, 1997); al-Bassam, *Khizanat al-tawarikh*, 9: 109, 111–12; 'Abd Allah ibn Sa'd al-Husayn, "Raghaba wa ansab sukkaniha" *al-Arab* 29 (1994): 547–552.

25. A factor that may have contributed to further detribalization in pre-Wahhabi Najd is the ability of women to inherit, which would have misaligned property interests and genealogical lines.

26. Though I am unaware of any scholarly treatment of the subject, it seems that in the extreme north and south, in Jabal Shammar and Wadi al-Dawasir, there are no discernible differences in the dialects of the *Hadari* and Bedouin populations.

27. The *Hadari*s peculiarly use their respective *nakhwa*s as a means of identification during the pilgrimage to Mecca. Regrettably, I am unaware of any studies of either *nakhwa*s or *wasm*s. My comments should therefore be considered tentative.

28. The richest collection of *nakhwa*s, though still limited, is found in ibn Khamis, *Mu'jam al-yamama*, under several town entries.

29. This is also the *nakhwa* used by the Wahhabis in general. It is not clear whether it pre-dates the movement. See ibn Khamis, *Mu'jam al-yamama*, 424, and 'Abd Allah ibn Muhammad ibn Khamis, *Tarikh al-yamama*, 7 Vols. (Riyadh: Matabi' al-Farazdaq, 1987), 6: 137–8.

30. ibn Khamis, *Mu'jam al-yamama*, 1: 343, 2: 125.

31. Al-'Awni's famous poem urging the Qasimi 'uqayl to come to the rescue of their homeland after the battle of Sarif (see later) invokes the term frequently. See al-Bassam, *Khizanat al-tawarikh*, 7: 356–8, and Saad Abdullah al-Sowayan, *Nabati Poetry* (Berkeley: University of California Press, 1985), 82–3.

32. Like many *nakhwa*s, its provenance is uncertain. There is an area by the name Juraysi in the town of Baq'a (near Ha'il) from which the original settlers in Zilfi came. A family of the clan was also called by that name but it no longer exists. The only family currently with the name is Khadiri. See Nasir ibn Hamad al-Fahd, *Mu'jam ansab al-'usar al-mutahaddira min 'ashirat al-asa'ida* (Riyadh: Dar al-Bara, 2000), 56, 108.

33. Another related matter is the *bayraq*, or war standard, where each town or region would march to battle under its own banner. It is not clear whether such regional *bayraq*s were generic or employed distinctive designs for each area.

34. We are addressing here the most significant of *wasm*s, i.e., of camels. Other animals, such as sheep and goats, are also branded but the identification tends to refer to smaller families and not larger units. There are tens, if not hundreds, of *wasm*s that differ in their shapes and their locations on the animal.

35. There is a quaint story circulating in the area about the origin of this *shahid*. It is said that the shaykhs of the al-Dafir tribe, the Al Suwayt, were forced to take refuge in `Alaqah in northern Zilfi and in gratitude to the *Hadari* assistance suggested that they add this *shahid* to their *wasm* so that Dafiri raiders would be able to recognize their camels and refrain from stealing them. al-Fahd, *Mu`jam ansab*, 197.

36. Another indicator of weakened tribal sentiment is the disappearance among the *Hadar* of the Bedouin practice of *tahyir/tahjir* through which a first cousin would have a claim to marry his first cousin and a right to block her marriage to others. Although difficult to document, it appears also that *Hadar* are much more exogamous than the nomads. Finally, the *Hadar* long ago lost the habit of maintaining their tribal identity as part of their names, and only Bedouins did (and still do) maintain this custom.

37. The centrality of *ghazw* to Bedouin life is nicely captured in the following, well-known anecdote. When Farhan (d. 1890), the great chief of the Jarba Shammar of Iraq, noticed the impressive physique of some Iraqi villagers, the following exchange took place:

> Farhan: Do you practice *ghazw*?
> Villagers: We do not know how.
> Farhan: Why not raid those shittier (*atga`*) than you?

The source is ibn `Aqil, *Al al-Jarba*, 194. On *ghazw* more generally, see L. E. Sweet, "Camel Raiding of North Arabian Bedouin," *American Anthropologist* 67 (1965): 1132–50, 1136; and Rosenfeld, "Military-Occupational Specialization," vi, 75.

38. Rosenfeld, "Military-Occupational Specialization," 65, 68–9, 71; and Sweet, "Camel Raiding," 1147. `Abd Allah al-Bassam, *Tuhfat al-mushtaq*, records not fewer than 40 *manakh*s between the beginning of his chronicle (A.H. 850) and the rise of Wahhabism and fewer than ten afterward. Ibn `Aqil, *Diwan al-shi`r*, 3:139–170, has a long section on the last of the *manakh*-type conflicts in upper Najd during the ascendancy of `Utayba in the late nineteenth century written by a contemporary.

39. *Khuwa* or *akhawa* both connote brotherhood/companionship.

40. A striking (and maybe understandable) feature of Najdi chronicles is their (almost) total silence on the issue of *khuwa* paid by Najdi towns to the Bedouins. See al-Juhany, "History of Najd," 270. It is of course possible that some towns, especially the larger ones, could resist payment but most did not have enough power to avoid it. The best documentation is available in writings about the nomads of northern Arabia, Iraq, and Syria, mostly by foreign

travelers. Rosenfeld, "Military-Occupational Specialization," 25; Carlo Guarmani, *Northern Najd, Journey from Jerusalem to Anaiza in Qasim* (London: The Argonaut Press, 1938), 17; John Lewis Bruckhardt, *Travels in Arabia* (London: Frank Cass, 1968), 3, 10, 193; Musil *Northern Najd*, 126, 257, 263. Tayma for a time was under Rashidi rule and simultaneously paying khuwa to the Bili tribe. 'Abd Allah al-Salih al-'Uthaymin, *Buhuth wa ta'liqat fi tarikh al-mamlaka al-'arabiyya al-sa'udiyya.* (n.p., 1984), 258. For the tributes paid by the interior towns of Najd, the evidence is mostly through nabati poetry, anecdotes, and the fleeting written reference. Ibn 'Aqil. *Diwan al-shi'r*, 3: 150–1. Some examples are also given by al-'Ubayyid, *al-Najm al-lami'* for several towns in upper Najd like Nifi (67) and Dariyya (315). He twice mentions a poetic exchange (67 and 282) between a Bedouin 'Utaybi and his *Hadari* counter-part, the famous ibn Subayyil (d. 1352/1933–34) from the town of Nifi. The former taunts the *Hadari* by his association with the cow (never possessed by Bedouins) and instructs him to pay up the *akhawa*. Ibn Subayyil retorts that he is simply giving him a bone like to a dog so that he would keep barking and protect the town. There is an edited version of a letter given by an 'Utaybi chief to Shaqra, a town in Washm, in which he renounces any claims to *akhawa* or *rafiq* rights. See al-Bassam, *Khizanat al-tawarikh*, 2: 236. During Ottoman rule in Hasa, the 'Ijman apparently collected *khuwa*. Ibn 'Aqil, *al-'ijman wa za'imuhum*, 160. The *ulama* found that *khuwa* that is paid by "some towns to the Bedouins" to "avoid their evil" to be permissible. See ibn Qasim, *al-Durar al-saniyya*, 9: 337.

41. The fears and worries (and costs) associated with desert travel as late as the early twentieth century are richly captured by a Danish traveler, Raunkiaer, *Through Wahhabiland*.

42. It is noticeable that on the periphery of Najd, the *Hadar* of several towns come from the same Bedouin tribe in whose *dira* the towns are located. In addition to Jabal Shammar, Khurma in eastern Hijaz is heavily identifiable with Subai', although more than half of the population were reckoned at one time to be non-*asil*. Some distance to the north, Turaba is considered a Buqum town; in the south, towns of Wadi al-Dawasir are inhabited mainly by the same groups as the Dawasir Bedouins. Ameen Rihani, *Tarikh najd al-hadith wa mulhaqatihi* (Beirut: Dar Rihani lil Tiba'a wa al-Nashr, 1954), 250.

43. For Wahhabism as a *Hadari* ideology, see Turki al-Hamad, "Tawhid al-jazira al-'arabiyya," *al-Mustaqbal al-'arabi* 93 (1986): 27–40. What is meant by Hanbalism here is not the legal school (*madhhab*) but the creed of *ahl al-hadith*, whose champions were the Hanbalis, but was widely held by members of other schools that had been developed in Muslim urban centers. In its intel-lectual genealogies, there is certainly nothing Bedouin about Wahhabism, but Musil, *Northern Najd*, 257, characterizes it as a religion of the nomads anyway.

44. The Shaykh's writings are full of references to the Bedouins and their tribes, whom he held to be pure *kafirs* as they would not even believe in resurrection and many basic Islamic tenets. See ibn Qasim *al-Durar al-saniyya* 8: 117–19, and 9: 385–95; and Sulayman ibn Sihman, *Irshad al-talib ila ahamm al-matalib* (Cairo: Mitba'at al-Manar, A.H. 1340), 4–5.

45. Apparently, `Arid is more resistant to the periodic droughts that afflict Najd since some of its water is obtained through springs (`uyun) that tap into ancient fossil aquifers as old as 20,000 years, making extensive *Hadari* settlements possible. See Leland Thatcher et. al., "Dating Desert Water," *Science* 134 (1961): 105–6. The area is also less hospitable to pastoral nomadism and fewer Bedouin tribes make it home. The population balance is therefore most likely to be to the advantage of the *Hadar*. It should be noted also that in 1136/1723–24 Najd suffered probably its worst drought in recorded history (named *sihhi*). See al-Bassam, *Tuhfat al-mushtaq*, 98. The Bedouins of Najd and the northern *Hadari* areas, which depend on non-aquifer waters, were more affected (i.e., `Attar in Sudayr was left with only four men and four water wells), which would leave the demographic balance in favor of the southern *Hadar* vis-à-vis both other *Hadar* and nomads. Assertions that Najdi nomads are superior in numbers to *Hadar* (al-Juhany, "History of Najd," 130; Kostiner, "Transforming Dualities," 226) are potentially misleading. First, they are at best conjectures, and second, distribution of nomads and *Hadar* is uneven throughout Najd, varying according to climatic conditions.

46. See ibn Bishr, `Unwan al-majd, 1: 40. Ibn Humayd must have also feared the reformer's views on the legitimacy of taxes he was collecting. See Husayn ibn Ghannam, *Tarikh najd*. 2 vols. (Cairo: Mustafa al-Babi al-Halabi, 1949), 3.

47. The circumstances of his becoming chief of the town were bloody and his position was not very secure which may have contributed to his support of the Shaykh. See al-Juhany, "History of Najd," 189.

48. According to ibn Bishr, the Shaykh explained to the Saudi ruler the power of the idea of *tawhid*, saying that those who champion it "shall rule over people and land," with the hope that the ruler would unify the Muslims and be their imam and his sons afterward. When Ibn Saud asked for exemption to continue collecting the extra-*shar`i* taxes, the Shaykh declined to accept and it had to be abandoned. See `Unwan al-majd, 1: 42. The conspicuous political nature of Wahhabism is further attested to by al-Dhukayr who explains that the tough resistance over 27 years by the Riyadh chief, Diham ibn Dawwas, as well as by other local Najdi chiefs, was based on their political fears and not necessarily their rejection of revivalist Islam per se. See al-Bassam, *Khizanat al-Tawarikh*, 7: 112–13.

49. ibn Bishr, `Unwan al-majd, 2: 23, is one example of a Wahhabi authority who is unambiguous about the Sa`ud family's descent from the Banu Hanifa. The confusion about origins is due to a number of factors. One is that both Banu Hanifa and `Anaza are considered by some to share a common ancestor, Wa'il. Another is the historical coincidence of the rise of the Sa`ud family at a time when `Anaza was the hegemonic tribe in Najd. See ibn Khamis, *Tarikh al-yamama*, 4: 29. King `Abd al-`Aziz, moreover, found it expedient to claim this affinity to further his territorial gains, especially in his negotiations with the British. Rihani, *Tarikh najd al-hadith*, 308–9, 311. Finally, it is not unusual for weaker groups to identify (or be identified) with more successful ones, as commonly observed in many Najdi families, both Bedouin and *Hadar*. This is certainly the case with the other ascendant *Hadari* families at the time, the

'Utub of Kuwait and Bahrayn (Al Sabah and Al Khalifa) who are also described as 'Anaza. For a full discussion of these controversies, see ibn 'Aqil's introduction to Rashid ibn 'Ali ibn Jurays, *Muthir al-wajd fi ansab muluk najd* (Riyadh: Darat al-Malik 'Abd al-'Aziz, 1999), 11–66; Hamad al-Jasir, *Jamharat ansab al-usar al-mutahaddira fi najd*, 2 vols. (Riyadh: Dar al-Yamama lil Tiba'a wa al-Nashr, n.d.), 2: 860–8; al-Juhany, *History of Najd*, 230 n. 53.

50. That the Saudis never had the numbers nor the '*asabiya* that Bedouins had is clearly understood. Shaykh 'Abd al-Rahman ibn Hasan described them as "a small family" (*hathihi al-hamula 'ala qillatihim*). See ibn Qasim, *al-Durar al-saniyya*, 8: 86. See as well ibn Khamis, *Mu'jam al-yamama*, 1: 417, and *Tarikh al-yamama*, 6: 132, 173, and Wahba, *Jazirat al-'arab*, 215.

51. M. S. El-Shaafy, "The Military Organization of the First Saudi State," *Annals of Leeds University Oriental Society* 7 (1969–73): 61–74; Jerzy Zdanowski, "Military Organization of the Wahhabi Amirates (1750–1932)," *New Arabian Studies* 2 (1994): 130–9; and Wahba, *Jazirat al-'arab*, 10, 287. "War" for the Bedouin is not a lethal affair as a rule and a nomad would not lose his life in order to protect his camel. He knows that next time he would be able to recover it or pilfer someone else's. He would not be expected to fight in the determined way of the *Hadari*s and in many historical battles the first to flee were the nomads, which usually caused their side to lose. War for him, in addition, is an enterprise for loot; thus a common tactic in *Hadari* battles is to ensure that loot is available for the opposing forces to distract them and cause their Bedouins to busy themselves with booty. See al-'Ubayyid, *al-Najm al-lami'*, 54.

52. Not only were the Wahhabis cognizant of the importance of maintaining this coalition, but ibn 'Abd al-Wahhab himself was aware of the dangers of allowing the Al Sa'ud to assume the *imara* of newly conquered towns. Thus, when Imam 'Abd al-'Aziz, on the conquest of Riyadh in 1187/1773, wished to appoint his brother 'Abd Allah to be the town's *amir*, ibn 'Abd al-Wahhab vetoed the decision viewing it as a threat to the unity of the realm. Ibn Qasim, *al-Durar al-saniyya*, 9: 80.

53. They also attacked their customary laws and imposed *shari'a* judges on them. The *ulama* hold that Bedouin customary law (*sawalif*), if applied, is ground for *kufr*, and characterize Bedouin judges as *taghut*s. Burckhardt, *Travels in Arabia*, 288; ibn Qasim, *al-Durar al-saniyya*, 10: 426, 502–11.

54. See ibn Bishr, *'Unwan al-majd*, 1: 268–74. Imam 'Abd al-'Aziz is considered the first Imam to abolish the Bedouins' custom of collecting *khuwa* from towns and wayfarers. See ibn Khamis, *Tarikh al-yamama*, 6: 190.

55. Ibn Bishr, *'Unwan al-majd*, 1: 271, For a reaffirmation of this principle by the most successful of Saudi leaders, King 'Abd al-'Aziz, see Rihani, *Tarikh najd al-hadith*, 309. Local folklore also corroborates the view of the natural differences and conflict between the two communities. The "classical" legend encompassing some attitudes held by Bedouins toward the *Hadar* (lack of courage in battle) is immortalized by a well-known poem by a *Hadari* protesting such denigration after his success in battle in recovering his Bedouin neighbors' losses. Sowayan, *Nabati Poetry*, 21–3. A humerous example of some attitudes held by the *Hadar* is given by a famous nineteenth Hijazi 'Utaybi

(*Hadari*) poet, Budaywi al-Waqdani, who admonishes his son for keeping company with the Bedouins and advises him to avoid them, because their "ways are not your ways," they would steal your belongings if they had a chance, etc.

56. Ibn Bishr, `*Unwan al-majd*, 1: 271. The Imam also shackled that chief together with the chief of Mutayr (al-Bassam, *Tuhfat al-mushtaq*, 137). Al-Dhukayr supports this claim and further emphasizes that the Imam imposed on the tribal chiefs the task of maintaining law and order within their *dira*s and held them personally responsible for their tribesmen's offenses. See al-Bassam, *Khizanat al-tawarikh*, 7: 152–3.

57. For the biographis of `Abd al-Latif and `Abd al-Rahman Al al-Shaykh, see al-Bassam, `*Ulama najd khilal thamaniyat qurun*, 1: 202–14 and 180–201.

58. See Wahba, *Jazirat al-`arab*, 220, for the practice of Imam Sa`ud (d. 1229/1814). There is an interesting letter sent by `Abd al-`Aziz to a Bedouin chief addressing some issues, including how he would hold the tribe collectively responsible for certain acts by individual tribesmen. See ibn Khamis, *Mu`jam al-yamama*, 2: 367–8.

59. ibn Qasim, *al-durar al-saniyya*, 6: 422–3. There are other legally sanctioned anti-Bedouin practices that would require a separate treatment.

60. This is perhaps understandable. The Bedouins are assumed to be unskilled administratively and, more important, the feelings of group solidarity, `*asabiya*, among the Bedouins is a great disadvantage as the *Hadari*s could never trust them to administer a town fairly. For a list of Saudi-appointed amirs, see ibn Bishr, `*Unwan al-majd*, 1: 278, 362, 423.

61. See ibn Bishr, `*Unwan al-majd*, 2: 230. A clue to determine the background of a person is the name. Practically all Bedouin names terminate with their tribal identity, a practice that survives to this day. Accordingly, ibn Bishr mentions only a few: three commanders from the Mutayr tribe and one `Utaybi leader of the cavalry, who was accused of being too quick to surrender to the invading Egyptians.

62. ibid, 2: 237.

63. The `Ijman (an offshoot of the large Yam tribe of Najran) migrated into Najd in small numbers from around the end of the eighteenth century and were cause for a major Wahhabi defeat when the Yamis invaded in 1178/1764–65. Imam Turki, fleeing the Egyptians, resided with an `Ajmi clan and married into them. Later, he encouraged them to settle in the Hasa area as counterweight to the Banu Khalid. The `Ijman proved a major challenge to any Saudi ruler well into the 1930s. See ibn Bishr, `*Unwan al-majd*, 1: 93. `Utayba made its presence felt in upper Najd as early as 1236/1820; however, there are references to `Utaybi raiders in upper Najd as early as 1148/1735–36. By the early twentieth century, they became the dominant tribe in that area, creating further pressures on the rest of the nomads and causing a major redistribution of nomadic clans within Najd. al-`Ubayyid, *al-Najm al-lami`*, 315; al-Bassam, *Tuhfat al-mushtaq*, 106.

64. Whereas pre-Wahhabi Najd was dominated by `Arid and Sudayr, by the nineteenth century a shift in population size and economic resources was clearly discernible. This may have been related to growth in trade and trade routes between these areas and the outside world, especially the Levant. Although pre-dating Wahhabism, it was toward the end of the eighteenth and

beginning of the nineteenth centuries that the `uqayl emerged as a significant factor in the economy of the region. See al-Juhany, "History of Najd Prior to the Wahhabis," 225.

65. The Humaydi dynasty in the east that preceded Wahhabism was similarly built on a tribal power base; the Rashidis, however, enjoyed the advantage of the loyalty of both *Hadar* and Bedouin groups in the Jabal, something the Humaydis were not able to achieve due to the detribalization of the *Hadari* communities in Hasa.

66. For a discussion of the relationship between the Bedouin and *Hadari* leaderships, see ibn `Aqil, *Al al-Jarba*, 84–7. It seems that, unlike his kinsmen, the Rashids, ibn `Ali was in the traditional *Hadari* mold with little attachment to or influence with the Shammar Bedouins. See al-`Uthaymin, *Buhuth wa ta`liqat*, 46.

67. Dari ibn Fuhayd ibn Rashid, *Nubtha tarikhiyya `an najd*, Hamid al-Jasir, ed. (Riyadh: Dar al-Yamama lil Tiba`a wa al-Nashr, 1966), 61, 65; al-`Uthaymin, *Buhuth wa ta`liqat*, 74–5; ibn `Aqil, *Diwan al-shi`r*, 2: 132–8. Although the Rashidis were clearly *Hadari*, they emphasized that their concerns were not typically *Hadari* and that they were like Bedouins in their pre-occupation with warfare. See ibn `Aqil, *Diwan al-shi`r*, 2: 91.

68. The identification between *Hadar* and Bedouin in the Rashidi *amirate* was practically total, thus even their *nakhwa* was none other than that of their `Abda (nomadic) clan, *al-sana`is*. Indeed, chronicles often describe ibn Rashid as the "chief of Shammar Bedouins and villages of the Jabal." See e.g., al-Bassam, *Khizanat al-tawarikh*, 3: 152. For more local *nakhwa*s in Ha'il, see Rihani, *Tarikh najd al-hadith*, 221.

69. Al-`Ubayyid, *al-Najm al-lami`*, 36. Both Muhammad ibn `Abd Allah al-Salman, *al-Ahwal al-siyasiyya fi al-qasim fi `ahd al-dawlah al-sa`udiyya al-thanya: 1238–1309/1823–1891* (n.p., 1999) and Sowayan, *Nabati Poetry*, 75–87, who carefully studied the region during this period, never take their own analyses to their logical conclusions, independence.

70. In fact, Qasim was so strongly identified with camel exports that the traders' name, `uqayl, almost became synonymous with the inhabitants of the region despite the fact it was not exclusive to them.

71. There were many bloody encounters between the two sides with Qasim often on the losing side. Baq`a, the earliest, major battle (1257/1841), was caused by Qasim's attempt to help their `Anaza allies and the battle of Mulayda (1308/1891) was caused by, *inter alia*, friction over collection of *zakat* from neighboring Bedouins. See al-`Ubayyid, *al-Najm al-lami`*, 24–5, 36; al-Bassam, *Khizanat al-tawarikh*, 7: 217–18, 284–6; and al-Salman, *al-ahwal al-siyasiyya*, 122–32, 253–79.

72. The best example of these alliance advocates is the Bassam family. Upon King `Abd al-`Aziz's conquest of `Unayza, he expelled a number of their leading men. See al-Bassam, *Khizanat al-tawarikh*, 7: 389–90; 5: 138–41. `Uqayl and `Uqaylat, whose etymology is of uncertain origin, and who mostly came from Qasim, are originally the camel traders from central Arabia, but the meaning over time came to cover all people who go outside Najd and were either traders or mercenaries. With the pre-occupation with tribes, some westerners dubbed `uqayl a tribe or even a "race." Since its membership represents a cross section

of Najdi *Hadari* society, including Khadiri elements, Dickson, the British agent in Kuwait, describes them not only as a tribe but a non-*asil* one at that. Rosenfeld, who is otherwise insightful, erroneously suggests that `*uqayl* may be a "caste-like group" and claims that *asil* nomads would not intermarry with `*uqayli*, which is untrue so long as the person is of *asil* origin. This group further reflects the depth of *Hadari* Najdi detribalization as many of its most influential members are Khadiri. In early nineteenth-century Baghdad, the chief of the `Arid `*uqayl* was ibn Ghannam, a Khadiri. See Guarmani, *Northern Najd*, 142; John B. Glubb, *Mudhakkarat glubb basha*, translated by S. Takriti (Baghdad: al-Fajr, 1988) [translation of Glubb's *The Changing Scenes of Life: An Autobiography*], 106; Rosenfeld, "Military-Occupational Specialization," 46, 116; and al-Bassam, *Tufhat al-mushtaq*, 174.

73. Unlike the Saudis, the Rashidis failed to develop a system of succession, though it is said that `Abd Allah and his brother, `Ubayd, made a pact that succession would be through `Abd Allah's line only. Within that branch, the first succession was smooth but the second occurred laterally and subsequent successions happened usually through regicide. The Rashidis appear to have inherited the worst of *Hadari* traits, disorderly succession. Among the Bedouins, succession to the position of the chief, as a rule, is peaceful even when no rules of primogeniture exist. The only exception for Najd is the assumption by Faysal al-Duwish of the leadership of Mutayr through the murder of his predecessor in 1312/1894–95, a harbinger of things to come. See al-`Ubayyid, *al-Najm al-lami`*, 107; and al-Bassam, *Tufhat al-mushtaq*, 202.

74. Al-`Ubayyid, *al-Najm al-lami`*, 31, quotes him saying that he never knew of a *Hadari* wronging a Bedouin. This book is a valuable source for the less-known parts of the history and ethnography of Najd, especially for the period to which he was an eyewitness. He was an itinerant *Hadari* trader from al-Qasim; he lived in Mecca, Ta'if, and Khurma, where he was prayer *imam* for Khalid ibn Lu'ay. He was also an *imam* for the chief of the Shayabin clan of `Utayba. For his biography, see al-Bassam, `*Ulama najd*, 6: 306–11.

75. Passage found in al-`Ubayyid, *al-Najm al-lami`*, 45. `Abd al-Rahman was not the only or first Saudi leader to articulate a pro-*Hadari* stand as a basis for rule; his cousin, `Abd Allah ibn Thunayyan, who ruled between Faysal's two reigns, vowed that if he lived long enough he would not "leave even one horse with the Bedouins." See ibn Rashid, *Nubtha tarikhiyya*, 34. `Abd al-Rahman's pro-*Hadar* views are further corroborated in al-Bassam, *Khizanat al-tawarikh*, 4: 133; 7: 318–19.

76. Rihani, *Tarikh najd al-hadith*, 149, 151; Ibrahim ibn `Ubayd ibn `Abd al-Muhsin, *Tadhkirat uli al-nuha wa al-`irfan bi ayyam al-wahid al-dayyan wa dhikr hawadith al-zaman*, 5 vols. (Riyadh: Mu'assat al-Nur, n.d.), 2: 49.

77. Madawi al-Rasheed, "Durable and Non-Durable Dynasties," *British Society for Middle Eastern Studies Bulletin* 19 (1992): 144–58, 156; idem, *Politics in an Arabian Oasis City: The Rashidi Tribal Dynasty* (London: I. B. Tauris, 1991). The famed Philby also subscribes to this view. See John Habib, *Ibn Sa'ud's Warriors of Islam: The Ikhwan of Najd and their Role in the Creation of the Sa'udi Kingdom, 1910–1930* (Leiden: E.J. Brill, 1978), 23.

78. That the House of Rashid, the population of Ha'il, and the surrounding areas were Wahhabis are amply documented. Muhammad al-Za'arir, *Imarat al-rashid fi ha'il* (Amman: Bisan lil Nashr wa al-Tawzi', 1995), 34; ibn 'Aqil, *Masa'il min tarikh*, 254, 257; 'Abd All al-Salih al-'Uthaymin, *Nash'at imarat al-rashid* (n.p., 1991), 184–5. For comments on their "fanaticism" see Guarmani, *Northern Najd*, 56, 91. The famous 'Ubayd al-Rashid, for all his bloody history, is often described as a supporter of Wahhabism. See al-Rashid *Nubtha tarikhiyya*, 9. Even the Rashidi flag is identical to the Saudi with its Islamic inscriptions and unsheathed sword. The *ulama* of the Rashidi realm as well as its judges were the same as those of the Saudi State. See al-Za'arir, *Imarat al-rashid*, 106–7. It is true that for the people of southern Najd, the relaxed ways of the north (e.g., smoking) were frowned upon, but in the essentials no differences existed. Nonetheless, a close scrutiny of the *ulama's* polemics during the days of the Rashidi *amirate* and the first few decades of the Saudi restoration, reveals an interesting yet barely perceptible difference between the *ulama* supporting the competing houses; it revolves around the question of to what extent the Ottomans may be seen as true Muslims? Since the Rashidis were allied to the Ottomans, the pro-Saudi *ulama* maintained that the Ottomans were simply non-Muslims which led to the Rashidi *amirs* persecuting those who held such views. This difference must, however, be seen in context. It was the Saudi ruler, 'Abd Allah (d. 1889), who first requested Ottoman help against his brother, Sa'ud, splitting his own *ulama* in the process. King 'Abd al-'Aziz's intercourse with the definitely non-Muslim British presented the same challenge to the Wahhabi *ulama* but they still managed to maintain their support for that House. The best sources covering this subject are ibn Qasim, *al-Durar al-saniyya*, and al-Bassam, *'Ulama najd.*

79. Al-Rasheed, "Durable and Non-Durable Dynasties," 155, recognizes that the dominance of Shammar, as reflected in the Rashidi dynasty, was not something other groups were going to accept easily, hence it would take a non-tribally based alternative to appeal to the non-Shammar groups, something the Saudis offered.

80. The logic behind this, according to the Bedouins, is that since the allies are going to lose their possessions anyway, they may as well be kept by their "friends." See Wahba, *Jazirat al-'arab*, 10.

81. During 'Abd al-'Aziz's campaigns, he was also to suffer from Bedouin unreliability; in the battle of Jurab (1915), he was defeated mostly due to the plundering of his camp by his own Bedouin forces, in contrast with the loyal Shammar Bedouins who stood their ground with their leaders; also the 'Ijman retreated prematurely. His uncle, 'Abd Allah, suffered a similar fate in the battle of Juda (1287/1870–71) when Subay' retreated and plundered their own allies. See ibn 'Aqil, *Masa'il min tarikh*, 149, 150, 163; idem, *Ansab al-'usar*, 66–7, 78, 153; Rihani, *Najd al-hadith*, 99, 222, 224; al-Bassam, *Khizanat al-tawarikh*, 7: 504–5; ibn 'Aqil, *al-'ijman wa za'imuhjum*, 79; ibn Khamis, *Mu'jam al-yamama*, 1: 68; and ibn 'Ubayd, *Tadhkirat uli al-nuha*, 2: 183–4.

82. Ibn 'Ubayd, *Tadhkirat uli al-nuha*, 2: 81, 92; Rihani, *Najd al-hadith*, 174, 179, 185, 186.

83. See, e.g., the poem accusing the tribe of Qahtan of insulting one of the *matawi`a* sent by Imam Faysal by plucking his beard. Ibn `Aqil. *al-`ijman wa zaimuhum*, 240.

84. Ibn Khamis, *Tarikh al-yamama*, 3: 287. The *imam* invariably had to be *Hadari* since even rudimentary learning was not available to Bedouins.

85. For the *imam*, see al-`Ubayyid, *al-Najm al-lami`*, 265. Much of his poetry is published in the usual *nabati* collections. See ibn `Aqil, *Diwan al-shi`r*, 1: 115–206.

86. This equally applies to the paramount `Utaybi chief, Muhammad ibn Hindi ibn Humayd (d. 1914/15), who is reported to have had the same attitude. See ibn `Aqil, *Diwan al-shi`r*, 3: 156, 193.

87. Al-`Ubayyid, *al-Najm al-lami`*, 123–4. This transformation in outlook is attested in oral and written tradition. Al-Ubayyid (279) relates the story of the hapless *qadi* of Ranya who was robbed by Bedouins while traveling. When it was time for prayer, the robbers respectfully asked the *qadi* to be the *imam*. When he inquired why their fear of God would not extend to his property, the answer was blunt, "We do not wish to make enemies of God," but were willing to have the *qadi* as an enemy. A similar incident is still being reported in Zilfi in which the pilgrims were watering near a Bedouin encampment in Upper Najd when they noticed an `Utaybi chief performing his prayers, a sight they could only snicker at. When he had completed his prayer, the chief turned to the *Hadari* detractors and declared that they were senseless since he had no intention of fighting God on *all* fronts (i.e., robbing as well as not praying). Further north, Musil observes that Ruwala did not pray in 1908–9 but were doing so by 1914. See Rosenfeld, "Military-Occupational Specialization," 136.

88. The creation of the Ikhwan, as is well known, involved the copying of early Muslim models. Thus the *Hijar*, connoting, *inter alia*, the flight from unbelief to Islam, became the generic name of their numerous settlements. The Bedouin became a *muhajir*, left his old, errant ways, and embraced the faith. The nomad settlers sold their camels and tried to pursue a life of learning and agriculture with varying degrees of success. Rihani, *Najd al-hadith*, 262–3. He has a list (454–6) of the *Hijar* and their tribal affiliation. Habib, *Ibn Sa'ud's Warriors*, remains the best study on the subject though inaccurate on some points. He exaggerates the Ikhwan's military contributions (65, 156); and his assertion that conquest was the *raison d'etre* of the movement (117) is a simplification of a more complex process. He also implies that proselytism was the work of Bedouins.

89. Al-`Ubayyid, *al-Najm al-lami`*, 178. Some authors attribute to this force a critical role in the formation of the third state. Al-Rasheed, "Durable and Non-Durable Dynasties," 150, considers the "creation of a religious fighting force" to be the "most crucial step in Ibn Saud's expansion." For another view, see `Abd Allah al-Salih al-`Uthaymin, *Buhuth wa ta`liqat fi tarikh al-mamlaka al-`arabiyya al-su`udiyya* (n.p, 1984), 219.

90. The Sharifis were first to recognize the military potential of the Ikhwan, and in the early stage of conflict offered to end hostilities in return for certain concessions, including the Ikhwan's reversion to nomadic life. See Rihani, *Tarikh najd al-hadith*, 249.

91. It seems that the ascendance of this group of "half-learned" individuals with extreme views began with the Saudi civil war. See ibn 'Aqil, *Masa'il min tarikh*, 50–1. One interesting person, ibn Biti, is credited with some of the successes (and excesses) of the Ikhwan and engaged ibn Sihman and other *ulama* in polemics, e.g., ibn Qasim, *al-Durar al-saniyya*, 8: 421. For his role and his subsequent demise, see ibn 'Aqil, *Masa'il min tarikh*, 52–4. In Riyadh, I have heard some prominent Wahhabi names suspected of having been at least sympathetic with Ikhwan excesses. Sihman, *Minhaj ahl al-haqq*, 72, mentions one, 'Abd Allah al-Damigh. Two other names are mentioned in ibn 'Aqil, *Masa'il min tarikh*, 78, but no further information is given.

92. This is also observed by Troeller, *Birth of Saudi Arabia*, 210.

93. Barrington Moore, *Moral Purity and Persecution in History* (Princeton: Princeton University Press, 2000).

94. They would resent the *Hadar* generally for knowing the truth and taking so long to relay it; anyone not ready to declare that Sharif Husayn was a *kafir* would forfeit his life; they would not grant the traditional Bedouin *man'*, bodily safety after surrender; they would take no prisoners; and in their role as roving inquisitors, if they asked a man about his religion and he happened to answer correctly, they would simply declare that his knowledge was useless since he would not practice anyway. See al-'Ubayyid, *al-Najm al-lami'*, 189–190.

95. One of the interesting anecdotes related by al-'Ubayyid shows that as far as some Ikhwan were concerned, the new belief simply provided a different basis for plunder and not necessarily precluded it. The story goes as follows (*al-Najm al-lami'*, 190):

> I [al-'Ubayyid] have been told by a member of the Ikhwan that once while traveling in the desert they were met by a man with a donkey. The donkey was carrying two goat-skin bags full of ghee [*samn*] on his way to al-Khurma [a town on the border between Hijaz and Najd] to sell there. They were eight people; some said to the others, "ask him whether or not he knows his religion." They asked about his knowledge of religion and he answered all their questions competently and correctly and they failed to find a [single] mistake in his response. He and they almost went on their [separate] ways when they discussed [his fate] among themselves and one addressed him saying, "are you among those who believed then did not believe or among those who did not believe and then believed?" [The man] sensed that they were planning to kill him and take the donkey along with its load so he answered them saying, "I am among those who abandoned the donkey and fled," and he ran away. Since they were from 'Utayba and he was from Shalawa he feared he would be assassinated in this wilderness where no one was around to help him.

96. A major part of al-'Ubayyid's manuscript, *al-Najm al-lami'*, is a recording of Ikhwan's deeds and misdeeds, including many first hand experiences. One worthy of mention is the Ikhwan's murder of the brother of Khalid ibn Lu'ay, the famous sharif of Khurma and leader of the Wahhabi campaigns in Hijaz, for "worthless" reasons. Despite his power and influence, Khalid could not act

against these murderers who were cloaked by religious untouchability (191). Their impertinence spread all over Najd and was not confined to specific areas. My uncle Muhammad (b. 1914) tells me that he once went with his uncle (d. 1960) to look for some stray camels and needed to spend the night in the Bedouin *hijra* of Mulaih, about 25 miles south of Zilfi. When the last evening prayer was due, the Ikhwan summoned them to prayer. They tried to explain to them that they were travelers and as such had availed themselves of the permission to perform this prayer earlier, to which the answer was a contemptuous "you are *sfiri* [travelers, another of the sins invented by the Ikhwan] and would not even pray?" The two men, sensing imminent danger, hastened to obey the Ikhwan and perform the prayer one more time. In the same vein, Ahmad al-Nadawi (d. 1950s), a townsman from Zilfi, was friends with a Mutayri Ikhwan from the nearby *hijra* of Artawiyya, but this friendship had to stop at its gates. Once when Nadawi was praying in the *hijra*'s mosque and his friend was seated next to him, the latter, having no choice but to avoid greeting his polluted *Hadari* friend (he was a "traveler" after all), whispered under his breath "what kind of a heaven is this, oh Nadawi" (*ya jannat 'l-brekah ya'nnedawi!*).

97. Although the Saudis accept some responsibility for the events, they still maintained that much of the killing and looting was done by Hijazi Bedouins pretending to be Ikhwan.

98. Kostiner, "On Instruments and Their Designers," 308, claims that the early interests of the Ikhwan were to "mould the entire Najdi population of Najd in their own likeness." This is a generous reading of their interests; freedom to raid and wage *jihad* were what they were most interested in.

99. As early as 1338 (1919), the *ulama* were taking a strong position on Ikhwan raids of others and urging the Imam to prevent these transgressions. See ibn Qasim, *al-Durar al-saniyya*, 9: 94–6.

100. Thus al-Duwish declares that "we are neither Moslems fighting the unbelievers nor are we Arabs and Bedouins raiding each other and living on what we get from each other." Habib, *Ibn Sa'ud's Warriors of Islam*, 136.

101. See ibn Sihman, *Irshad al-talib*, 63, and *Minhaj ahl al-haqq*. Also see Rihani, *Tarikh najd al-hadith*, 433, and ibn ʿAbd al-Muhsin, *Tadhkirat uli al-nuha*, 2: 259–60.

102. While condemning these excesses, the Wahhabi *ulama*, nonetheless, would not deviate from the strict orthodox position that "*taʿarrub*" after the *hijra* is a major sin and may rise to total unbelief if done with certain intentions and attitudes. Ibn Qasim *al-Durar al-saniyya*, 8: 81–2, 454–5; 10: 452. For *taʿarrub*, see C. E. Bosworth, "A Note on *Taʿarrub* in Early Islam," *Journal of Semitic Studies* 34 (1989): 355–62.

103. Ibn Sihman, *Minhaj ahl al-haqq*, 72. It is not clear whether the ʿ*imama* itself, as opposed to the legal rules pertaining to its use, was a new innovation. *Nabati* poetry is replete with reference to it, and one of ibn ʿAbd al-Wahhab's sons is described as wearing one similar to the one worn by the Prophet. See ibn ʿAqil, *Masaʾil min tarikh*, 76.

104. For further elaboration on the exchange at that time, see ibn 'Aqil, *Masa'il min tarikh*, 52–81.

105. Azmeh, *Islamic Modernities*, 116, misunderstands the issue when he finds the "Wahhabite polity" imposing such a code.

106. The rules are conveniently listed, according to the various legal schools, under "albisa," *al-Mawsu'a al-fiqhiya*, vol. 6 (Kuwait: Wizarat al-Awqaf, 1986), 104. Of all Ikhwan beliefs and practices, this issue seems to be the most difficult to interpret rationally. First, they seem to address it mostly to other Bedouins and not to the *Hadar*. Second, to the extent it was meant to be a means of identification (e.g., another *wasm*), it was easily thwarted by wearing the piece to avoid danger. Finally, and this may be an indication of the original motive, the attacks against the *'iqal* are justified sometimes by the fact that "soldiers" wore it. Since Najd really had no soldiers at the time, it must have been a reference to Sharifi forces. See al-'Ubayyid, *al-Najm al-lami'*, 286; ibn Sihman, *Minhaj ahl al-haqq*, 94.

107. The objection to this device was made easier by an earlier fatwa, where the *ulama* had declined to declare it *haram*, but also refused to say it was legal. The professed an inability to understand its nature and, thus, to make a ruling. See ibn 'Abd al-Muhsin, *Tadhkirat uli al-nuha*, 3: 182. Perhaps the Ikhwan's hostility was based on the technological advantage the telegraph would give the central government, something they must have known through the experiences of the Hijazi and Iraqi Bedouins.

108. Ibn 'Abd al-Muhsin, *Tadhkirat uli al-nuha*, 3: 178, 186. The Ikhwan also objected to his use of non-Muslims such as Philby. Interestingly, one of their demands was the abolition of extra-*shar'i* taxes. Reflecting his preoccupation, Kostiner, "On Instruments and Their Designers," 312, speaks of such taxes on the "tribes." The objectionable taxation is simply custom duties imposed on (almost always exclusively) *Hadari* traders (or perhaps dues collected from pilgrims), which were hardly targeted at any tribe. The *ulama*, in typical fashion, objected to the "*ta'shir*" of Muslims and declared it impermissible. See ibn Qasim *al-Durar al-saniyya*, 9: 302–10. The state needed the money and the rulings were conveniently ignored.

109. The *ulama* were later to urge *jihad* against the Iraqis. See ibn Qasim, *al-Durar al-saniyya*, 9: 349–52.

110. The story is told in detail by Glubb, *War in the Desert*.

111. Ibn Khamis, *Tarikh al-yamama*, 7: 268; Wahba, *Jazirat al-'arab*, 294; al-'Ubayyid, *al-Najm al-lami'*, 239; al-Bassam, *Khizanat al-tawarikh*, 6: 228, says 30 men, including a major *'uqayli* merchant, who were returning from Iraq were murdered. It should be noted that the non-*asil* tribe of Al-'Awazim in Hasa region was very effective in defeating two combined Ikhwan forces shortly after the battle of Sabala. See ibn 'Aqil, *Ansab al-'usar*, 98–9.

112. Al-'Ubayyid, *al-Najm al-lami'*, 234–5. 'Utayba would be in charge of most of Hijaz and Qasim; Mutayr, most of central Najd; Harb, the areas around Medina and Yanbu'; 'Ijman, the Hasa region; 'Anaza the northern territories. For other, thwarted ambitions, see ibn Khamis, *Tarikh al-yamama*, 7: 254–5.

113. When an eminent jurist came to talk to al-Duwish, he responded by tapping the jurist's belly: "speak, oh money," an accusation that he was simply doing Ibn Saud's and not God's bidding. Ibn ʿAbd al-Muhsin, *Tadhkirat uli al-nuha*, 3: 203.

114. It should be noted that Ibn Saud's army in this battle was not exclusively *Hadari*; the Wahhabi call had managed to split tribal coalitions and many loyal sections entered the battle against their own tribesmen, e.g., the chief of the Ruwiqa section of ʿUtayba.

115. It is generally assumed that he had come to assess ʿAbd al-ʿAziz's power. He is reported to have informed his camp upon his return that he saw easy booty. "I saw a *Hadari* (Ibn Saud) trembling with fear, surrounded by a bunch of cooks only good for sleeping on cushy mattresses." Wahba, *Jazirat al-ʿarab*, 296; ibn ʿAbd al-Muhsin, *Tadhkirat uli al-nuha*, 3: 206.

116. Al-Duwish was not alone; several Bedouin chiefs launched their own raids in a direct challenge to the government, but all were eventually defeated. ibn Khamis, *Tarikh al-yamama*, 7: 287. The ʿIjman did not participate in the battle, but the Saudi governor of the eastern area pursued them and killed their chief, losing his own son in the process. Ibn ʿAbd al-Muhsin, *Tadhkirat uli al-nuha*, 3: 210–11.

117. See John Frederick Williamson, "A Political History of the Shammar Jarba Tribe of al-Jazira: 1800–1958," Ph.D. diss., Indiana University, 1975. I have not come across any document specifying the relationship between the central authority and Najdi tribes. After the conquest of the Hijaz, however, there is ample documentation of the "covenant" (ʿahd) entered into by the Hijazi tribes with the government. The texts are available in the first few issues of the Saudi official Gazette, *Umm al-Qura*, and they are conveniently grouped in al-Bassam, *Khizanat al-tawarikh*, 10: 203–10, 302–3. It is reasonable to assume that the same terms would govern relations with the Najdi tribes.

118. In the military, only over the last few years were Bedouins promoted to command major defense forces (e.g., Land Forces). The National Guard, which is heavily manned by Bedouins, is also commanded by *Hadari* officers. While this may reflect the understandable *Hadari* advantage in education, it is difficult not to see it as a carryover from old prejudices and fears (especially of divided loyalty between tribe and state).

119. See Hassan Hamza Hajrah, *Public Land Distribution in Saudi Arabia* (London: Longman, 1982). The formal order was issued in 1953 and later clarified to exclude the traditional *hima* system of the non-nomadic groups in the southwestern mountains. Legally speaking, the *ulama* find no justification for any *hima* except that set up by the Imam for public interest, but the jurists still would acknowledge a right of *Hadar* to preclude Bedouins from access to pasture lands in the immediate vicinity of their towns. See ibn Qasim, *al-Durar al-saniyya*, 6: 459.

120. For example, Burckhardt, *Travels in Arabia*, is full of compliments for the Bedouins and their character. There is a charming passage (1: 363–4) that displays his interpretation of the negative effects of mingling of Bedouins with townsmen; see also 367–8.

121. It is inconceivable for a Najdi *Hadari* to name his son after a Christian. For a Bedouin, so long as such a person possessed the requisite "manliness" (*merjleh* = *rujula*), religion was of no importance; thus the chiefly family of the Ruwala tribe named their son Orans, after the famous Lawrence of Arabia, who had died only recently.

122. References to raiding pilgrims are found in the very early history of Islam; thus the ancient tribes of Ghifar, Aslam, Muzayna, and Juhayna were nicknamed "*surraq al-hajj*," an epithet still hurled at some tribes today, principally Harb and 'Utayba. See Uri Rubin, "Muhammad's Curse of Mudar and the Blockade of Mecca," *Journal of the Economic and Social History of the Orient* 31(1988): 249–64, 260.

123. One exception is Rihani, *Tarikh najd al-hadith*, e.g., 258–290, whose experience in Najd educated him about the profound differences between the two communities and who in many ways internalized the attitudes of the *Hadar* toward the Bedouins. The same applies to Wahba, Jazirat al-'arab, 10, 286–7.

Chapter 3

Ecology, Knowledge, and Trade in Central Arabia (*Najd*) during the Nineteenth and Early Twentieth Centuries

Guido Steinberg

Introduction

Most scholars dealing with Saudi Arabia still write its history by focusing exclusively either on political, economic, or cultural matters. For example, treatment of religious aspects in writings on politics and economy are often confined to some superficial remarks insufficient to clarify the interrelations among the Weberian dimensions of culture, politics, and economy, which still dominate writings on the region. On the other hand, many of those dealing with religious issues still seem to think that a treatment of religious developments alone provides us with valuable insights into the region's history. While historians of other parts of the world and other countries of the Middle East have realized that an artificial isolation of dimensions of history—even if only for analytic purposes—should be considered a thing of the past, studies of Saudi Arabia still suffer from a serious lack of methodological sophistication, not only in this regard. Not surprisingly, anthropologists have become the better historians of the Peninsula in general and Saudi Arabia in particular. One possible method of applying up-to-date historical methodology on the Peninsula could be to focus on the various interrelations between the historical "dimensions," thereby identifying new directions for historical research concerning

Saudi Arabia. While writings on religious aspects neglect the decisive role of ecological factors and material conditions for the intellectual history of Arabia, the most serious gap in the literature is its pre-oil economic history. In the following, I will therefore try to focus on the interrelations between economy and culture in Central Arabian society during the nineteenth and early twentieth centuries.

Ecology and History in Central Arabia

Up to the 1950s, life was precarious in Central Arabia and the living conditions of its inhabitants more than humble. The climate was generally very hot and dry, with temperatures rising over 45° centigrade in summer. In winter, cold winds blew over the open deserts and the temperature quite frequently fell several degrees below zero. In some cases, extraordinarily cold weather destroyed the crops and even killed animals. For example, in 1879/80, the "*bard*" (arab.: cold) took a pilgrimage caravan in southwestern Qasim, that is Central Najd, by surprise. The Qasimi pilgrims had to interrupt their journey for 18 days and when the weather improved, most of their riding camels had perished.[1] Even in cold winters, however, it rained only rarely, so that water became the one commodity on which life and death in Central Arabia ultimately depended. In good years, the winter rains filled the underground basins and streams, which ultimately found their outlet in Eastern Arabia, in the oases of al-Hasa and Qatif. Where this water was closest to the surface, in the wadis like the Wadi al-Dawasir, the Wadi Hanifa, and the Wadi Rimma, the inhabitants of Central Arabia had established urban settlements, some of which became centers of economic, political, and cultural life on the Peninsula. However, if compared with the cities of the neighboring territories like Mecca, Medina, and al-Hufuf, cities in Najd were merely big villages, where economic life was based on agriculture and modest trade with the bedouin and the trading centers of the surrounding regions.

Around 1900, the biggest towns in Najd were Ha'il in Northern Najd, `Unaiza and Buraida in Central Najd or Qasim and Riyadh in Southern Najd. Ha'il was the main transit point on the trade route between Damascus and Najd and, from the 1860s on, the capital of the Rashidi state, which dominated Najd for several decades until the early twentieth century. While Ha'il is said to have hosted a population of up to 20,000 people during the reign of Muhammad ibn Rashid (d. 1897), the decline of the Rashidi state in the early twentieth century was accompanied by falling population numbers.[2] `Unaiza and Buraida, the big trading centers of

Central Arabia, were situated conveniently on the Darb Zubaida, the ancient pilgrimage route between Iraq and the Hijaz. `Unaiza became the center of long-distance trade in the central peninsula, while the inhabitants of Buraida were specialized in organizing transport by camel caravans all over the region. However, each town was inhabited by a population of only about 10,000 to 20,000 persons.[3] Riyadh, until the early 1870s the capital of the second Saudi state, was even smaller. After Muhammad Ibn Rashid had finally destroyed the Saudi state in 1891, Riyadh was in fact reduced to a village with a population of less than 10,000 souls.[4] All the other big towns of central Najd hosted a population of not more than 5,000 persons.

These low population numbers had several causes. First and foremost, ecological and medical catastrophes reduced the population of the region every couple of years. Water was considered to be a divine gift, but often it turned into a deadly threat. The winter rains more often than not turned into floods, filling the wadis with torrent streams within minutes. The Najdi annals are full of episodes about these flood catastrophes.[5] They destroyed gardens, palm groves, and even parts of the towns, which—in order to reach the underground water that they needed for irrigation—had to be built as close as possible to the ground of the wadis or in hollows, which proved to be equally dangerous when rain fell. As a consequence, the farmers tried to protect their crops by building mud walls around their groves and by leaving ample space for the torrents to pass the city. This proved to be only an insufficient protection against the floods. Living close to the underground water necessary for irrigation meant being periodically threatened by the floods. Besides, even in the nineteenth century Najd mankind—with its then still limited destructive capabilities—proved to be one of the most serious ecological catastrophes. Whenever a city was belea-guered by an enemy force—which happened quite frequently during the nineteenth century—one of its first measures was to cut down the palm groves surrounding the city walls. Since a palm tree has to grow several years before carrying the first consumable dates cutting down the trees meant seriously threatening the future livelihood of the city's inhabitants. In many cases, survivors were forced to leave their hometowns for lack of food. Furthermore, the winter rains were frequently followed by the arrival of locust swarms. Their former generation had left its larvae buried in the desert and these only hatched out from their eggs when the falling rains gave them the signal that there would be food in abundance in a short time. These locust swarms crossed huge parts of the Arabian Peninsula, destroy-ing the pasture grounds of the bedouin as well as the groves and fields of the city dwellers. Although some townspeople developed methods to catch and kill the larvae, other swarms were left unmolested in more distant parts of the Peninsula, eventually leaving the Najdis helpless.[6]

Even more devastating were the periods of drought, which hit Central
Arabia quite frequently, sometimes for several years in succession. These
droughts hit bedouin and townspeople alike and for centuries forced large
parts of the Najdi population to emigrate to the neighboring countries,
especially Eastern Arabia and Iraq. These periods were often accompanied
by political and religious strife, and in most cases it seems as if the ecological crises had triggered the turmoil or were at least among its major causes.
The emergence of the Wahhabi movement, for example, followed pro-
longed periods of ecological disaster in the early eighteenth century. Given
recent studies on the causal relations between the little ice age in Europe
and the witch hunts of the early seventeenth century or studies about the
interrelations between cholera and the European revolutions of the nineteenth
century, these and similar speculations do not seem so unlikely any more.[7]
In fact, Arabian history is full of examples of political and social turmoil
coinciding with ecological disaster. In 1918/19, for example, Ibn Saud—
who ruled between 1902 and 1953—was hardly able to quell the rebellion
of starving bedouin tribes after several years of drought, the results of which
were aggravated by the blockade of Ottoman territory during the war.

At times, devastating medical catastrophes aggravated ecological disasters and caused crises encompassing the whole region. In many cases, it is
impossible to establish which disease hit the region in certain years. Najdi
historians frequently mention *"al-waba'"* ("epidemic") or *"al-ta`un"*
("plague") without giving any information about the exact nature of the
disease. For example, in 1872, `Unaiza was hit by an unknown disease,
which caused severe headaches and killed a considerable number of its citizens.[8] In this case, the mention of one of the symptoms allows us to speculate that the disease must have been either typhus or typhoid fever. In
most other cases, however, we don't know anything about the disease. But
although we know only a small fraction of what really happened, the Najdi
medical record remains frightening: One of the most common diseases
until the early twentieth century was smallpox, which hit Najd periodically.
Children especially fell prey to this disease, which left many of the survivors
blind. Eye diseases were therefore common in Najd as elsewhere in the
Middle East. Caused by smallpox, trachoma, or conjunctivitis, up to
20 percent of the male population was affected by severe eye diseases, leaving an important part of the population economically unproductive.[9] The
second deadly scourge up to 1912 was cholera, *the* disease of the nineteenth
century. From 1830, several cholera pandemics broke out, which spread
along the major shipping lines and overland trade routes in the region.
Whenever a new cholera epidemic had broken out in India and found its
way to the Middle East, it entered Najd either from the Persian Gulf
or—more frequently because of the Hajj—from Mecca and killed major

portions of the population. During the third cholera pandemic between 1841 and 1859, Najd was hit in the mid-1850s as well. Riyadh is reported to have lost up to a third of its population at that time.[10] Not surprisingly, Najdi society was severely affected by this visit. During a wave of religious fanaticism, the predecessors of what today have become the religious police cleaned Riyadh and its environs of everything that might have caused God to punish his chosen people by sending them this deadly scourge.[11]

Modern transport caused other epidemics to reach Najd. Just as the introduction of steam traffic had brought cholera to the Middle East, the expansion of international traffic during the age of European imperialism intensified the globalization of epidemic diseases. The most dreadful among them was influenza, which had already affected the region in 1890, but as "Spanish flu" it resurfaced again and this time in a much more virulent form, in 1918/19. Several features of this epidemic, which lasted for about three months, had an important impact on the history of Najd in the early twentieth century. First, thousands were killed, among them the Saudi heir apparent and other members of the Saud family. In Riyadh, nearly 100 persons per day are reported to have died.[12] The death toll among the bedouin seems to have been even larger.[13] Second, the influenza mainly killed young males between the ages of 20 and 40. For example, many young *ulama* and younger members of the big merchant families were killed. Thereby, the disease focused on those persons who would have formed the cultural, economic, and political backbone of Najdi society during the next decades. Furthermore, it hit Najd at the end of World War I, after a period of droughts that had ruined the Najdi economy from 1915 and which had been aggravated by the results of the aforementioned blockade of Ottoman territories. As a result, the Ikhwan movement in 1918/19 was on the verge of open rebellion against Ibn Saud. The crisis threatened their way of life and the material basis of their existence as well, leading them to raid bedouins who had not joined their movement. While the sources do not allow us yet to elaborate the exact causes of the crisis of 1918–20, it has been established that ecological and medical factors deeply influenced Najdi history up to the twentieth century.[14]

Agriculture and Trade

Until the twentieth century, agriculture and the breeding of camels, horses, and sheep were the main pillars of the Najdi economy. All the agricultural lands were situated in the oases within or close to the towns. Date palms in large orchards surrounded by mud walls dominated the pictures of Najdi towns. On the ground, the peasants grew grain, mainly wheat and barley, but also millet, lucerne, lime and fig trees, vegetables and fruits like peaches, melons, and pumpkins, the parcels being irrigated by wells, which were run by camels, sometimes by cattle and donkeys. The peasants often used the irrigated space between the date palms for other produce, mainly lucerne, which was used as fodder for the valuable camels and horses. However, although every piece of cultivable land was used as intensively as traditional techniques allowed, Najdi towns were seldom self-sufficient.[15] This was definitely true in times of crisis, when harvests were destroyed by the above-mentioned catastrophes, but also in ordinary times, when considerable quantities of food—rice, wheat, and barley—had to be imported. If one compares the description of what was being produced locally with what was being consumed in the towns, this becomes quite clear. In the early twentieth century, at least the upper echelons of urban society seem to have consumed large amounts of rice. While the date in that period still seems to have been the staple of the bedouin, in the towns it had already lost most of its importance to rice, which was imported from India and—in much smaller quantities—Arabistan and Eastern Arabia. Furthermore, the Najdis had to import tea, coffee, tobacco, textiles, weapons, ammunition, timber, and luxury items such as spices, paper, watches, and printed books.

The bedouin in the desert mainly produced livestock, hides, wool, milk, and butter ghee, which was used for cooking. But although the urban and the bedouin sphere each had their respective economic function, it is impossible to analyze their characteristics independently of each other. Interrelations between the towns and the desert were rather symbiotic: one's very existence depended on the economic success of the other. First, there was no clear-cut spatial separation between the bedouin and the town dwellers. Important parts of the bedouin tribes had settled in towns and villages and—if their settlement had taken place in rather recent times—they still remained in contact with their nomadizing kinsmen. Some nomadic tribes owned gardens in the towns and lived there during parts of the year after which they left again for the pasture grounds of their tribe. In other cases, they leased the plots to peasants. In the hot season, the bedouin in general moved closer to the cities because water was then only available in the urban wells. On the other hand, town dwellers owned animals—mainly sheep and goats—which they sent with the bedouin herds to their pastures in the desert. Furthermore, in order to purchase agricultural and imported products, the bedouin depended on the urban markets. The towns served as the markets for a wider region, comprising the surrounding deserts and villages. Thereby, the markets strengthened the economic (and cultural) interdependence between the desert and the towns.

In general, Najd had to import considerable amounts of foodstuff and commodities from eastern Arabia and abroad. This by itself was a big problem for a country suffering from a serious scarcity of natural resources. The inhabitants of Najd had to export something in order to pay for their imports. These exports consisted mainly of the produce of the bedouin sphere of economic life: horses, camels, sheep, butter ghee, and hides. Horses went to Iraq and India, camels to Egypt, Syria, and Iraq. One of the biggest markets for these products was the yearly pilgrimage, when enormous amounts of sheep were slaughtered for and by the pilgrims. However, Mecca and the Hijaz were not the most important trading partners of Najd. Equally important was the trade route to Damascus, which had been one of the busiest during the eighteenth and nineteenth centuries. However, the share of trade with Syria declined after 1900, when the route to Iraq and Kuwait replaced the one to Damascus.[16] Equally important, if more so for Riyadh and Southern Najd, was the trade route to al-Hasa in eastern Arabia. The oases of al-Hasa and Qatif were the only region close to Central Arabia where water was abundant. Therefore, its inhabitants were usually able to produce a surplus of agricultural produce and livestock, which they exported to Najd and other parts of the region. Furthermore, the whole coast of the Persian Gulf between Kuwait and the so-called Pirate Coast (today the United Arab Emirates) was the region's center of pearl fishing up to the early 1930s.

During the season between June and October, the pearl industry needed an enormous amount of manpower, which the small coastal cities couldn't provide.[17] Here, local demand and supply from Najd met. This is one of the reasons why manpower became the principal Najdi export item. Every year, a considerable, but unknown number of men mainly from Southern Najd moved to Bahrain, Kuwait, and the smaller Emirates in order to work as divers and pullers on the pearling boats. Most prominent among them were (settled) members of the Dawasir tribe, who each year left their villages in the Wadi al-Dawasir in Southwestern Najd, in order to fish pearls on the Gulf Coast.[18] The poverty of their home country didn't leave them any alternative.

A similar phenomenon can be traced in the Qasim region around the trading cities of 'Unaiza and Buraida. This region was a lot more prosperous than southern Najd. Agriculture was more successful here than in the South. The pilgrimage caravans along the Darb Zubaida and trade with the Hijaz, Syria, Iraq, and the Persian Gulf region were important sources of income, which Southern Najd didn't have. Nevertheless, even in Qasim, many people had to leave the country. This was caused by a number of reasons, insufficient material conditions and the quest for alternative sources of income being but two of the factors leading to the exodus of the Qasimis to Iraq, Syria, the Hijaz, and even Egypt. First and foremost, the ecological situation of Qasim invited its inhabitants to engage in trade. For the Saharan context, it has been shown quite convincingly that the inhabitants of date-producing oases more often than not had to engage in trade in order to survive in a hostile environment.[19] Although dates were available in sufficient amounts, their extremely high sugar content make them only a supplement to a certain diet, not a staple. In the oases on the Saharan desert edge just as in central Arabia, the production of food other than dates was always precarious so that their inhabitants had to look for alternative sources of foodstuff outside their oases. In many cases, the bedouin in the deserts surrounding the oases could provide them with butter and meat, but not with carbohydrates. However, they raised camels and thereby a superior means of transport in this environment. The bedouin themselves had to sell their produce in order to acquire dates, grain, and other necessities of daily life in the market towns. Thereby, the town dwellers gained control of the means of transport in order to deal with neighboring territories. As a consequence, trade and transport became the major occupations of the inhabitants of these date-producing oases.

Political reasons forced others to leave Najd. Since the eighteenth century, many inhabitants had left the Qasim and other areas in Najd because of the internal conflicts caused by the rise of the Wahhabiyya. This movement was mainly supported by the inhabitants of southern Najd, who until today are the staunchest supporters of the Wahhabiyya. In central and northern Najd, its opponents seem to have constituted a majority. This is why the Saudi rulers only overcame the resistance in Qasim, especially in 'Unaiza, in the early twentieth century.[20] Whenever Saudi troops conquered a town in the eighteenth and nineteenth centuries, parts of the population, that is *ulama* who rejected the Wahhabiyya, other anti-Saudi parts of the political elite and their followers either left the town or were exiled by the new rulers. Therefore, a Najdi–Qasimi diaspora community grew in Iraq, with smaller branches in the Hijaz and Syria. As a result, in the nineteenth century, Zubair, the Iraqi "gate to Najd" on the trade route between Qasim and Southern Iraq became a purely Najdi city and an important center of learning for the Hanbali school of law, which dominated in Najd.[21] Other big Najdi communities settled in Basra, Baghdad, al-Hasa, and Kuwait. In Ottoman Iraq, the "'uqailat", as the Najdis were called here, served as local militia in the Ottoman army and worked in the transport business and overland trade. Many Qasimis were among the workers who constructed the Suez Canal.[22]

Besides those who worked in agriculture, most people from Qasim were busy in the transport business and in long-distance trade. Especially the inhabitants of Buraida, itself an important local center of camel and livestock trade, became active in the camel-based transport sector.[23] Those who didn't own any camels were employed as personnel for the caravans. Others who owned camels hired these out to merchants and pilgrims crossing the deserts all over the Peninsula. Small "cameleers," as Philby called these inhabitants of Buraida, accompanied the camels that they had hired out. In 1877, Charles Doughty wrote that about a third of (presumably the male part of) the population of Buraida was active in the international caravan trade. Several of the city's notables owned whole caravans.[24] As a result, many of them became extremely rich, at least by Najdi standards.[25]

Money that the merchants of Qasim didn't invest in their businesses was used in order to purchase land, especially date gardens in their respective hometowns. Date gardens were a relatively secure source of income, and—just as all over the Peninsula—a status symbol and a source of considerable social prestige.[26] As a consequence, the big merchant families became the largest landowners in their hometowns. Some merchants from 'Unaiza even invested large sums in date gardens in Southern Iraq.[27]

During the nineteenth century, 'Unaiza became the most important trading center in Central Arabia. It was home to some of the most important merchant families of Najd, like the Bassam, Shubaili, Sulaim, Qadi, Fadl, and Dhukair.[28] These families established trade networks between 'Unaiza, Jidda, Mecca, Damascus, Zubair, Basra, Baghdad, Bahrain, and Bombay, thereby encompassing all the important international trade routes that were connected with Najd. They traded in all the above-mentioned commodities, family members leading the respective branches of the business abroad. The introduction of modern transport in the early 1930s constituted a severe blow for the merchants of Qasim, especially for those engaged in the transport business. The caravan trade between Najd, Syria, Iraq, and the Hijaz had always needed transit towns, where the slow camel caravans could refurbish their provisions. This is how Buraida and 'Unaiza had gained their importance. Their services became obsolete when automobiles, trucks and, some years later, the airplane became the main means of transport.[29] The Darb Zubaida quickly lost its former importance. Only those merchants, who, like the Bassam family, had established branches in other cities and had diversified their businesses in time, that is who were also engaged in other activities than the declining transport business and pearl trade, could retain their former position at least partially.

Material Conditions and Intellectual Life

Ulama, Books and Education

Until the 1950s, intellectual life in Najd was decisively shaped by the hostile environment and insufficient material conditions. First, and perhaps most importantly, the number of religious scholars (*ulama,*

Sg. `*alim*) was very low. In fact, until the 1950s, Najd suffered from a serious lack of *ulama* and—because only religious education was available up to the mid-1930s—a lack of educated people in general. Education was a luxury, which little village communities couldn't afford at all and which existed only on a very limited scale in the cities. The Najdi biographical collections are full of remarks that in a certain town at a certain time there was no teacher qualified even to teach the Qur'an or other basics of Muslim education. Besides, many village Imams seem to have shown a deplorable level of instruction, some hardly able to read and write, which didn't encourage the inhabitants to send children to their lessons.[30]

In order to receive a decent religious education, young students had to move to towns where qualified scholars were teaching. In order to become an important `*alim*, students had to study in the big Najdi intellectual centers, namely Riyadh, `Unaiza, Ha'il, or Buraida. However, such a trip was dangerous during most of the nineteenth century and up to 1930 and it cost money. More importantly, nearly all the young men were needed to secure the economic survival of the urban communities. They either produced food as peasants or fishermen, worked as craftsmen, artisans, or pearl divers, or earned their money as merchants and camel drivers. Therefore, even in the big centers, material conditions hindered the development of a strong educational sector. Whenever a central authority in Najd existed in the eighteenth and nineteenth centuries, the rulers supported the students financially. However, instability was the rule and therefore the students generally had to rely on financial support from their professors, donations by merchants or other rich personalities, and *waqf* income. In short, a student's life was miserable, if he didn't have the support of a rich and influential family. This is why the number of students was generally low. Many of those who learned to read and write left the schools as soon as they had finished the basics in order to become merchants. Others left because they had to assist their families in agriculture. Several times, this situation became the topic of controversies between Ibn Saud and influential scholars in Riyadh. For example, in or before 1940 Ibn Saud convened some of them in Riyadh and complained about the low number of students, many of them blind or otherwise physically handicapped.[31] The scholars replied that students didn't receive sufficient financial support. However, money was the one thing that the Saudi government never had, or was not willing to invest in education. As a consequence, the situation only improved when oil royalties began to flow in the second half of the 1940s.

It is interesting that Ibn Saud mentioned the disproportionate number of physically handicapped and especially the blind among the students. This remark again shows that the above-mentioned eye diseases had an important negative impact on Najdi society. Until today, many important

Wahhabi scholars from Najd are blind, the best-known example being the former Saudi Grand-Mufti `Abd al-`Aziz ibn Baz (1912–99). Among the 15 *ulama* who signed an important *fatwa* on February 11, 1927, three had been blind since their childhood and one could hardly see any more. Two others had become blind when already in their sixties.[32] Since education was mainly based on memorizing the Qur'an and other authoritative texts, it is possible that blind students—because they were not distracted by visual stimuli—developed better abilities in this regard than their sighted colleagues. Until today, Ibn Baz is famous for having known an enormous number of texts by heart. However, the memorizing abilities of blind students don't seem to have been the factor responsible for the high number of blind *ulama*. Rather, blind boys were not able to work in agriculture, trade, or the crafts, meaning that they were economically unproductive and therefore a potentially heavy burden if their family was poor. In the early twentieth century, their only chance to learn a profession and to ease the burden on their families was to study religion. This was the main reason why so many *ulama* were blind.

Disease also took its toll. There is no evidence that the death rate among *ulama* or students was higher than among other parts of the male population. However, the characteristics of some diseases, which tend to focus on relatively young persons, that is on men between 20 and 40, had a strong negative impact on the number of *ulama*. For example, the Spanish flu of 1918/19 killed at least ten prominent students. The three killed in `Unaiza were among the most talented among the students of their generation and—if they had not died so early—would each have educated dozens of future merchants and *ulama*. Their death was more than an individual tragedy; it was a social catastrophe. Society had invested relatively large sums in their long education—much larger sums than what was needed for the education of merchants or craftsmen—which had now been spent in vain.

As for the Saudi state, the lack of qualified religious personnel had other serious results. Together with the governors, the judges had always been an important tool of Saudi policy in newly conquered provinces. They reorganized justice and education according to Wahhabi principles and tried to control Saudi–Wahhabi rules of conduct, thereby becoming a (potentially) standardizing element in a state trying to grapple with the enormous social and cultural differences between its provinces. They reported directly to the central authority in Riyadh. However, their number was insufficient even to replace the majority of judges in the provinces. Partly as a result of this shortcoming, Saudi rule in the Hijaz, `Asir and al-Hasa, which were conquered between 1913 and 1925, remained superficial even in some of the most important fields of state activity.

The impact of material conditions on intellectual life reached even deeper. At least until the 1930s, most books available in Najd were manuscripts. The lack of writing materials was a big obstacle that students and professors in Najd had to face. At least until the 1930s, a teacher had to dictate the whole text first. Then the students added their comments and explanations by writing them down in the margins of the text.[33] Complete manuscripts were rare and expensive. First and foremost, paper and perhaps also ink were luxury items, which had to be imported from abroad. Pens were made out of certain stable branches of trees, which were locally available but rare, or of reed, which had to be imported from Eastern Arabia.[34] Furthermore, many of the few persons able to read and write spent a substantial portion of their time copying manuscripts, which either they themselves needed or which were considered to be important. Even leading *ulama* from time to time copied manuscripts.[35] Other *ulama* chose copying as a profession in order to earn a living. Furthermore, besides the big effort it required to produce a significant number of manuscripts, books in general were threatened by ecological catastrophes and—as all the merchandise that was being transported by camel caravans—subject to bedouin raids and robbery. Many biographers mention the destruction of whole libraries as a result of flood catastrophes.[36] Such a flood could destroy the work of decades. The same held true when a city was conquered in the case of war and subsequently plundered and/or burnt. Since most of the Najdi manuscripts existed only in a very limited number, their loss had far more serious consequences than the loss of printed books. Only in 1924, after Ibn Saud had conquered Mecca, did the Wahhabis first gain access to a printing press. During the nineteenth century, printed books had to be imported from abroad. Only in 1897, did the Wahhabi scholar Ibn Suhman have the first Wahhabi writing printed in Amritsar/India. Thanks to intensive economic and cultural relations with India, Ibn Saud had more books printed in the subcontinent and subsequently in Cairo.[37] Even after the 1920s, however, many Wahhabi *ulama* continued to write and copy manuscripts without having them printed. Only the introduction of the first printing press in Najd (Riyadh) in 1953 paved the way for the introduction of printed matter on a larger scale, and, ultimately the emergence of a modern public sphere.

Repercussions of this situation on the intellectual and religious development of Najd were serious. First and foremost, students and teachers alike lost time by copying manuscript after manuscript instead of dealing with their contents. Second, books were extremely rare. In 1862, William Palgrave called a collection of 40 books in Riyadh "a very fair library for Arabia." This was one of the reasons why the level of religious studies in Najd was relatively low.[38] On the educational level, the lack of books and the danger of losing them resulted in the practice of memorizing only those books that were available. Important texts had to be memorized because the *ulama* always kept in mind that a certain text in case of need might not be available. This is one of the reasons why they let the students learn those texts by heart that they considered to be of utmost importance or simply those texts that they owned (they might not have seen a difference anyway). On the other hand, only the limitation of the number of books allows students to memorize a larger amount of what is being read. The biographies are full of remarks about the astonishing memorizing abilities of certain *ulama*. For example, knowing the *hadith* collection of Bukhari by heart seems to have been considered an outstanding intellectual and religious achievement. In order to facilitate the memorization of texts, many shorter treatises were put into verses. This is a method that was not only popular (and successful) in Muslim education through the ages, but also in medieval and early modern Europe.[39]

Furthermore, memorization formed the basis of an educational system in which the monopoly of the transmission of knowledge was held by a small group of religious experts: "But one common feature of societies where literacy is confined to a particular group (that is to say, virtually all communities before recent times) is that the content of certain literate texts is communicated by literates to non-literates, though this material is of course transmitted only between the literates themselves."[40] Only the *ulama* understood the texts, the transmission of which thereby became primarily an oral and perhaps even sacral action.[41] Only after long and arduous years in school did the students learn to read and write and to understand the texts that they had memorized. Thereby, the students became *ulama*. Not surprisingly, the *ulama* tried to preserve this educational method even when "modern" schools and larger numbers of printed books had already been introduced to Najd in the mid-1930s. Then, the educational method became a political issue. However, resistance was futile. The fact that students now learned to read and write a lot earlier and because they were not educated with the ultimate goal to become men of religion, the *ulama* slowly lost their monopoly on knowledge and its transmission.

Material Conditions and their Impact on Legal Thought and Practice

Insufficient material conditions also had their impact on the realization of ideas central to the ideology of the Wahhabi reform movement. One of the main goals of Muhammad ibn ʿAbd al-Wahhab had been a return to the life of the pious forefathers, thereby establishing an Islamic ideal society organized according to the model of the glorified period of early Islam in Medina. One of the ways to achieve this aim was to return to the sources of the faith, the Qur'an and Sunna. According to Muhammad ibn 'Abd al-Wahhab's views, the development of the Sunni schools of law and "blind" obedience to their rulings and positions (*taqlid*) had divided the Muslim community. In fact, his main concern was the rejection of the *fiqh* of the schools of law, including the Hanbaliya. He concentrated on theology (*'aqida*), which he thought had hitherto been neglected. His preference for theology, which he tried to reconstitute to its central position in Muslim lore, also shaped his views with regard to the issue of *ijtihad* and *taqlid*, that is the question to what extent a legal expert was allowed to derive his judgments independently from the sources. For Muhammad ibn 'Abd al-Wahhab, this was a secondary problem. He was more concerned with the conflict between *fiqh* on the one hand and the Qur'an and Sunna on the other than with the (alleged) conflict between *ijtihad* and *taqlid*.[42]

Muhammad ibn 'Abd al-Wahhab had good reasons for his complaints about his Hanbali colleagues in Najd. When the reform movement emerged in the middle of the eighteenth century, scholars in Najd concentrated on Hanbali *fiqh*, neglecting important fields like *hadith*, *'aqida* and *tafsir*. They used the works of some younger authorities in *fiqh*, especially *al-Muntaha* by Ibn an-Najjar[43] and *al-Iqna'*, by al-Hujawi[44] as standard references and as the basic textbooks in their lessons. However, the Wahhabi *ulama* rejected these books as containing positions not compatible with the Qur'an and Sunna and the rulings of Ahmad ibn Hanbal himself.[45]

As an alternative, they promoted the use of the *fiqh* manuals by the Hanbali scholar Muwaffaq al-Din ibn Qudama (1146–1223), especially al-ibn *'Umda*, *al-Muqni'*, *al-Kafi*, and *al-Mughni*, from which all later Hanbali writings had derived.[46] However, the Wahhabis were predominantly concerned with theology. Therefore, at least theoretically, the emergence of the Wahhabiya brought with it a shift in religious paradigms: *fiqh* as the dominant field of interest should have been replaced by *'aqida*, and especially the doctrine of the absolute oneness of God. Practically, however, the Wahhabis didn't succeed in replacing the existing paradigm and this is not due only to the lack of interest in *fiqh* on the part of Muhammad ibn 'Abd al-Wahhab. In 'Unaiza for instance, scholars kept concentrating on Hanbali *fiqh* until the early twentieth century. Since 'Unaiza was one of the most important centers of learning in Najd, its *ulamas*' refusal to follow the lead of the Wahhabi theologians from Riyadh shows quite clearly, that the Wahhabiyya was not able to fundamentally change religious and legal thought and practice in Najd. All over Najd, judges continued to use the aforementioned manuals. Perhaps because of a lack of practical alternatives, they even became standard manuals for all Saudi Arabian judges from 1928 on.[47]

In the case of ʿUnaiza, the rejection of Wahhabi theology and legal thought is not that surprising. From the eighteenth century, ʿUnaiza had been one of the main centers of resistance against the Saudi–Wahhabi expansion and its *ulama* were no exception to that. If not all of them were steadfast opponents of the Wahhabiyya, most showed a marked distance toward the leading Wahhabi *ulama* in Riyadh, notably toward the Al al-Shaykh ("the Shaykh's family"), the descendants of Muhammad ibn ʿAbd al-Wahhab.[48] However, in smaller towns with no particular record of opposition to the Wahhabis, a different explanation for the deep-rootedness of the pre-Wahhabi legal tradition must be found. Especially in Southern Najd, in the small towns south and southwest of Riyadh, where the staunchest and most radical supporters of the Wahhabis lived, this phenomenon has to be explained. Here, material conditions played an important role. Their concentration on *fiqh* might be explained by the fact that the administration of justice was simply a necessary condition for the small urban communities to survive, while theology was not. Najdi scholars simply dealt with all those issues that had a major practical importance for their society. These were primarily the settlement of disputes and the rules of inheritance (*al-faraʾid*). In their society, theology was a luxury. Most *ulama* had to earn a living and therefore didn't have the time to deal with issues that were not of primary importance in everyday life. Furthermore, books and writing materials were expensive and therefore the copyists were forced to focus on a selection of important books. Again for practical reasons, legal writings providing the judge with the authoritative views of the Hanbali law school had to be copied first. This explains why Najdi *ulama* so rarely dealt with topics like theoretical grammar (*nahw*), *hadith*, and *tafsir*. There is even evidence that the most important Hanbali writing on comparative law, Ibn Qudama's *Mughni*, was not available in a complete manuscript before the mid-1920s. Although the book must have existed in Najd during the nineteenth century, manuscripts had been destroyed or had otherwise disappeared. Once the book was lost, it was an arduous undertaking to obtain a new copy from outside Najd. This is how ecological, economic, and political conditions took part in preventing the reform of legal thought.[49]

With regard to Muhammad ibn ʿAbd al-Wahhab's teachings on *ijtihad*, material conditions again proved to be a major obstacle to reform. In principle, the above-mentioned return to the Qurʾan and Sunna—a characteristic of all reformers in the eighteenth and nineteenth centuries—implied a positive predisposition toward "independent legal reasoning" (*ijtihad*). Not surprisingly, this tendency can clearly be discerned in the writings of Muhammad ibn ʿAbd al-Wahhab and the most important Wahhabi *ulama* of the following generations. Nevertheless, it took the Wahhabiyya several decades before an authoritative doctrine of *ijtihad* had been worked out. But even afterward, most Wahhabi scholars evaded the issue and until today it has remained somewhat sensitive.[50] This problem has its roots in the early history of the movement. Muhammad ibn `Abd al-Wahhab himself was not a legal specialist. In his writings, he rather concentrated on theological problems and on how society had to be reformed on the basis of his vision of early Muslim society. This is why no theoretical treatise by the founder of the Wahhabiyya has come down on us. Nevertheless, the question had to be settled authoritatively, so that a second-generation Wahhabi scholar, Hamad ibn Mu`ammar (1747–1810), took it up and defined the Wahhabi position toward *ijtihad* and *taqlid*. This is not the place to expound Wahhabi legal theory *in toto*.[51] However, it is important to understand its main characteristics. One of these characteristics is that Ibn Mu`ammar allowed even judges and *ulama* to follow the positions of their school of law (*taqlid*), if they hadn't obtained the necessary qualifications for independent reasoning during their legal studies. These *ulama*, he wrote, knew the standard compendia of younger legal authorities like the *Iqna'* and the *Muntaha*, but were not able to trace a proof (*dalil*) in the sources, that is the Qur'an and Sunna. Furthermore, these persons were not able to compare the positions of the different schools of law and choose the right one for their case. These scholars had to follow the accepted positions of their own schools of law, that is they had to apply *taqlid*. In fact, Ibn Mu`ammar in this paragraph of his treatise presented a compromise between the ideals of the Wahhabiyya and the actual situation in Najd, where *taqlid* of Hanbali positions was still the rule.

He continued, that only those *ulama* able to apply the *ijtihad* were obliged to do so. But even here Ibn Mu'ammar argued much more restrictively than for example Ibn Taymiyya. Interestingly, he called the *ijtihad* that he promoted "an *ijtihad* mixed with *taqlid*" ("*fa-huwa jtihad mashhub bi-l-taqlid*"). The `alim who acted according to his theory would look for the positions in which the founders of the four schools of law (*a'imma*) had agreed. He would accept these positions as the "consensus doctorum" (*ijma'*) and rule accordingly. In those cases where the four had differed from each other, he would check the proofs in the texts that the authors had quoted. If he thought that one of the *a'imma* had quoted the correct proof, he should follow his opinion. If he didn't find any reference in their writings, he should stick to the majority view among the four. If there was no majority view, he should compare the positions and evaluate them. He should then choose the position that he preferred or rather stick to the view of his own Imam. This is how *ijtihad* among the Wahhabi scholars should work. It shows that the scope for independent legal reasoning for the early Wahhabis was not very wide.

In this treatise, Ibn Mu`ammar advocated the most conservative approach toward the *ijtihad* of all the eighteenth- and early nineteenth-century reformers.[52] He rather legitimized the existing methods of legal reasoning in Najd, where material conditions and legal tradition didn't allow a single judge to come to a conclusion other than that which he found in the few (possibly even only one) standard manuals that he called his own. This point again becomes clearer when one recalls that the most important Hanbali book in comparative law, the *Mughni*, was available only in parts. For a student to study comparative law, he needed a book in which the positions of all the schools were treated on a comparative basis. Every school of law had its standard works in this field, which were called the *kutub al-khilaf*. For the Hanbalis, their standard manual was Ibn Qudama's *Mughni*. Besides his famous treatise on legal methodology, *Rawdat an-nazir, al-Mughni* was Ibn Qudama's most demanding work.[53] It contained the positions of the four Sunni schools of law and his own point of view on the problem in question. It is hardly conceivable that other *kutub al-khilaf* were available in Najd at that time. For a student, however, it was impossible to develop an understanding of what the different schools of law taught without such a book. On the basis of a discussion of the content of the *kutub al-khilaf*, the student should have developed his ability to apply his own *ijtihad*. It is typical of the pitiful situation of intellectual life in Najd around 1900, that this book was only available in parts scattered all over the region. Only in the 1920s, Ibn Saud instructed an `alim to collect the manuscripts and prepare a printed version of the book. When it had appeared in 1926/27, scholars began using *al-Mughni* in their lessons.[54]

A very striking example for the problems this situation caused for the activities of a provincial judge is found in the biography of `Abd al-`Aziz ibn Muhammad al-Shithri (1887/88–1967). During his tenure in Wadi Rain in Western Najd between 1920 and 1954/55 he used the Hanbali standard manuals in order to find the right judgments. He didn't own books of the other schools of law. Only when in 1954/55 he was transferred to Riyadh, did he gain access to the works of comparative legal studies and begin teaching their contents. Now he started to choose positions and look for differences and conflicts of opinion. In his case, and probably in many others as well, only the availability of books made the difference between a *muqallid* and a *mujtahid*, that is between a scholar sticking to the rulings and positions of his own school and one who came to his own, independent positions.

Generally, rank-and-file judges have applied Hanbali law until today.[55] However, the application of the *ijtihad* became much more common from the 1930s, although political pressure to stick to a common set of Hanbali legal norms continued to exist from the nineteenth century on. As we have just seen, the availability of books gave many *ulama* the opportunity to diversify their legal arsenal and rethink Hanbali norms. It is not mere coincidence that scholars started to engage in independent legal reasoning, if still on a very limited scale, when—in the 1920s and 1930s—the first printed books in considerable quantity appeared on the Najdi market. Especially the works of Ibn Taymiyya and Ibn Qudama seem to have encouraged the more adventurous among the Wahhabi scholars to show a higher degree of independence in their legal reasoning.[56]

However, intellectual developments in the wider Islamic world now became influential in Najd as well. The influx of books from the end of the nineteenth century was accompanied by a growing influence of Islamic Modernism as represented by Muhammad 'Abduh and wider networks of Salafi scholars in the Middle East and around the Indian Ocean. These ideas spread over Najd but had their center in 'Unaiza, where the level of intellectual achievement seems already to have been higher than in other regions in the nineteenth century. Scholars and students used the trade relations of the city's merchants by joining them on their journeys between the Hijaz, Iraq, Syria, the Gulf, and even India. This is how the city's scholars became part of the aforementioned Salafi networks and developed contacts all over the Islamic world. 'Unaiza was the place where Islamic modernism including its tendency to apply *ijtihad* had its stronghold in a society that at first wasn't very receptive to ideas coming from abroad. Here, Salih ibn 'Uthman al-Qadi (1865–1932) and his student 'Abd al-Rahman al-Sa'di (1889/90–1956) founded a tradition of scholarship which in many of its aspects proved to be fundamentally different from the scripturalist Wahhabi school in Riyadh. In 'Unaiza, openness towards intellectual developments in the outside world corresponded with intensive trade relations with neighboring countries.

Scholars and Merchants

The itineraries of the Najdi *ulama* show clearly that they followed the merchants and/or the pilgrimage caravans when traveling in the pursuit of knowledge. The main centers of learning in Najd during the nineteenth and twentieth centuries were Riyadh, Buraida, 'Unaiza and, until the early 1920s, Ha'il. However, many students traveled abroad. Already in the seventeenth and eighteenth centuries many Najdi *ulama* had studied in the Hanbali centers, Damascus, Cairo, and al-Hasa.[57] These choices were as much influenced by the presence of famous Hanbali scholars in these cities as by their geographical proximity and the respective chances to obtain financial aid and/or earn a living by engaging in trade. During the nineteenth century, this principle didn't change; only the destinations did. From around 1880, Delhi and Bhopal became very popular among Najdi students.[58] They went there in order to study with the *hadith* scholars of the *ahl al-hadith*, most notably Siddiq Hasan (1832–90) and Nadhir Husain al-Dihlawi (d. 1902/03) and their students. By the end of the nineteenth century, these scholars were the most celebrated *hadith* experts in the Muslim world.[59]

If one considers the ideological affinity between the *ahl al-hadith* and the Wahhabis, it is not very surprising that Wahhabi students traveled to study with them. However, India was far and the journey dangerous and expensive. Furthermore, India had never been a particularly popular destination for young students from Najd. What is especially puzzling about the journeys to India is the fact that the Wahhabis were well aware that India was governed by a Christian power. At the end of the nineteenth century, though, radical Wahhabi scholars even prohibited the journey to Ottoman territories because they considered their inhabitants as unbelievers. Therefore, it seems unlikely that these scholars sent their students to a country under Christian rule. It must have rather been the ardent desire to improve in *hadith* studies and the sorry state of Najdi society during the civil wars that prompted the students to travel to India. However, our understanding of this episode would remain incomplete if we didn't consider the economic relations between Najd and India. For the Najdi merchants, at least for those living close to the Persian Gulf shore, journeys to India were quite a common phenomenon. During the nineteenth century, especially from 1850, trade relations between the Gulf and India intensified.[60] Since Najd imported a considerable part of its food and merchandise from India, it was no logistic problem to travel to India via Bahrain. Besides the steamships operating between Bombay and Basra and other ports of the Persian Gulf, there were hundreds of dhows crossing the Arabian Sea to Karachi and Bombay every year. In fact, most of the big Najdi family enterprises ran a branch in Bombay, because considerable parts of their business depended on their trade with India. Furthermore, up to the early 1930s, pearls were transported to Bombay and thence to Europe. Even merchants from Hawtat Bani Tamim in the relatively isolated Southern Najd were known to travel to India quite frequently.[61] If we consider that Najdi students had followed all the important trade routes for some centuries, it seems only logical that they did so in the Indian case as well.

These journeys clearly hint at the fact that knowledge and trade were closely interrelated spheres of social activity. Any clear-cut differentiation between economic and cultural dimensions would obscure these interrelations. Quite apart from intellectual considerations, students and scholars needed money. Only where merchants or rulers were able and willing to support scholars and students, did the *ulama* find a basis for a flourishing intellectual life. In many Middle Eastern cities, the *ulama* and students were supported by the returns of rich pious foundations (*waqf*, pl. *awqaf*) or were given a part of the *zakat*. However, this support could only be financed in cities where peasants and merchants produced a considerable surplus. This was not the case in most Najdi cities, where pious foundations were extremely rare.[62] As a result, religious centers existed only on a very limited scale, hardly comparable with those in the big Muslim cities like Cairo or even Mecca. Furthermore, ecological, economic, and political upheavals could threaten these sources of income. This is why intellectual centers developed and declined parallel to the overall development of certain towns.

However, the *ulama* were not only passive recipients of financial aid. Rather, most students and *ulama* engaged in trade and other professions in order to earn a living. Especially the members of the notable families—which supplied the majority of important *ulama* and merchants—were active in trade. The `*alim* who owned a small shop in an urban market, where sometimes he even gave his lessons was quite a common phenomenon. These *ulama*-shopkeepers existed all over the Muslim world. Others traded while traveling abroad. They took Najdi merchandise with them, sold it, and lived on their profits until they were running out of money again. As members of the notable families, many *ulama* owned gardens in Najdi towns and sold their produce on the market. In a transaction called *salam*, others bought the harvest of a certain garden several months in advance and thereby pocketed large profits.[63] This was a common method of obtaining long-term credit in Central Arabia. How profitable this method could become for the person owning the capital was proved by the judge of Buraida between 1932 and 1943, `Umar ibn Salim (d. 1943). He started off as a poor man but became one of the richest personalities in Buraida in the 1930s.[64]

On the other hand, many merchants in Najd themselves had studied and some had even obtained religious knowledge up to a level that qualified them to be called *ulama*. From the 1850s, more and more persons can be traced in the sources who had received a conventional education, but afterward became merchants and continued their intellectual career by dealing (actively and passively) with literature, poetry, history, and genealogy.[65] These were not parts of the formal religious curriculum, but were rather taught in the private literary and intellectual circles in the parlors (*majlis*, pl. *majalis*) of the big merchants and *ulama* or among study groups that certain students had established.[66] All these persons were members of the big merchant families of Qasim, mainly the Bassam family, not sur-prisingly from `Unaiza. This development was clearly linked to economic factors. The Bassam family had become—again by Najdi standards—extremely rich in the second half of the nineteenth century. Therefore, we can assume that it was their unprecedented prosperity that prompted the Bassam to pursue their intellectual interests to an extent hitherto unknown. In Najd, only the richest families could afford to spend considerable parts of their time economically unproductive. Unfortunately, there is no evi-dence as to whether this was a new phenomenon among the merchants or whether their ancestors had already pursued similar interests on a similar scale.[67] It is intriguing, though, that the growth of the family enterprises coincided with the emergence of this group of "intellectuals."

The Al Bassam were the most important merchant family in Najd and one of the leading notable families in `Unaiza.[68] Many of its members were important merchants, but spent their spare time in intellectual, mainly nonreligious activities. Especially their historical and genealogical writings, some of which have not yet been printed testify that the Bassams were among the most important thinkers of Najd.[69] In many cases, it is hardly possible to distinguish whether the person in question was a merchant or an `alim/intellectual. It seems, however, that commercial success was con-sidered to be more important than intellectual interests. Although most of the young Bassams received a religious education, they hardly ever reached the level necessary to become important ulama. Rather, they interrupted their studies as soon as they had obtained the knowledge they needed in order to become successful merchants and as soon they were able to pursue their intellectual interests independently. Once having reached a certain level of knowledge, their favorite means of transmitting it seems to have been the informal majalis. Although the development of these circles was not limited to `Unaiza, reports about similar meetings in other cities are relatively rare. Thereby, they threatened the ulama's monopoly on knowledge and its transmission. However, because they only dealt with issues that had always been an informal part of the religious curriculum, this development at first had no serious implications for the ulama.

It is intriguing that this development coincided not only with an inten-sification of foreign trade, but also with the first massive influx of printed books into Central Arabia. For example, Charles Doughty in 1877 visited a local notable in `Unaiza, `Abdallah al-Khunaini. There he saw the first volume of Butrus al-Bustani's encyclopedia, which had only appeared in 1876. At that time, several young merchants read this book, and further-more dealt with genealogy, history, and poetry and spoke foreign languages such as English or Hindi.[70] Whenever possible, they read newspapers from Beirut or Cairo. If we consider how printed books in early modern Europe fostered the emergence of a group of humanists, it is not very likely that this was a mere coincidence in the case of 'Unaiza. Just like the early humanists in Europe, the Najdi intellectuals' education didn't differ fundamentally from that of the *ulama*. However, as in Europe, the first intellectuals gradually distanced themselves from the purely religious core of the Wahhabi curriculum. The emergence of secularist intellectual circles, which occurred—if at all—only in the 1950s, had its origins in these nineteenth-century developments.[71] A clear-cut differentiation between *ulama* and intellectuals is therefore neither necessary nor useful for this period.[72]

In general, nineteenth-century Najdi history testifies to the fact that a differentiation between cultural and economic motives is difficult. Even the economic and cultural orientations of regions or cities reinforced each other. This was for example the case in 'Unaiza. Its inhabitants not only traveled all over the Middle East, but also had close relations with the inhabitants of the neighboring Ottoman territories. Many of its citizens were deeply influenced by Ottoman culture and religion.[73] In the second half of the nineteenth century, a public debate broke out in Najd, mainly in Ha'il, 'Unaiza, and Buraida, about whether a true (i.e. Wahhabi) Muslim should be allowed to travel to non-Muslim (i.e. non-Wahhabi) countries, namely the neighboring Ottoman provinces. The debate seems to have been triggered by radical Wahhabi *ulama* from Riyadh in order to delegitimize Rashidi rule in Najd.[74] Since the rulers of the Rashid family were known for their close relations with Istanbul and their—according to Wahhabi standards—relative laxity in religious matters, this strategy proved to be quite successful in the long run. In Qasim, the debate—in spite of the religious terms in which these topics were discussed—rather revolved around commercial necessities. The majority of the citizens of 'Unaiza were of the opinion that the inhabitants of the Ottoman territories were Muslims indeed and that their excommunication (*takfir*) was an error and a grave sin. If the Hijaz, Iraq, and Egypt were inhabited by Muslims, then these were Muslim territories and, as a consequence, traveling there was strictly legal. Commercial interests, cultural, and religious orientation and opposition against Saudi–Wahhabi hegemony combined here and predefined the opinion of the citizens of 'Unaiza.

In this debate, the Wahhabis in Southern Najd combined their claim to cultural and political hegemony in central Arabia with what was a genuine religious conviction in the South. Ottomans (and Shiites) were the unbelievers par excellence. However, the southern Najdis maintained only very limited trade relations with the Ottoman territories. This is why it was relatively uncomplicated for them to defend radical isolationist views. Once again, political, economic, and cultural motives combined. Their relevance only becomes clear when we focus on the interrelations of history's dimensions. In fact, the ecological and geographical situation of 'Unaiza forced its inhabitants to engage in trade with the surrounding territories. These trade relations helped the development of cultural links with the Ottoman world. In their turn, these links together with commercial interests and the desire to stay independent from Riyad predefined 'Unaiza's position toward the radical Wahhabiyya and the Saudi state in Riyad. Therefore, the ensuing debate was triggered by a number of mutually inseparable causes, comprising ecological, economic, cultural, and political ones.

Notes

1. `Abdallah ibn `Abd al-Rahman ibn Salih al-Bassam, ed., *Khizanat al-tawarikh al-najdiyya, al-juz' al-khamis* (n.p.: 1419/1999), 95.
2. Muhammad al-Zaarir, *Imarat al rashid fi ha'il* (n.p.: Birsan, 1997), 32.
3. India Office Library and Records (IOR): L/P&S/18/B 446: Independent Arabian States, 9.
4. In 1917, the British official Hamilton estimated that its population numbered about 5,000–8,000. IOR: R/15/5/104: Diary Colonel Hamilton, 18.
5. See e.g. Bassam, *Khizanat al-tawarikh al-najdiyya*, 38.
6. Harry St. John Philby, *Arabia of the Wahhabis* (London: Constable & Co., 1928), 248 f.
7. Hartmut Lehmann, "Frömmigkeitsgeschichtliche Auswirkungen der "Kleinen Eiszeit," in Schieder, Wolfgang, *Volksreligiosität in der modernen Sozialgeschichte* (= GG Sonderheft 11) (Göttingen: V&R, 1986), 31–50; Richard J. Evans, "Epidemics and Revolutions: Cholera in Nineteenth-Century Europe," *Past and Present* 120 (1988), 123–46.
8. Bassam, *Khizanat al-tawarikh al-najdiyya*, 96.
9. William G. Palgrave, *Narrative of a Year's Journey through Central and Eastern Arabia* (1862–63), 2 vols. (London: Macmillan, 1865), II, 34; Charles M. Doughty, *Travels in Arabia Deserta*, 2 vols. (Cambridge: Cambridge University Press, 1888), II, 4 and 348; Harold R.P. Dickson, *The Arab of the Desert: A Glimpse into Badawin Life in Kuwait and Sa'udi Arabia* (London: George Allen & Unwin, 1951), 506 f. and 510.
10. R. Bayly Winder, *Saudi Arabia in the Nineteenth Century* (London: Macmillan/St. Martin's Press, 1965), 56 f., 90 f., 168; F.E. Peters, *The Hajj. The Muslim Pilgrimage to Mecca and the Holy Places* (Princeton: Princeton University Press, 1994), 274, 301.
11. Palgrave, *Narrative of a Year's Journey*, 407–13.
12. Eleanor Abdella Doumato, *Getting God's Ear: Women, Islam, and Healing in Saudi Arabia and the Gulf* (New York: Columbia University Press, 1999), 173, n.2.
13. Philby, *Arabia of the Wahhabis*, 254.
14. Guido Steinberg, *Religion und Staat in Saudi-Arabien. Eine Sozialgeschichte der wahhabitischen Gelehrten 1912–1953* (unpublished Ph.D. dissertation, FU Berlin, 2000), 389–96.

15. Philby, *Arabia of the Wahhabis*, 217.

16. IOR: L/P&S/20/E85: *Handbook of Arabia*, April 1919, 94.

17. Mohamed G. Rumaihi, "The Mode of Production in the Arab Gulf before the Discovery of Oil," in Niblock, Tim, ed., *Social and Economic Development in the Arab Gulf* (London: Croom Helm), 49–60.

18. Harry St. John Philby, *The Empty Quarter: Being a Description of the Great South Desert of Arabia Known as Rub'al Khali* (London: Constable & Co., 1933), 362.

19. Philip D. Curtin, *Cross-Cultural Trade in World History* (Cambridge: Cambridge University Press, 1984), 23 f.

20. Steinberg, *Religion und Staat in Saudi-Arabien. 1912–1953*, 161–75.

21. Yusuf b. Hamad al-Bassam, *al-Zubair qabla khamsina `amman ma`a nubdha tarikhiyya `an najd wa-l-kuwait* (Riyadh, al-Farazdaq, 1391/1971).

22. `Abd al-`Aziz `Abd al-Ghani Ibrahim, *Najdiyun wara'a l-hudud. al-`Uqailat wa-dawruhum fi `alaqat najd al-`askariyya wa-l-iqtisadiyya bi-l-`iraq wa-l-sham wa-misr (m1750-m1950)* (London: al-Saqi, 1991); Doughty, *Travels in Arabia Deserta*, II, 312.

23. IOR: L/P&S/20/E85: *Handbook of Arabia*, April 1919, 94–7.

24. Doughty, *Travels in Arabia Deserta*, II, 312 and 319; Philby, *Arabia of the Wahhabis*, 191.

25. Muhammad ibn `Uthman ibn Salih al-Qadi, *Rawdat al-nazirin `an ma`athir` ulama' najd wa-hawadith al-sinin* (vol. 1, Cairo: al-Halabi; vol. 2, Cairo: al-Halabi, 1403/1983 and 1400/1980), II, 126; al-Bassam, `Abdallah ibn `Abd al-Rahman ibn Salih, *`Ulama' najd khilal thamaniyat qurun*, 6 vols. (Riyadh: Dar al-Asima, 1419/1998) 5: 303.

26. Palgrave, *Narrative of a Year's Journey*, 379, 387, 392; Philby, *Arabia of the Wahhabis*, 279.

27. Philby, *Arabia of the Wahhabis*, 239.

28. Ameen Rihani, *Ibn Sa'oud of Arabia. His People and His Land* (Delmar, N.Y.: Caravan (Original edition London: Constable, 1928), 1983), 286.

29. Soraya Altorki/Donald P. Cole, " 'Unaizah, le 'Paris du Najd': le changement en Arabie saoudite," *Monde Arabe: Maghreb-Machrek* 156 (Avril–Juin 1997), 7.

30. Ahmad ibn Zayd al-Da`ajani, *al-Shaykh muhammad ibn ibrahim al-bawaridi* (Riyadh: al-`Ubaikan, 1419/1998), 120.

31. Ibrahim ibn `Ubaid Al `Abd al-Muhsin. *Tadhkirat uli al-nuha wa-l-`irfan bi-ayyam allah al-wahid w-l-dayyan wa-dhikr hawadith al-zaman*, 4 vols. (Buraida: as-Salman, 1406), 4: 110.

32. Steinberg, *Religion und Staat in Saudi-Arabien. 1912–1953*, 51.

33. Snouck Hurgronje has described this method in his book about Mecca. There is no evidence that the Najdis employed the same method, but I see no alternative that the Najdi students might have used. Snouck Hurgronje, C., *Mekka*, 2 vols. (Haag: Martinus Nijhoff, 1888/1889), II, 264.

34. `Abd al-Rahman ibn Zayd al-Suwayda`, *Najd fi l-ams al-qarib. Suwar wa-malamih min utur al-hayat al-sa'ida qabla thalathina `amman* (Riyadh: Dar al-`Ulum, 1403/1983), 214.

35. `Abd al-Rahman ibn `Abd al-Latif ibn `Abdallah Al al-Shaikh. *Mashahir `ulama' najd wa-ghayrihim*, (Riyadh: Dar al-Yamama, 1974), 291 f.

36. al-Qadi, 1:181; *ibid.*, 2: 109–14.

37. Steinberg, *Religion und Staat in Saudi-Arabien. 1912–1953*, 52–4.

38. Ibid., 71–121.

39. Norbert Elias, *Über den Prozeß der Zivilisation. Soziogenetische und psychogenetische Untersuchungen*, 2 vols. (Frankfurt a. M.: Suhrkamp, 1993), I, 77; Jonathan P. Berkey, *The Transmission of Knowledge in Medieval Cairo. A Social History of Islamic Education* (Princeton: Princeton University Press, 1992), 28.

40. Jack Goody, *The Domestication of the Savage Mind* (Cambridge: Cambridge University Press, 1977), 151.

41. Malika Zeghal, *Gardiens de l'Islam: Les oulémas d'al-Azhar dans l'Egypte contemporaine* (Paris: Presses de Sciences Po, 1996), 119 and 116 ff.

42. Esther Peskes, *Muhammad b. 'Abdalwahhab (1703–92) im Widerstreit. Untersuchungen zuz Rekonstruktion der Frühgeschichte der Wahhabiya* (Beirut: Steiner, 1993), 41–7. For a detailed discussion of law and justice in the first half of the twentieth century, see Guido Steinberg, *Religion und Staat in Saudi-Arabien. Die wahhabitischen Gelehrten 1902–1953*. (Würzburg: Ergon, 2002), chs. 6 and 7. For the second half of the century see Frank E. Vogel, *Islamic Law and Legal System: Studies of Saudi Arabia* (Leiden: Brill, 2000).

43. *Muntaha l-iradat fi jam` al-muqni`ma`a l-tanqih wa-ziyadat* by Abu l-Baqa' Muhammad ibn Ahmad al-Futuhi (gest. 972/1564), commonly known as Ibn al-Najjar.

44. *Kitab al-iqna` li-talib al-intifa`* by Musa al-Hujawi (d. 1560–61).

45. Ibn Qasim al-`Asimi al-Qahtani al-Najdi, *al-Durar al-saniyya fi l-ajwiba al-najdiyya*, 12 vols. (Bayrut: Matabi` al-Maktab al-Islami, 1385/1965), 4:6 and 55; Frank E. Vogel, *Islamic Law and Legal System: Studies of Saudi Arabia* (Diss., Harvard 1993, Ann Arbor, 1997), 191 and 204 f.

46. M.J. Crawford, *Wahhabi `Ulama and the Law 1745–1932 A.D.* (unpubl. M.A. Thesis, Oxford University, 1980), 78.

47. Su`ud ibn Sa`d al-Duraib, *al-Malik `abd al-`aziz wa-wad` qawa`id al-tanzim al-qada'i fi l-mamlaka* (Jidda: Dar al-Matbu'at al-Haditha, 1408/1988), 86.

48. Steinberg, *Religion und Staat in Saudi-Arabien. 1912–1953*, 161–75.

49. On the political aspects see ibid., 288–95.

50. Reinhard Schulze, *Islamischer Internationalismus im 20. Jahrhundert: Untersuchungen zur Geschichte der Islamischen Weltliga* (Leiden: Brill, 1990), 352.

51. For a detailed discussion see Crawford, *Wahhabi `Ulama and the Law 1745–1932 A.D.*, 73–7; Rudolph, Peters, *"Idjtihad and Taqlid in 18th and 19th Century Islam,"* WI 20 (1980): 3/4, 131–45; Vogel, *Studies of Saudi Arabia*, 1997, 163–65.

52. Peters, *"Idjtihad and Taqlid in 18th and 19th Century Islam,"*, 143 f.

53. Crawford, *Wahhabi `Ulama and the Law 1745–1932 A.D.*, 78.

54. Duraib, *al-Malik `abd al-`aziz wa-wad`qawa`id al-tanzim al-qada'i fi l-mamlaka*, 9; Bassam, *`Ulama' najd khilal thamaniyat qurun*, 1: 365; ibid., 3: 501.

55. Vogel, *Studies of Saudi Arabia*, 1997, 204 f.

56. Steinberg, *Religion und Staat in Saudi-Arabien. 1912–1953*, 298–302.

57. Uwaida Metaireek Al-Juhany, The history of Najd prior to the Wahhabis: a study of social, political and, religious conditions in Najd during three centuries preceding the Wahhabi reform movement, Ph.D. diss, University of Washington, 1983, 242–8.

58. Steinberg, *Religion und Staat in Saudi-Arabien. 1912–1953*, 96–100.

59. Barbara Daly Metcalf, *Islamic Revival in British India: Deoband, 1860–1900* (Princeton: Princeton University Press, 1982), 264–96.

60. For an overview of trade in the Persian Gulf see Hala, Fattah, *The Politics of Regional Trade in Iraq, Arabia, and the Gulf, 1745–1900* (Albany: State University of New York Press, 1997).

61. J.G. Lorimer, *Gazetteer of the Persian Gulf, 'Oman, and Central Arabia* (Calcutta: Indian Government Press (Reprint Shannon/Westmeah: Irish University Press/Gregg International 1970: 6 vols. in 2 parts), 1915), II B, 1357.

62. Bassam, *Khizanat al-tawarikh al-najdiyya*.

63. Al al-Shaykh, *Mashahir `ulama' najd waghayrihim*, 355 and 359.

64. Al al-Shaykh, *Mashahir `ulama' najd waghayrihim*, 359; Al `Abd al-Muhsin, *Tadhkirat uli al-nuha wa-l-`irfan bi-ayyam allah al-wahid w-l-dayyan wa-dhikr hawadith al-zaman*, 4: 148.

65. Cp. the authors' biographies in Bassam 1419/1999, and the respective entries in the biographical dictionaries.

66. Abdallah ibn `Abd al-Rahman ibn Salih al-Bassam, *`Ulama' najd khilal sittat qurun*, 3 vols. (Mecca: an-Nahda al-Haditha, 1398/1978/79), 2: 456f.

67. There is some evidence that single members of the family have dealt with non-religious disciplines since the seventeenth century.

68. Bassam, *Khizanat al-tawarikh al-najdiyya*.

69. Bassam, *`Ulama' Najd khilal sittat qurun*, 2: 346; Bassam `*Ulama' Najd khilal thamaniyat qurun*, 5: 5ff.

70. Doughty, *Travels in Arabia Deserta*, 2: 359.

71. Even in the 1950s, these new intellectuals were often former judges or had received at least a religious education.

72. In general this differentiation does not seem to be supported by the facts. For an example see Schulze, *Islamischer Internationalismus im 20*, 1 ff. and 27.

73. Philby, *Arabia of the Wahhabis*, 275.

74. Steinberg, *Religion und Staat in Saudi-Arabien. 1912–1953*, 122–74.

Chapter 4

Shifting Loyalties and Failed Empire: A New Look at the Social History of Late Ottoman Yemen, 1872–1918[1]

Isa Blumi

Introduction

On the night of July 16, 1898, British soldiers patrolling the unmarked "frontier tribal region" of the Hawashib, a group of communities living along the borders of the British-held area of southern Yemen, came upon a caravan of mules and camels. According to the commander of the unit, the caravan was clearly attempting to enter "illegally" the neighboring British-held territory of Dhali. During its attempt to halt the caravan, the British soldiers came under fire and four soldiers were killed. In the subsequent "complaint" posted to Ottoman officials who administered the region from where the caravan was coming, the figure of one "Shaykh Muhammad Nazir Muqbil" is mentioned with great frequency.[2] Over the next three years the man known variably as "Shaykh of the Hawashib," "Muqbil," and "Muhammad Nazir" became the main point of tension between the British and Ottoman administrations in Yemen. The subsequent violence along the porous mountain trails that made up the then unmarked frontier created a diplomatic and administrative crisis for the British and Ottoman empires. This crisis provides for the reader in the twenty-first century a perfect case study of how our conventional wisdom about the nineteenth-century history of the Arabian Peninsula is in need of revision.[3]

The Muqbil case has been noted in a number of studies on Ottoman–British relations in the Yemen during the 1874–1918 period. Much of the focus, however, has remained on the level of the actual diplomatic exchange between the two imperial states involved. Contrary to this diplomatic focus, what the acts of a local power holder (Muqbil) demonstrate is that two world powers were vulnerable to pressure from within Yemen. As will be demonstrated throughout this chapter, it was a local potentate who became the central animating factor behind the "modern" transformations taking place in Yemen, often at the expense of larger imperial strategies that had been drawn up in imperial capitals. Put differently, it is these very "subjects" whose ability to manipulate imperial rivalries and capitalize on the economic demands of an entire population redefined the nature of international commerce, diplomacy, and law. Moreover, Muqbil and others' actions in Yemen forced the two principal powers of the region to institute dramatic changes in the shape, composition, and solidity of the frontiers meant to permanently delineate British spheres of influence from those under Ottoman rule. This chapter, therefore, reinterprets the context in which this transformation in the imperial relationship with its imperial rivals and territorial possessions took place and explores possible new angles of interpreting the period as a whole, angles that ultimately return to the local actor a significant role in the modern world.

The interpretative approach adopted here is helpful as it focuses on "local" factors that contributed to regional and imperial politics usually reserved for imperial actors. This focus adapts the analytical scope of Latin American, South Asian, and African studies that emphasized the importance of reinterpreting power and the forces behind social, commercial, and political change.[4] Unfortunately, far too little has been done among historians of the Ottoman Empire and those working on Yemen in particular, to study events beyond what transpired between the imperial capitals, their diplomatic representatives and at best, those local figures serving as interlocutors between states.

Regarding these local "paramount chiefs," it is suggested here that while clearly a force to be reckoned with in the region, they cannot be understood exclusive of their temperamental base of support. Indeed, recent work has highlighted that these local figures, often as lowly as a village elder, had the ability to incite a chain of events, leading to diplomatic crisis and the downfall of important local figures like Muqbil. What is lacking in this body of work, however, is an understanding of the interrelationship between the modern states that were eagerly seeking to implement structures of domination and centralized control in Yemen and how local communities adapted to these factors of modernity.[5] As will be made clear, Muqbil eventually loses out to other, more adept local actors who use the very forces of the imperial states involved to loosen his grip over the region's economic resources.

Bringing Muqbil to the Surface

The Muqbil case dominates much of the diplomatic correspondence in the British and Ottoman archives during the 1898–1903 period. While not stated in actual terms within the documents, it is clear that Muqbil's raids on British "protected" villages within the Hawashib set the tone of the region's imperial relationship for long periods of time, in large part because they impacted the region's trade. This is evident with the plethora of communications that focus on the sudden need to delineate a frontier between the two powers as disputes over the trade routes crisscrossing the region begin to involve imperial troops.[6] While much ink is spilt over Muqbil, little is written in these documents about why he attacked the British "lines of defense" in 1898 and who were those "hundreds" of men supporting him. Ostensibly, we are left to understand the events that ultimately led to the formal delimitation of the frontiers between Ottoman and British Yemen in 1905 from the perspective of the two states eager to criminalize Muqbil's actions. By accepting this perspective, we would erroneously accept that he was the central personality driving these events. Such methods of interpretation, linking a chain of events to one personality, obscure the often precarious political ground upon which such figures sit. In addition, there is a danger in reading Muqbil's actions as "criminal" or "insubordinate" as depicted in the documents. Such a marking of participants in events needlessly distorts the analysis of events to the point where local factors are of marginal importance.[7] On the other hand, by interpreting Muqbil's actions in terms of a contentious political, economic, and social space within the region, we may begin to appreciate the complex dynamics behind such "men of history."

The principle incident that animated the two powers was Muqbil's "occupation" of an abandoned fort in the middle of his home district of Darayjah, an area that had lain within the British zone of influence since 1895. It is clear once we scratch the surface of the events that Muqbil, while a prominent player in regional commerce for at least ten years, was not identified by Britain to be the key "figure" with whom they would negotiate a "treaty" in the 1890s. In a process not yet clear, the British identified Muhsin bin Ali Mani as the "Hawashib Sultan" and signed a "protectorate treaty" with him on August 6, 1895.[8] The problem with this, as with the eight other "treaties" Britain signed with local "sultans," was that much of the legitimacy of these selected "chiefs" was under constant challenge by others. It is clear that Muqbil did not recognize Muhsin bin Ali Mani's privileged position and most probably was acting within his normal sphere of influence when the British began to claim Darayjah as territory under Ali Mani's (and by treaty, British) control.

As noted earlier, the British first tried to police its areas of influence on its own with patrols, ultimately costing them four British lives in what was ostensibly an attempt to assert British sovereignty over Muqbil's territory.[9] Upon learning of his presence and resistance to British patrols, the British formally complained to Istanbul, demanding support from the Porte to forcibly evict Muqbil from the fortress, in large part because Muqbil posed an "unacceptable threat" to caravan traffic. In first conducting "disciplinary" raids on Muqbil and then demanding Ottoman assistance, the British were beginning to show signs of a new operational interest in securing control of trade in the region, which had only recently been formally claimed under their sovereignty. Such tactics would be key to how the region changed over the next ten years and plays a central role in our inquiry into new approaches to studying the history of the region.

The first impression one takes from the files on these incidents (and one adopted by historians) suggests that Muqbil was acting out of sheer belligerence, threatening a well-established order that needed righting again by a joint Ottoman and British strategy. Once we scratch the surface of this case, however, the familiar veneer of categorical niceties breaks down and the imperial sense of "order" suddenly becomes one in which the source of regional instability does not clearly originate from Muqbil. It is this fragility of order that is intriguing and inspires much of my research into the region's history.

After realizing who Muqbil was, one begins to surmise from a close reading of the evidence that Muqbil was actively seeking to sustain or even expand his commercial network when he took on British "border" guards in his home district. Muqbil's confidence in taking on the British is indicative of both Britain's still wavering military strength in the region and of Muqbil's power. As a reflection of his local power, Muqbil was appointed by Ottoman officials in the 1890s to administer its key southern hinterland regions that linked the coastal trading posts of Mukha (Mocha) with the recently conquered southern Yemeni highlands. His jurisdiction extended from Mukha and Perim along the coast and the Ta'iz/Lahej highlands further east, constituting a lucrative channel of exchange between the Arabian Peninsula's Indian Ocean links and trade emerging from the Red Sea. Since Muqbil was also charged with levying taxes on the region's agricultural production as well as the power to administer this trade, it is not difficult to imagine the man becoming quite wealthy over the short period between his appointment and the events of July 1898.[10]

That such figures existed in southern Yemen is nothing new. The British, too, were well aware of the limitations to their rule in many parts of southern Yemen and practiced a similar policy of awarding local "leaders/sultans/shaykhs" with "treaties" that directly linked them to British interests. These recognized (or imposed) "tribal representatives," in return for a percentage of the revenue generated by taxation and trade (identified in British documents as "stipends"), were required to create a secure and stable environment for the imperial state that claimed legal sovereignty over the territory. By signing "treaties" with nine identified "sultans" along the disputed regions separating British Aden from Ottoman territory, the British effectively manipulated commercial and diplomatic "law" to expand its influence beyond Aden from the 1890s onward.[11]

This, again, was much the case with Ottoman relations with men like Muqbil and various Zaydi Imams. The issue remains, however, what lies behind the power of such "leaders." As Muqbil's case reveals, local power granted by an imperial patron sometimes created counterproductive local relations in which abusive leaders like Muqbil and Imam Yahya inspired resistance that ultimately led to instability, often taking the shape of large-scale insurgencies against the empire and their local allies.[12]

The source of concern that Aden/London had expressed to Istanbul over Dhali and Hawashib was Muqbil's commercial influence in areas Britain had every intention of monopolizing for itself. At one point in the diplomatic correspondence, Muqbil was formally accused of taking part in unsanctioned commercial activities in the region, resulting in a sudden imbalance of local conditions. Involved in the "illegal" shipment of goods between the Ottoman port of Mukha and the highland districts that Britain considered its own, Muqbil had crossed an as-of-yet unidentified threshold of British power.[13] That Muqbil would actually stake a claim to a piece of that trade was all the more difficult to entertain by British officials as it became clear to them that he was an Ottoman subject. The relationship between Muqbil and the Ottoman administration meant in theory that his actions were either directly sanctioned by the Ottoman state or could be halted by the Sublime Porte with the proper pressure.

The rigid semantics of imperial power and the diplomacy surrounding Muqbil's actions clearly erase the extent to which local agency was determining the direction of events largely beyond the control of the states claiming sovereignty over the territories in question. Although Muqbil first appeared on the scene in 1898 as a leader of a brief but violent exchange, his continued efforts to expand what I suggest was his personal control over these lucrative trade routes forces us to reconsider the nature of local political and economic affairs. Attempts by the British to resist Muqbil's power grab and the diplomatic means through which they sought to do so

become of paramount importance to understanding Yemeni history as
a whole.[14]

Placing the Blame: Asserting Sovereignty and Imperial Relations

For London, the problem was that it could neither buy Muqbil's loyalty nor
coerce him as they opted to support his rival, bin Ali Mani. When the
British failed to evict Muqbil using their own methods of coercion, they
resorted to diplomatically pressuring Istanbul, which initially proved able
to avoid British claims that it was solely responsible for the events taking
place in Yemen. As the British phrased it to their Ottoman counterparts
through a series of correspondence between London and Istanbul, a faction
of the Hawashib "tribe," supposedly under the control of "Shaykh Nazir
Muqbil," was considered the direct responsibility of the Ottoman state.
Operating under this logic of association, London had hoped to shift an
increasingly dangerous problem of regional control to the Ottoman state.
Istanbul's response equally sheds light on this operational dynamic between
imperial states. While Istanbul conceded that Muqbil was the responsibility of the Ottoman administration, it reminded London that the Hawashib
territory actually flowed into British-claimed valleys, meaning some members of the "tribe" engaging in acts of resistance were "British" subjects. This
imperial method of selectively identifying sources of local power in order to
control them is indicative of the British and Ottoman regimes' evolution in
Yemen at the turn of the century. It is also indicative of just how vulnerable these two states were to local factors beyond their control.

Missing in these documents is any analysis of the motivating factors for
this confrontation. As understood in the documentation of both
represented states, the assumed unity of the local population is predicated
on labeling the inhabitants of Hawashib as a "tribe" who simply followed
the lead of their "shaykh." As anthropologists in recent years have correctly
noted, the operational logic of such social categories was not necessarily
reflective of political and economic currents at play in societies traditionally labeled "tribal" in the literature. Much like in Africa and South Asia,
the imperial categories of tribe meant to assert political and cultural
affiliation to a portion of the indigenous population in the region failed to
represent the local realities. Indeed, as in the case of Muqbil, the method of
placing him at the center of the violence in the area does not reflect the
local dynamics surrounding commercial activity. As research reveals, locals
living in the border region had only developed a temporary allegiance to

Muqbil in the 1898–1902 period. Muqbil, who had successfully created a commercial network which connected him to markets in Ottoman Yemen, other ports in the Red Sea, and British Aden, had been able to buy the allegiance of certain communities and groups at the time. By the time the British patrols in 1898 and again in 1901 were engaging "Muqbil's tribe" however, shifts in local trading patterns were taking place.

For locals whose livelihood depended on assuring the safe passage of their trade in and out of the area, anyone who either threatened or promised to protect the flow of goods had a great deal of influence. At the time, there was economic instability because of the challenges of regional trade by the Italians and French taking place in the Red Sea. In addition, there was an ongoing drought in much of the southern Arabian Peninsula. Initially, these conditions favored Muqbil, who promised access to trade routes under his protection, essential for the survival of communities and their merchants located in Yemen's hinterland. For village leaders, not aligning with Muqbil could mean political suicide. It was clearly in the interest of locals to have a stake in the lucrative business by way of aligning with Muqbil, who by that time secured a monthly stipend from Ottoman administrators in Ta'iz as well and served as a local governor, collecting taxes and maintaining the local militia. These communities would, in turn, supply Muqbil with armed support as he took on British troops and assist him to enforce his monopoly of trade on the Ottoman side of the frontier. As a result of this privileged position, Muqbil was able to gain the upper hand in the regional flow of trade by the time he battled with the British and commanded, as a consequence, the loyalties of these communities.

Britain began to understand that the main problem lay in that there was no formal frontier between the two states. The ambiguous territorial areas of control in the Hawashib allowed these local "subjects" to threaten the state's interest in maintaining "law and order" in its respective territory by monitoring this lucrative trade. The key appears to be how the respective imperial powers negotiated these local problems. While Istanbul initially resisted British tactics of placing the blame directly on Ottoman officials for not controlling their "subjects," the Sublime Porte soon adopted key points of London's argument, causing a significant shift in how the empire operated in Yemen and inducing a dramatic shift in local political relations.

Reconfiguring the Imperial State

Based on the logic of patronage actively being installed throughout its own "tribal" areas, the British diplomatic attempts to assert "order" in an area normally beyond its reach quickly enforced a discursive order in terms of its relations with "Shaykhs," "tribes," and it appears, Istanbul. Diplomatic correspondence demonstrates perfectly that the discursive rigidities explicitly under scrutiny in this chapter were becoming instrumental to British imperial logic and eventually Istanbul's as well.[15] While first able to shift the blame, London and Bombay's rhetorical move of asserting ultimate responsibility to Istanbul for the actions of an autonomous population temporarily attached to an identifiable individual effectively tied the hands of the Ottomans to a method of imperialism it did not yet practice in Yemen. Subsequent inquiries about "Shaykh Nazir Muqbil," therefore, confirmed in the operational language of all modern empires, that the Ottoman state was indeed "responsible" for Muqbil's actions. Since the "*Hawashib Kabilesi*" was a "subject" receiving Ottoman money, Istanbul had no recourse but to ascribe the methods of abstraction to its administration of the area, methods that suddenly rendered Muqbil a danger to British–Ottoman relations and therefore, had to be eliminated.

This, I argue, represents a dramatic shift in Ottoman governing tactics and signals a sudden ascendancy of Istanbul-based diplomacy and "reform" over previously locally developed methods of administration.[16] As a result of British pressure to change the methods of administration in Yemen, no effort was made by Istanbul to find out the reasons behind the initial process of funding Muqbil or why he may have "attacked" the British. Instead, probably sensing its weakness in the larger world, Istanbul's bureaucrats ordered that Yemen's administrators halt its friendly relationship with Muqbil in order not to cause needless tension with the British Empire. Just months earlier, such a policy of funding a local would not have attracted Istanbul's attention, let alone condemnation; paying off Muhammad Nazir Muqbil was clearly part of a larger program to incorporate locals into the smooth governance of the vilayet.[17] The modified discourse surrounding subject and ruler immediately forced local administrators to abandon successful governing practices in order to placate diplomatic concessions granted far away from Yemen.

This had serious consequences on how the Ottoman Empire would function over the next ten years. If Istanbul had not agreed to the terms established by these "formal" diplomatic methods and had allowed local administrators to figure out a solution reflective of local conditions, the issue may have been resolved in a way more in keeping with how local problems had been solved in the past. It is clear from documents that the British position in Yemen was vulnerable, with local actors distrustful of British ambitions, a fact that could have worked to Istanbul's advantage. But, by being rigidly tied to the logic of modern imperialism, the officials in Istanbul were obliged to cooperate in an effort to "reclaim order" in the area by using force against their local ally. The consequences are quite visible, both as concerns Muhammad Nazir Muqbil, and the others living in a region that would become the focal point of an evolving imperial drama.[18] The subsequent efforts to confront Muqbil signaled to many among his former allies that power was shifting in the region and that Muqbil may have bitten off more than he could chew and the Ottomans were incapable of protecting their client.

Containing the Empire

Often, as the case with Muqbil suggests, local politics took on the parameters of the larger, inter-empire political rivalry beginning to surface throughout the Red Sea region. This dynamic provided a key cipher for British or Italian agents to both affect and effect change in Ottoman-held territories through the patronage of figures such as Asir-based Muhammad Idrisi and coastal communities south of the key port of Hudaydah.[19] This may be better appreciated by thinking how the imperial frontiers that were beginning to gain greater diplomatic importance became key components in local attempts to dictate the terms of engagement between these imperial states and their assumed subjects.[20] How the process of delineating territorial frontiers affected local perceptions of their own limitations and "possibilities," may offer a key component to our appreciation for social diversity and political opportunities available to communities and individuals throughout the Arabian Peninsula over the last century and half.

As demonstrated in the case mentioned above, Shaykh Muhammad Nazir Muqbil was considered a threat to the quickly evolving British interests in the region. His last major show of force in July 1901 ultimately had the effect of upsetting perceptions of a local balance of power among Muqbil's temporary allies. The consequences for Muqbil would be immediate. Soon after the joint Ottoman and British force chased Muqbil from his fortress, Ottoman troops, ordered to "police the imperial borders" were reportedly clashing with factions at first assumed to be loyal to Muhammad Nazir Muqbil.[21] What local officials soon learned, however, was that Muqbil's many trading partners involved in the trade (or smuggling) of high-value goods from Mukha into British areas were not entirely dependent on Muqbil. While Muqbil was clearly outgunned when facing the powers head-on, his former subordinates were quickly able to assert their own power by escaping the immediate thrust of the two imperial armies. Much to both Empires' frustration, clashes between locals and imperial forces continued into August and September over the use of trade routes and the "illegal" trade of essential commodities. Since the Ottomans and the British were both still fixated on the "tribal" hierarchies conceived in order to better articulate policy in the region, they understood these new manifestations of local resistance as Muqbil's continued ability to project power. In the subsequent struggle over these ambiguously drawn frontier areas, Britain and the Ottoman state began to blame each other for funding the fugitive Muqbil, creating new tensions in London and Istanbul that would lead to a formal delineation of the frontier.[22]

In time, Ottoman officials, at first eager to match Britain step by step, realized that their capacity to physically coerce loyalty led to greater instability in the entire vilayet.[23] As Britain, Italy, and France expanded their interests in the region, any hope of quietly administrating the areas south of Ta'iz became more and more difficult for locally based Ottoman officials who were being criticized and even persecuted by Istanbul-based "reformers" wanting to see "results" in Yemen. It must be stressed that the origin of these tensions should not be solely pinned to Britain's decision to shift gears diplomatically. As demonstrated in the case of Muhammad Nazir Muqbil and his Mukha-based trade network, the rising instability in the area may also be attributed to the decreasing power of imperial states and the ascendancy (and confidence) of local circles of power.

Over time, therefore, one observes that officials stationed in Yemen (both Ottoman and British) had to eventually abandon the ambitious and largely unrealistic reforms sent from the metropole, often on terms dictated by local factors such as those in the Hawashib. For the sake of survival, local officials faced with heightened distrust and increasing "foreign" involvement would eventually court perspective allies in Yemen in ways that contradicted assumptions the "state/subject" relationship implied in the documents exchanged between imperial states in 1901. Importantly, how this develops over time in no way substantiates British or Ottoman manipulation of local communities or their organization into tribal sections. Instead, what happened was a constantly changing dynamic of negotiation and struggle for ascendancy with local figures playing off rival imperial interests to facilitate, or at times, circumvent, current structures of power, economic flows, or diplomatic convention.

What can easily be forgotten when reading the documented exchanges between imperial powers, therefore, are the finite qualities of local power, which by July 1901 had completely marginalized Muqbil. It is clear that those formally associated with Muqbil were beginning to play off both states in search of room to operate in the region's now wide-open commercial arena. A myriad of interests succeeding for the most part because both states failed to recognize the dispersal of power went well beyond the central figure of Muqbil, who was in hiding and ostensibly finished.[24]

Again, this may be best appreciated by looking more closely at the process surrounding the formal delineation of the frontier, a process that entailed asserting official imperial control over territory left to local players in the past. That this process would clearly change over time provides us with a key sociological basis to appreciating my concern with past methods of interpretation. What appears, for instance, at any given time as "order" in the imperial scheme, may be a reflection of momentary realities that jell around particular configurations of local power brokers who operate within impurely confined spaces. This "order" may but last for two years but these moments of "order" can settle into peoples' lives, creating what appears to be "patterns" others have observed when they write Yemen's history. Market relationships, commercial partnerships, and the financial long-term goals of the region's merchants and of those who protect them are set around this temporary order, often beyond the capacity of any single entity to "control." That men like Muqbil can disrupt this order and become the major animating factor, which constitutes a key period in the history of places like the Ta'iz highland region, suggests that any desire to constitute long-term sociological coherence to people's lives must address the frequent contingencies to such "order."

Clearly, by July 1901, imperial rivalries and the subsequent search for formal order produced the kind of disruption of people's lives that would cause a reconfiguration of that social order anthropologists want to fix by asserting permanent loyalties to people through the categories they use. The important factor suddenly animating local events in the Hawashib at the time was the conceptualization of "frontier," and not some primordial loyalty to "tribe," "shaykh," or "sect." Prior to 1905, therefore, the "frontier" between Aden and Ottoman was demarcated neither by geographic line nor cultural boundary.[25] A process that was neither unilateral nor unilinear enveloped its very conception. Rather, the frontier was dotted by zones of multiple, intermittent, and complex interpenetrations among factions endowed with unequal power in contest over territorial space and access to resources such as modern guns, the local drug qat, or gold coin.[26] Although constructed in binary terms as an ideological foundation for core areas and the bureaucrats running them, the frontier may be better conceptualized in terms of networks of social linkages and understandings, a large proportion of whose relations, experiences, and meanings transcend bounded notions of place. Critically, these frontier regions, like others, have been marked by the state's tenuous ability to exercise hegemony through mechanisms of consensus and consent and to monopolize the use of violence. When that exclusive use of violence is challenged, however, a new set of dynamics to the frontier emerges.[27]

Ottoman officials in Ta'iz, perhaps at a loss as to how to stop the violence in the area, report to Istanbul that there are daily clashes in the Ta'iz area, all involving British "paid" agents.[28] Such recognition of direct imperial involvement in the actions of locals temporarily removed the balance of power between state and subject. For Istanbul, Muqbil could no longer represent the figurehead of instability. For a while, it would be British intrigue. The power of the local, I argue, is significantly increased in this context of formal ambiguity. The significance of these circles of power begins to shift the imperial capital's focus away from catering to local interests, at least in the abstract of diplomacy, to one of trying to formalize techniques of control through its administrative categories. As a response to "British" intrigue, Ottoman state patronage of the "native" became one of imperial importance rather than one based locally, as in the past. The subsequent empowerment of certain elements of local society because of this shift translated into yet another generation of administrative innovations, new military strategies and indeed, a new order of life for those living in the affected areas. Such shifts may signal a time when formal boundaries in regions historically fluid become the primary tool of imperial administration.

Conclusion

Recent work on bringing voice to those formally distinguished as "marginal" in the hierarchies presumed to exist in "tribal" and patriarchal societies demonstrates that there is a way to replicate a past's complexities by actively disengaging from using certain categories as the foundation of inquiry. I sought to reproduce that same voice here. It has been demonstrated that power in Yemen is not negotiated solely along terms set by state institutions or ethnographic conventions that assert a position of authority onto "tribal shaykhs." The social order predicated on uniform notions of power was shown to be constantly transcended by social actors whose worlds were not locked in perpetual isolation from the outside world and who were not dependent on local, "tribal" claims to their loyalties.

By strategically calling into question the epistemological assumptions that units such as "tribe" carried through a historical study of Ottoman Yemen until World War I, it is hoped that studying these forgotten events clarifies the otherwise confused and highly un "conventional" behavior of history's agents. Such an approach to identify agency beyond the categories of the ethnographer and historian may prove to be an attractive alternative to the scholarship on empire. By suggesting Yemeni society is not static, but in a process of constant change (as much as European societies were during the same period) we conceptually open up new avenues of interpretation that allow us to reconsider the parameters of modernity. Asking new questions of the late Ottoman period in Yemen allows us to discover that human beings are not rigidly inclined to any one standard of interaction entombed in "tradition" and immune from modern sentiments and agency. Customs, social allegiances, religious associations, and legal traditions are fluid, reflecting the contingencies that make up life, a fact that has similar consequences to our appreciation of events that take place on the Arabian Peninsula or elsewhere.

Notes

1. The author would like to thank the staff at the Public Records Office in London (PRO), and The Prime Minister's Archives in Istanbul (BBA). Special thanks are reserved for Ebru Sönmez for her years of support and friendship. Funding for research has been provided by the SSRC IDRF and Near and Middle East Dissertation Fellowship programs.
2. See BBA HR.SYS 85/4, dated March 30, 1901 for various documents recounting these first encounters in the Hawashib.
3. A helpful summary of the events leading to the eventual signing of a border treaty in 1905 may be found in BBA HR.HMS.ISO 140/1, dated 30 Rebiyülevvel 1335 (January 25, 1917) files 14 and 18.
4. For interesting work along these lines, see the theme issue of Cultural Anthropology James Ferguson and Akhil Gupta, eds. "Space, Identity, and the Politics of Difference," *Cultural Anthropology* 7/1 (1989).
5. While Eugene Rogan's recently published work is to be applauded, the author still relies far too much on how the Ottoman state itself understood its frontier region in trans—Jordan, a shortcoming I am addressing here. Eugene Rogan, *Frontier of the State in the Ottoman Empire: Transjordan, 1850–1921* (Cambridge: Cambridge University Press, 1999).
6. See, for instance, BBA HR.SYS 85/24, dated September 19, 1902 as a joint border committee travel the length of the region in order to inspect the various points of conflict. What is often noted in the commission briefings is how local communities were actively engaged in the process, suggesting that more attention should be paid by the historian in regard to who and why certain actors get embroiled in the events.
7. Farah's exasperating habit of using derogatory and imprecise labels like "rascal" for nameless individuals rebelling against Ottoman rule highlights the epistemological limitations of past studies on Yemen. Caesar Farah, *The Sultan's Yemen: Nineteenth-Century Challenges to Ottoman Rule* (London: I.B. Tauris, 2002).
8. The treaty was reportedly delayed because of clashes between bin Ali Mani and the Lahej "Sultan" Abdali who was selected as Britain's key interlocutor in the region. It appears that bin Ali Mani objected to being a subordinate of Abdali within Britain's artificial hierarchy and actively sought the assistance of the Ottoman authorities throughout 1894 to gain more leverage. Such tactics did win more concessions from the British, but the reasons behind bin Ali Mani's eagerness to sign such a "protectorate treaty" most probably rests in the fact that his immediate rival, Muqbil, was already a key ally of the Ottomans and proved a threat to him. PRO FO 78/5098 India Office report to London, dated Bombay, November 21, 1895.

9. PRO FO 78/5098 India Office, dated Bombay, March 14, 1900.

10. This is made clear in any number of files, including the correspondence between Ottoman officials in Yemen and the Sublime Porte. See BBA HR.SYS 85/21 dated July 10, 1902, documents 4 and 5.

11. See British correspondence between Aden and Bombay during the process of negotiating with hinterland communities and how Ottoman infiltration into these regions became of primary concern. PRO FO 78/5098, in particular, document 59, dated Aden, November 28, 1894, J.J. Jopp to Political Department in Bombay.

12. I have made a similar argument in the case of the Zaydi Imam Yahya, who from 1904 to 1911 battled with Ottoman administrators for local power in the northern Yemeni highlands. Ultimately, Yahya was forced by local threats to his power to sign a formal alliance with the Sublime Porte, giving him, much like Muqbil in the 1890s, tax-gathering powers in return for his cooperation. See Isa Blumi, "To Be Imam: Empire and the Quest for Power in Ottoman Yemen during World War I," *The Great Ottoman-Turkish Civilization*, vol. 1, Kemal Çiçek, Ilber Ortayli, and Ercüment Kuran, eds. (Istanbul: Yeni Türkiye Odasi, 2000), 731–42.

13. For extensive coverage on British fears of Muqbil and others' impact on local trade, see BBA DUIT 69/3 (1–23, 24, 28, and 39).

14. Demonstrations of the interconnectedness of regional economy, political ambitions of locals, and global flows of commodities such as salt may be found throughout the late Ottoman period in Yemen. BBA, Irade-i Shura Devlet: Report number 639, dated 21 Cemaziyelahir 1305 (March 10, 1888) for instance, discusses the impact of shortages of Indian salt on local relations in Ottoman Yemen. Likewise, Imam Yahya's official historian has noted the role of merchants in opposing his patron's rule during the late Ottoman period, suggesting that failure to sustain local merchants was politically dangerous. See `Abd al-Wasi` al-Wasi`i, *Ta'rikh al-yaman* (Cairo: al-Matba`at al-Salafiyya, 1928), 121.

15. Gavin's informative work helps flesh out some of the initial logistics of British imperial policy toward "tribes" and territory, R.J. Gavin, *Aden Under British Rule, 1839–1967* (London: C. Hurst & Company, 1975).

16. One can see that this slow process take place over a course of two years. A case in point is when an Istanbul-appointed "reformer," Muhammad Ali Bey, begins the disruptive process of assigning a large number of troops from other parts of the empire to repress local Yemenis who were not cooperating with his "reform" proposals. See BBA YA.RES 116/7, which covers events in Ibb and Ta'iz over the period of 1 Shaban 1318 (November 21, 1900) to 6 Muharrem 1320 (April 16, 1902). See especially document 6 in which the supreme council in Istanbul approves Muhammad Ali Bey's proposed budget and orders additional troops to be sent to Yemen, dated 4 Muharrem 1320 (April 14, 1902).

17. This approach had been in practice for years in the southern region, creating a strong administrative base that would produce positive results years later during World War I. See BBA YA.RES 108/45 Bab-i Ali dispatch number 2322, dated 18 Rebiyülahir 1318 (August 16, 1900) where local Nu'man is

appointed judge to a local court as a reward for his loyal service. For more on events in Ta'iz and the role this man and others played during this period, see my "The Ottoman Empire and Yemeni Politics in the Sancaq of Ta'izz, 1911–1918," in *Arab Provincial Capitals in the Late Ottoman Empire*, Hanssen, Weber, and Philipp, eds. (Berrut: Beiruter in Texte und Studien, 2003): 349–367.

18. Case is detailed in BBA YA.HUS 418/65, The bulk of the information discussed above was found in a letter sent by the Ottoman Ambassador in London to the Sublime Porte, dated, July 30, 1901.

19. For instance, significant money was invested in placating the Zeranik communities along the coast, whose loyalty could not be easily bought as first Italian and then British "stipends" constantly undermined Ottoman efforts. See BBA DH.MUI 82/17, dated 26 Rebiyülevvel 1328 (April 12, 1910) for a late example.

20. The Yemen boundary between Aden and Ta'iz was established on April 23, 1905, treaty found in PRO FO 94/953.

21. BBA YA.HUS 418/65, Bab-i Ali Darsadeet Sadrazam report No. 447, dated 16 Rebiyulahir 1319 (August 4, 1901).

22. BBA YA.HUS 418/65, document 5.

23. In BBA DH.MUI 1-1/10, Abdurrahman Ilyas Pasha sends a report to Istanbul on the conditions of Ottoman troops in Yemen. Due to events that took place over the years and the subsequent rise of external sources of money and weapons, Ilyas Pasha advocated the immediate alliance with local forces, which were at the time in open rebellion. His advocacy of aligning with either Muhammd Idrisi or Zaydi Imam Yahya, suggests *realpolitik* took precedence over imperial ambitions among Ottoman officials based in Yemen. Dated 24 Muharrem 1327 (February 16, 1909). See also extensive reports on Imam Yahya's activities in BBA YA.HUS 504/135, dated 30 Cemaziyelevvel 1324 (July 22, 1906).

24. See the following for further details as to how Muqbil's downfall led to increased violence in the area. BBA YA.HUS 418/65 Bab-i Ali Darsadeet Sadrazam report No. 447, dated 16 Rebiyülahir 1319 (August 4, 1901).

25. BBA YA.HUS 484/94 Bab-i Ali report 2660, dated 18 Cemaziyelahir 1322 (September 1, 1904), the Ottomans accuse British supported elements of infiltrating the Perim district, especially a key road linking Hudaydah and Mukha.

26. On frontiers as "contact zones" see Mary Louise Pratt, *Imperial Eyes: Travel Writing and Transculturation* (New York: Routledge, 1992).

27. See BBA YA.HUS 426/126 report 1685, dated 28 Cemaziyelevvel 1319 (September 13, 1901) in which a discussion around the function of the recently established border commission reveals the new anxieties of power that both capitals develop.

28. Reports of British troops reinforcing the informal points of exchange between Ottoman and British Yemen indicate to many in Istanbul that this indeed is a case of British adventurism. See BBA YA.HUS 418/65, Bab-i Ali 447, dated 16 Rebiyulahir 1319 (August 6, 1901).

Chapter 5

Leaving Only Question-Marks: Geographies of Rule in Modern Yemen

John M. Willis

And having stated at large what he means by saying that the same actions have not the same qualities in Asia and in Europe, we are to let your Lordships know that these gentlemen have formed a plan of geographical morality, by which the duties of men, in public and in private situations, are not to be governed by their relation to the great Governor of the Universe, or by their relation to mankind, but by climates, degrees of longitude, parallels, not of life, but of latitudes: as if, when you have crossed the equinoctial, all the virtues die . . . .

—Edmund Burke, in his speech in the impeachment trial of
Warren Hastings, February 16, 1788

Next I presented the King with a copy of Friso Heybroek's map of South Arabia made during our first season. He looked carefully at the border between the Aden Protectorates and Yemen, marked with a series of dashes and question-marks, and I wondered if he might be annoyed that our geologist had not put the boundary where the King thought it ought to be. But he smiled and said, "Next time, please remove the dashes and leave only question-marks."

—Wendell Phillips, in an account of his audience with Imam Ahmad

Introduction

The juxtaposition of these seemingly unrelated moments in Britain's colonial history, the trial of Warren Hastings and a conversation with Imam Ahmad concerning the borders of Britain's Aden Protectorate, is meant to suggest the importance of geography in the constitution of the state and its object of rule. As Burke realized even then, colonial rule was predicated on a geographical imagination that marked off spaces as modern and pre-modern and, therefore, justified particular forms of government. In South Yemen, the British quite consciously placed Aden and its hinterland under separate forms of rule based on a distinction between city and tribe. But as Imam Ahmad's statement indicates, the Zaydi Imamate of the Yemeni highlands was no less obsessed with space, albeit of a very different kind.

While the quote by Burke suggests a world already divided by "climates, degrees of longitude, and parallels of latitude" Imam Ahmed's comments suggest a geography of movement, of borders not yet written. While the space of the Aden hinterland was constructed as an abstract space through the rationalities of the modern state, the Zaydi Imamate of Yahya, Ahmad's father, would seem to have generated a conceptual space that recognized no borders save those created by the extension of the Imam's authority and the rule of Islam.

The rather modest aim of this chapter is to suggest, in a preliminary fashion, ways of reading the relationship between these two very different and competing conceptions of order and their relation to the geographic imagination of rule. In the end, I suggest that any history of modern Yemen should interrogate the ways in which these very different spatial regimes interacted, overlapped, constituted, and reconstituted local identities through the everyday practices of rule. Taking Dali`, a region on the border between the British and the Imamate, as an example, I shall attempt to suggest ways of writing the history of a locality between two spatial regimes and how this region on the margin revealed the internal tensions inherent to both the Imamate and the Protectorate.

Making Aden Tribal

Colonial rule in Aden and its hinterland was based on a distinction between city and tribe. The production of the city of Aden as a colonial space sought the transformation of the social and political identities of the colonized with the constitution of society and economy as objects of rule, and more specifically, urban commercial society. Shortly after occupation in 1839, property was literally given to members of the wealthy local merchant class, and in 1864 the Aden Act established a court system based on Indian legal procedure, which, among other things, relegated religious law to issues of personal status and inheritance. A new city was planned with care by colonial engineers to protect the small garrison and to foster what the British hoped would be a new Singapore. In 1850, the city was declared a free port in the hopes of increasing trade and strengthening the new commercial class that would be the basis of a colonial civil society.[1]

Colonial policy in the hinterland could not have been more different. The construction of fortifications and the strict policing of immigration into the town effectively cut off the hinterland from the port. Rather than deploying the tactics of colonial governance, policy outside Aden was based on the identification of what was thought to be local, social, and political practice in order to ensure its *preservation* and to justify a policy of ostensible nonintervention. These practices were defined by the social category of "tribe." Contrary to the notion that the colonial state and its rationalities were "totalizing and individualizing"[2] the practices of the colonial state in the Aden Protectorate were targeted at the social category of tribe, but did not engage in the types of official procedures that marked off the individual as an object of rule. As others have argued for colonialism in parts of India and Africa, while this type of indirect rule claimed to protect traditional, social, and political forms, it was predicated on the production of difference.[3]

With their Own Weapons

Prior to the British occupation, the port of Aden was ruled by the Sultan of Lahj of the `Abdali family. The `Abdali family had freed themselves from the control of the Zaydi Imamate in the early part of the eighteenth century, as did a number of the areas that would later be incorporated into the Protectorate. Until the British occupation, the majority of the Aden hinterland was under the nominal authority of the `Abdali sultan, who used his income from the port to pay out stipends to the surrounding tribes, thus maintaining a semblance of stability in the countryside. Aden's occupation in 1839 removed that source of income, forcing an immediate political realignment of the hinterland.

Although it was assumed that the port's primary purpose would be as a coaling station for the Indian Navy, strategically placed between the Red Sea and the Indian Ocean, Aden's first Political Agent, S.B. Haines, was more interested in the port's commercial revival. He immediately embarked upon a project to rebuild the town, repopulate the port with the region's merchant class, and increase security by rebuilding the town's fortifications. His immediate concerns with the hinterland, then, had to do mainly with protecting Aden from attack and provisioning the garrison and town. Hence, his earliest dealings with the hinterland tribes were based on achieving these immediate goals rather than establishing any presence beyond the town. But what is of particular interest is the way in which the hinterland and the role of the British in local politics were conceptualized.

The style of Haines and the early Aden government was characterized by his reliance on personal relationships rather than institutions or a trained civil service. In the city, Haines relied on his immediate supporters from the Indian Navy and local men of influence. In the immediate hinterland, he relied on the personal services of Mullah Ja`far, a Persian member of the local merchant class and, more importantly, the `Abdali sultan. It is of some importance that under Haines the treaty with the `Abdali sultan stated that all tribal relations would be conducted through his offices rather than through the British. The logic behind this policy, which was reflected also in the early treaties with the tribes of the Aden hinterland, was that it attempted to reproduce in practice the local political relationships that already existed prior to the British occupation. Agreements were made with the Fadli, the Amiri, the Yafi`i, the Hawshabi, the `Alawi, and the `Aqrabi among others in which they received stipends from the British in exchange for keeping the peace and the trade routes safe, all of which were channeled through the `Abdali sultan.[4] These agreements reveal the extent to which early policy was directed toward protecting the town and encouraging commercial activity in the port by protecting trade routes.

Haines was removed from his position in Aden and charged with embezzlement and confined to a debtor's prison only to die after his release in 1856.[5] The issue at stake was not merely the money but how Aden should be ruled. Despite the port's relative insignificance at this time, Haines's lack of modern bookkeeping skills, tendency to mix private and public funds, and habit of ruling authoritatively were seen fit to prosecute. Outside the city walls, Haines attempted to place himself squarely in the midst of local political practice. Relations were conceptualized in terms of individuals, the `Abdali sultan, the Fadli, and `Aqrabi shaykhs, who were dealt with personally by Haines. Tribal space was defined by the limits of the authority wielded by particular people, and Haines's policy was to ensure that these limits remained as they had in the eighteenth century. Although restricted by the Bombay government to a program of limited interference, the British extended their influence by proxy through the financial and political support of Lahj and other friendly hinterland chiefs and the occasional military action against those in opposition to the British efforts to control regional trade networks.

Creating a Tribal Population

In the period after Haines's dismissal and arrest, the British continued their policy of ostensible nonintervention in the Aden hinterland. However, by the late nineteenth century the Aden government had created an institutional framework through which information on the tribes was collected, the tribes themselves ranked according to an established hierarchy and incorporated into particular rituals of rule based in the space of the city. The Arabic Translation Department (ATD) was established in 1858 by the Political Resident at that time, William Coghlan. Although at this time the ATD comprised a single person, Hormuzd Rassam, an Iraqi archaeologist and employee of the British Museum, the department was responsible for all correspondence with the hinterland and the collection of information on its inhabitants. This situation changed with the establishment of the Arabic Guest House in 1869.[6] The Guest House became the "focal point in the conduct of tribal policy"[7] by orienting tribal relations toward the seat of colonial authority in the city, forming a body of knowledge on the tribes, and establishing a hierarchy of tribes linked to Aden through stipends and rituals of rule. Whereas gifts in the past had been dispensed to tribal chiefs according to rather arbitrary criteria, loosely corresponding to the importance of the tribe to British policy, entertainment in the Guest House was offered according to a carefully graded hierarchy, which not only determined the allowance given to the chiefs but also determined the number of retainers they were allowed to bring, and ultimately, their importance to the colonial state.[8]

As the Department grew in the later nineteenth century it came to be associated with Salih Ja`far, a descendant of Haines's informant, Mullah Ja`far. Working his way up through various positions he was, by 1869, Interpreter and Superintendent of the Arabic Guest House. It was he who drew up the lists of chiefs eligible for entertainment and the size of the presents they should be offered on their departure. The political and social landscape of the hinterland was thus made knowable according to criteria established by the ATD, the Guest House, and their native informants. Although the idioms were still seemingly rooted in the local practices of the hinterland—stipendiary relations, hospitality in the Guest House, and gift giving—they were now part of a bureaucratic language of rule rather than part of social practice.

The Ottoman occupation of the northern highlands and the city of San`a' in 1872, and the subsequent incorporation of the region into the empire provided the context in which the British formally brought the hinterland into treaties of protection. After establishing themselves in the north, Ottoman attempts to extend into the south pushed the British to establish the boundaries of their sphere of influence. In 1873, the British formally requested that the Ottoman government respect the independence of the "nine tribes" (often referred to as the "nine cantons") of the Aden hinterland with whom they had established treaty relations.[9] Afterward, the British attempted to situate the tribes of the hinterland both geographically and legally. They embarked on two major projects meant to mark off the hinterland geographically, the survey of the hinterland in 1891–92 and the joint Anglo-Turkish Boundary Commission of 1902–05, a period that coincided with the signing of treaties of protection by the nine tribes.

The geographical survey and the Boundary Commission provided the context for the placement of the tribes in space.[10] The survey established the northern boundary of the hinterland, the results of which were used as the basis for the British case ten years later during the delimitation of the boundary. Yet, these projects also revealed the extent to which the tribal landscape was a construct of colonial state practices. British attempts to delimit the geographic boundaries of tribal lands were challenged by Ottoman efforts to do the same. Moreover, attempts to establish relations with tribes as coherent political entities with stable leaderships were undermined as rival shaykhs turned to the Ottomans for support against those under British protection. As the activities of the Commission proceeded, the British found that the original "nine tribes" were not necessarily representative of the political and social geography of the hinterland, and the Protectorate treaties that were signed reflect a somewhat more complex view of the region.[11] Nonetheless, once brought into the Protectorate system, the British incorporated the new tribal elite into the imperial framework of the Indian Residencies. Friendly "native chiefs," as they were called, were invited to the Imperial Durbars of 1902 and 1911 in New Delhi, and local meetings within the Protectorate were referred to as durbars as well, in reference to the colonial reading of Mughal political practice.[12]

The Governmentalization of Tribe

The institutional framework of British rule in the Aden hinterland was motivated first and foremost by the need to secure the port's safety and its prosperity. The body of knowledge produced on the tribal hinterland was motivated then, by the needs of security, which comprised both the safety of the port from attack and also the safety of the trade routes on which the port depended for provisions and for export products. Tribe, as a form of colonial knowledge, reflected these concerns. With the establishment of the ATD and the Guest House and the increased involvement in the hinterland after the 1873 memo to the Ottoman government, the British published what would become the standard descriptive and statistical guide of the Protectorate population. In 1886, Hunter and Sealey's *An Account of the Arab Tribes in the Vicinity of Aden* was published less than ten years after the publication of Hunter's account of the settlement in Aden. Thus, the distinction between city and tribe was textualized in colonial knowledge itself, reaffirming that tribal society was a coherent object of analysis and rule.[13]

After the demarcation of the Protectorate boundary, the Indian government again published a series of handbooks on the hinterland. Hunter and

Sealey's 1886 account was revised and reissued in 1909 as *The Arab Tribes in the Vicinity of Aden.* The outbreak of World War I necessitated the printing of two more texts, the *Military Report on the Aden Protectorate* (1915) and the *Handbook of Arabia* (1916) by the War Office. These latter texts were written or compiled by the military, and updated the 1909 account with information gathered during the Geographical Survey and the Anglo-Turkish Boundary Commission.[14] Yet, neither text essentially changed the understanding of tribe presented in the Hunter and Sealey work, which, in its revised form, remained the basic reference on the Protectorate.

The remoteness and relative insignificance of Aden within the Indian Empire prevented the Residency from becoming the "ethnographic state," a term Nicholas Dirks uses to describe the relationship between the production of knowledge on caste and colonial rule in India.[15] Indeed, the handbooks did not engage in colonial ethnography in the volume and detail of such monumental works as the multivolume *People of India* (1868). Rather, the type of knowledge collected on the hinterland was largely instrumental, directed toward the limited requirements of indirect rule. As such, there was little information on customs, legal procedure, or land tenure. The handbooks were historical and empirical, including not only the genealogies of the ruling houses, but statistics on population and local geography. The tribal hinterland as represented in these texts was, in Foucault's terms, "a sort of complex composed of men and things."

> The things which in this sense government is to be concerned are in fact men, but men in their relations, their links, their imbrications with those other things which are wealth, resources, means of subsistence, the territory with its specific qualities, climate, irrigation, fertility, etc.; men in their relation to that other kind of things, customs, habits, ways of acting and thinking, etc.; lastly, men in their relation to that other kind of things, accidents and misfortunes such as famine, epidemics, death, etc.[16]

That is, the tribal hinterland was constituted as the object of colonial indirect rule as a form of population, quantified and reproduced in a series of texts, which represented the totality of knowledge on tribal social space. But the complex of men and things that was constituted through this body of knowledge had less to do with "... the welfare of the population, the improvement of its condition, the increase of its wealth, longevity, health, etc." than the need to make sense of what seemed to a be a chaotic social landscape in order to make secure and profitable the port of Aden.[17] In these texts and in administrative practice, the Protectorate comprised a complex of ruling "chiefs," which included the ruling sultans, shaykhs, and amirs, defined genealogically and legally through their signing of the Protectorate treaties, "fighting men," who were the armed tribesmen or mercenaries that they could command, and resources, which generally meant the amounts and types of agricultural products available that could sustain soldiers—either the forces commanded by the ruling chiefs or British forces.

The assumption, however, that the population of the hinterland could be neatly divided into "nine tribes" under particular figures of authority was based on the rather singular experience of the `Abdali sultanate of Lahj, despite its uniqueness. The `Abadil had ruled over Aden and the hinterland as appointees by the Zaydi Imams until 1745 (or 1728 according to the colonial tradition) when they became independent along with the rest of the local rulers. Not only had they provided most of the hinterland tribes with stipends as the British would later do, but as was mentioned, until the rise of the ATD, all relations with the hinterland were conducted through the offices of the `Abdali sultan. As for the `Abdali sultans, their genealogy was replicated in a number of official manuals, and unlike other hinterland chiefs, they could guarantee that the succession would remain in the family, especially with direct British support. The `Abdali sultans were honored with an eleven-gun salute when visiting Aden, attended the Delhi durbars in 1902 and 1911, and, perhaps most evident of their importance to Aden, Sultan Ahmad Fadl al-`Abdali was knighted (K.C.I.E.) in 1902. In fact, of all the Protectorate "chiefs," the `Abadil most resembled the independent rulers of the Indian Residency system, the implicit model with which the British were working.

Moreover, the area under the sultan's authority comprised the highly cultivated Tuban valley, which produced an agricultural surplus, satisfying the needs not only of the sultanate, but of Aden as well. This also meant that "the people are agricultural rather than warlike, and ... are by far the wealthiest of the tribes bordering Aden."[18] The major trade routes also met in Lahj before passing on to Aden on which the `Abadil levied transit dues. In light of its thriving agriculture, contracts in Aden for supplying the town with vegetables, transit dues on the Aden trade, and the highest stipend of all hinterland tribes it was little wonder that the `Abadil generally hired mercenaries, and those tribes that could send soldiers were considered "poor fighters."[19] The `Abdali sultans were so fully tied to the British regime, economically and politically, that they, in fact, did not sign a Protectorate agreement, nor did they need to, until 1915.

As historians of the colonial world have noted in recent years, the social and political categories deployed by the colonial state had a tendency to create a series of ambivalences, which undermined the colonial order itself. This was certainly true in the Aden Protectorate, and a good part of indirect rule in the hinterland was occupied with reconciling local practice with colonial typologies. But the failure of this order was made particularly acute in Dali' in the immediate postwar period when parts of the Protectorate were declared under the authority of the Imam, as we shall see below. Across the border in the northern highlands, the political order of the Imam and the space it inhabited was imagined in a much different way.

Marginalizing Tribes or the Moral Geography of the Imamate

Ameen Rihani, a Syrian American writer, wrote that Imam Yahya nursed great political ambitions, and "[h]e, therefore, abides his time, keeping the maps of Al-Yaman, of Arabia, before him. And there is Aden, the pearl in the crown of his ancestors. It is not only on the map, but also in his dream."[20] The image of the Imam pouring over maps of Yemen, like the quote by Imam Ahmad with which this essay began, again points to the importance of geography in the discursive construction of the Imamate. Whereas colonial rule in the south was based on the production of knowledge on the "nine tribes" and their submission to the normalizing practices of the colonial state, the Zaydi Imamate was inherently expansionist, at least in its own representation, determined by the Imam's ability to extend the rule of the shari`a. This section deals with the discursive construction of the space of the Imamate in the sirah, or biographical literature, devoted to Imam Yahya.

My reading will be guided in part by the sirah written by the Imam's chief secretary, Qadi `Abd al-Karim ibn Ahmad al-Mutahhar, which covers the period roughly between 1918 and 1923.[21] In a reading of similar literature, Paul Dresch, the foremost scholar on tribal society in Yemen, has written that in the history of the Zaydi Imamate, "there is something of a paradox involved: the tribes have always been politically important, and yet tribalism forms no part of the language of statecraft."[22] He places this rhetorical marginalization in the context of the reproduction of a learned religious tradition, that of Zaydi Islam, through genealogies of sayyid scholars. Inspired by Hayden White's work on narrativity, he suggests that the texts produced by the learned tradition engaged in a historical vision of the Zaydi community, which was synonymous with that of the Muslim community. The tribes, by contrast, could only generate random events set in a generic past; rather than a unified history they had only timeless custom (`urf).[23] Taken as such, the historical tradition of the learned class, and by implication, the Zaydi Imamate was based on an opposition between the learned tradition and the tribes.

As will become apparent below, my feeling is that this opposition is more an effect of reading the biographical and chronicle literature through the category of the tribe than an account of what this literature says. Instead, I would suggest that in the literature of the late Imamate the tribes themselves are not so important as their place in a shifting moral geography of obedience (ta`ah) and dissension (fitnah), defined by the presence of the Imam's authority and the application of the law.

Imam Yahya and the Imamate

In 1904, following the death of his father, Imam al-Mansur Muhammad ibn Yahya Hamid al-Din, Yahya ibn Muhammad Hamid al-Din announced his da`wah or summons to the Imamate and the "ulama" were called to discuss his nomination. As the historian `Abdalla ibn `Abd al-Karim al-Jirafi wrote, "their word was entirely in agreement that no one could take the place of the Imam like his son, so they gave the oath of allegiance and he was called "al-Mutawakkil `ala Allah'."[24] Afterward, we are told, delegations from a number of great sayyid houses and from the tribes of Hashid and Bakil came to give the oath of allegiance as well, all of whom "answered him [his summons] with obedience."[25]

The Imamate is the spiritual–temporal authority in the Zaydi language of statecraft. Zaydism itself, named for a fourth generation descendent of the Prophet (Zayd ibn `Ali, d. 740), requires the Imam to be a sayyid, descended through the wife of `Ali ibn Abi Talib, Fatimah. Beyond the genealogical requirement, however, there is a very specific group of criteria that must be met by likely candidates to the Imamate. Other than that he be an adult, free, sound in mind, senses, and body and that he be just, pious, and generous, the Imam was required also to be both a mujahid, a warrior in the name of religion, and a mujtahid, a shari`a interpreter.[26] He became Imam through his summons to allegiance (da`wa) and rising against illegitimate rule (khuruj). Since knowledge of the law was a prerequisite to the Imamate, would be Imams were generally schooled, as were other members of the sayyid class and the class of hereditary judges (qadi pl. qudat). The biographers and chroniclers of Imam Yahya, for example, note in some detail his ijazah, the certificate detailing the texts he had learned and with which scholars.[27]

The application of Islamic law was of considerable social capital and became the most important theme in the Zaydi discourse of opposition to the Ottoman occupation (1872–1918). Imam al-Mansur framed his resistance in terms of the protection of the shari`a from the irreligion of Ottoman rule, as did Imam Yahya as he continued the opposition after the death of his father. In 1908, during the Ottoman governorship of Hasan Tahsin Pasha, a treaty was concluded with Imam Yahya, which reinstated the *shari`a* as the legal system in the areas under his control.[28] In 1911, a renewed revolt under Imam Yahya's leadership forced the Ottoman government to sign a new agreement. The treaty of Da`an recognized the Imam's religious and temporal authority over the Zaydi highlands in the north, giving him the power to administer the *shari`a*, appoint governors and judges and collect taxes with some degree of freedom.[29] It was certainly not a complete independence; the Ottoman state still received a tenth of the taxes collected, appointed judges to deal with followers of the Shafi`i and Hanafi legal schools, and retained the right to approve the application of *qisas*. And as Blumi argues, the Imam still could not be said to wield power enough to claim full authority in the north without the aid of the Ottoman state.[30]

Nonetheless, the importance of the agreement was in its recognition of the Imam's authority as residing in his knowledge of the law and claim on its enforcement. Despite the fact that the Imam may not have fully controlled the regions and peoples theoretically under his rule, the social capital, which he still enjoyed through genealogy, recognition as Imam and knowledge of the law should not be ignored. The support the Imam generated, even outside the Zaydi highlands, is exemplified by a comment made by the Sharif of Bayhan, who, putting his hand to his head, said, "From this point and above I am pro-Turk; from my heart downwards I am with the Imam."[31] After the end of World War I, the Imam's campaign to gain control of the country evacuated by the Ottoman forces was couched in the discursive forms of the Imamate. This was especially true for the campaigns in the south, which had been under Ottoman rule and the Tihamah, most of which was under the rule of Muhammad al-Idrisi, who claimed spiritual authority and the support of the British.[32] Central to the discourse deployed during these campaigns, was the Imam's spiritual authority in applying the tenets of Islam, the law, and collection of *zakat*.

In the period after the end of World War I, the application of the *shari`a* and the *hudud* punishments for criminal acts became a sign of legitimate authority, sanctioned by God, in Imam Yahya's claim to rule the rest of the country. In general appeals to the tribes, the foundation of the *shari`a* was used as a rallying cry to encourage opposition to the British and to the Idrisi.[33] Similarly, the state-sponsored newspaper, *al-Iman* reported application of the *hudud* punishments in its back pages. In his initial contacts with the British, the Imam invoked his historical and spiritual claims over the area of the Aden Protectorate in an attempt to incorporate those areas diplomatically. Although the British rejected any outright secession of the Protectorate tribes, the Imam further suggested that he be given the authority to appoint judges and hear legal cases, assuring the British that he would respect differences between the Zaydi and Shafi`i schools of jurisprudence. Furthermore, he also suggested that he be given the right to collect *zakat* among them as well. But the Imam also directly contacted local sultans within the British sphere in which he spoke of his military victories, his implementation of Islamic law (*iqamat shari`at allah*) and of people's "whole-hearted desire to enter into God's obedience and our [the Imam's] obedience" (*al-mahabbah bi samim al-qalb li-l-inkhirat fi silk ta`at allah wa ta`atina*).[34] The reference to obedience is important and will be elaborated shortly, but for the moment what is important about the Imamate's self-representation is the way in which it was framed by his knowledge, practice, and enforcement of the law.

It should be noted, however, that this legitimacy based on the law was not as a rule framed as the antithesis of the tribes and customary law (*`urf* or *taghut*). While a number of historians have taken seriously Imam Yahya's attempts to eradicate tribal law, Dresch has rightfully noted that in practice the Imam's intervention in tribal law was more a matter of jurisdiction than an opposition between *`urf* and the *shari`a*.[35] Indeed, the Imam continuously appropriated local practices associated with customary law, leading Dresch to note: "The rhetorical opposition between the two forms of law obscures whatever accommodation there may have been between them in practice."[36] But even this rhetorical opposition was not consistent. Although references to tribal custom can be found in the later biographies they are not as prevalent as Dresch suggests, and the fact that they are indeed tribal does not seem especially important.[37] On the contrary, although the tribes are frequently mentioned in relation to their ignorance of Islamic law or of religion in general, their role as tribes in the religious and historical imagination of the late Imamate seems secondary to whether or not they had submitted to the authority of the Imam.

I would like to suggest an alternative way of thinking about the discursive space of the Imamate and offer this quote from al-Mutahhar's biography of Imam Yahya as a point of departure. For the beginning of the *hijri* year 1338 (1919) he writes, "most areas of Yemen are connected to the state of our lord the Imam, peace be upon him, and have entered into obedience," after which he lists those areas under the authority of the Imam.[38] There is no mention of the tribes in particular, nor any other social groups for that matter. What is important is the word "obedience" within which all particular social groups are subsumed. The fact that the tribes are following local custom is not so important as the fact that they are not following the tenets of Islam in a way deemed acceptable by the learned class, and in this sense they are not obeying the Imam as the representative of God's authority. It is this sense of obedience, within which tribes and all other segments of the population may or may not belong, that is important in the religious and historical imagination of the late Imamate.

Disorder and the Domain of Obedience

In the period after World War I, Imam Yahya waged successive campaigns against Hashid and Bakil, the Zaraniq, and the tribes of the Jawf. But arguably more important to the foundation of Yahya's state, were the campaigns conducted in the agricultural, non-tribal south. Mutahhar's chronicle is largely interested in these campaigns, and the tribes, in fact, play only a minor role in his history. The rhetorical opposition between tribes and the Imamate is, likewise, rarely evident. I would suggest that the historiography originating in Imam Yahya's state *does not invoke this opposition*, but is engaged in a Zaydi-Islamic discursive tradition *whose categories are moral not social*. Instead, when speaking of the state discourse of Imam Yahya's period, I would suggest that "tribe" itself was not nearly as important as its position within a shifting moral geography defined by religious dissension (*fitnah*), opposition (*khilaf*), and corruption (*fasad*) or its opposite, the domain of obedience (*hazirat al-ta`ah*).

In Brinkley Messick's discussion of the discursive-political tradition, which he terms the calligraphic state, he alludes to its spatiality. This tradition, based on the importance of the spoken word, was reproduced in genealogies of learning and embodied in "spiral texts." He notes that these texts, as spatial metaphors, reflect the authority of "presence" rather than that of the abstract form, which can be extended to the domains of administrative practice, city planning, and the "space of the state."[39] Like Islamic legal texts, he argues that the space of the state was defined by the authority of the Imam's presence as it moved through geographic space.[40] Quite the opposite of the abstract space of the Protectorate produced by the British, the borders of the Imamate were marked by the presence of the Imam, his sons and appointed administrators, and the application of the law. Beyond these limits were spaces defined conceptually by dissension (*fitnah*), disorder (*fawda*), or opposition (*khilaf*). Using Messick's brief discussion as a point of departure, I would like to suggest a similar, though differently nuanced, reading of the space of the Imamate.

At the beginning of the *hijri* year 1337 (1918), al-Mutahhar records the names of the places that have been conquered by the armies of the Imam:

> So entered the year 1337. The Imam was resident in al-Rawdah. The following countries were under *obedience and the order of our lord the Imam*, especially Sa`dah, and all areas to the edge of Bani Juma`ah and Razih, and all of the places in the far north (*qibli*), and al-Ahnum, Hajur al-Sham, Sharafayn, al-Sudah, Kuhlan Taj al-Din, `Affar; all of the middle areas to the edges of Yarim and al-`Awd were held jointly by him and the Ottoman state.[41]

These places indicate not only the conquests of the Imam, but also the moral limits of the Imam's authority and all that it implied. The space of the Imam's state during the conquests after the withdrawal of the Ottomans in 1918 was based on the extension of what is often referred to in the texts as the "domain of obedience" (*hazirat al-ta`ah*). What this term implies in the texts is a moral space in which the tenets of Islam are observed, the *zakat* is paid, the Imam's subjects (*ra`iyah*) are respected, and the orders of the Imam are obeyed.

The basis for obedience to the Imam derives from the Qur'an, as the Imam al-Mahdi Ahmad ibn Yahya al-Murtada (d. A.H. 840) wrote in the fifteenth century: "It is incumbent upon the *ra`iyah* to obey the Imam, to advise him and assist him and obey his orders, as was said on high 'obey God and obey His messenger and those charged with authority among you' and they are the Imams."[42] By meeting the requirements of the Imamate and being recognized by other *ulama* the Imam was invested with God's authority and was thus owed obedience. In his study of Ottoman Lebanon, Ussama Makdisi notes that in Ottoman state discourse, the domain of obedience was a "metaphorical domain," which "… encompassed politics and religion, public and private—all that contributed to a stable and tranquil social order."[43] But the particular salience the concept had in the period of Imam Yahya had to do specifically with the transformation of the juridical foundations of the Imamate in the late eighteenth century, and a renewed emphasis on these foundations after the end of Ottoman rule in Yemen.

By the eighteenth century, the once highly centralized Qasimi Imamate had lost its control of southern districts, including Aden, and was increasingly challenged in the Zaydi highlands. The loss of revenue from these lands as well as the decline in the coffee export trade severely weakened the state. Moreover, Bernard Haykel has suggested that a series of Qasimi Imams, who no longer fulfilled the conditions of the Zaydi doctrine of the Imamate, encouraged a reassessment of the legal foundations of the position. The appointment of Muhammad ibn. `Ali al-Shawkani to the position of *qadi al-qudat* was intended to remedy this situation. Shawkani, using Sunni traditions (*hadith*), argued that it was not necessary that the Imam be a *mujtahid* or that he be descended from `Ali through Fatimah. He also argued that the *da`wa* was not the only way of attaining the Imamate, but that one could do so by receiving allegiance from people of importance or through one Imam delegating the position to another. Most importantly in the context of this discussion, he argued, "Muslims are forbidden to rise (*khuruj*) against an unjust Imam (*zalim*) so long as he prays and performs no public act of unbelief."[44] Obedience to the Imam was now incumbent upon all Muslims according to the Qasimi state as it was in Sunni doctrine, a doctrine that was implicitly supported during the Imamate of Yahya Hamid al-Din.

Haykel goes on to suggest that the Hamid al-Din Imams, despite their own self-presentation as defenders of the Zaydi Imamate in light of what was represented as the decidedly un-Islamic character of Ottoman rule, were inheritors of the Qasimi state tradition of the eighteenth century rather than the early Zaydis. Not only did Imam Yahya replicate the outward manifestations of the Qasimi Imamate by taking San`a' as his capital and by relying on the same rituals and processions as symbols of his authority, but his state continued the same reliance on Sunni oriented scholars and a Sunni oriented theory of state as the Qasimis. As Haykel has shown, not only did Yahya see that a number of critical Sunni legal works were printed in Cairo for mass consumption but his own legal decisions (*ikhtiyarat*) tended toward Sunni interpretations. More directly in line with Sunni theories of state and the Qasimi legacy, Yahya installed his son as crown prince (*wali al-`ahd*) and declared Yemen a kingdom (*al-mamlakah al-mutawakkiliyyah*).[45]

The chronicle literature from this period is, in effect, a record of opposition to the formation of this new state, which is framed in moral terms. In Mutahhar's text, resistance to the expansion of Imam Yahya's state generally begins with phrases such as "the fires of dissension were ignited" (*insha`alat niran al-fitnah*) in such and such a place, followed by the admonition that the local *a`yan* had "withdrew from obedience to the Imam" (*kharaju `an ta`at al-Imam*). Contrary to Dresch's reading of the *sirah* literature, this opposition to authority is only occasionally couched in the terms of the "tribes," but more frequently in the opposition to this rather open category of "obedience." On the one hand, the return to the domain of obedience implied restoring the Imam's authority, application of the *shari`a* and the *hudud*, and collection of the *zakat*. But on the other it indicated a type of obedience located in local practice, generally symbolized by the slaughtering of "bulls of obedience" (*`aqa'ir al-ta`ah*) or the offering of "hostages of obedience" (*raha'in al-ta`ah*), neither of which is generally located in a specifically local practice.

To take the example of the district of `Udayn, southwest of San`a', we can see how this moral geography is created in al-Mutahhar's narrative. We are told that `Ali ibn `Abdallah al-Wazir was ordered to Jabalayn in `Udayn after `Id al-Fitr in 1337, "the authority (*haybah*) of the Imam having grown great in the hearts [of the inhabitants]."[46] In this case, the mashayikh and notables (*a`yan*) from `Udayn and surrounding areas came to see al-Wazir and "and exerted all in their power to obey (*al-ta`ah*) and submit (*al-inqiyad*)."[47] Once the area was returned to the domain of obedience, the Imam's presence was made continuous by the appointment of new administrators to the surrounding areas, and `Ali ibn `Abdallah went into the countryside, returning the surrounding population to obedience and securing hostages from the *ru'asa'*, which they did "without reticence (*tarakh*) or anger (*ta`bis*)." From then on, he continued to settle the affairs of al-Sada, al-Ba`dan, and al-Mazahim, and the mashayikh of the region returned to obedience in a way that would surprise "any reasonable person" (`ijab kulli `aqil).[48] This instance in which the Imam's authority (haybah), embodied by the presence of al-Wazir and his soldiers, so inspired the inhabitants of 'Udayn that they immediately returned to obedience was not typical.

The majority of regions evacuated by the Ottoman forces did not submit so quickly to the forces of Imam Yahya, which in the moral universe of Mutahhar's text meant that their inhabitants had removed themselves from obedience and entered the land of either dissension (fitnah), chaos (fawda), or opposition (khilaf). To note one of many such examples, that same year, the author narrates, the people of Jabal Bur'ah in the Tihamah leaned toward opposition (al-khilaf) in support of Muhammad al-Idrisi. They besieged the fort of the Imam-appointed governor and his troops until the Imam himself was alerted and sent reinforcements. At the head of this force was `Abdallah ibn. Qasim Hamid al-Din who immediately declared amnesty to those who returned to obedience. Although the siege was lifted, the inhabitants turned to the Quhrah tribe and attacked the Imamic garrison. Troops were gathered from the regular army in San'a', which proceeded to al-Haymah, where the governor of Mafhaq, Yahya ibn Ahmad al-Kibsi gathered another force, and they both proceeded to Bur'ah, conquering all villages along the way. Once there, they engaged the mukhalifin in a battle "that would make a newborn go gray."[49] Like his accounts of so many other campaigns in this period, we are told that the locals returned to obedience, slaughtered bulls, and requested protection or amnesty.[50]

The author's account of the conquest of Jabal Bur'ah is one of many such episodes in his narration of the Imam's campaigns to bring the country into obedience. Although the specifics of person and place might change, the discursive field in which it engages is surprisingly uniform. Uprisings are generally indicated by some variation on the phrase "error ignited the fire of dissension in the majority of the Tihamah" or certain areas "announced their opposition." The Imam generally responds by ordering one of his amirs to gather a force and proceed to the area, giving them the opportunity to submit. If that offer is rejected, there follows the account of the battle itself and the general descriptions of the feats of the mujahidin. With the victory of the "soldiers of truth" the Imam generally offers amnesty to those who fled and appoints a new administrator who proceeds to settle the area or bring it to order, ushering in a period of prosperity and justice.

To return to the example of `Udayn, the return to the domain of obedience meant the beginning of an era of reform under the benevolence of the Imam and a return to the tenets of Islam. al-Mutahhar writes that "the district of al-`Udayn realized a new age."[51] Under Ottoman authority, he continues, scholars and places of learning had been wiped out, the place had been marked by hostility (ta`adi) among its people and the domination of the strong over the weak, "and every shaykh, wearing the garb of the state (ziyy al-dawlah), did whatever he wanted with his subjects (*ra`aya*)." Under the authority of the Imam and the state of righteousness (*dawlat al-haqq*), he writes, God released the weak from this severity and secured their wealth, fields, and persons from oppression. Most importantly, the return to obedience meant the application of the *shari`ah* "and justice was demanded for the oppressed."[52] In more quotidian terms, Mutahhar narrates the conquest of Sa`fan during the coffee harvest. The Imam forbade anyone from harvesting the fruit since the inhabitants had fled and he ordered that any who returned and submitted should be returned their property. Many did return and "it was said by more than one of the residents of Sa`fan that there had not been such fruit in terms of quantity and purity in forty years."[53] The return to obedience not only signified a return to justice and the rule of Islam but found expression in general prosperity for all.

As Makdisi suggests regarding the use of the term in the discourse of provincial rule in Ottoman Lebanon, the domain of obedience invoked a cyclical view of history as well.[54] The domain of obedience could be left as is commonly seen in the chronicle literature in the phrase *kharaju `an ta`at al-imam* (they withdrew from obedience to the Imam) or some variation thereof, but one could just as easily return to obedience by accepting the Imam's authority by accepting his administrators, offering hostages, and paying the *zakat*. By returning to the domain of obedience memories of corruption, dissension, and pollution are erased; in the language of the chronicles, lands are "purified from filth" (*tuhhirat min al-adran*). Contrary to the abstract social space of the British Protectorate based on the conceptually immutable category of tribe, one is either in the domain of obedience or one is without it; it is not inscribed into geography as the Protectorate but defined by "presence" as Messick argues. What this means is that the domain of obedience constantly shifts with the movement of the Imam, his administrators and soldiers through space, and that the Imam's subjects can leave obedience but can just as easily reenter it. In the period directly following World War I these two very different ways of conceptualizing social and moral space were to come into conflict and reveal the tensions inherent to both.

Leaving Only Question Marks

Ma yadkhul al-Dali` wa fiha `askari Zaydi
Don't enter Dali` if there are Zaydi soldiers there

—*Anon.*

Kalam al-Imam la budda minhu
There is no withstanding the Imam's authority

—*Anon.*[55]

When the forces of Imam Yahya entered the area of the Aden Protectorate in 1919, the British construct of tribe and the moral geography of the Imamate collided. The tensions between these were not reducible to language or representations but were embodied in practices as well. The Zaydi claim to authority was just as much based on the collection of *zakat* and the taking of hostages from Protectorate tribes as it was on the application of law. For the British, the Protectorate relationship demanded that the tribes defend their borders according to their agreements.[56] But as the quotes above suggest, the relationships between the population of the Aden hinterland, the Zaydi Imam, and the British were ambivalent at best. Even though the presence of Zaydi soldiers was often not welcomed, the moral authority of the Imam could draw supporters, especially as reports of his military successes were circulated. And although for the British the questions surrounding the future of the Protectorate were momentarily resolved by the presumed need to support their stipendiaries, the responses of the local population were not so clear-cut. This section attempts to juxtapose the narratives of the British authorities concerning the incursions of the Zaydi state into the Protectorate with the chronicle accounts of the Zaydis themselves in order to reveal the disjunctures in the ways by which the tribes of the Protectorate were "known" and thus narrated.

Constructing the Amiri Tribe

The so-called Amiri tribe of Dali` bore little resemblance to the ideal British conception of tribe. Unlike the genealogies established for other tribes, the Amiri had a somewhat different history. The Amirs descended from *muwallad* (mixed parentage) slaves owned by the sayyids who ruled the region in the name of the Imam. In the sixteenth century, these slaves established themselves as local rulers, having evicted the sayyids.[57] The "Amiri," then were not a tribe but a loose coalition of tribes who in some way recognized the authority of these local rulers; to refer to this following as the "Amiri" tribe was little more than a matter of convenience. The British first entered treaty relations with the Amir in 1880, when `Ali ibn Muqbil agreed to keep the trade routes open and take responsibility for security in the area under his authority. In 1904, during the delimitation of the boundary, the Amir Shayif ibn Sayf signed a treaty of protection with the British. A Dali` Agency was created and a garrison posted there until 1907.

Despite the British recognition of the Amir's authority over the surrounding regions and tribes, in practice it was rarely exhibited without the direct financial and military support of Aden. For example, in 1881, the

Qutaybi, nominally under the authority of the Amir, began exacting dues on the Hardabah trade route until a British force from Aden stopped them. Likewise, in 1885, Turkish forces were able to levy tribute from a number of Amiri villages and to buy the support of the Sha`iri tribe.[58] In fact, the authority of the Amir was found to be extremely limited and could be exercised only over "… his own kindred, adherents and dependents."[59] As for the rest of the groups theoretically under his authority, it becomes clear that this, again, was only an appearance of order. The Ahl Jahhaf acknowledged the Amir as their "chief" and leased lands from him, and the Ma`fari also leased lands from the Amir while he appointed their shaykhs. The Dakkam paid nothing in terms of tribute but made annual visits to the Amir's household, bringing him gifts. The Azraqi and Mihrabi both declared themselves the Amir's subjects and paid annual tribute and taxes on land, as did, it seems, the Ahmadi and Humaydi. As for the Sha`iri, Ahl Halimayn, and Ahl Aj`ud, they paid no revenues and were obligated to join the Amir only in "time of war."

The type of authority wielded by the Amir of Dali` and masked by the colonial desire for order was of an extremely varied type. Rather than representing a single authority to all theoretically under his rule, the relationship between the Amir and the local population was defined by very different legal relationships and practices. The Amir was landlord, for example, leasing or farming out land and collecting taxes, legal authority for some who accepted his decisions, and mostly, it seems, an arbiter for disputes not solved by local qadis.[60] According to the logic of the Protectorate system, however, the Amir was the ultimate authority in the region, responsible both for local security, for the trade routes specifically, and maintaining transit dues agreed upon with the British. For the British, the Amirs were the authority of the region by virtue of the treaties and Protectorate agreements, by accepting the financial and military aid of the Aden authorities, and by participating in the rituals of colonial rule embodied in the annual visits to Aden and the Delhi durbars. Yet, the limits to the Amir's authority became increasingly evident, especially during the Anglo-Turkish Boundary Commission and after.

The Amir's relationship with one of its theoretical subjects, the Qutaybi tribe, will serve as an example. The Qutaybi tribe, residing primarily in the valleys around Jabal Radfan, was part of the Ahl Aj`ud and often referred to within the larger category of "the Radfan tribes." The Amir of Dali` considered them under his authority; as the Handbook points out: "[t]he Sultan of the Amiri … claims suzerainty over them, but cannot enforce it, nor do they admit the claim."[61] As was noted earlier, the British came into direct conflict with the Qutaybi concerning the exaction of transit dues along the Hardabah road on the Dali` route to Aden at the end of the nineteenth century. In 1903, the Qutaybi declared independence from the

Amir, and the British forced them into submission during a short military campaign.[62] Nonetheless, it became clear during the Boundary Commission and the Dali` Agency that the Amir's authority over the local tribes was limited as was his ability to secure the trade route to Aden.

So long as a British garrison was present in Dali` there was no immediate need to deal with the issue, but the knowledge that evacuation was necessary to conform to any policy of nonintervention pushed the resolution of the problem. It was certain that the Amir could not effectively rule the area he claimed as the British expected of him, as Harold Jacob, the Political Agent in Dali`, noted:

> ... the Amir is after all only the "dejure" suzerain of the Radfan tribes. He is called "Abu Jeban" (i.e. "father-of-two-pockets" viz of the Halmin and Radfan peoples who pay him no tribute but are expected to furnish him with warriors on occasion). As a matter of fact he is not all powerful. Their's is a paper allegiance, and where the house is divided against itself, it were unwise to pretend he can check them, or that they will lend a willing ear to his overtures, charm he never so wisely.[63]

With the realization that the Amir could not fulfill his obligations to provide security on the roads and consistent transit dues, those in the field suggested concluding a treaty of friendship with the Qutaybi shaykh, Muhammad Salih al-Akhram, granting him some sort of stipend in return for his protection of the roads. But rather than concluding such an agreement with the Qutaybis and undermining the "nine cantons" recognized by the Ottoman government and used as the conceptual frame for the Protectorate, it was argued that any stipend paid to them must be administered through the Amir of Dali`.

There was no confusion as to why the Qutaybis were not to be paid directly; Jacob suggested quite plainly that the necessity of maintaining the appearance of colonial order required that the funds be channeled to the Qutaybis through the Amir. "In other words," he wrote, "the Amir will be paying the allowance; it will be paid through him so as to enhance the suzerain's importance, and the Amir will be able to withhold the amount if the tribesmen ever display any contumacy. This is administration by and through Arabs."[64] It was decided that Muhammad Salih should receive a stipend of 50 rupees and a supply of rifles and ammunition as a gift. Thus according to the draft text of the agreement, first written in 1904, the Qutaybi shaykh was to receive the same benefits as the other chiefs of the "nine cantons" who were later to sign Protectorate treaties.[65] Like the other treaties, the Qutaybi shaykh and his heirs or successors were taken as legal subjects and held responsible for security on the roads and discontinuing any new transit taxes. In return, the Qutaybi shaykh was entitled to an annual stipend, gifts of weapons and ammunition, and the honor of visiting Aden at the government's expense. However, the need to justify a particular appearance of order based on the agreements with the nine tribes made it necessary to bestow these honors through the Amir of Dali`, who, despite all evidence to the contrary, was still considered to be the sovereign authority over the population of what were called the "Amiri lands." In effect (and contrary to Jacob's Arabist sentiment), the Qutaybis were to be made subject to the Amir whether or not they could be said to be his subjects.[66]

The withdrawal of British troops and the Political Officer from Dali` in 1907 made more urgent the issue of security and authority along the Dali`–Aden trade route. Early on, the British had realized the limitations on the Amir's authority, and by extension, the authority of most all of the Protectorate chiefs. The subjects of the Amir were also fully aware that British power stood behind him, as was noted by the Political Resident in 1907 when he quoted a saying common among the Sha`iris, Jabal Jahhafis, Azraqis, and Radfanis: "We are not children of the Amir, but children of the British Government."[67] Already by 1912, the Imam was making overtures to the Amir, and during World War I the Amir allied himself with the Ottomans, for which he was deposed for a short time by the British at the end of the war. The self-proclaimed "children of the British" behaved no more predictably.

Between Protection and Obedience

After the evacuation of Ottoman forces in 1918, Imam Yahya sent troops to occupy the Shafi`i south, not only those areas that were under Ottoman rule but the border areas of the Protectorate as well, and Dali` in particular. By early 1919, rumors reached Aden that the Imam had called together shaykhs from the south and demanded that they recognize him as their suzerain. More alarming were the more explicit rumors that Zaydi troops were sent to Qa`tabah on the border, and from there to Dali` and Jabal Jahhaf, within the British Protectorate. In hindsight it seems ironic that the Political Resident could respond to these reports, writing calmly that "[a]t the same time, I don't think the imam has any designs on our protectorate."[68] In his account of the *hijri* year 1338, Yahya ibn `Ali al-Haddad begins by noting that the "people of Milhan revolted, announced their opposition (*khilaf*) and removed themselves from obedience (*kharaju `an al-ta`ah*)." From there he narrates a series of movements through areas characterized by disorder and their pacification by the "soldiers of truth." In an otherwise generic account of the Imam's campaigns what is particular about this year is his narration of their movement into the area of the Protectorate about which he writes,

> in this year [there was] the conquest of Dali` and the areas connected to it, and the conquest of the lands of al-Sha`iri on the part of the Imam's soldiers led by the sayyid `Imad al-Din Yahya b. Muhammad b. `Abbas, and Jabal Jahhaf, and the occupation of Jabal Harir with the Imam's soldiers led by the sayyid Muhammad b. Muhammad al-Shami, and the entrance of the Maflahi into obedience, the conquest of al-Shuk`ah, the fall of al-Naja, the destruction of al-Quz`ah, the obedience of al-Shu`ayb, the conquest of al-Aj`ud, the conquest of the fort of Halimayn and the villages around it.[69]

The fact that this account is so remarkably similar to al-Mutahhar's account of the year 1337 is important. al-Haddad is charting a geography of Islamic authority represented by the movement of the Imam's commanders through a space defined morally as a land of disorder or irreligion, the discursive equivalent of "stamping a territory with ritual signs of dominance," as Geertz has written in another context.[70] al-Mutahhar begins narrating this series of events in another familiar way: by noting that a representative of the Imam's authority, Yahya ibn Muhammad ibn `Abbas, was ordered to proceed from al-Nadirah to al-Qa`tabah (directly north of Dali`) from which he was to descend south.

His account of the conquest of Dali`, however, makes no mention of a British sphere of influence or the border agreement concluded with the Ottoman government. Instead al-Mutahhar writes of the Amir Nasir ibn Shayif that, "because of his deviousness and disdain for religion, Satan the deceiver, made preferable to him the breaking of the covenant and the return to the fold of the unbelievers."[71] He went to Aden and requested their aid, thinking that it would be enough to withstand the forces of the Imam.[72] As is typical in the representation of other campaigns, the Imam's agent Yahya ibn Muhammad sent letters of advice and warning, pointing to the fact that the Amir's grandfather was a servant (*mamluk*) of previous Imams. And by not heeding this advice, "he judged for himself that nothing would avail him but the sword and cannon."[73] The Amir's forces were defeated in the ensuing battle and afterward the tribes of the region and the shaykh of Jabal Jahhaf entered into obedience. With their submission, the Imam's authority was made continuous through the appointment of Sayyid Muhammad ibn Muhammad ibn Ahmad al-Shami as the administrator (`amil) of Dali`, from where he called on the surrounding regions to return to the domain of obedience. Indeed, the entire episode is narrated as the extension of the domain of obedience.[74]

To continue with al-Mutahhar's narrative, the general call to the surrounding regions brought immediate responses. Despite Nasir ibn Shayif's intrigues there, the people of Jabal Harir "desired to enter the door of peace in obedience" and submitted to the Imam's forces. The Maflahi's were contacted and submitted, and as an indication of the peace and security that was brought with the return to the domain of obedience, al-Mutahhar can write that "the cutting of roads was eradicated" (*qata`a dabir qutta` al-tariq*), a metaphor for the establishment of just Islamic rule. Similarly, the call went out to the al-Shu`ayb in Yafi`i country, who split into two camps, both pro- and anti-Imam. And "knowing that the foundation of these parts in obedience was not possible without a conclusive battle (*darbah hasimah*) due to the evil of this group of oppressors," Yahya ibn Muhammad attacked al-Shu`ayb and defeated them in two days after which the *mujahidin* collected much booty (*ghana'im wasi`ah*).[75]

By the end of 1919, the Imam's forces were making substantial incursions into parts of the Amiri territories. Jabal Jahhaf was occupied, and, as the British represented the events, shaykhs from various villages in the region were forcibly taken to audiences with the local Zaydi commanders. But while the Zaydi chronicles narrate these events as episodes in the institution of the domain of obedience, the British saw the collapse of the Protectorate as a direct threat to security. Charting a geography of colonial insecurity, the Political Resident wrote that "[e]ighty-five Zaidis visited the Ahmadi, Mehrabi and Azraki tracts, and carried away the sheikhs from the villages of Al Hakl, Husan Kohlan and Dar-al-Miqtar (or Muktar). The sheikh's names are Abdul Karim Awwas the Ahmadi, Abdalla Ahmed the Mihrabi and Hussain Ahmed the Azraki. The informant saw these sheikhs at Dala on the November 16. They are all from our protectorate."[76]

The Protectorate signatories, for their part, responded to the crisis by invoking their treaties of protection and Aden's responsibility to come to their defense, often noting their willingness to ally themselves to the Imam in the absence of British support. While this suggests a canny reading of the treaties by the signatories, it also points to the fragile basis of the Protectorate itself. As Jacob realized earlier, the Protectorate tribes did not view the treaty relationship as one that excluded relations with other authorities, noting that "[t]he late Amir Shaif of Dala; his son, the present Amir Nasr; Sultan Saleh bin Umar of Upper Yafa`; the Radfan tribes; the Alawi Sheikh; certain other Yafais;—and even at one time the Kadi Atik of Behan—have all coquetted with the Zeidis."[77] Indeed, once it was clear that the forces of the Imam intended to incorporate the south, the tribes of the Protectorate deployed tactics other than armed resistance.

In the face of armed invasion, many of the inhabitants of the border regions simply prepared to submit to the Imam's forces. Despite Nasr b. Shayif's position as Amir, he could hardly force those supposedly under his authority to resist invasion, as the Resident noted when he wrote that "[t]he Koteibi Sheikh has already warned his people to get a bullock ready and kill it before the Zeidis can do any damage in his country."[78] He also noted that the Saqladi section of the Sha`ib were reported to have approached the

Zaydi forces with "sacrifices and hostages" in a token of "submission" unbeknownst to the naqibs of Mawsattah. According to al-Mutahhar, the news of the Imam's victories encouraged others to return to the domain of obedience. Thus, we see a group from the Ahl Aj`ud submitting as well as the `Alawi shaykh and the shaykh of Jabal Radfan, both of whom continued on to San`a' to submit personally to the Imam. Sayyid Muhammad ibn `Ali ibn Ahmad ibn Ishaq was sent to become `amil of Shu`ayb and troops were sent on to Halimayn, whose inhabitants returned to obedience and offered hostages. And although the British had supplied ammunition somewhat freely and specifically raised his stipend, the lack of any determined defense of the Protectorate borders drove Nasr ibn Shayif to force the issue, and it could be reported that "… the Amir has become tired of waiting, and has come down to settle the issue once for all [sic]. If the British can do nothing for him, he is said to have made up his mind to join the Imam, with whom he has been in communication for some time."[79]

These responses to the Imam's encroachments are telling on a number of levels. It is on these borders that the tenuousness of maintaining the appearance of order in the hinterland is most evident. It is nearly impossible to find the inhabitants of the Aden Protectorate acting wholly within the conceptual framework established by the British colonial project. But perhaps more surprising is the deft manner in which the signatories of treaties of protection invoked the language of the agreements in ways that the British had not quite anticipated. As the report on the Amir of Dali` indicates, they expected military support from the British as part of their Protectorate agreements and were just as willing to ally themselves with the Imam, or at least threaten to do so, to encourage assistance from Aden.

But it serves us well to consider other modes of representing these same events if the British construction of tribe as a social category is part of a greater narrative of security. The narrative of the chronicle literature is that of the Imamate triumphant, which by its very nature means the triumph of Islam as well. Tribes exist in this narrative, but their categorization as such is secondary to their place in the domain of obedience, whether or not they have submitted to the Imam's authority. The tribes of the Protectorate were similarly skillful in their dealings with the Imam's forces by showing their mastery of the practices associated with the domain of obedience.

After his account of a battle at the village of al-Quz`ah in Yafi`i country, al-Mutahhar goes on to suggest that the victory was one of the "miracles" (*karamat*) worked by the Imam—proof of his righteousness as commander of the faithful. "More than one said" that the Yafi`i had gathered 5,000 men, and the Imam's forces only half of that. Yet, "what was strangest of all was the paucity of martyrs from among the mujahidin in all of these wars … and all of that when what was expected was a great number of martyrs and fewer of the enemy killed; and the inverse of the issue can be but one of Mawlana al-Imam's miracles, God grant him victory."[80] But only a few years later, such confidence in the Imam's mission was perhaps less strong. In 1922, the British first used air power against the Imam's forces, which had occupied Hawshabi and Subayhi country.[81] In 1928, al-Jirafi reports that Nasir b. Shayif and some of the Qutaybis fled to Aden from the collection of the *zakat*, at which Aden sent in planes to bomb Yemeni positions.[82] It was in 1927 that the Royal Air Force officially took over the responsibility for the defense of Aden, indicating at least from the point of view of defense, a turn toward the "forward policy" of the 1930s. Ameen Rihani came upon a group whom he referred to as the "Imam's men" who had taken refuge in Hawshabi country after their base in Mawiyah was bombed in 1928. One of them, commenting on their condition there, said

> We complain, but only to Allah. Our friends are here, but up there is the Dog (meaning the Governor of Mawia). We fought for him—never turned our backs. We fight who meets us in the fight, but what can we do when the enemy is in the air, and is armed? We run to a shelter from the lead that was raining upon us, and the Dog says we betrayed the Imam. The Dog confiscates our homes, our cattle, everything, and we escape slaughter. We come here and find peace and friendship.[83]

This account bears much resemblance to the poetry that would come out of the Protectorate in later years as the British began to rely ever more on air power in the defense of their forward policy. Yet, one should not assume that the defeat of the Imam's soldiers also defeated the ability to conceptualize the events in the same Zaydi narrative of which al-Mutahhar's text is a part. As he approached San'a', Rihani happened to meet a young sayyid on the road, wearing the white turban that signified his genealogy. The young man told Rihani of the campaign in Dali', proudly claiming that "We were 2000, and we had one cannon. We killed twenty-three of the enemy and we lost five of our men ... Yes, the *taiyara* (aeroplane) came and threw two bombs at us. But we read the Fatihah (opening chapter of the Koran) against it, and she straightway disappeared."[84] At least to some members of the learned class, then, the Zaydi social and moral imagination still provided a meaningful way for conceptualizing the world and its events.

Conclusion

Edward Said has famously asserted the importance of the geographical imagination in the constitution of the non-Western world, writing "Just as none of us is outside or beyond geography, none of us is completely free from the struggle over geography. That struggle is complex and interesting because it is not only about soldiers and cannons but also about ideas, about forms, about images and imaginings."[85] The purpose of this chapter has been to locate the relationship between the geographical imagination and the everyday practices of rule in the constitution of both the Aden Protectorate and the late Zaydi Imamate. While it is in no way unique to argue that the logic of colonial rule in south Yemen was based on the production of difference in the form of pre-modern tribal society and the elaboration of a complex of discourses and practices that made this difference real, I have tried to suggest that the Imamate was no less dependent on ordering discourses and practices in the imagination of its space. The virtue, I believe, of this approach is that it allows us to interrogate more fruitfully, and within a common framework, the tensions in both the colonial order and the Imamate in the period after 1918, in which the fate of the hinterland was in question.

As I have suggested, the clash between the British and Imam Yahya in the Aden hinterland was a conflict between two opposing understandings of what the space of the state was and how it was to be organized. Both the Protectorate and the domain of obedience as discursive orders embodied in local practices of rule fell to pieces as the local populations on the border evaded, manipulated, and resisted both the British and the Imam. Although the border agreed upon by the Anglo-Turkish Boundary Commission was reconfirmed in a treaty between the Imam and the British in 1934, the conflict pushed both the Imamate and the colonial state to redefine themselves and push for greater centralization and intervention in the affairs of their populations. While I have only dealt with these issues in a tentative fashion here, I would suggest that the impetus for the spatial constitution of both states came not from the centers, but from the margins. The modern history of Yemen should, in fact, pay much more attention to the borders and the spaces they create.

Notes

My research in Yemen was conducted during September 1999–July 2000 as a pre-dissertation fellow supported by the SSRC Program in the Near and Middle East and the American Institute of Yemeni Studies. In Yemen, I would like to thank the staff of the General Organization for Antiquities, Museums, and Manuscripts, Dar al-Makhtutat in San`a' and the Say'un branch of al-Markaz al-Watani li-l-Watha'iq. Jessica Winegar provided helpful comments on earlier drafts.

1. As several studies have suggested. See David Scott, "Colonial Governmentality," *Social Text*, no. 43 (Fall 1995): 191–220; Talal Asad, "Conscripts of Western Civilization," in *Dialectical Anthropology: Essays in Honor of Stanley Diamond*, vol. 1 (Gainesville, FL: University Press of Florida, 1992), 333–51; Bernard S. Cohn and Nicholas B. Dirks, "Beyond the Fringe: The Nation State, Colonialism, and the Technologies of Power," *Journal of Historical Sociology*, vol. 1, no. 2 (June 1988), 224–9.

2. Scott, "Colonial Governmentality," 202; Cohn and Dirks, "Beyond the Fringe," 226.

3. See the very different approaches to a similar subject in Mahmood Mamdani, *Citizen and Subject* (Princeton: Princeton University Press, 1996), Anne Phillips, *The Enigma of Colonialism: British Policy in West Africa* (London: James Currey, 1989); Leroy Vail, ed. *The Creation of Tribalism in Southern Africa* (London: James Currey, 1989).

4. Z.H. Kour, *The History of Aden, 1839–1872* (London: Frank Cass, 1981), 113–18.

5. Gordon Waterfield, *Sultans of Aden* (London: John Murray, 1968), 225. Waterfield treats the trial at length, 205–41.

6. See Kour, *The History of Aden*, 219–20 for Rassam's biography.

7. R.J. Gavin, *Aden under British Rule, 1839–1967* (London: C. Hurst & Company, 1975), 127.

8. Ibid., 127–9. The minutiae of these transactions can be followed in the correspondence of the ATD, which are to be found in IOR R/20A/4520-847.

9. Ibid., 140. These were the `Abdali, `Aqrabi, `Alawi, Amiri, `Awlaqi, Fadli, Hawshabi, Subayhi, and Yafi`i tribes.

10. See Gavin, *Aden under British Rule*, 195–226.

11. Those who signed Protectorate treaties in this period were the `Aqrabi (1888), `Alawi (1895), Amiri (1904), Upper `Awlaqi (1903), Lower `Awlaqi (1903), Fadli (1888), Hawshabi (1894), `Atifi and Barhimi (subsections of the Subayhi), (1890), Upper Yafi`i (1903), and Lower Yafi`i (1895). Even then, several subsections of tribes signed separate Protectorate agreements indicating the difficulties the British faced in enframing the political geography of the hinterland within their conceptualization of tribe.

12. It should be kept in mind that until 1937 (1921 for the Protectorate), Aden was a political extension of Bombay, not the British government. Not only were Aden and the Protectorate ruled by veterans of the Indian government but many of the idioms of rule deployed in Aden were taken directly from Indian practice, especially from the princely states. The fact that a heterogenous group of hinterland shaikhs, sultans, and sayyids were referred to collectively as "chiefs" was perhaps less obvious then the practice of saluting the most important with cannonades and inviting them to the Delhi durbars and later coronation celebrations. Cf. Bernard Cohn, "Representing Authority in Victorian India," in *The Invention of Tradition*, Eric Hobsbawm and Terence Ranger, eds. (Cambridge: Cambridge University Press, 1984), 165–209.

13. F.M. Hunter, *An Account of the British Settlement of Aden in Arabia* (1877; reprint, London: Frank Cass and Company Limited, 1968); F.M. Hunter and

C.W.H. Sealy, *An Account of the Arab Tribes in the Vicinity of Aden* (Bombay: Government Central Press, 1886).

14. F.M. Hunter and C.W.H. Sealy, *The Arab Tribes in the Vicinity of Aden* (1909; reprint, London: Darf Publishers, 1986); General Staff, India, *Military Report on the Aden Protectorate* (Simla: Government Press, 1915) in *Military Handbooks of Arabia, 1913–1917*, vol. 1 (London: Archive Editions, 1988) (Hereafter cited as MRAP, followed by page number) and "Handbook of Arabia (1916)," in *Military Handbooks of Arabia, 1913–1917*, vol. 4 (London: Archive Editions, 1988). (Hereafter cited as HA followed by page number).

15. Nicholas B. Dirks, *Castes of Mind* (Princeton: Princeton University Press, 2001).

16. Michel Foucault, "On Governmentality," in *The Foucault Effect*, Graham Burchell, Colin Gordon, and Peter Miller, eds. (Chicago: The University of Chicago Press, 1991), 93.

17. Foucault, "On Governmentality," 100.

18. HA, 208. See also MRAP, 182 For a short account of agriculture.

19. MRAP, 199.

20. Ameen Rihani, *Arabian Peak and Desert* (New York: Caravan Books, 1982), 142.

21. `Abd al-Karim ibn Ahmad al-Mutahhar, *Sirat al-imam yahya bin muhammad hamid al-din*, 2 vols., Muhammad `Isa al-Salihiyyah, ed. (`Amman: Dar al-Bashir, 1998). Al-Mutahhar worked as a *katib* for the Imam from 1918 until his death in 1946. See his biography in Muhammad ibn Muhammad al-Zabarah, *Nuzhat al-nazar fi rijal al-qarn al-rabi` `ashar* (San`a': Markaz al-Dirasat wa al-Abhath al-Yamaniyyah, 1979), 356–8.

22. Paul Dresch, "Tribal Relations and Political History in Upper Yemen," in *Contemporary Yemen*, B.R. Pridham, ed. (London: Croom Helm, 1984), 154.

23. Paul Dresch, *Tribes, Government, and History in Yemen* (Oxford: Clarendon Press, 1993). See especially ch. 5, "Sayyid History and Historiography."

24. `Abdalla ibn `Abd al-Karim al-Jirafi, *al-Muqtataf min tarikh al-yaman* (Beirut: Manshurat al-`Asr al-Hadith, [1951] 1987), 285. For al-Jirafi's biography, see al-Zabarah, *Nuzhat al-nazar*, 380–1.

25. `Abd al-Wasi` ibn Yahya al-Wasi`i, *Tarikh al-yaman* (San`a': Maktabat al-Yaman al-Kubra, [1928] 1990), 299. See also al-Jirafi, *al-Muqtataf*, 290. For al-Wasi`i's biography, see Zabarah, *Nuzhat al-nazar*, 410–11.

26. Brinkley Messick, *The Calligraphic State* (Berkeley: University of California Press, 1993), 38 and Manfred Wenner, *Modern Yemen, 1918–1966* (Baltimore: Johns Hopkins University Press, 1967), 31.

27. See al-Wasi`i's rendition of Imam Yahya's *ijazah*, 298–9.

28. al-Wasi`i, *Tarikh al-yaman*, 308 and Wenner, *Modern Yemen*, 46.

29. See the text of the agreement in al-Wasi`i, *Tarikh al-yaman*, 367–8 and Muhammad b. Muhammad al-Zabarah, *A'immat al-yaman bi-l-qarn al-rabi` `ashar*, vol. 2 (al-Matba`ah al-Salafiyyah, A.H. 1396), 213–15.

30. Isa Blumi, "Looking Beyond the Tribe: Abandoning Paradigms to Write Social History in Yemen during World War I," *New Perspectives on Turkey* (Spring 2000): 117–43.

31. Harold F. Jacob, *Kings of Arabia* (London: Mills & Boon, Ltd., 1923), 115.

32. And it should be noted that the shaykhs of Hashid and Bakil who allied themselves with the Idrisi, couched their alliance in terms of the Imamate. As their argument went, by signing a treaty with the irrelgious Ottoman government, Yahya Hamid al-Din was no longer fulfilling the conditions of the Imamate, and hence their support of the Idrisi as imam was justified. See the letter from shaykhs of Hashid and Bakil to the Resident in Aden, 14 Rabi` al-Awwal 1337/December 18, 1918. IOR R/20/A/4892.

33. See his general announcement to the "*ashraf,* `*ulama',* *masha'ikh* and *a`yan* of Yemen" from the post-Da``an period [photocopy in my possession], his announcement to the people of the Tihamah, dated 27 Jumadi al-Awwal 1338/February 17, 1920 in IOR R/20/A/1441, and his letter to the tribes of the Protectorate dated A.H. 1341 in IOR R/20/A/3075.

34. See two letters from Imam Yahya to Sultan Mansur b. Ghalib al-Kathiri in the Hadramawt, 22. Rabi` al-Awwal, 1333. Say'un, al-Markaz al-Watani li-l-Watha'iq, Category II: 42 and 47.

35. Manfred W. Wenner, *Modern Yemen, 1918–1966* (Baltimore: Johns Hopkins University Press, 1967), 70–1 and Robert Stookey, *Yemen: The Politics of the Yemen Arab Republic* (Boulder: Westview Press, 1978), 178.

36. Paul Dresch, "Guaranty of the Market at Huth," *Arabian Studies,* vol. 8, R.B. Serjeant and R.L. Bidwell, eds. (Cambridge: Cambridge University Press, 1990), 64. See also his "Keeping the Imam's Peace: A Response to Tribal Disorder in the late 1950's," *Peuples Mediterranéens,* no. 46 (January–March 1989), 77–95 and the 1910 *tahjir* document of Dhi Bin in Sayyid Mustafa Salim, *Watha'iq yamaniyyah* (Cairo: al-Matba`ah al-Fanniyyah, 1985), 207–22.

37. In al-Mutahhar's *sirah,* e.g., there are only two references to *taghut* among the northern tribes; these are in the context of the campaigns against Bani Bukhayt and Khawlan. *Sirat al-imam,* vol. 2, 40–1 and 80.

38. al-Mutahhar, *Sirat al-imam,* vol. 2, 109–10.

39. Messick, *The Calligraphic State,* 231–50.

40. Ibid., 248.

41. al-Mutahhar, *Sirat al-imam,* vol. 2, 22–3 (my emphasis).

42. Surat al-Nisa', vs. 59. Ahmad ibn Yahya al-Murtada, *al-Bahr al-zakhkhar,* vol. 5 (San`a': Dar al-Hikmah al-Yamaniyyah, 1988), 387–90.

43. Ussama Makdisi, *The Culture of Sectarianism* (Berkeley: University of California Press, 2000), 42.

44. Bernard Haykel, "Al-Shawkani and the Jurisprudential Unity of Yemen," *Revue du Monde Musulman et de la Méditerranée,* no. 67 (Summer 1993), 56. See also, Muhammad ibn `Ali al-Shawkani, *al-Sayl al-jarrar,* Muhammad Subhi ibn Hasan Hallaq, ed., vol. 3 (Damascus: Dar Ibn al-Kathir, 2000), 696–707.

45. Bernard Haykel, *Order and Righteousness: Muhammad `Ali al-Shawkani and the Nature of the Islamic State in Yemen.* Unpublished D.Phil. thesis, Oxford (1997), especially ch. 8.

46. al-Mutahhar, *Sirat al-imam,* vol. 2, 91.

47. Ibid., 92.

48. Ibid., 93.

49. al-Mutahhar, *Sirat al-imam,* vol. 2, 126.

50. For example al-Mutahhar, *Sirat al-imam*, vol. 2, 127.
51. al-Mutahhar, *Sirat al-imam*, vol. 2, 93.
52. Ibid., 93.
53. al-Mutahhar, *Sirat al-imam*, vol. 2, 179.
54. Makdisi, *The Culture of Sectarianism*, 50.
55. The former quote is in Muhammad ʿAli al-Akwaʿ Hawali, *Hayat ʿalim wa amir*, vol. 2 (Sanʿaʾ: printed by the author, 1996), 25; the latter and its translation is in Jacob, *Kings of Arabia*, 136.
56. The weekly Aden newsletters from the period regularly commented on Zaydi tax-gathering and hostage taking in the area of the Protectorate. See PRO CO 725/1, 2, 3, 5, 6, and 7 and PRO CO 725/11/2.
57. MRAP, 12 and HA, 5. Although Hamilton would later write that "[t]o see that they have no slave blood in them requires no more than ordinary eyesight, and it would be impossible for an Imam of San'a to appoint a slave to any post, since there are no slaves in the Yemen at all, slavery being forbidden by the tenets of the Zeidi sect." R.A.B. Hamilton, "The Social Organization of the Tribes of the Aden Protectorate," *Journal of the Royal Central Asian Society*, vol. 30 (1943), 144.
58. MRAP, 12–15.
59. MRAP, 232.
60. MRAP, 232–4 and Gavin, *Aden under British Rule*, 201–2.
61. HA, 53.
62. Ibid., 53.
63. H. Jacob to Pol. Res. Aden, January 31, 1905. Richard Trench, ed., *Gazeteer of Arabian Tribes*, vol. 11 (London: Archive Editions, 1996), 13. (Hereafter cited as GAT, followed by volume and page number.)
64. H. Jacob to Pol. Res. Aden, December 8, 1906. GAT, vol. 11, 33. A policy supported by the Political Resident, DeBrath. See DeBrath to Pol. Dept., Bombay, January 27, 1907. GAT, vol. 11, 35.
65. See the draft of the treaty text. GAT, vol. 11, 8–9.
66. The urgency of maintaining this appearance of order had already arisen in 1894 when the Hawshabi's elected the ʿAbdali sultan as their own sultan, thus eliminating the Hawshabi sultanate and one of the "nine cantons" recognized by the British. See Gavin, *Aden under British Rule*, 210. As for the Qutaybi, Hamilton would later say that placing them under the authority of the Amir of Daliʿ was a "political mistake." Hamilton, "Social Organization of the Tribes," 155.
67. E. DeBrath to Pol. Dept., Bombay, January 27, 1907. GAT, vol. 11, 39.
68. Stewart to Wingate, February 5, 1919. RY, vol. 6, 427.
69. Yahya b. ʿAli b. Naji al-Haddad. ʿ*Umdat al-qari fi sirat imam zamanina sayf al-bari.*" Western Library of the Great Mosque, Sanʿaʾ. Tarikh: 2594, 144.
70. Clifford Geertz, "Centers, Kings and Charisma: Reflections on the Symbolics of Power," in *Local Knowledge* (New York: Basic Books, 1983), 125.
71. al-Mutahhar, *Sirat al-imam*, vol. 2, 144.
72. al-Haddad, ʿ*Umdat al-qari*," 144.
73. Ibid., 144–5.

74. In fact, this narrative is reflected in the correspondence between Imam Yahya and the Protectorate "chiefs" as early as 1909. The majority of this correspondence, which will be considered more fully in my dissertation, is located in IOR R/20/A/1257–60 and in IOR R/20/E/301.

75. al-Mutahhar, *Sirat al-imam*, vol. 2, 147.

76. 9th Aden News Letter, December 10, 1919. RY, vol. 6, 460. Al-Wasi`i suggests that the invasion of the Protectorate was in response to the British handing over Hudayda to the Idrisi and argues further that this caused the British to change their policy toward the Imam, a view that al-Jirafi also held. al-Wasi`i, *Tarikh al-Yaman*, 327–8 and al-Jirafi, *al-Muqtataf*, 298.

77. Jacob to High Commissioner, Cairo, November 18, 1917, in RY, vol. 6, 208. See also a note by Jacob concerning the relations between the Protectorate tribes and the Imam, June 10, 1918. GAT, vol. 1, 291.

78. Stewart to High Commissioner, Cairo, January 1, 1920. RY, vol. 6, 466.

79. American consul to Sec. of State, March 20, 1923. Reginald W. Sinclair, ed. *Documents on the History of Southwest Arabia*, vol. 1 (Salisbury, NC: Documentary Publications, 1976), 60. The Amir's stipend was raised in 1920 to 700 Rs. and in 1926 to 800 Rs. "in compensation for his financial losses due to his enforced exile." GAT, vol. 11, 6.

80. al-Mutahhar, *Sirat al-imam*, vol. 2, 150.

81. Gavin, *Aden under British Rule*, 262–3.

82. al-Jirafi, *al-Muqtataf*, 310.

83. Rihani, *Arabian Peak and Desert*, 31.

84. Ibid., 69.

85. Edward Said, *Culture and Imperialism* (New York: Vintage Books, 1993), 7.

Chapter 6

Aramco World: Business and Culture on the Arabian Oil Frontier

Robert Vitalis

On a warm and windy day late in January 1947, 3,000 visitors gathered at the U.S. Air Force base in Dhahran to await the arrival of King `Abd al-`Aziz ibn Sa`ud. The American ambassador, J. Rives Childs, the patrician from Virginia who collected the works of Henry Miller, had come from Jidda to crown the king's welcoming committee to Aramco's settlement on the Persian Gulf coast.[1] The visit was only the king's second in the 14 years since the Americans originally splashed ashore. Once, on the eve of the war in 1939, `Abd al-`Aziz had traveled by motorcade from his palace in Riyadh to witness the loading of the first tanker of Saudi crude. As the Americans liked to say, since that time Dhahran had been transformed.

Shortly after 12 noon, all six of the Kingdom's TWA-piloted Douglas twin engine DC-3s appeared overhead, flying wing-to-wing. When the king's plane landed, the first up the ramp to welcome him was Sa`ud al-Jiluwi, the governor of Hasa Province, son of a first cousin and trusted ally of `Abd al-`Aziz, and probably the country's second largest land- and slave-holder after the king himself. Behind him came Ambassador Childs. To gauge from photographs, the American ambassador occupied the place of honor at the king's side at virtually every one of the highly choreographed events of the weekend, from the official airport reception to the endless round of banquets at Aramco's compound, in the king's makeshift camp atop an abandoned well site, and at Jiluwi's estate in the lush Hasa oasis.

Childs's report to Washington later described the visit as one more instance of Aramco executives, employees of a private American firm, improperly usurping prerogatives that belonged to the U.S. government and its representative. The company's visiting committee had coordinated with Jiluwi to control access to the various events, but the passes issued to Childs and his staff were seen as an affront. "[T]here was no American authority in Saudi Arabia competent to 'authorize' me or any member of my party to attend the King."[2] The ambassador was also unhappy with his place in the caravan to the new refinery and pier at Ras Tanura. These personal slights were appended to a longer list of instances where Aramco executives overstepped the boundaries between "commercial" and "diplomatic functions," said Childs, who reminded his colleagues of the root of the problem. "Unfortunately the Arabian American Oil Company was in Saudi Arabia before the Legation at Jidda or the Consulate at Dhahran," and the king and his ministers had grown used "to dealing with Aramco as they would with representatives of a foreign government."

The ambassador's complaint was a standard one in the cable traffic between Washington and Jidda. The flag had followed drilling rigs to the domains of Ibn Sa'ud. Aramco's owners had an exclusive lease on the largest oilfields in the world, and virtually every subject that crossed the desks of the small and overworked embassy staff in its ramshackle house on the western Red Sea coast was linked to oil and the wealth that it was suddenly generating inside the Kingdom.[3] The large influx of soldiers and civilians to Dhahran, which Aramco officials described as the largest single overseas postwar American settlement, led in turn to the opening of the consulate there. The same claim is still made today about the American community in Dhahran. Back in the 1940s, this new outpost of the United States, thousands of miles away from Washington, relied on Aramco's organization and expertise for reporting on developments in Dhahran and its hinterlands. The consul and his staff even depended on Aramco for housing.[4]

Aramco thus loomed large in the minds of those whose job it was to observe and report on the firm and its operations in eastern Saudi Arabia, and, arguably, loomed even larger in the minds of those men and women who were drawn to places such as Dhahran, Abqaiq, al-Khobar, and Dammam by the work created in the beginning stages of the oil boom. New migrants moved to the coast from as close as Hofuf, the oasis town to the southwest and for a long time before oil the center of economic life in Hasa, and as far away as Caracas and Coalinga.

Earlier migrations and empire-building episodes had marked the Hasawi landscape. Bare foundations of metropolitan civil administration had been laid in the previous decades by Egyptian and then Ottoman reformers. The nineteenth-century British state had incorporated pieces of the southwestern and eastern Arabian coasts in stages into its global empire via a treaty system ("protectorates"). The last such treaty was signed in 1915 with `Abd al-`Aziz, a chief from the Arabian interior of Najd who had successfully occupied and annexed Hasa in the name of his family two years earlier. From then on, the Al Sa`ud was forced to grapple with the consequences of its having laid claim to an emerging hinterland of the capitalist world economy.

We have few, if any, accounts of the processes of market and state formation on the Hasa frontier. Most studies of the political economy, written from the vantage point of the late 1970s when the hegemony of the Al Sa`ud over a national-territorial space seemed secure, are either unconcerned with the details or else simply adopt a Saudi or Najdi (that is, the central region of the country from which the Al Sa`ud hailed) perspective. Similarly, the nationalization of the American holdings in the 1970s and 1980s and the related analytic debate over state versus firm in the oil sector have left their mark on historical work in terms of a single-minded focus on Aramco's bargains with various Saudi monarchs and their agents.

This chapter uses the concept of the frontier in order to bring together the related strands of "new" social history of (European) imperialism and "process school" accounts of Western (American) expansion. These two traditions parallel one another quite closely. When Cronon, Miles, and Gitlin depict the eighteenth- and nineteenth-century history of the trans-Mississippi borderlands in terms of "species shifting," "market making," "land taking," "boundary setting," "state forming," and "self shaping" transformations, they are describing *global* processes.[5] Their ideas are familiar to anyone today working on the history of state and market formation in the European and Ottoman peripheries. In the same way, the controversies associated with Patricia Limerick's *Unbroken Conquest* and the questioning of the legacy of Frederick Jackson Turner echo wider debates about how to narrate and ultimately judge the course of empire in Africa, Asia, and the Middle East.[6]

The critique of exceptionalism—the belief that some country or people has escaped the current of history in which most others are trapped—that underpins the work of Limerick and other Americanists will remain incomplete as long as we continue to imagine a boundary line in time and space dividing processes and eras of expansion at "home" and, after 1898, "abroad." The record of life in the Aramco settlement at Dhahran and of the clash of cultures on the Arabian oil frontier provides scant support for conventional periodizations and truth claims about a unique American form of *empire-lite*. Rather, an unbroken line leads from the places, institutions, and agents of nineteenth-century expansion in the western United States to eastern Saudi Arabia and other hinterlands of the twentieth-century world economy. No essential collective American cultural character

or creed can therefore explain the different and significant *political* outcomes—conquest and territorial consolidation in the 1800s, the emergence
of an international sovereignty regime to replace protectorates in the
1900s.[7]

America's twentieth-century imperial rivals and theorists of the new
global anticolonial movements routinely compared U.S. conquest of the
North American continent with the projects Europeans pursued "overseas."
Leaders of the American imperial state repeatedly conceded the force of
these arguments through the concerted efforts to deny the application of
international conventions and rights norms to the territories it ruled, from
the Jim Crow south and the remnants of the native American states to
"Central and South America and the Philippines."[8] The myths about the
past that the new regionalist and process school historians have
demolished—grounds that others have not yet ceased to defend—are the
same foundations on which rest beliefs about the distinctiveness of
America's mission abroad in comparison with all other, alleged "earlier"
national imperial projects.[9]

The significance of the water's edge is one more still-intact frontier myth
that obscures the ways in which American continental empire-building
coincided with and in basic ways shaped each moment of the "late" wave
of European imperialism. One of the most obvious ways in which this is
true is in the adaptation in the 1920s and 1930s in Africa of the race
development and uplift models invented in the post-reconstruction south
and in the Dawes era reservation system in the West, which were repack-
aged later in a variety of British and French "colonial development acts."[10]
The same progressive paternalism underlay the development "concessions"
that oil companies and other early multinationals reluctantly began to offer
in their confrontations with populist and nationalist forces in Mexico, Iran,
and elsewhere after World War I.

Even as workers' movements in these older production zones challenged
firms and their privileges, American oilmen and managers recreated the
world of Jim Crow in Dhahran and in the satellite settlements and pipeline
stations across Hasa province. Norms of separate and unequal rights and
privileges structured work and life inside the camps in the 1940s and 1950s.
The racial geography of American mining enclaves was a familiar world, "cut
in two" in Frantz Fanon's memorable phrase. "The zone where the natives
live is not complementary to the zone inhabited by the settlers . . . .
The settler's town is a town of white people, of foreigners . . . . [T]he native
town is a crouching village, a town on its knees, a town wallowing in the
mire. It is a town of niggers and dirty Arabs."[11]

Visitors to Dhahran, paid to document the feats of postwar U.S.
enterprise abroad, frequently depicted a different world. For instance, the

novelist Wallace Stegner set his romance of the early Aramco pioneers, *Discovery*, in Hasa's vast, seemingly unpopulated wilderness. The same familiar images filled the 70-mm screen during the Saudi segment of Lowell Thomas's 1956 Cinerama spectacular, *Seven Wonders of the World*. "The meeting of the old and the new, *in the midst of the wasteland*, oil derricks, pumping wealth out of the ground, a million dollars a day for King Saud; the Arabian–American Oil Co. establishment in Dhahran, where American boys are Cub Scouts and play baseball."[12]

This myth of a virtual empty quarter, like other stock images intended for consumption in the United States and, later, in Cairo and Beirut, had little impact on the oil industry's operations in Dhahran. Soon after the war Aramco took the unprecedented step of creating an in-house research division in order to map the changing cultural geography of Hasa province and assess the impact for industrial relations.[13] Aramco's agents proved themselves more adept at designating place names and charting tribal lineages than at understanding the culture inside the camps of what the firm's public relations men began in 1949 to call "Aramco World."

This chapter is divided into three parts. It begins by describing some basic characteristics of the region in which Aramco began oil production in 1939 and the changes wrought on and underway in Hasa as a result. The fact that the company imported forms and built on a scale that had never been seen before in Hasa may have distracted some otherwise keen observers from considering the myriad long-standing signs of settled, urban–oasis–agricultural life. The rapid development of the coastal triangle of Dammam–Dhahran–Khobar as an alternative population and economic center to the interior oases and the first capital of Hasa is probably the most important obvious regional change. By 1952, the rudimentary Saudi provincial administration relocated from Hofuf to Damman. Though agents of the Al Sa`ud there would attempt to exercise a degree of oversight over the U.S. firm's operations, Aramco was probably the only institution in the entire kingdom engaged in any kind of local planning for Hasa, and the notion of development of the region in this period is best understood as a loose and somewhat misleading categorization of total company investments and expenditures there.

The second part turns to the place that the company designed for its employees: a segregated, fenced-in compound in Dhahran originally known as American camp. In effect, an audacious attempt to manage the clash of cultures on the Arabian oil frontier, Aramco's enormous influence on the shaping of Hasa's landscape begins here. The details pose a strong challenge to the company's carefully cultivated image of a firm that was unique in the annals of multinational enterprise.[14] It turns out that in the 1940s and 1950s, Aramco managers acted like Standard Oil and its rivals in Venezuela and

Anglo-Iranian (BP) in Abadan in the 1930s where even minimal changes toward equality in housing, education, wages, and basic needs depended on workers first acting collectively to claim them as rights.[15]

The third part looks inside the enclave at the building of Aramco's Government Relations Organization and especially its Arabian Affairs Division. Aramco's Arabists defined their purpose as solving "the problem of establishing a common meeting ground for two vastly different civilizations . . . based on . . . securing the full truth about the life, character and background of the Arab people."[16] These action intellectuals seemed particularly prone to exceptionalist beliefs, for instance, in imagining that Saudi Arabia could, like America, continue to escape the consequences of modernity. Their counsel was thus of little use to the firm when thousands of Saudi workers launched the largest mass strike in the Kingdom's history in October 1953 and began the process of overturning Jim Crow in Hasa.

The Nearest Faraway Place

For most American settlers and travelers in the 1940s and 1950s, their first views of Dhahran were from the air, on the last Cairo or Beirut leg of the long flight from home. Returnees would scan the landscape intently and describe the changes in their letters. By 1950, the 30-inch trans-Arabian pipeline was in place, a project that California builder, Steve Bechtel, called "the biggest news since Boulder Dam" for his firm, snaking 1,000 miles from the Gulf to Sidon on the Mediterranean.[17] Close to the Hasa oasis, Aramco's newest well sites were expanding southward. The railway, running to the Al Sa'ud's capital, Riyadh, crossed there as well. At the approach to the coast, the new deep-water port of Dammam was crowded with tankers and cargo. One would swear that buildings had seemed to sprout up and down the eastern shore. It was worse on the ground where it was hard to find the "old" landmarks to the Aramco reservation.

On the eve of the oil discoveries of the 1930s, and as an outcome of prior cultural encounters in this borderland, Hasa province comprised two main population centers, Qatif oasis, a strong Shi'a redoubt on the coast where Indian merchants were active, and, 50 miles inland, the mixed Shi'a–Sunni Hasa oasis, which was dominated by the town of Hofuf. The place that would begin to emerge in the 1950s as the region's new core, Dammam, was a hinterland of Qatif, a one-time pirate's refuge, a Wahhabi preserve in the mid-nineteenth century, and finally a tiny fishing village.[18] Farther south on the coast, the larger village of Uqair served as the port for the goods that Hofuf's big merchant families handled in the trade circuits that linked the Peninsula's towns, however tenuously, with Indian and European producers.[19]

The identification of these distinct places as parts of a larger regional entity was itself an effect of the intensification of "overlapping processes of conquest, colonization, and capitalist consolidation" in the Persian Gulf and Arab East generally associated with the era of British hegemony.[20] Specifically, its foundations are the administrative reforms introduced when the Ottomans occupied Qatif and Hasa in the 1870s, drove out the Al Sa'ud, and began to rule the territories as a single district or *sanjak* of the southern (now Iraqi) province of Basra.[21] While the Americans adopted the Ottoman custom, it seems that as late as the 1940s this particular imagining still fitted uneasily with the local geographies of townspeople and nomads.[22] The Al Sa'ud later depended on Aramco's maps in renaming and fixing the boundaries of "the Eastern Province" in the 1950s, which is more or less used interchangeably with Hasa in contemporary texts. Relative to Najd, Hasa was a wealthy region—which explains much about the relentless campaigns of the Al Sa'ud in the 1800s and 1900s to occupy its towns. The Hasa oasis was the largest and richest tract in what became the Saudi kingdom, comprising 30,000 spring-fed acres, fabled for its date palms. Handicraft production was on an extremely small scale (no factory yet existed anywhere in the country). Dates were Hasa's main export to markets such as Jidda, Bahrain, Qatar, Najd, Oman, Iran, and India, and the source ultimately of the largest sums extracted in the form of taxes and tribute from any place or tribe under Saudi protection.[23] As al-Nuaim argues, many Hasa merchants ultimately accepted rule by the Al Sa'ud as a reasonable price to pay in return for an end to the menace of marauding tribes who preyed on the caravans.

It is not particularly hard to imagine some of the basic effects of oil production on the place that has just been described, even in the absence of conventional economic data. Toward the end of World War II, Aramco began to employ large numbers of local and migrant workers in its three main production sites: Dhahran, where no indigenous settlement then existed, Ras Tanura, where the first Saudi refinery and loading terminal were built, and Abqaiq, 40 miles southwest of Dhahran. Workers were trucked to other close-by fields, while the company built smaller settlements at the pumping stations along the pipeline route. Before this time wage work in the province had been rare.[24]

Labor demand during the late-war and early postwar period of large-scale construction was especially strong. Aramco counted 12,000 Saudi workers on its payroll in the late 1940s. The Bechtel Brothers' operations employed additional thousands of Saudis in three distinct spheres: building directly for the Aramco account, on the Tapline project, and on the roads, ports, and power stations that it undertook as the de facto public works department of the Saudi Arabian government between 1947 and 1951. Construction and maintenance on the U.S. airfield required still more workers. An employee census conducted by Aramco in 1954 found that 60 percent of its Saudi workforce originated from Hasa, and of these, 67 percent were from the two oases.[25] The combined numbers then would represent roughly 5–10 percent of the entire population of the region, which Aramco's researchers guessed to be 160,000 in the early 1950s.

While most accounts of this period emphasize the rapid accumulation of wealth in the hands of the Al Sa`ud as Aramco expanded production and royalties climbed from $5 million in 1945 to $110 million in 1951, these sums represented a massive transfer of resources *from* the Hasa frontier to Hijaz and to Najd. The fortunes of the eastern hinterland were, by contrast, tied much more directly to the pattern of Aramco's own investments and operating expenditures. U.S. embassy officials reported that the company's payroll had reached SR1 million weekly by 1948, the equivalent of $15.6 million, annually. By comparison, estimates of the Saudi government's own payroll in this period were around SR2–2.2 million weekly, though these payments were also three to four months or longer in arrears during most of the decade.[26]

The effects of these flows were easily visible, for example, in the new import and consumption patterns emerging in the area, and in the rising towns. Al-Khobar, the tiny fishing village where Aramco had built its first makeshift port, grew into a bustling commercial center, servicing both the American compound and the nearby separate workers' barracks the Americans called Saudi camp.[27] As rents in al-Khobar soared, Saudis began to move to Dammam where, once plans for the new port there were finalized, company officials envisioned the development of a new model modern city.[28] The direction that the new and unregulated building followed in this early stage reinforced the need in the minds of the Aramco Americans for careful planning of Dammam's future.

By comparison, the role of the Al Sa`ud or its agents in shaping the contours of Hasa during the 1940s and early 1950s was extremely modest. Previous discussions of this place and period cite the $32 million Dammam port and railroad projects in Hasa either as evidence of Ibn Sa`ud's role as modernizer or, even more anachronistically, of a nascent strain of developmentalism on the Saudi government's part. The company itself did much to promote the image of "partners in development" but the reality is that Aramco sited and designed the port as a routine part of its business, much as it made decisions on where and when to drill for oil. The king, however, insisted on formal Saudi ownership. He also insisted, against the advice of a phalanx of engineering consultants, that a railroad be built from

Dammam as a means of solving the bottlenecks in supplying his palace's, and Riyadh's, seemingly sudden, voracious appetite for imports. Aramco advanced the funds and contracted the firms to build and run the trains, with all such desires of Ibn Sa'ud and his sons charged (liberally) against royalties. The benefits to Hasawis were primarily in the form of jobs and, for a handful of clients, in windfalls from the king's earlier gifts of property along what became the right of way.[29]

The expansion of Aramco's operations rapidly spawned a variety of services and subcontracting agencies, for example transport, labor contracting, laundries, supplies, often with direct support from the company. The most important were the local private power plants that were erected in al-Khobar and Dammam, along with the first factories for building materials. Members of the largest merchant family in Hasa, the Gosaibis (al-Qusaybi), were natural early intermediaries, but a number of new and now large local investors had their beginnings in business arrangements with Aramco.[30] The most notable is Sulayman Olayan whose global holdings by the 1970s had gained him entrée to the pages of *Fortune* and the like. Backed by the company, Olayan began a trucking firm that worked on the Tapline project. Aramco then helped him set up the National Gas Company, which created a market for the butane and propane produced at the Ras Tanura refinery. Olayan distributed gas to customers in Hasa and in the Saudi capital of Riyadh where refrigerators and air conditioners were becoming fixtures in the palaces.[31]

For those who observed them, the effects of Aramco's operations on the Hasa frontier were indeed dramatic. By the end of the 1940s the first branches of European banks had opened east coast offices. Ships were backed up at the new port of Dammam virtually as soon as it opened, the pier clogged with goods destined for Hasa's oil fields and air base, but also, unexpectedly, Riyadh, then in the beginning stages of a building boom of its own. Local merchants no doubt viewed with alarm the first appearance on the east coast of Hijazi trading firms and concessionaires, though the reality is that for the moment the leading merchants of the Kingdom were largely content to feed on the enormous sums spent by the Al Sa'ud and its agents in the Hijaz, the "core" region where the population of the two largest cities, Mecca and Jidda, alone equaled that of the entire eastern, Aramco-dominated hinterland.

Inside the walls of the rapidly expanding American enclave, the settlers reached instinctively for the images, symbols, and iconography of other frontier chronicles that seemed so resonant with the rigors of daily existence, the world of oil camps and company towns, immigrants, and economic change. For example, U.S. counsel Parker Hart thought it important to report to Washington in August 1949 on the march of "cosmopolitanism and prosperity" in al-Khobar: the grand opening of "a thriving brothel section, which also includes two houses occupied by boys."[32] There is, nonetheless, never a hint of irony when the frontier's exceptionalist premises are invoked, as when William Eddy and other representatives of the firm asserted that the world Aramco sought to build on the coast of Hasa was unique in the annals of foreign enterprise and empire.[33] The Americans who believed this generally had little trouble dismissing as grossly unfair exaggerations the claims of the Pakistani clerks who were fired in 1949 while trying to organize a union to improve living conditions in their outlying camp: "American officers, drunk with racial arrogance, are all too primed to subject young Muslims to an unscrupulous 'lynch-the-nigger' treatment. And when the 'niggers' muster enough courage to protest against the treatment meted out to them, they are first handed over to the Police and then dispatched to Pakistan without any regard for the terms of contract."[34] Yet it was also well known, according to an internal memo to Aramco's top manager, Tom Barger, that many of the Americans routinely referred to the company's Saudi workforce as "coolies."[35]

Such fragments of the record of the clash of cultures in Hasa in the 1940s and 1950s need to be considered in the context of perhaps the most glaring problem for any claim that Americans were not like other, earlier settlers in the Gulf: Aramco's rigidly segregated world was an all too familiar one.[36]

White Man's Camp

In Dhahran . . . there are, except in rare cases, no grandparents, widows, orphans, or socially maladjusted people. There are no teenage gangs or in-law problems. There are no restaurants, hotels, bars, nightclubs, or department stores. There are no crimes or juries, no package stores, Sunday Sabbaths, fireplaces, radiators, or snow, no maids, pediatricians, Jews, haunted houses, or churches . . . .

There are streets of single-story houses, surrounded by lawns or high walls. The streets are wide and clean, blazing white and empty . . .

The people who live in the houses are married couples, frequently young and usually with children. The two other kinds of people in Dhahran are the bachelors and the bachelorettes, who live in "barastis," portables for four which look like the beat-up dormitories of a college with no endowments. Bachelors and husbands, vice-presidents and houseboys, all the males in town wear white ducks, white buck, white sports shirts, and sunglasses; the houseboys are indistinguishable from their employers except for the color of their faces. This is a kind of democracy that doesn't exist in Cairo or Beirut, where the houseboys wear robes of brocade and golden tarbooshes.

Nora Johnson, *You Can Go Home Again*

Novelist and critic Nora Johnson, the daughter of filmmaker, Nunnally Johnson, fled Aramco's American camp in 1958, after three years there with her husband, a young Arabist in the company's research division. The sarcasm drips from this diary entry faster than the sweat off the brows of the stray relations man caught out in one of those blazing streets in summer. But it was only after beginning to understand that there was a spatial order of race and class in Dhahran that her stress on whiteness came to dominate my reading of this text.

The town that Aramco founded in Hasa was built around a fenced enclave, originally referred to as American camp until the 1950s when the firm's public relations men renamed it Senior Staff camp.[37] American camp was laid out like one of the ubiquitous housing tracts then sprouting up in the hills outside Los Angeles. A gently curving semicircle of paved streets filled with neat Californian ranch homes radiating out from a hub where the main administration building was located. Residents called it the Kremlin. Nearby was the gate where one entered or exited the compound. Company buses drove past the freshly mowed lawns, the jasmine hedges, and water sprinklers, took the sons and daughters of Aramco personnel who lived in these coveted family quarters to school or to the pool, and shuttled the single men from the dining halls and clubhouse to their plaster and plywood dorms at the far end of the camp (Whiskey Gulch).

The thousands of Saudis employed by Aramco in Dhahran were housed outside the bounds of the American colony, originally in palm frond huts. The huts were slowly replaced by barracks that were still in use in the 1980s as dormitories for Dhahran's new University of Petroleum and Minerals. Saudi camp was starkly different from the facilities built for the Americans. Saudi camp was open and unfenced, and, at first, bereft of all basic services: water, power, sewers, and so on. These came later, and slowly, after a series of strikes by its residents.

At the same time, nonemployees attracted to the area built "traditional" style two- and three-story houses and stores on *awqaf* (religious endowment) land in streets laid out by Aramco engineers in familiar "block" style, names running in one direction, numbers running in the other. Both the mosque and market were located between eleventh and twelfth streets, where a small network of alleys and cafes created a feel of a *hara* or quarter for its residents.[38] When large numbers of Saudi workers began to move with their families to the area in the 1950s, however, Aramco encouraged them to settle in Dammam, and Dhahran's growth slowed.

Italian, Indian, and Pakistani contingents in the original Aramco workforce were likewise quartered in separate and isolated reservations. The Italians had been imported from Eritrea to build the refinery at Ras Tanura, where they lived in four-man tents or in Dhahran in barastis with dirt floors. In the wake of a strike in 1947, the U.S. consul general was forced to tour the camps and condemned the residences of the non-American workforce as "a disgrace to American enterprise."[39] Compounding this stark judgment is the company's own view of its skilled Italian workers at the time as a solution to the extraordinarily high turnover rates and thus added costs of American labor. The Italians did the same work for lower rates of pay and the sharply reduced overhead that characterized all the non-American quarters ("no recreation facilities, no movies, no swimming pool, etc.").[40] By the mid-1950s the various nonindigenous but non-American worker camps had been consolidated in one large somewhat improved compound, Intermediate camp, housing ostensibly all skilled manual and clerical labor, which triggered the last serious protests by the Italians now outraged because, unlike Americans, they were being forced to live with "Orientals."[41]

Numerous accounts of life inside American camp in the 1940s and 1950s remark about its uniquely democratic and egalitarian character, though usually without even a hint of the irony found in Nora Johnson.[42] Of course, they do not mean democracy in the formal sense of participating in the governing of the community or workplace. It was, after all, a company town, jointly ruled by representatives of the parent firms in San Francisco and the Al Sa'ud. Rather they seek to describe the enclave experience of white families drawn from different worlds of work and origin, as seen by its most urbane and cosmopolitan quarter. This same cohort, which played the preponderant role in production of the official ideology of Aramco World as an Arabian–American partnership in development, also tended to dismiss racism and related currents within American camp as the folkways of the drillers from Texarkana.[43]

At moments such as the Pakistani or Italian protests it became easier for outsiders to see more of the ways in which a hierarchy was constituted in the buildings and spaces of Dhahran, and reproduced in (rather than simply being limited to) the more common slurs and stereotypes. Aramco's senior staff of Arabists had a custom of building models of King Sa'ud, whom they called "Banana Nose." One of these dolls laid exploding eggs. Another sat on a seesaw with Prince Faysal, drinking martinis. A third was a motorized toy dog, with the head of the king, which stood on its hind legs, "waving his hands rather idiotically," as if it were praying.[44] It is likely that they drew no connection in this instance between themselves and the less suave Aramcons.

At other moments, the effects of the community's dominant values became too obvious to ignore. In an unpublished reminiscence, Aramco's folk historian decries the "Texas herrenvolk atmosphere" inside the colony that made life miserable for Sophie Basili, the wife of the company's senior Orientalist, George Rentz, and the first Arab permitted to live inside American camp. "Not only was Sophie an Arabic speaking Egyptian, she was, though attractive, dark skinned," Mulligan writes. "Despite life long friendships established with a wide circle of friends, Sophie was never happy in Dhahran. Her unhappiness stemmed from far more than a Cairene's traditional homesickness for family and the city on the Nile."[45]

Numerous barriers operated to restrict cultural encounters in American camp, apart from the fence surrounding it. At the time of his abrupt dismissal from the company in June 1944, an American named William Lutz charged that Aramco actively discouraged his fraternization with Arab employees, which the company's senior representative in Dhahran reassured superiors, was "entirely groundless" since "many of us have numerous friends among the Arabs." Lutz was different, however, in that unlike any other Aramco employee he spent his off hours outside American camp, "living for days at a time in the Saudi camp," and he had become a Muslim. His failure to follow enclave norms led directly to his being terminated.[46]

The comparison with the case of Willard Beling is instructive. Employed in the same Arab personnel section as Lutz between 1949 and 1958 and head of the section during the period of intense labor unrest, Beling made sure he was noticed. A Princeton Ph.D., he was the star of the camp's football and baseball teams, drove a white Jaguar around Dhahran, and, according to one account, was "offensively aggressive, self centered, coldly calculating, unprincipled and amoral." One of the king's trusted agents in Hasa, Turki ibn Utayshan, who led the Saudi forces in the area, "said he had never known an Aramco American who hated Arabs as much as Beling did."[47] Yet Beling won regular promotions and special benefits before leaving Aramco. His lucrative post-Dhahran career as academic consultant, originally at Harvard's Middle East Center and later as the first King Faisal Professor at the University of Southern California, only began to fizzle in the late 1970s, as reporters traced the money trail used to buy his chair, and he was convicted in Los Angeles of defrauding a Kuwaiti in a land deal.

A final example to contrast with Beling, who invested a great deal of energy in a particular kind of aggressively heterosexual identity, is informative about the official policing of desire in a community that at the time was overwhelmingly male.[48] I had been at a loss about how to judge a recently published account of labor recruitment policy on the Tapline: "Cooley also refused to hire homosexuals. According to his associates during that period, his means for discovering a prospective employee's sexual proclivities was to ask, 'Are you a cocksucker?' If the candidate reacted by cursing Cooley or hitting him, he was hired. Those who hesitated or stammered were abruptly dismissed."[49]

An internal Aramco memo is, however, equally explicit and only slightly more refined: "We had had our share of kooks, weirdos, homosexuals, et. al. and had gotten rid of them over the years. We were not about to start in again."[50] In this case from the late 1960s, the manager of the company's research division had called in an employee to answer the charge by unnamed members of the camp that he knowingly violated "generally accepted norms of behavior," which included his housing a nonemployee in his room and dressing in a *thaub* (the full-length gown that Saudi men wore) in public. There can be little doubt that powerful norms of intolerance operated inside the enclave, side by side with an ethos among white drillers and managers that we are all in it together. The norms we are chiefly interested in here worked to reinforce the effects of the segregation of races in the founding of Dhahran. When a ship of the U.S. merchant marines landed in Ras Tanura in 1944, an Aramco relations man boarded and insisted that Saudi law forbid Jews and Blacks to set foot in Hasa. In the report later by the Congress of Industrial Organizations, which filed a protest, the U.S. vice counsel was described as refusing to answer questions regarding Saudi law. Parker Hart, the official in question, squirmed to protect himself in arch bureaucratic fashion. "At no time while I was aboard the ship was I consulted by any member of the crew other than the Captain and consequently had no occasion to refuse to answer any questions which might have been put. In view of the delicate nature of the complaint, I felt it better to 'let sleeping dogs lie,' and I did not seek out any crew members in order to go into the matter further." Needless to say, no such law existed. Aramco and other U.S. firms did explicitly screen against Jews in deference to Ibn Sa`ud's "sensibilities," a fact that the State Department massaged endlessly when pressed by Congress and the public. As for the ban on Blacks, all Hart could note was that Saudis had no particular feelings about this, and that Hasa's population was itself racially diverse. Parker ended by parroting the company's line: "it should be passed off as an ill-advised action of an individual member of Aramco's staff" who acted "on his own initiative and without company sanction . . . ."[51]

Inside the grounds of the nearby Dhahran Air Base, where a new pool was opened for use of all the field's employees, American soldiers fought to keep Saudi and Italian workers out. There was obviously less chance of such conflicts erupting inside Aramco's American Camp since the "non-nationals" working there were not permitted inside the grounds in their off hours. Nonetheless, Aramco executives were at times obliged to accommodate visits by the younger princes of the Al Sa'ud for "medical treatment," for instance, when the 19-year-old Prince Talal, who later led the democratic movement of Free Princes, and his companions spent the month of Ramadan in 1949 in a drinking binge, holed up in the company's guest house. The U.S. counsel in Dhahran dutifully reported the fears among the American community that were caused by Talal, "known to have syphilis" and other Saudis using the pool.[52]

Alcohol fueled many but by no means all the less memorable encounters along the Hasa frontier. For instance, U.S. and Saudi soldiers engaged in a rock-throwing brawl in June 1949, which escalated when a drunken Saudi commanding officer on the air base drew his pistol.[53] Aramco was plagued a great deal of the time by theft, and its relations men inside and outside Dhahran spent similar amounts of time interceding with Hasa's authorities on behalf of employees. For example, in September 1950, after allegedly fleeing the scene of an accident near a Tapline camp, the amir of the area had the American whipped. The result was a work stoppage, "general mob tension," and an unsuccessful attempt to have the Saudi punished in turn.[54] This is not to claim that every missing piece of reinforcing bar or every roughneck hauled off to jail represented an act of resistance, but it may help explain why residents of American camp were seemingly so mystified by encounters "that got hundreds of Americans in very hot water through no real fault of their own."

> It was difficult to predict just what might strike the Saudi as an insult. To actually swear at him was a criminal offense, for which many Americans were hauled into court and even deported, after paying fines. And, as the end product of centuries of starvation, the Saudi was less than brawny, if remarkably durable. A chummy slap on the back from a beefy Oklahoman might therefore strike him as assault and battery . . . .
>
> To strike a Saudi, even in self-defense, was a sure ticket to the calaboose. Once in jail on such a charge, usually the best a foreigner could hope for was deportation. The testimony of Christian witnesses is not valid in Saudi courts. That of Muslims, on the other hand, is good as gold, and as readily negotiable among them . . . .
>
> In this shadeless land, it was unwise to jump into a vehicle and drive away without checking first to see if anyone was sleeping in the shade underneath. We were discouraged, too, from giving Saudis lifts in our cars and trucks. Still unused to speed, they might, on reaching their destination, simply step out while the vehicle was still traveling at forty miles an hour. The driver invariably then went to jail on a manslaughter charge.[55]

This piece of folklore notwithstanding, the relations organization was actually fairly effective through quiet appeals to Jiluwi in extraditing imprisoned Aramcons or at least arranging for them not to have to serve their sentences in the miserable cells of the local jail. And, finally, the company participated in designing the governorate's new prison system, in order to better house and segregate foreigners. But the early American encounters in Hasa become much less puzzling once we realize that the jail cells they sometimes found themselves in resembled, if they were not superior to, Aramco's own workers' quarters.[56]

Slaves of Aramco

The world women built in Aramco's American camp was the one that impressed the *Life* photographers and the one that the company liked to portray in the pages of *Aramco World*: a world crowded with cub scout dens, choral groups, fashion shows, art classes, and plays (by the *Drama*ramcons). "[F]or a moment or two you have the illusion that you're not in Arabia, but in, oh, White Plains, and that Kathleen [Barger] is just back from Saturday shopping at Saks-Fifth Avenue and an hour at Elizabeth Arden's . . . . Then the door closes and over the greens, beiges and pale golds of the living room you suddenly notice the view: in the foreground a carpet of green lawn; beyond, the rough shape of a jabal ['mountain'] and the twin minarets of a mosque."[57]

Late one morning in the spring of 1957, John W. Pendleton drove from his office in Dammam to a meeting in a living room like Kathleen's on the King's Road. He had agreed to address the Dhahran's Women's Group on the activities of the Arab Affairs Division (AAD) and its importance to Aramco. He told them that he was among the 100 people working fulltime to try to understand the culture in which they and the rest of Aramco were operating. The field workers needed information about the customs of local tribes, those in Government Relations required up-to-the-minute studies of Saudi ministries and personalities, New York made use of the summaries they produced of Arab world radio broadcasts, and virtually all parts of the Aramco organization made demands on their translators, the biggest single part of his division. Pendleton knew that the work was actually more exciting than he was making it sound and he looked for a way to jazz up the talk.

You might be interested in hearing a word about . . . the Bedouins who frequent the offices in Dammam and *are known as relators*. A few of them are on the regular payroll; the majority are casuals. They come from various parts of the Kingdom, and are what I might call homespun authorities in general on the areas which they represent. Some of them are expert guides and are used as such by the Exploration Department. Others are content to lead a more sedentary existence, answering countless questions about geography and sociology of particular areas under study. Some are especially useful in establishing names of remote places . . . *All of them are colorful and friendly*, and they have become a vital part of the Division.[58]

The Government Relations Organization or what was informally referred to as "Local Relations" or just "Relations," emerged as Aramco's early management found increasing amounts of its time diverted from production issues to negotiations with `Abd al-`Aziz's court in Riyadh and the minister of finance in Jidda. The new department was given responsibility for day-to-day intermediary activities of all types, from dealing with tribal shaykhs in the vicinity of the oil fields to the myriad services performed for the king's sons, for example outfitting special hunting cars and staffing Crown Prince Sa`ud's kitchen.[59] The company's first relations head, Floyd Ohliger, who critics derided for his too slavish devotion to the whims of his hosts, apparently loved the custom in the early days of donning Saudi dress for visits to Riyadh, "accompanied by his trusty interpreter, Ajab Khan."[60]

If Relations was Aramco's equivalent mini-State Department, then the AAD, created within it in 1946, was its intelligence branch. The key figure in the organization of the AAD was George Rentz, Aramco's most famous orientalist. Rentz was an American working toward a Ph.D. in Near Eastern History at Berkeley when the United States entered World War II. He went to Cairo where he was put in charge of research and translation in the Office of War Information. At the end of the war, Aramco was desperate for an American staff member with Arabic language skills because the company did not want its Saudi translators involved with negotiations then taking place with Dhahran's amir over treatment of Saudi workers. Rentz was wooed to accept a permanent position with the promise that he would head a full-fledged research organization, where he worked for the next 17 years before retiring to Stanford's Hoover Institution.[61]

Rentz had to battle against competing claims for resources, space, and personnel at a moment when the company's operations were growing rapidly. He began work at a spare desk in a tiny prefab that housed the company's Safety Department. While management ignored its promises of a support staff (three to four Americans, 15–20 Arabs) he struggled for a year or more with only three Arab assistants and waged an endless campaign for other divisions' old mimeo machines and typewriters. In these difficult conditions, Rentz's new organization handled all the company's

confidential translation and correspondence work, while sharing more routine translation and interpreting duties with the three Saudi employees in
relations who were regularly featured in early accounts of Aramco's commitment to training Saudi white collar staff.[62] In their spare moments the
AAD staff made desultory progress on the various early projects—standardizing place names used by the company's geologists, creating a list of all
Saudi government officials and royal family members, preparing a handbook on Saudi Arabia for new employees, building the company's knowledge base in Islamic law, and bedouin and tribal affairs, and starting a
reference library—and Rentz earned his reputation as a hard partying, hard
drinking Aramcon with a penchant for what today we might call sexual
harassment.[63]

Rentz eventually obtained the larger staff and quarters he wanted as a
result of Aramco's growing involvement in the long and protracted conflict
with Great Britain over Saudi Arabia's borders with Qatar and Oman (the
Buraimi crisis).[64] Intent on limiting the access of other firms to Persian
Gulf oil, the company supported the maximalist claims of the Al Sa'ud.
Rentz's division worked up the evidence in support of the Saudi position,
in coordination with the U.S. law firms on company retainer. Much of
Aramco's classic research, for instance, on Hasa, on the eastern tribes and
on the non-Arabic dialects in use along the coast, was driven by the boundary question.[65] Rentz went on Arabist-hunting expeditions in Cairo and
elsewhere, the funds allocated for local informants—relators—increased,
and the AAD grew into an essential part of the company's operations.

The AAD also gained through its backing by some of the most important figures in Aramco, including James Terry Duce, the Texaco executive
who was the company's representative in Washington, DC and through the
internationalist currents that governed the postwar American state. Duce,
for instance, helped forge Aramco's relationship with the newly founded
Central Intelligence Agency, and Aramco drew liberally on ex–OSS
employees for its relations personnel (e.g., William Eddy, who worked for
the CIA while serving in Aramco, David Dodge of Tapline, Rentz, and
others).[66] Duce's protégé Tom Barger, the head of relations in Dhahran and
by 1959 Aramco's president, was another of the AAD's patrons. They
banked on Rentz's claim that engineering or technical know-how alone was
not sufficient to secure the company's position on the Hasa frontier. "The
problem of establishing a common meeting ground for two vastly different
civilizations must be faced and overcome," he wrote in 1951, through an
organization devoted to "securing the full truth about the life, character and
background of the Arab people."[67] For a time, Aramco's Arabists took over
a floor of a new office building outside the camp in Dammam, in pursuit
of the "intimate knowledge" that might protect the "large, rich and

powerful American industrial corporation operating at full blast" at a time and in a region that seemed surrounded on all sides—Egypt, the Arab East, and Iran—by powerful national and populist political currents.

Unsurprisingly, this faith in a social–scientific strand of Orientalism failed America's homegrown experts or led them to bet wrong in Hasa. Starting in the late 1940s, the company had faced increasing complaints from members of the Al Sa`ud and the coterie around the finance minister for its desultory fulfillment of various commitments to training workers, improving working conditions, or building schools for Saudis like those in American camp. There is little doubt that the Americans tended to see much of this essentially as Saudis posturing to various quarters: themselves, the Hijazis, critics in Cairo or Baghdad, and so on. Their "intimate knowledge" seemingly confirmed a sense of Hasawi (or bedouin) difference vis à vis workers elsewhere, and the company's self-defined "enlightened" industrial labor relations policies were apparently working at least as well as its policing power. "Of even greater, although intangible, value is the increased respect of the Arabs because of their realization that the Company's system of identification is infallible. There can be no doubt that Arab American relations have been bettered by the system" (plastic badge bearing photograph number, thumbprint, etc.).[68]

Yet, as the reporting of the U.S. consulate in Dhahran attests, Aramco was taken by surprise and its intelligence division thrown into disarray by a strike of virtually the entire non-American workforce in October 1953. The protest's roots were in the Jim Crow settlement that the company had constructed.[69] In May 1953, the company had received a petition from 155 intermediate employees calling for a cost of living allowance similar to Americans and for improved working conditions more generally. The company agreed to discuss the petition with a small delegation. Seven workers met with company officials at the end of June, but the oilmen, viscerally antiunion, stonewalled when confronted with the workers' complaints of discrimination and the demand to be recognized as representatives of all of Aramco's Saudi employees.[70]

Of the seven, the company singled out `Abd al-`Aziz Abu Sunayd as the leader of the fledgling movement.[71] Sunayd had migrated to Hasa from southern Iraq. He worked as a trainer in the company's orientation and vocational education programs, and had been sent both to the U.S. and to the American University in Beirut for advanced training. The evidence is also clearest in Sunayd's case that the workers' grievances against the company included the sense of bigotry that permeated camp life. Most no doubt saw the hierarchy as a religion-based one, institutionalized by Christians against Muslims, but at one point Sunayd had written to Aramco's president complaining that he had been refused admission to the

senior staff's movie theater and comparing the incident to the color ban
that he had found when he and other Saudi students visited Washington.[72]
William Eddy, the CIA agent on the company's payroll as special advisor,
extended the point to the large mass of Saudi workers who, he said, had no
trouble comparing "this primitive land of low pay, slaves, eunuchs, and
harems to the comfortable conditions of U.S. residents in Dhahran."[73]
Company officials, however, countered that there was no sense in supplying Saudis with Western amenities because they did not really want them.

Many other Americans read the psychology of the workers differently in
constructing an account of its leaders aggrandizing power for its own sake.
Thus, they were "not interested so much in alleged grievances over working conditions and privileges as they were in obtaining for themselves position of spokesmen for Aramco's laborers."[74] The company's early strategy of
brinkmanship backfired, however, and instead catalyzed the movement that
eventually swept the camps.

Aramco refused the demand by Sunayd and his comrades that they be
recognized as leaders of a formal Saudi workers' movement, and the nego-
tiators terminated all contacts. They were instead directed to act through
the government's official representative for labor relations in Dammam, the
normal channel for negotiations with the company. The government representative surprised the Americans by insisting that the company settle
matters directly with the petition signers. Armed with backing from
Dammam, Sunayd forced the company into a new round of meetings in
September with an expanded agenda that included the formation of a
union among company employees.[75] The organizers mobilized support in
mosques and villages throughout the summer, and the Bahraini press as
well as a Beiruti left wing paper publicized their views. New petitions were
circulated, calling for Crown Prince Sa`ud to recognize Sunayd and his
comrades as the bargaining agent for all Aramco employees, and the company estimated that 6,000–7,000 of the 14,000 employees signed these
petitions.[76] Aramco pressed its own government contacts to take the movement seriously as a threat to public security. Aramco fed the amir's brother,
`Abd al-Muhsin Ibn Jiluwi, all the materials they had collected on the
movement, and pressed him to end it. Aramco was insisting that the target
of the movement was the government and not the company, although the
workers' petitions and telegrams to the crown prince and his agents were
customarily deferential and made clear that their demands were for the end
of discrimination against them.

The crown prince sent a royal commission from Jidda to Hasa in
October 1953 to hear the complaints of the workers in person. Aramco
provided its members with the personnel files of the leadership, and if their
account is accurate, then the workers overplayed their hand by demanding

formal recognition as a condition for participating in the commission's proceedings. The chairman of the commission, `Abdallah Adwan, instead had the leaders arrested and imprisoned in Hofuf on October 15. At the same time, the Saudi colonel in charge of the Dhahran air base was given control of all military forces in Hasa, and he moved 1,000 troops into the vicinity of the camps. On October 16, demonstrations broke out in Saudi camp and in nearby villages, and residents staged a march to the American consulate and the air base. Private cars and a U.S. Air Force bus were stoned, although no one was injured, before Saudi troops were ordered to crush the protest.

A strike was called on October 17 in protest at the arrest of the movement's leaders, and workers staged massed meetings in various camps and towns. What shocked the company was the effectiveness of the boycott and the size of the crowds that assembled in public. For the next ten days, the company's Saudi workforce stayed off the job. Many returned to their villages. And the strike spread to the U.S. base in Dhahran. The consulate was reporting that local authority had begun to break down. Saudi officials in Hasa ordered employees back to work by October 20 under threat of permanent dismissal, but the order was ignored (and, later, forgotten). By October 21, hundreds of Saudis had been jailed and the army moved into the workers' camps in Dhahran, Abqaiq, and Ras Tanura. Aramco officials cooperated with the authorities in interrogating workers while the army searched the quarters for communist literature. Fifty Aramco workers were deported to Riyadh before the strike finally collapsed on October 27.

At the same time, Aramco officials were compelled to renew negotiations with the government commission, first on the original issues of pay raises and equitable cost of living allowances, and later on an expanded list of demands for more hospitals, more schools, better housing, more drinking fountains, and the training of Saudis at foreign universities.[77] An agreement was finally reached at the end of November 1953, with the firm making concessions it had long resisted. The Americans continued to debate the meaning of the strike—was it aimed at the company or the government? was it communist led or inspired?—but the State Department postmortem reached one firm conclusion. Although Aramco officials had always insisted that labor unions were illegal in Saudi Arabia, there was in fact "no known basis for the belief."[78]

The Frontier Closes

Americans were witnesses as well as agents of Hasa's incorporation as a hinterland both of the world economy and of an emerging Saudi state.

Not surprisingly, many facets of the world that Aramco created on the Hasa frontier seemed innately familiar. For instance, the American ambassador Rives Childs early on described Aramco in Saudi Arabia as an "octopus" whose tentacles "extended into almost every domain and phase of the economic life of Saudi Arabia."[79] The reference to Frank Norris was undoubtedly deliberate, and if the railroads were not a perfect analogy, Ida Tarbell had never managed to produce as powerful a metaphor for the Standard Oil Trust from which Aramco was descended.

"Westernization" went far beyond Childs's faux populism, however. In *Angle of Repose*, a later and much better book than *Discovery*, the one he wrote about Saudi Arabia, Wallace Stegner describes a settler's first view of a mining town's racial geography ca. 1880: Mexican camp abutting Cornish camp and the Chinese town. Fifty years later and thousands of miles away, Aramco's engineers began to lay out the districts of Dhahran along similar lines: Saudi camp, Italian camp, and American camp. General Patrick Hurley, who visited Dammam in 1943 as President Roosevelt's special envoy to Ibn Sa`ud, made the linkage between old and new frontiers explicit. Born and raised in Oklahoma Indian territory, Hurley felt compelled to stand up at a banquet given by Hasa's amir in his honor and to let loose a "Choctaw war whoop."[80]

Along with ideas about hierarchy, the settlers brought their ideas about American exceptionalism to Hasa's shores, insisting that both they and the domains ruled by the Al Sa`ud had somehow managed to escape the history that had trapped others. The firm's principals and agents never tired of contrasting their own enlightened policies with those of all other overseas investors from the time of the East India Company on.[81] The labor reporting by U.S. embassy officials attached little value or credence to such claims, and internal company documents in fact described their policies as distinctly backward when compared with labor policies in place in their Latin American operations, but local Aramco men never abandoned this doctrine.[82] They clung to it even after the October 1953 strike, as Saudi Arabia entered a period of rising political tensions and the government relations organization sought to analyze the company's increasing difficulties. Thus, as the future company chairman Tom Barger insisted, Aramco's troubles were the product of a host of forces beyond its control: the creation of Israel, the rise of nationalism region-wide, the influence of Arabic magazines and newspapers on an unsophisticated and easily swayed population, and even the U.S. Federal Trade Commission's suit against the oil firms, all of which allegedly contributed to nascent anti-American currents in Saudi society. The company's policies could not be the problem, except residually and inadvertently, the "growing dislike for Americans . . . in some instances has been justified by the attitude and behavior of *some* of our own people."[83]

While some of the Arabists similarly may have clung to their romantic constructions of tribal culture and notions of Saudi exceptionalism—prior to the October strike various Aramco officials had insisted that Hasawis were simply incapable of such an action—the reality is that the firm's policies were designed as if it were possible to avoid or else tame historical change. This is the logic ultimately underpinning the enclave that Aramco built in Hasa. The company sought to insulate the larger population of the hinterland from the effects of capitalist incorporation. As the state department's labor attaché for the region put it in his review of the October uprising, Aramco officials were anxious "to postpone . . . westernization" in Hasa rather than promote it.[84] He pointed to the company's continued resistance to fulfilling its commitment to building housing and schools in the region and argued that the fear entailed more than rising production costs. Interviews with executives in New York, where he found them wringing their hands "over the fact that most of the original, known leaders in the strike had been trained in Beirut at company expense" seemingly reinforced these views.

Exceptionalist arguments notwithstanding, this attempt by the Americans to monitor and regulate the American–Saudi encounter on the Hasa frontier resembled colonial practices of the British in Nigeria and the French in Morocco. Unlike Lyautey in Rabat, however, there were no walled old towns and quarters where natives could be contained, and around which foreigners could build garden cities. Instead, American planners erected fencing around their modern compound in Dhahran and discouraged Hasawis from settling permanently in the vicinity. If the firm later altered their labor policies, the short-term response to the October 1953 uprising gave no hint of the developmentalist current of the late 1950s and early 1960s.[85] Rather, the response on the part of American and Saudi officials alike in the wake of the strike was to focus on improving the surveillance capacity in place in Hasa. One landmark not usually commemorated in accounts of the transition from frontier to state is the creation in 1954 of an official intelligence unit in the Saudi military's headquarters in Dammam.[86]

Notes

Author's Note: I researched and wrote this chapter during a remarkable fellowship year in 1995–96 at the Shelby Cullom Davis Center. I am grateful to Bill Jordan, who directed the Davis seminar, Kari Hoover, who runs the center, to their colleagues in Princeton's history department, and to other seminar members. I learned much from scholars there and at Stanford, Berkeley, Brown,

Harvard, SUNY New Paltz and U. Mass Amherst where I presented some of the arguments. For their help along the way, I would like to thank Steve Aron, `Abd al-Muhsin Akkas, Joel Beinin, Eleanor Doumato, Ellis Goldberg, Larry Michalak, Karen Merrill, Anne Norton, Roger Owen, Marsha Posusney, Paul Sabin, Eileen Scully, John Vanderlippe, and Mary Wilson. Two others deserve special mention: Debi Harrold, from whom I stole the idea of "empire-lite," and Geoff Hartman, who housed me when I was in Washington.

1. "Report on the Visit of King `Abdul `Aziz ibn Sa`ud to the Arabian American Oil Company, January 1947," Box 6, Folder 6, William E. Mulligan Papers, Georgetown University Library, Special Collections Division, Washington, DC [hereafter Mulligan Papers].

2. Jidda to State, Desp. 150, February 13, 1947, General Records of the Department of State, Record Group 59, 1945–49, 890F.001/Abdul Aziz/ 2-1347, National Archives, Washington, DC [hereafter cited as RG 59, with filing information].

3. The original concession was signed by representatives of Standard Oil of California (Socal or, more recently, Chevron). Socal formed a partnership with the Texas Oil Company (Texaco) to explore for and market oil from its concession there and in Bahrain, an island off the east coast. The Saudi subsidiary was first known as the California Arabian Standard Oil Company and later Aramco. In 1947, Standard Oil of New York (Socony-Vacuum or, later, Mobil) and Standard Oil of New Jersey (Esso/Exxon) obtained a long-sought share in the Saudi concession. Both sets of original owners have recently merged. They are now ChevronTexaco and MobilExxon.

4. The "dependency upon ARAMCO places the Consul and his staff in a position of subordination to the officials of the Oil Company which has adversely affected their relations with the concern. This situation is not lost upon the officials of the Government of Saudi Arabia, who now think of the Consulate as a dependency of the Oil Company." See Memo from Thorp to Henderson, June 3, 1947, RG 59, 890F.24/6-347.

5. William Cronon, George Miles, and Jay Gitlin, "Becoming West: Toward a New Meaning for Western History," in Cronon, Miles, and Gitlin, eds., *Under an Open Sky: Rethinking America's Western Past* (New York: Norton, 1992).

6. Michael Adas, *"High" Imperialism and the "New" History* (Washington, DC: American Historical Association, 1994).

7. See Robert H. Jackson, *Quasi-States: Sovereignty, International Relations, and the Third World* (Cambridge: Cambridge University Press, 1990).

8. Christopher Simpson, *The Splendid Blond Beast: Money, Law, and Genocide in the Twentieth Century* (New York: Grove Press, 1993), 18; Paul Gordon Lauren, *Power and Prejudice: The Politics and Diplomacy of Racial Discrimination*, second edition (Boulder: Westview, 1996); Penny M. Von Eschen, *Race Against Empire: Black Americans and Anticolonialism 1937–1957* (Ithaca: Cornell University Press, 1997).

9. Tony Smith, *America's Mission: The United States and the Worldwide Struggle for Democracy in the Twentieth Century* (Princeton: Princeton University Press, 1994).

10. Begin with Michael O. West, "The Tuskegee Model of Development in Africa: Another Dimension of the African/African–American Connection," *Diplomatic History* 16 (1992): 371–88.

11. Frantz Fanon, *The Wretched of the Earth* (New York: Grove Press, 1963 [1961]), 38–9.

12. Program booklet, 7 (for which I am grateful to Tom Levin), emphasis is mine.

13. A "vital question that has attracted the Company's interest with regard to the oasis, refers to the composition of the population of Hasa in terms of groups with different cultures. Aside from the more obvious components of religious denomination and residence patterns, how many and how large are the cultural differences between Sunnite farmers, Shiite farmers and craftsmen, and Sunnite Bedouins? Do these differences concern only the more superficial aspects of material culture . . . or do they reach into the deeper-lying, more covert elements of social structure and value systems? Are there any significant physical differences between the three groups? . . . We may not therefore at the present moment have reliable information on the Hasawis' readiness or reluctance to accept employment with the Company . . . Neither do we know the extent, cirucmstances and effects of the changes now being brought about in both the sedentary and Bedouin groups by industrialization." Frederico S. Vidal, *The Oasis of Al-Hasa*, Local Government Relations, Arabian Research Division, Aramco (New York: Aramco, 1955), preface, n.p.

14. George Lenczowski, *Oil and State in the Middle East* (Ithaca: Cornell University Press, 1960); Wallace Stegner, *Discovery! The Search for Arabian Oil* (Beirut: Middle East Export Press, 1971); Irvine Anderson, *Aramco the United States and Saudi Arabia: A Study of the Dynamics of Foreign Oil Policy 1933–1950* (Princeton: Princeton University Press, 1981), 123, 199–200.

15. J.H. Bamberg, *The History of the British Petroleum Company*, vol. 2, *The Anglo-Iranian Years, 1928–1954* (Cambridge: Cambridge University Press, 1994), 63–105; Henrietta Larson, Evelyn Knowlton, and Charles Popple, *New Horizons, 1927–1950: History of the Standard Oil Company (New Jersey)*, vol. 3 (New York: Harper and Row, 1971), 116, 139–43, 345; Rómulo Betancourt, *Venezuela: Oil and Politics* (Boston: Houghton Mifflin, 1978), 52–9.

16. George Rentz, Memorandum draft dated February 1, 1951, "Why a Research Divison?," Box 2, Folder 16, ART, AAD, etc., 1951, Mulligan Papers.

17. Laton McCartney, *Friends in High Places: The Bechtel Story: The Most Secret Corporation and How it Engineered the World* (New York: Simon and Schuster, 1988), 86; Douglas Little, "Pipeline Politics: American, Tapline, and the Arabs," *Business History Review* 64 (1990): 255–85.

18. Gary Anderson, "Differential Urban Growth in the Eastern Province of Saudi Arabia: A Study of the Historical Interaction of Economic Development and Socio-Political Change," Ph.D. diss., Johns Hopkins University, 1985, 41–67.

19. For Hasa's merchants and merchant networks, see Mishary Abdalrahman al-Nuaim, "State Building in a Non-Capitalist Social Formation: The Dialectics of Two Modes of Production and the Role of the Merchant Class, Saudi Arabia, 1902–1932," Ph.D. diss., UCLA, 1987, 96–102, 113–52. The now indispensible account of the Peninsula's political economies more generally is

Khaldoun Hasan al-Naqeeb, *Society and State in the Gulf and Arab Peninsula: A Different Perspective* (London: Routledge, 1990) [translation of *Mujtama` wa al-dawlah fi al-khalij wa al-jazirah al-`Arabiyya*, trans. L. Kenny, emended by Ibrahim Hayani].

20. al-Naqeeb, *Society and State in the Gulf and Arab Peninsula*, 58–64.

21. R. Bayly Winder, *Saudi Arabia in the Nineteenth Century* (New York: St. Martins Press, 1965), 206–7, who in classic Princeton fashion of the time, naturalized Al Saud/Najdi/Wahhabi "expansion" against Turkish "invasion" ("ever grasping at useless and embarrassing possessions, ever willing to annex fresh hostile subjects and barren sands."); Muhammad `Arabi Nakhlah, *Tarikh al-ihsa` al-siyasiya* [*The Political History of Hasa*] 1818–1913 (Fat al-Salusil, n.d.), 145–81.

22. See Vidal, 4–9, "it is a fact that the Bedouins of al-Ruayyiqah and al-Hazm do not consider themselves, nor are they considered by the other inhabitants of the oasis, to be proper Hasawis. It is another fact that Bedouins from these two localities have learned through experience that answering 'al-Ruayyiqah' or 'al-Hazm' to questions on their locale of residence left most Americans in the dark, and have consequently taken to declaring themselves as coming from 'Hofuf.' As a result, not only have people with widely differing backgrounds and origins been lumped together in the same classificatory group of 'from Hofuf,' but terms have been adopted in regular usage such as 'Hofuf caves,' 'Hofuf gardens,' 'Hofuf springs'—all of them misnomers" (preface, n.p.).

23. Vidal, *The Oasis of Al-Hasa*, 149–52; Winder, *Saudi Arabia in the Nineteenth Century*, 211–16; al-Nuaim, *State Building in a Non-Capitalist Social Formation*, 97–100.

24. Vidal, *The Oasis of Al-Hasa*, 192 argues that cash wages in the nascent oil sector led to the adoption of wages in oasis production, where payment in kind had been common.

25. See Ian Seccombe and Richard Lawless, *Work Camps and Company Towns: Settlement Patterns and the Gulf Oil Industry* (Durham: University of Durham, 1987), 37–9. They caution that an unknown number of workers from Bahrain and other nearby territories were present on the company rolls but identified as Saudis with the aid of identity documents easily purchased from the police in Hasa (19).

26. See Jidda to State, 730, December 31, 1947, RG 59, 890F.51/12-3147; and Jidda to State, 266, December 31, 1949, RG 59, 890F.51/12-3149.

27. "In the 1930s Alkhobar had been just a dozen *barasti* [thatched frond huts] and a coral stone mosque. By 1951 a banker described it as: 'A mud village by the sea—one dusty street of little shops, mostly food stores, with several exchange dealers and a few consumer goods shops.' The Aramco employees began using Alkhobar for buying foreign currencies and air tickets before they left the Kingdom . . . . The first banks in the eastern Province were set up in Alkhobar and the more modern-minded merchants established themselves there. While Dammam developed as a Saudi town, Alkhobar became a center for the expatriate community and foreign businessmen." Michael Field, *The Merchants: The Big Business Families of Saudi Arabia and the Gulf States* (Woodstock: Overlook Press, 1985), 212.

28. See Memorandum of Conversation on Arabian–American Oil Company Plans, June 6, 1947, William Moore (Aramco president), James Terry Duce (Aramco vice president), Loy Henderson, and Richard Sanger, Near Eastern Affairs, Department of State, RG 59, 890F.6363/6-647.

29. See Jidda to State, A-498, December 29, 1949, RG 59, 890F.6363/12-2349.

30. On the Gosaibis, see Field, *Merchants*, 217–46.

31. Jidda to State, 64, August 20, 1952, Survey Trip of Embassy Officer to Riyadh and Eastern Arabia, RG 59, 886A.00/8-2052; Field, *Merchants*, 311–21. Aramco's public relations department specialized in the rags-to-riches boiler-plate, e.g., "Oil Helps People to Help Themselves," *The Standard Oiler*, February 1959, that is now disseminated directly by the Olayan group. See Folder 41, Olayan, Suleiman S Correspondence, and Folder 42, Olayan, Suleiman S Bio Materials and Photos, Box 1, Mulligan Papers.

32. Dhahran to State, 125, August 20, 1949, RG59, 890F.00/8-2049.

33. See the stock speech of Eddy, an Aramco consultant and the CIA's first agent inside the company, "Impact of an American Industry," August 13, 1952, Box 15, Folder 19, William Alfred Eddy Papers, 1859–1978, Mudd Library, Princeton University, Princeton, NJ.

34. "Where Yankees Misbehave," *Freedom*, March 25, 1949, enclosed in Karachi to State, 99, March 31, 1949, 890F.6363/3-1349.

35. See Memo, Rentz to Barger, Dhahran, January 12, 1948, Folder 13, ART, AAD, etc., 1947–48, Box 3, Mulligan Papers.

36. In considering British oil enterprise in Abadan and Qatar, Seccombe and Lawless, *Work Camps*, draw on Janet Abu-Lughod, *Rabat: Urban Apartheid in Morocco* (Princeton: Princeton University Press, 1980).

37. See the account by a former employee of the public relations department, Michael Sheldon Cheney, *Big Oil Man from Arabia: From Cambel Back to Cadillac—Or the Amazing Adventures of Aramco, the American Overseas Oil Company that is Transforming Saudi Arabia* (New York: Ballantine, 1958), 218–19.

38. See Jon Parssinen and Kaizir Talib, "A Traditional Community and Modernization: Saudi Camp, Dhahran," *Journal of Architectural Education* 35 (1982): 14–17. The hara was destroyed in the 1970s by the University.

39. See Ian J. Seccombe, "A Disgrace to American Enterprise: Italian Labour and the Arabian American Oil Company in Saudi Arabia 1944–56," *Immigrants and Minorities* 5 (1986): 233–57, 248.

40. J.B. McComb (Supervisor, Employee Relations Deptartment, Aramco) to State, August 10, 1945, RG 59, 890F.504/8-1045; Memorandum of Conversation, "Treatment of Indian and Pakistani Workers by the Arabian–American Oil Company in Saudi Arabia," various participants, April 14, 1949, RG 59, 890F.6363/4-1449; Seccombe, "Disgrace to American Enterprise," 242.

41. Seccombe, "Disgrace to American Enterprise," 253.

42. See, e.g., Cheney, *Big Oil Man*; David Holden, *Farewell to Arabia* (London: Faber, 1966).

43. On the Arabian–American "Partnership," see Roy Lebkicker, *The Work and Life of Aramco Employees*, American Employees Handbook Series, Part II (Aramco, 1950), 1–6.

44. See "Cake Parties, Pin Presentations, and Cape Cana-Vidal, "ms., Folder 64, Vidal, Federico S., Rick-Miscellaneous, Box 1, Mulligan Papers.

45. Notes by Mulligan, Folder 57, "Rentz, George S – Notes Re," Box 1, Mulligan Papers.

46. "Mr Lutz, however, could not seem to understand that, isolated as we are in Arabia, it was important in the interests of community spirit and harmony that we all work together . . . it is regrettable that Bill did not fit into the organization because he liked the Saudi Arab employees, acclimated himself nicely to the country and was progressing well with his study of the Arabic language." See Garry Owen to W.E. Palmer, Memorandum, copy [and apparently redacted], Dhahran May 13, 1947, Enclosure No. 2 to Jidda to State, desp. 257, "Transmitting Memoranda Concerning Activities of W.E. Abdur Rahman Lutz, Secretary of the Council, American Muslim Congress," May 21, 1947, RG 59, 890F.404/5-2147.

47. Biographical ms. by Mulligan, Folder 6, ARAMCO-Miscellaneous Biographies, Box 2, Mulligan Papers. The account in this paragraph also draws on various newspaper clippings enclosed with the Beling ms.

48. Mulligan makes it appear as if Beling's Jaguar and "his attractive blond wife Betty Mae" were equivalent status symbols. But he also testifies to Beling's fondness for "boasting to his associates of the feminine conquests he had made on his not infrequent business trips outside the kingdom," ibid. This is not to suggest that all heterosexuals were treated equally. See the account of the female secretary in the relations department who was terminated within 24 hours and flown out of the country after her gynecological exam ("for an unmentionable physical problem") came back positive. Letter from Hoel to Mandis, Idaho Fall, March 19, 1956, Folder 8 Aramco—Miscellaneous Biographies, Box 2, Mulligan Papers.

49. McCartney, *Friends in High Places*, 87. Technically, the description is of a Bechtel employee, but the author goes on to point out that in their closely linked operations with Aramco they screened in the same ways, e.g. against Jews.

50. William Mulligan, Memo to File, April 9, 1968, J.P. Horgen-Counseling Session, Folder 8, Aramco—Miscellaneous Biographies, Box 2, Mulligan Papers.

51. Quotations from memorandum by Hart, July 24, 1945, RG 59, 890F.4016/7-2445; original report of incident found in Jack Winocur, President American Communications Association, CIO, to State, May 8, 1945, RG 59, 890F.4016/5-845.

52. Dhahran to State, 108, July 25, 1949, RG59, 890F.00/7-2549.

53. Dhahran to State, 100, July 9, 1949, RG 59, 890F.00/7-949.

54. See report by Mandis, September 24, 1950, "N.Z. Howe Incident/American Beaten by Government Station Leader at Turaif—18 September 1950," enclosure to Duce (Aramco) to Awalt (State Department), October 17, 1950, RG 59, 886A.2553/10-1750.

55. Cheney, *Big Oil Man*, 39–40.

56. The jail in Ras Tanura where an Aramco employee was housed after severely beating a Pakistani coworker was a 15 × 15 × 15 room with running water, a toilet, and electric lights. Rooms in Saudi camp had none of these amenities until the 1950s. See Dhahran to State, 280, September 23, 1949, RG 59, 890F.6363/9-2349; Seccombe, "Disgrace to American Enterprise."

57. Mary Norton, "His Fair Lady," *Aramco World Magazine*, September–October 1969. Kathleen Barger was the wife of Tom Barger, and the article is part of an issue commemorating the latter's retirement as chief executive officer and chairman of the board of Aramco after 30 years' residence in the Kingdom. During the 1940s and 1950s he was a top official in the Government Relations Department. See Folder 5, Barger, Thomas C. Biographical Info and Obits, Box 1, Mulligan Papers.

58. From the ms. titled "Speech by John W. Pendleton for the Dhahran Women's Group," Folder 56, ARD, Chronological Files, April–June 1957, Box 2, Mulligan Papers (emphasis mine).

59. See confidential document titled "Local Government Relations Department Program, Endorsed by Management Committee," p. 10, Folder 19, Barger 1955 Paper, Box 4, Mulligan Papers.

60. Ms. by Mulligan, Folder 39, Ohliger, Floyd W., Box 1, Mulligan Papers.

61. See memo by G. Owen to W. Spurlock, Dhahran, October 27, 1945, SZ-251, Aramco, San Francisco, subject: George Rentz, Folder 52, Rentz, George S.— Correspondence Re, 1945–52; and ms. by Mulligan, Folder 53, Rentz, George S.—Correspondence Re, 1963–87, Box 1 Mulligan Papers.

62. Rentz's memos at the time and Mulligan's retrospective accounts of the department's operations nonetheless attest that none of the Saudis (notably Olayan and Ahmad al-Qusaybi) were competent to do the work ("not a one of them could conceivably have passed the tests the company now administers for its lowest ranking translator jobs" and "only one . . . could be said to speak and write good Arabic"). Rentz's new hires were all from Palestine, Egypt, Iraq, etc. See ms. by Mulligan, Folder 57 Rentz, George S.—Notes Re, Box 1; and Memo by Rentz, Dhahran, February 8, 1947, Arabic Research and Translation Section, Folder 13, ART, AAD, etc., 1947–48, Box 2, Mulligan Papers. It should also be noted that Rentz warned the company that when hired he probably did not have the skills to do official English into Arabic translation work. See Memo, Hamilton Osborne, Cairo to Aramco, Bahrein Island, Letter # 270, George Rentz, November 27, 1945, Box 1, Mulligan Papers.

63. See Mulligan's handwritten notes: "heavy drinking, affection for the girls (pinch/pat) . . . loved . . . drinking-partying." Folder 57 Rentz, George S.—Notes Re, Box 1, Mulligan Papers.

64. For examples of the company's politically inspired research see memo by C. Matthews, Dhahran, September 9, 1956, Present Service to the company—With Plans for Future Work, Folder 36, Matthews, Charles D. Biographical Materials, Box 1; and ms. by Mulligan, Robert Leigh Headley Jr., Folder 8 Aramco—Miscellaneous Biographies, Box 2, Mulligan Papers.

65. See e.g. Jidda to State, 65 and 2 enclosures, February 20, 1950, Transmittal of a Copy of an Aramco Study of Eastern Hasa and the Trucial Coast, RG 59, 786A.022/2-2050.

66. On Duce, see Anderson, *Aramco*, 71–2, 110. My argument on the company's linkages to the war and postwar intelligence community are based on work in the Eddy and Mulligan Papers.

67. See memo draft dated 2-1-51 titled "Why a Research Divison," Folder 16 ART, AAD etc., 1951, Box 2, Mulligan Papers.

68. See Garry Owen to Terry Duce, Dhahran, Saudi Arabia, November 28, 1945, SZ-366, "Identification System" RG 59, 890F.6363/12-2945.

69. See Dhahran to State, desp. 22, August 30, 1951, Labor: Revised Service Allowance Plan for Senior Staff Employees of Arabian American Oil Company, RG 59, 886A.06/8-3051.

70. Dhahran to State, 61, November 4, 1953, RG 59, 886A.062/11-453.

71. The others were Saliy al-Zayd, `Abdallah `Ali al-Ganim, Ibrahim al-Faraj, `Abd al-Rahman al-Bahijan, Umar Wazna, and `Abd al-`Aziz al-Sufayyan. See Dhahran to State, 52, October 13, 1953, RG 59, 886A.06/10-1353.

72. Dhahran to State, 61, November 4, 1953, RG 59, 886A.062/11-453.

73. See Department of State Instruction, No CA—3384, December 29, 1953, "Comment on the October–November 1953 Strike at the Arabian American Oil Company Installations in Saudi Arabia," p. 6, RG 59, 886A.062/12-2953.

74. Dhahran to State, 52, October 13, 1953, RG 59, 886A.06/10-1353.

75. Dhahran to State, 61, November 4, 1953, RG 59, 886A.062/11-453.

76. Ibid.

77. Dhahran to State, 61, November 4, 1953, Labor Disturbances in Eastern Saudi Arabia, p 10, RG 59, 886A.062/11-453.

78. Department of State Instruction, No CA—3384, December 29, 1953, "Comment on the October–November 1953 Strike at the Arabian American Oil Company Installations in Saudi Arabia," section titled " The legal Roots of the Strike Itself," 10, RG 59, 886A.062/12-2953.

79. Jidda to State, 186, March 11, 1947, RG 59, 711.90F/3-1147.

80. Mulligan notes, "this was not the ghastly dud it proved when Hurley used it in Chiang Kai-shek's china, since in Dammam an Arab force from Riyadh responded with a war cry of that region." Untitled ms., Folder 39, Ohliger, Floyd, W., Box 1, Mulligan Papers.

81. William Eddy, "Impact of an American Industry," text and notes for a speech given August 13, 1952, Folder 19, Box 15, Eddy Papers.

82. For the discussion of comparative labor policies see Tehran to State, 138, August 1, 1951, Labor Attache's Comments on Dhahran, Saudi Arabia, RG 59, 886A.2553/8-151.

83. "Confidential, Local Government Relations Department Program, Endorsed by Management Committee," 5, Folder 19, Barger 1955 Paper, Box 4, Mulligan Papers, emphasis mine.

84. Department of State Instruction, No CA—3384, December 29, 1953, "Comment on the October–November 1953 Strike at the Arabian American

Oil Company Installations in Saudi Arabia," 18, RG 59, 886A.062/12-2953.

85. Helen Lackner, *A House Built on Sand: A Political Economy of Saudi Arabia* (London: Ithaca Press, 1978), 98, describes a shift in the firm's orientation toward labor later in the decade.

86. See Dhahran to State, 185, May 23, 1954, RG 59, 886A.062/5-2354.

Chapter 7

The Capture of Riyadh Revisited: Shaping Historical Imagination in Saudi Arabia

Madawi Al-Rasheed

During the centennial celebrations, all talk was about the 'liberation' of Riyadh by Ibn Saud. One was led to imagine that the British or the French had been there.

—Western Scholar: *oral communication*

The Saudi state of 1932 is one of the new states of the Arab world born after the collapse of the Ottoman Empire following World War I. It dedicates large financial resources to historical research, publications, and dissemination of information about the past in an attempt to define its uniqueness as a national and political entity.[1] The state publishes history textbooks, encyclopedias, local chronicles, and archival material inside the country but mainly abroad. These are constantly reproduced, printed, and distributed. So far one of the main preoccupations of this vast literature is defining the key historical event that led to the birth of Saudi Arabia in the twentieth century. State sponsored historiography remains predominantly a history of the origins of the state, the role of important historical agents, and the material modernization of the country following the discovery of oil. This is an ideological history concerned with political legitimacy[2] rather than analytical interpretations of the past. Unfortunately, with few exceptions, the majority of contemporary Saudi historians work in state institutions and academic research centers that militate against critical evaluation of the past. Most historical research is sponsored by the state. Since the

1970s oil wealth has allowed the state to increasingly dominate constructions and interpretations of the past.

The state's concern with its ideological history is neither unique nor
exceptional. Saudi Arabia shares its desire to manipulate, glorify, and invent
its past with other states not only in the Arab world but also elsewhere.
National mythologies, state rituals, pomp, and state narratives are powerful
political instruments, the analysis of which escapes the attention of
scholars, with few exceptions.[3]

Since the oil boom of the 1970s, wealth has allowed the Saudi state to
invest heavily in the production of national mythologies, that is, the totality of those narratives and rituals that glorify the story of the unification of
the country under Saudi rule. A fixation with the origin of the state,
together with a glorification of a single historical event, namely the capture
of the capital Riyadh by `Abd al-`Aziz Ibn `Abd al-Rahman Al Sa`ud
(known as Ibn Saud) in 1902 dominate the national narrative. The capture
of Riyadh is the key historical event. It is projected as marking two
contrasted historical periods: one before the establishment of the Al Sa`ud
leadership in Riyadh, a period commonly understood in Saudi history
textbooks as a second Arabian *jahiliyya* (age of ignorance), and one after
the Al Sa`ud assumed leadership of the country, referred to as *nahda*
(renaissance or awakening).

The story of the capture of Riyadh by Ibn Saud is mythologized in Saudi
history textbooks. An eminent Saudi historian describes the event:

> Ibn Saud and his men arrived at night at the gates of Riyadh. They secretly
> entered the house of the Riyadh governor, Ajlan, who ruled on behalf of the
> Rashidi emirate of Hail. They immediately found the governor's wife, who
> informed the raiding party that the governor was in Qasr al-Masmak with
> his garrison. Ibn Saud and his men waited until the morning in the
> governor's private quarters. When the governor emerged after the dawn
> prayers, he was attacked by Ibn Saud's men. The governor was killed. News
> of this heroic act spread across Riyadh. The inhabitants rushed to greet their
> legitimate Saudi ruler and swear allegiance to him. This is how Ibn Saud was
> successful in the battle of Riyadh, his first attempt to unify the country.[4]

According to this narrative, the capture of Riyadh does not correspond
to a "battle" as understood and described in early twentieth-century
Arabia. In fact, the story unfolds events marked by surprise attack (the raiding party arrives at night), the manipulation of female fears (in some oral
accounts, Ajlan's wife was tied with a rope throughout the night), female
jealousies (in the context of a polygamous society (in oral narratives Ajlan's
wife provided information that her husband was spending the night with

his other wife) and treacherous killing (Ajlan was killed in a surprise attack as he emerged from morning prayers). Both in written and oral narratives, the so-called battle of Riyadh has its own poetics. Far from an historical event that can be described as a battle, the capture of Riyadh is, nevertheless, elevated to the status of a key historical event that marks the origins of the Saudi state of the twentieth century. It is also the event that anchors the process of state and nation building, unification, and more importantly the reestablishment of Al Sa'ud rule in the Arabian Peninsula in "concrete historical facts." We shall see how this event became the central narrative in the 1999 centennial celebrations.

Since 1902 the story of the capture of Riyadh is dominant as a narrative in the Al Sa'ud oral tradition. The founder of the Kingdom, Ibn Saud, regularly told the story in his famous *majlis* (council). His audience consisted of tribal sheikhs, Arab functionaries, foreign guests, and writers who later popularized the story in print. In scholarly and journalistic accounts of the reestablishment of Al-Sa'ud rule in Arabia, the core of the story of Riyadh is repeated with minor variations in details. Archival sources, mainly British, reiterate the oral narrative and offer no serious possibility for alternative interpretations. Local Saudi chronicles also repeat the story as it was "told by Ibn Saud" and his companions. In some of the early historical accounts, Ibn Saud was supported by 40 companions. In later publications, a figure of 60 men was given. The latest official count indicates that 63 men accompanied Ibn Saud from Kuwait to Riyadh. Their names are now documented in a book entitled, *al-ruwwad* (The Pioneers) and published by the King 'Abd al-'Aziz Foundation. In 1999 the descendants of the 63 men received medals in recognition of their pioneering effort in the "unification of Arabia."

In addition to dominating Saudi history school textbooks and political rhetoric,[5] the story of the capture of Riyadh occupies central space in monographs as different as that of Amin Rihani,[6] Khayr al-Din al-Zirkili,[7] Fuad Hamza,[8] Hafiz Wahba,[9] Abdullah al-Uthaymin,[10] St. John Philby,[11] Robert Lacey,[12] Leslie McLoughlin,[13] and David Long.[14]

Given the predominance of the story in oral and written sources, it is surprising that the capture of Riyadh was never celebrated as an event at the national level. In 1950 Ibn Saud intended to launch the Jubilee celebrations of this event, but festivities were cancelled one week before they were due to commence. The Deputy Minister of Foreign Affairs at the time explained to invited foreign diplomats that cancellation was due to objections from the king's religious advisors who declared that in Islam only '*id al-fitr*, marking the end of *Ramadan* and '*id al-adha*, marking the *hajj* season were occasions for festivities. Rumor had it that the king was greatly bereaved over the death of his sister and did not wish to indulge in festivities.[15] The circumstances were different 50 years later when the state launched the centennial celebrations of the capture of Riyadh in January 1999.

Although the Kingdom of Saudi Arabia was declared in September 1932, the government surprised its citizens and outside observers when it celebrated its hundredth anniversary on January 22, 1999 when the Kingdom was only 67 years old. The confusion stemmed from the fact that the capture of Riyadh by Ibn Saud (in the Muslim calendar this took place on 5 Shawal A.H. 1319) was chosen to mark the beginning of the process of unification that culminated in the declaration of the Kingdom in 1932. In January 1999 the capture of Riyadh was 100 years old. The event became the legend around which the government mobilized its resources to shape the historical imagination not only of its own citizens but also of invited foreign guests and a large international audience, thanks to publicity made possible as a result of revolutionary communication technology including print media, electronic communication, and satellite television.

While pressures from religious scholars resulted in the cancellation of the jubilee celebrations in 1950, similar objections did not result in the cancellation of the centennial celebrations of 1999. Just before the 1999 festivities began, it was reported that Sheikh `Abd al-`Aziz ibn Baz, the highest religious authority in Saudi Arabia issued a *fatwa* (religious decree) in which he declared that the festivities were *bida* (innovation), considered an imitation of nonbelievers. He considered such celebrations as alien to the "authentic" Islamic tradition. One week before the celebrations, copies of the sheikh's *fatwa* appeared in the capital and near mosques, distributed possibly by Islamist groups opposed to the celebrations. While the government proceeded with its plan to launch the celebrations, it was reported that senior government officials and prominent princes advised the Centennial Committee to play down public manifestations of the festivities. Days after Ibn Baz's *fatwa* was made public, colored lights and elaborate decorations vanished from shop windows in Riyadh.[16]

The spirit of the centennial celebrations was conveyed in a poem that appeared not only in local publications sponsored by the Ministry of Information but also in international newspapers, for example the *Financial Times*.[17] The poem was meant to embody the thoughts and emotions of Ibn Saud as he was preparing for his legendary capture of his "ancestor's" capital with his most loyal companions. The poem documents the slaughter of Ibn Rashid's governor, Ajlan, in Qasr al-Masmak, a mud brick fortress turned now into a national museum in the old quarter of Riyadh. The poem begins with Ibn Saud lamenting his exile in Kuwait following his father's failure to defend Riyadh against the marching troops of the Rashidis, a rival emirate established in the middle of the nineteenth century. This emirate emerged in northern central Arabia at a time when the Al Sa'ud's leadership was weakened by internal rivalries and power struggles.[18] The poem begins with these lines:

Banished was I from the heart of Arabia,
Riyadh, my home, had been stolen by others:
Banished was I, and my father and mother,
Brothers and sisters, deprived of our birthright.
Sadness we felt for the years that denied us
The feel of the sand of the Nejd in our hand.

After describing the kindness and hospitality encountered during exile in Kuwait, Ibn Saud is believed to have asked, "Who will ride at my side on this perilous venture?" The raiding party arrived at night in Riyadh and waited for the governor, Ajlan to appear after the early morning prayers:

The fate of the Amir of Riyadh was sealed.
He must die for Who will risk life and limb to expel Al Rashid?
Sixty answered my call, young and brave, one and all.
"With all our strength, we will give what you need:
we will stand by your side when the battle is joined
until each of us falls-or Riyadh is freed."
When Ajlan, the Amir, appeared in the open,
We struck as the lion descends on its prey.
Bin Jelawi forced open the gate of the fortress
The rest of our brothers then joined in the fray.
The garrison knew that resistance was futile;
Al Saud had returned to its home on that day.

The act of capturing Riyadh was completed and Ibn Saud reflects on the event:

Looking back through the decades, the taking of Riyadh
Was merely one step on a path, hard and long.
After many a battle, I put my heart into
building a nation, devout, proud and strong,
with justice its sword and faith as its shield,
in the land where the message of God was revealed.

With this focus on the capture of Riyadh, the centennial celebrations were obviously not meant to mobilize the country along broader national themes. The spectacle was marking 100 years of Al Sa'ud's dynastic rule. More specifically, the celebrations were a glorification of the era of Ibn Saud and a homage to the achievements of a single man rather than to the achievements of the "people" or the "nation," who are defined in general and vague Islamic terms as part of an Islamic *umma* (community). The "people" were projected as recipients of *ni'ma*, gift and were expected to renew their allegiance to its sources.

The state mobilized vast resources to mark the event. Its control over print, visual, and electronic media enabled unprecedented coverage of the celebrations, both in Saudi Arabia and abroad. Saudis followed the spectacle on their domestic screens while the rest of the world watched on satellite television. The Ministry of Information published hundreds of leaflets, booklets, and publicity literature documenting phases of the renaissance during the last 100 years. The slogan of the festivities was "hundred years of unification and construction." Special glossy photographic books documenting pictures taken of Ibn Saud during various phases of his life were distributed among Saudi and foreign guests. This was accompanied by the production of biographies of his life on CD-ROM and video. Saudi embassies distributed this vast literature abroad.

Saudi public and private institutions including financial companies, banks, hospitals, universities, and schools placed congratulatory statements to the royal family in Saudi newspapers. Saudi readers are familiar with these kinds of advertisements, which often appear during Muslim festivals. The centennial advertisements addressed King Fahd, Crown Prince Abdullah, and other senior members of the royal family with words of gratitude for 100 years of *amn* (peace) and *istiqrar* (stability). Advertisements included poetic and Quranic verses intercepted by portraits of Ibn Saud occupying the central part and surrounded by photographs of King Fahd, Crown Prince Abdullah, and Interior Minister, Prince Nayef. One advertisement included seven photographs of senior members of the royal family in addition to the central one of Ibn Saud, printed on the background of a map of the whole of the Arabian Peninsula.[19] Sometimes the background consisted of a photograph of Ibn Saud riding on a horse or camel. The centennial celebrations were an occasion for the renewal of allegiance to present members of the royal family, who could capitalize on the heritage and memory of the founding father.

Newspapers were also full of heroic poetry in Nabati (colloquial) and classical style. Saudi poets celebrated the life of Ibn Saud and his conquests. The above poem was one among several compositions. It was, however, unusual in the way it captured the spirit of the festivities; it was published not only in the Saudi press, but also in international newspapers with wide circulation and prestige. In historical literature and in poetry, the language invokes images of chivalry, piety, military skills, heroism, generosity, bravery, justice, scholarship, and other qualities attributed to the founder, *al-muassis*. The image of Ibn Saud as *asad al-jazira* (lion of the Peninsula) and *saqr al-jazira* (falcon of the Peninsula) establish him in historical memory as an extraordinary figure to be remembered for his legendary qualities. Other qualities emerge from the usage of labels such as *imam* and king, thus anchoring royal power in an Islamic framework.

A special theatrical performance, *malhamat al-tawhid*, "The Epic of Unification," written by Badr ibn `Abd al-Muhsin, a grandson of Ibn Saud, was performed on stage in Riyadh to mark the event. The epic's title draws on the double meaning of *tawhid*, both the unification of the country and the oneness of God. It tells the story of a man and a woman and their reflections on the political, social, and economic situation in Riyadh prior to its capture by Ibn Saud. The epic culminates with the dramatic capture of Riyadh, bringing a new era of *nahda* (renaissance) and prosperity for the country. Several popular Saudi singers took part in the event, together with over a thousand participants in minor roles. The performance was produced by a British producer and recorded on cassette, video, and CD-ROM.

The centennial celebrations sealed the development of an "ancestor cult" around Ibn Saud, which has so far been embedded in state-sponsored historiography. While in other Arab countries, states are preoccupied with consolidating personality cults around living presidents, for example Asad in Syria (d. 2000)[20] and Saddam Hussain in Iraq,[21] in Saudi Arabia, the cult venerates a dead ancestor. Ibn Saud has become a totem, a symbol around which national unity is expected to revolve. He is a symbolic figure invested with a whole range of meanings; his name invokes the beginning of historical time. The name is also associated with the present *nahda* and the transformation of the country.

The ancestor cult of Ibn Saud is consolidated by the restoration of his artefacts, each capturing an aspect of his eminence. Ibn Saud's first car, airplane, sword, Qur'an, royal seal, and other objects were restored. These were displayed for the public to see and appreciate his grandeur. Artefacts known to have belonged to Ibn Saud have become icons, representing his many attributes. His Qur'an represents his piety and commitment to Islam, his sword stands for his bravery and vitality, his car and aeroplane symbolize his technological innovations. In this iconography, the pious Ibn Saud is also a modernist. The man of the sword is also a scholar.

The Pictorial Book of King `Abd al-`Aziz published by the Saudi Ministry of Information[22] captures all these attributes in portraits of the king. Individual photographs of the "young warrior" are followed by those of the "wise statesman" seated on elaborate chairs in his palaces and surrounded by his advisors and retainers. A special collection of portraits of the king with his sons, brothers, and other members of the royal family conjure images of the benevolent father (al-majala December 1999, 12–18). One photograph of Ibn Saud participating in the famous tribal dance, *ardah*, in

Riyadh amidst his "sons and people" invokes images of ra'y (shepherd/leader) and ra'yya (herd/followers). Other photographs show him hosting lavish feasts for foreign guests. Early meetings with British officers and envoys are documented in pictures followed by portraits of the king with world leaders, including Roosevelt, Churchill, King Faruq of Egypt, and King Abdullah of Jordan. Images of Ibn Saud in various local and international contexts encourage a sense of his imminence as a world leader in public imagination. The "local" Ibn Saud is also a "global" figure that features prominently in the political scene of the 1940s.

Ibn Saud's words were remembered and documented in several volumes. One publication lists his sayings as they were documented by foreign observers, thus casting an aura of international recognition of his wisdom. Here is a sample of Ibn Saud's words as listed in one of the publications of the Ministry of Information: "I have conquered my Kingdom with my sword and by my own efforts; let my sons exert their own efforts after me" (Ministry of Information 1998: 68). "Go into battle sure of victory from God. Have no doubt of his sustenance and support" (ibid.).

And his final words on his deathbed:

> Faysal, Sa`ud is your brother.
> Sa`ud, Faysal is your brother.
> There is no power and no strength save in God. (Ibid.)

In a society where "sayings" are usually attributed to the Prophet Muhammad in the *Hadith* tradition, the documentation of Ibn Saud's words bestows on him a sense of sacredness, celebrated at the time of the centennial festivities. His advice to his sons before his death in 1953 is remembered for its underlying wisdom and insight; it is relevant to the 1990s when succession to the throne is subject to speculation given the deterioration of King Fahd's health. Ibn Saud's words reflect the apprehensions of an aging father/king, sensing early signs of competition and rivalry among his most senior sons, Sa`ud and Faysal. Ibn Saud's words became a self-fulfilling prophecy with the power struggle between Sa`ud and Faysal that unfolded after his death in 1953.[23] To invoke Ibn Saud's advice in 1999 reflects the same sense of apprehension among a royal family that is perhaps not so sure of its consensus over who should succeed King Fahd.

Had it not been for possible objections from religious scholars against the erection of human statues, it would have been conceivable to erect a monument in one of Riyadh's central squares as homage to the ancestor. Instead, Qasr al-Masmak, the site where the slaughter of the governor of Riyadh took place, has become the "historical site," the monument that has acquired a sacred significance. In a country where so far the only sacred shrine is the holy mosque around the Kaaba, Qasr al-Masmak, a site associated with the act of murder, is elevated to the status of sanctity. While most Saudis are familiar with the official story of the capture of Riyadh, now it is possible to visualize it. The door leading to the interior courtyard of the palace is marked with special reference in publicity literature: "This door has witnessed the fighting between the ruler of Riyadh Ajlan and the late King `Abd al-`Aziz when the main fight occurred at this gate. The spearhead of the lancer of King `Abd al-`Aziz can still be seen pierced in the door."[24]

Although in the historical narrative, Ajlan was killed by Ibn Saud's cousin, Ibn Juluwi, the founder's participation in the so-called battle of Riyadh is marked by the trace of his lancer's spearhead. The interpretation of the event centers on projecting the act of murder as a heroic act, against a background of fear and apprehension. While Ibn Saud remains invisible as a figure at the gate of Qasr al-Masmak, the attention of visitors to the site is drawn to the trace of his spearhead. The mystification of Ibn Saud's legacy continues. He emerges as a venerated totem. His immortality is ensured by constant references to his images, words, deeds, and historical sites.

Qasr al-Masmak was one site among several buildings that form the "Historical Centre of King Abd al-Aziz," a series of restored buildings in Riyadh inaugurated by King Fahd during the celebrations. The cost of the restoration was estimated at $166 million.[25] The center includes Ibn Saud's mosque, Muraba' Palace, al-dara, a public research and publishing foundation hosting among other things Ibn Saud's private book collection, and King Abd al-Aziz Conference Hall. The complex of buildings has become a national monument, a constant reminder that Ibn Saud's memory can be anchored in several shrines, each with its own sanctity.

In addition to paying homage to the central totemic figure, the centennial spectacle celebrated the life and achievements of his descendants. The ancestor cult of Ibn Saud includes other revered personalities. His descendants are recognized as important perpetuators of the founder's legacy. In printed material, photographs of previous Saudi kings accompanied that of the founding father, though smaller in size. Where images of previous kings were occasionally included, the main focus was on King Fahd and the present most senior members of the royal family. Although no images of female relatives of Ibn Saud appeared in the centennial literature, his sister Nura deserved an article, published in a Saudi newspaper with wide international circulation.[26] In a society where the feminine voice is silenced in the public sphere, it was surprising that the celebrations justified the inclusion of a biography of this earlier female companion of Ibn Saud. The article highlights her contribution as she was a "constant support and a source of inspiration for her brother during his various battles to unify the country."[27]

Foreign and Arab testimonies enhance the credibility of the narrative. Not only do contemporary Saudi poets and scholars venerate the totem, but also outside observers and commentators. The credibility of the ancestor cult is anchored in a wider international context. Citations from well-known foreign sources in praise of Ibn Saud are assembled and printed as slogans celebrating his achievement, wisdom, and political genius. Citations from the works of Philby, Rihani, Van der Meullen, Bell, and de Gaury among others permeate the historical narrative as testimony of his extraordinary life and effort.

Contemporary Arab and foreign scholars were drawn into the celebrations as participants in the "Conference of Saudi Arabia in 100 Years," organized as part of the celebrations. The opening statement of this unprecedented scholarly meeting described the event: "The conference will inform the whole world of the most successful experiment in progress and civilisation. The secret behind it is the attachment of this nation and its leadership and people to Islam. The foundation was laid by King `Abd al-`Aziz, may God rest him in peace, and it was maintained by his grateful sons up to the reign of the Servant of the Two Holy Mosques, King Fahd, may God protect him and bestow on him health."[28]

The conference had eight stated objectives, which fell within three broad themes. First: highlighting the importance of the Islamic foundation of the Kingdom, second: highlighting aspects of *nahda* during the reign of Ibn Saud and his sons, and third: highlighting the role of the Kingdom in the Gulf, Islamic, Arab, and international contexts.[29] These objectives are not new; they are a reiteration of the main focus of the official historical narratives. They are a restatement of the well-rehearsed rhetoric in official historiography.

Saudi and international academic circles were mobilized. Participants presented 200 papers in more than 60 panels over a period of three days. The scholarly spectacle was intercepted by visits to the national museum, poetry recital, lavish feasts, and the display of national heritage. The conference was organized along the lines of major international academic meetings, but the content was different. In the Saudi version of a centennial conference, a monolithic historical narrative was on display. This was an occasion for establishing a historical truth rather than an occasion for debate or reinterpretations. Both Saudi citizens and foreign guests were participants in the consolidation of the ancestor's cult. The official historical narrative is internalized and reproduced in a consistent manner. The state defines the parameters of speech, images, and symbols, which are in turn converted into the language of academic and scientific research. The process conveys an "objective" dimension on state propaganda. Official rhetoric is then endowed with a symbolic power of its own.

The ancestor cult of Ibn Saud is dominant in Saudi Arabia. It is founded on the belief in an epical ancestor whose name is generalized to the whole population. The state shares with its people a preoccupation with genealogy. Without a genealogy, the state is outside the comprehension of its citizens, who in spite of decades of *nahda* and official rhetoric in favor of a universal Muslim *umma*, still cherish descent. The official narrative is contradictory in the way it condemns people's identifications with genealogies (e.g. when belonging to a Muslim *umma* is celebrated in state controlled education literature) while it fixes its own as a historical truth in social memory. The state demands from its citizens a kind of historical amnesia vis à vis their own genealogies, while subjecting them to a celebration of its own line of descent, a journey that always begins with that of Ibn Saud, the founder.

The centennial celebrations can be read as a text whose main objective was to delineate the genealogy of the state at a time when this seemed to be doubtful and could even be subjected to competing interpretations. As the majority of Saudis have access to sources of information beyond state control, it is now imperative for the state to formulate its own narrative about its origins and invite Saudis themselves to participate in its construction. Their participation as poets, scholars, academics, and artists is a testimony that the official text is successfully internalized by some but not all Saudis to the extent that it can be reproduced without variation or betrayal. The internalization of the rhetoric of the state by some Saudi citizens after decades of being subjected to it indicates that in a society where language is always power, a set of contentious vocabulary and utterances has become hegemonic.

The ancestor cult of Ibn Saud is central to national unity. It is a symbol that mobilizes a country divided by regional differences (Hasa, Najd, Hijaz, and Asir), and differences within each region (in Najd one can point to differences between Jabal Shammar, Qasim, and Wadi Hanifa). Other divisions emerge from strong local cultural traditions, tribal allegiances, and unequal economic and social development. The ancestor cult plays a role similar to that played by the rhetoric of Islam. Ibn Saud's cult is meant to mask localized identities and alternative sources of loyalty and belonging. Official narratives capitalize on the transformation of society under the auspices of Ibn Saud. The narratives invite people to abandon their own ancestors in favor of an omnipotent symbolic ancestor, projected as the "ancestor" of the nation. Although a latecomer to the game of manipulating the historical imagination, Saudi Arabia has now joined the race to manipulate the historical imagination of its own people. Ibn Saud joins other totemic figures in the region, for example Kemal Ataturk, Gamal Abd al-Nasir, Ayatollah Khomeini, Hafiz Asad, and Saddam Hussain.

Veneration in Saudi Arabia is destined to be more ostentatious given the country's resources.

At a different level, the centennial celebrations are a rite of passage for Saudis. The rite not only marks 100 years of their modern history, but also initiates them into the ancestor cult. The rite unfolds the story of a mystified past, the pre–Ibn Saud era where chaos, violence, and political instability reigned among a "fragmented" and "backward" population. Separation from that dark past followed the capture of Riyadh in 1902. Between 1902 and 1932, a period of liminality and apprehension is juxtaposed on Ibn Saud's various battles of unification. According to Saudi historiography, over 52 battles were fought by Ibn Saud between 1902 and 1932. This rite of passage is a journey from "darkness," "poverty," "moral, social and political decay" to "affluence," "prosperity," "peace," and "civilization." In this rite Saudis are turned into "novices" under the authority of ritual elders, in this case their own historians, scholars, and intellectuals who control a sacred knowledge about the past. The contrasted images of the past and present are documented in words, pictures, and sounds. Crucial for this rite of passage is the role of the ancestor, who was prematurely venerated and revered in 1999 even before his realm reached its hundredth anniversary. In a society that is not known for elaborate public rituals and festivities, the centennial spectacle was outstanding. Given Wahhabi condemnation of saint worship and ancestor cults common in other parts of the Arab and Islamic world, the staging of the spectacle represented the triumph of the Saudi royal family over its *ulama* and their doctrines. The celebrations confirmed the state as master of the symbolic world and historical interpretation.

The capture of Riyadh dominates official narratives as the historical event that marked the unification of four regions (Najd, Hasa, Hijaz, and Asir) into what became the Kingdom of Saudi Arabia. Riyadh was important because its capture led to the establishment of Saudi rule in an area defined by the ruling group as "belonging to their ancestors." It is worth noting that after Riyadh Ibn Saud occupied Hasa in 1913, thus leading to the termination of Ottoman rule in this vital region. Later in 1921, Ibn Saud succeeded in undermining the leadership of a rival local power in northern Najd, the Rashidi emirate. In 1922 Asir fell within the Saudi sphere of influence. In 1925 the old Hashemite leadership in the Hijaz collapsed under Saudi pressure. None of these major historical events that were associated with famous battles well documented in archives and oral popular narratives feature as key historical events in the centennial narrative. The conquest of Hasa and Hijaz are far more important as historical events than the capture of a small provincial town such as Riyadh in 1902. Hasa allowed the Saudis access to the Gulf with its trade, diplomatic, and international networks whereas Hijaz was the province of Islam's holiest shrines, the center of a global trade and pilgrimage, the main source of revenue for Saudi Arabia in the pre-oil era. A possible interpretation of the invisibility of the conquest of Hijaz and Hasa (and other regions) in the centennial narratives is perhaps the reluctance to reactivate dormant sentiments in regions and among people who after almost 70 years still regard Saudi rule as an imposition of an alien Najdi leadership. It is understandable why the Saudis play down their conquests in areas where they had no historical claims. In the absence of real social and cultural integration and genuine political representation and participation, the capture of Riyadh remains the key historical event.

The Centennial Celebrations Challenged

The centennial celebrations generated alternative discourses that undermine their hegemonic images, slogans, and rhetoric. Above all, this alternative discourse questions the eminence of Ibn Saud and members of the royal family. It casts doubt on their leading role in the historical process. While alternative narratives are not expressed in public, they feature strongly in private domains and abroad. State control prevents any public debate on the validity of the celebrations, timing, and images. But so far censorship cannot completely silence people in the privacy of their homes.

Reactions to the centennial celebrations ranged from apathy to objections. Some Saudis refused to become participants in the festivities. Those included Saudis who did not place congratulatory statements or poetic praise of the capture of Riyadh in local newspapers. Other Saudis prefer to see the celebrations as mere ceremonial, corresponding to what is commonly described as "snow, an insubstantial pageant, soon melted into thin air."[30]

Among Islamist circles, objections to the celebrations centered on rehearsing an old reservation that such festivities represent a form of *bida*, innovation, thus reiterating the *fatwa* against them mentioned earlier. An Islamist expressed that the capture of Riyadh was a minor incident in the unification process. As such it did not deserve an ostentatious spectacle. Instead, the state should have celebrated 250 years of reformist Islam, which had a greater impact on the modern history of Saudi Arabia. Some Islamists expressed doubt regarding whether the unification of the country was at all possible without the message of Muhammad ibn `Abd al-Wahhab (1703–92). In their views, the centennial celebration shifted the focus to a later incident in modern history, whose significance remains minor compared with the impetus of the Wahhabi *dawa*, call.

One Islamist group, the Movement for Islamic Reform in Arabia (MIRA), criticized the glorification of Ibn Saud. In one publication, Ibn Saud is described as having become *masum*, infallible, invoking images of the infallible *imam* in the Shia tradition. Objections were voiced regarding how the ancestor cult turned Ibn Saud into a "sacred figure": "`Abd al-`Aziz is scholar, generous, brave, pious, clever, warrior, honest, forgiving, and just. These are qualities often associated with prophets. Some Saudis see him as a king among other kings whereas others consider him a criminal and a traitor made by the British."[31]

While such criticism cannot be expressed publicly in print in Saudi Arabia, it finds expression electronically and through the medium of the fax machine. The messages of the Islamist opposition were transmitted from abroad by fax and email. These messages touch upon sentiments that remain dormant under censorship. While Islamists may refer to the celebrations as *bida*, yet the heart of the matter lies in the fact that celebrating the last 100 years is bound to marginalize an important date in Islamists' historical imagination, that is the Wahhabi reform movement of 1744. Islamists consider Wahhabism as the historical event that shaped the history and character of Saudi Arabia. The debate about whether such celebrations constitute an un-Islamic *bida* masks a deeper cleavage in Saudi society and a struggle between the state and people over the manipulation of historical consciousness.

Educated Saudis who are products of state modernization regularly challenge state narratives. Islamists are now capable of producing their own historical narratives, thanks to formal education, literacy, and training in state universities and abroad. They also produce their own poetry and video tapes to counter state sponsored artistic work.[32]

While Islamist criticism remains grounded in religious principles, others criticized the celebrations on the basis of their "vulgarity" and ostentatious display of empty slogans during times of economic hardship. The fall in oil prices since 1986 and successive budget deficits could not have been a worst moment for extra spending, according to some Saudi bankers and merchants. These views were expressed privately; they circulated among a close network of intimate and trusted friends.

Young Saudis pointed out the contradiction involved in displaying in public portraits of senior princes after decades of banning statues, images, and even paintings of human figures by the government. While art that uses human figures as a source of inspiration remains controversial and frowned upon in the country, the display of royal portraits in the main avenues of the cities is regarded as hypocrisy. A Hijazi who belongs to a family associated with a famous Sufi tradition described how upset she was when she saw "vulgar portraits of the King" when she visited Mecca in

January 1999. She pointed out what she described as a contradiction. In her opinion, in Saudi Arabia Sufism is mistakenly depicted as "saint worship" and is strongly condemned by Wahhabi doctrine, but portraits of the king and other members of the royal family continue to dominate the public sphere as "icons ready to be worshiped."

With the repetitive images and a constant set of words that accompanied the celebrations in January 1999, Saudis broke monotony and boredom with jokes, undermining the slogans of the centennial celebrations. The humor represented what Scott calls "hidden transcripts."[33] One popular joke at the time was: "Question: why did the Saudi government change the number of Ibn Saud's companions who helped him capture Riyadh from forty to sixty men? Answer: this was done in order to avoid Ibn Saud being described as Ali Baba and the forty thieves."

The story of Ali Baba and the 40 thieves is well known in Arabic popular culture. This humor undermines state efforts to alter history for its own purposes.

Many Saudis are aware of the manipulation of historical imagination by the state. With the exception of those who participated in the celebrations in various capacities, the majority of Saudis remained spectators. Their constant search for alternative sources of information about their past and different interpretations of their current affairs is a testimony that state control over the historical imagination is neither complete nor successful. So far this control generates compliance, accompanied by minor resistance of the kind discussed above. The voices of dissent remain scattered and lacking any form of organization. While this is the case, the state struggles to dominate the historical imagination and draw Saudis into the process of its construction according to well-defined rhetoric, images and symbols.

The Centennial Celebrations and Saudi Politics in the 1990s

The centennial spectacle was launched at the end of one of the most turbulent decades in Saudi history. To understand why the Saudi state needed to reinvent itself and assert the role of Ibn Saud as the founding father, we must consider the political and economic context in the 1990s.

Although the stability of the Saudi state was occasionally undermined by internal dissent within the royal family,[34] in the 1990s the state was challenged by previous supporters of the regime, namely a group of Saudi *ulama* and activists, who draw on the Wahhabi tradition for inspiration.

Following the Iraqi invasion of Kuwait in 1990s and Saudi resort to American military assistance to reverse this invasion, a Saudi Islamist opposition became more articulate in its criticism of the regime.[35] Members of the royal family were regularly attacked for mismanaging the economy, plundering wealth, and more importantly, resorting to American troops to defend the country and liberate Kuwait. That this criticism circulated widely abroad, thanks to new communication technology, exposed the Saudi royal family and undermined its legitimacy.[36] This coupled with a stagnating economy, falling oil prices, and increasing debts following the Gulf War did little to boost the popularity of the royal family. Unemployment among a new generation of educated Saudis, who are themselves a product of the state sponsored modernization and expansion of education, became more responsive to calls for reform and wider political participation. The state responded by reasserting its own legitimacy as it drew on past success and foundation myths to rejuvenate its image among a population not easily manipulated, thanks to literacy, education, and alternative sources of information. The project of the centennial celebrations became more urgent in the mid-1990s as Saudi Arabia began to witness terrorist attacks targeting its military and economic infrastructure and the American presence in the country. The turmoil of the 1990s, both political and economic, led to unusual dissent in a country not used to political confrontations in public, criticism within the country and abroad of the leadership, and terrorist acts on its own soil. The Saudi leadership needed to mobilize the population in search of a new *baya*, oath of allegiance. What aggravated the situation was the deteriorating health of King Fahd and the unresolved problem of succession among an aging ruling group. By 1999, it was clear that Saudi internal politics was reaching a stalemate. The centennial spectacle was a response to this context. As Saudis approached the twenty-first century, this stalemate is still perpetuated. Consequently, in the future they are more likely to witness similar spectacles staged by a leadership eager to redefine itself in a desperate attempt to deal with unforeseen challenges and diffuse new alternative discourses.

Notes

1. Madawi Al-Rasheed, *A History of Saudi Arabia* (Cambridge: Cambridge University Press, 2002).
2. Madawi Al-Rasheed, "Political Legitimacy and the Production of History: The Case of Saudi Arabia," in *New Frontiers in Middle East Security*, L. Martin, ed. (New York: St. Martin's Press, 1999).

3. Rahma Bourqia and Susan Gilson Miller, eds., *In the Shadow of the Sultan: Culture, Power, and Politics in Morocco* (Cambridge, Mass.: Cambridge University Press, 1999); Lisa Wedeen, *Ambiguities of Domination: Politics, Rhetoric, and Symbols in Contemporary Syria* (Chicago: Chicago University Press, 1999); Jill Crystal, *Oil and Politics in the Gulf: Rulers and Merchants in Kuwait and Qatar* (Cambridge: Cambridge University Press, 1990); Eric Davis and Nicolas Gavrielides, eds., *Statecraft in the Middle East: Oil, Historical Memory and Popular Culture* (Miami: Florida International University Press).

4. A. Abdullah al-Uthaymin, *tarikh al-mamlaka al-`arabiyya al-sa`udiyya* (History of the Kingdom of Saudi Arabia) (Riyadh: Wizarat al-Ma`arif, 1993), vol. 3, 72–3.

5. Madawi Al-Rasheed. "God, the King and the Nation: Political Rhetoric in Saudi Arabia in the 1990s," *Middle East Journal* 50, 3 (1996), 359–71.

6. Ameen Rihani, *Ibn Saud of Arabia* (London: Constable and Co. Ltd., 1928).

7. Khayr al-Din al-Zirkili, *shibh al-jazira fi ahd al-malik `abd al-`aziz (The Arabian Peninsula during the Reign of King `abd al-`aziz)*, first edition, 4 vols. (Beirut: Dar al-Qalam, 1970).

8. Fuad Hamza, *al-bilad al-`arabiyya al-sa`udiyya* (Saudi Arabia) (Riyadh: Maktabat al-Nasr al-Haditha).

9. Hafiz Wahba, *Arabian Days* (London: Arthur Barker Ltd., 1964).

10. Abdullah al-Uthaymin, *tarikh al-mamlaka al-`arabiyya al-sa`udiyya* (History of the Kingdom of Saudi Arabia), vol. II, Riyadh, 1995

11. Harry St. John Philby, *Saudi Arabia* (London: Benn, 1955).

12. Robert Lacey, *The Kingdom* (London: Hutchinson and Co., 1981).

13. Leslie McLoughlin, *Ibn Saud: Founder of a Kingdom* (London: Macmillan, 1993). Philby, *Saudi Arabia* (London: Benn, 1955).

14. David E. Long, *The Kingdom of Saudi Arabia* (Gainsville: University of Florida Press, 1997).

15. Madawi Al-Rasheed, *Politics in an Arabian Oasis: The Rashidi Tribal Dynasty* (London: I.B. Tauris, 1991).

16. *al-Quds al-`Arabi*, January 4, 1999.

17. *Financial Times*, September 23, 1998.

18. Al-Rasheed, *Politics in an Arabian Oasis*.

19. *al-Sharq al-Awsat* January 25, 1999, 6.

20. Wedeen, *Ambiguities of Domination*.

21. Samir Al-Khalil, *Republic of Fear: The Politics of Modern Iraq* (London: Hutchinson and Radius, 1989).

22. Saudi Arabia, 1996.

23. Al-Rasheed. *A History of Saudi Arabia*, 106.

24. Ministry of Education Publicity Literature, 1997.

25. Firman's Fund: Saudi Arabia Economic Trends and Outlook, November 30, 1999, 5.

26. *al-Sharq al-Awsat*, February 11, 1999.

27. Ibid.

28. Directorate of the Centennial Celebrations, 1999, 8–9.

29. Ibid., 16.

30. D. David Cannadine and Simon Price, *Rituals of Royalty: Power and Ceremonial in Traditional Society* (Cambridge: Cambridge University Press, 1987), 1.
31. MIRA: Communiqué, 147.
32. CDLR, 1995.
33. James C. Scott, *Domination and the Arts of Resistance: Hidden Transcripts* (New Haven: Yale University Press, 1990).
34. Al-Rasheed, *A History of Saudi Arabia*, 106–20.
35. Madawi Al-Rasheed, "God, the King and the Nation"; Mamoun Fandy, *Saudi Arabia and the Politics of Dissent* (Basingstoke: Macmillan, 1999).
36. Madawi Al-Rasheed. "Le couronne et le turban: l'etat saoudien a la rechereche d'une nouvelle legitimite," in *Les Etats arabes face a la contestation islamiste*, B. Kudmani-Darwish and M. Chartouni-Dubarry, eds. (Paris: Armand Colin, 1997).

Chapter 8

Struggles Over History and Identity: "Opening the Gates" of the Kingdom to Tourism

Gwenn Okruhlik

International tourism is at the nexus of global capitalism and national identity. Thus, it provides a powerful vantage point from which to examine the tensions between the imperatives of global capitalism and the protection of domestic jurisdiction. Global capitalism, as articulated by the World Trade Organization (WTO), mandates a free-er flow of information, capital, and people. A part of "opening up" is the promotion of tourism in countries that were previously difficult to access. This chapter is about the politics of tourism.

Tourism, as a dynamic of capital accumulation, is about creating and marketing experiences, in which place is commodified and reduced to an image for consumption.[1] The production of a national image has internal and external components[2] and it can be negotiated and revised even as the producers of the dominant image promote its authentic essence. Tourism suggests an invitation to come in and view your self, so it prompts the questions: What image of self is offered for viewing? What representation of self do you want to project?

These questions are especially provocative in Saudi Arabia where the state seeks, on the one hand, to accommodate global capitalism (by joining the WTO, inviting in investors, and foreign tourists) as it attempts, on the other hand, to forge a national identity that transcends diverse domestic voices (such as Islamism, class, gender, and region). In my view, the pursuit of the former exposes tender spots in the pursuit of the latter. The state attempts to project to tourists a homogenized version of "being Saudi" that is consistent with its desire to forge a national identity. As I illustrate, however, the experience of tourism makes evident contested voices over identity issues, through both glaring omissions and muddy edges (or, unintended encounters). My particular interest is in two aspects of tourism: (a) capturing the dominant representation through the official itinerary, choice of sites, and museum exhibits, and (b) distilling the muddy edges of controlled tourism, that is, incidents and observations that were not on the official itinerary.

To comprehend tourism, it must be situated in the post–Gulf War political economy of Saudi Arabia. I seek to articulate the rational and material reasons for the promotion of tourism, and to locate its meaning as part of a nationalist project. I make three primary arguments. First, I claim that a particular representation of the founding of the Kingdom and its development over the decades has been constructed, institutionalized, and consolidated and is being marketed to foreign audiences even before it is fully accepted (or experienced) by Saudi Arabian citizens. The idealized narrative on "what it means to be a Saudi" is interesting not only for what it does represent, but also for its exclusions, silences, and ambiguities. Second, I argue that the muddy edges of controlled tourism expose the internal complexity of Saudi Arabia. At these edges, when the official itinerary goes awry, international tourists encounter and contest local voices that seek to define and protect an identity. Examples are numerous and include such incidents as negotiations with *mutawwa* (enforcers of behavior) over covering and photography, the missing *igama* (residence permit) of a foreign bus driver, frustrations with the severe restrictions on mobility and interaction, and the unintentional exposure to substandard housing for foreign laborers. Finally, I argue that one of the unintended consequences of controlled tourism is that the Saudi Arabian state is losing its long-standing control of the external discourse on its development.

The politics of tourism are evident throughout the world; in the Middle East it is certainly so in Egypt, Israel, Jordan, and Morocco. What makes Saudi Arabia especially interesting is timing. Saudi Arabians are only now struggling to (re)construct the content of national identity (including citizenship and belonging) quite independently of tourism or the WTO. The coincidence of the two processes provides a fertile field for examining debates over national image.

In 2000, during which this research was conducted, the tourism sector was taking root and the stage was set for rapid expansion.[3] There were extensive development projects including investment programs, training sessions for service providers, media coverage, and the construction of a tourist infrastructure. Multiple groups toured the country and many more were scheduled for arrival. The tours came to a screeching halt after September 11, 2001. Consumer demand plummeted amid security fears. Media portrayals of Saudi Arabian culture and society further dampened the enthusiasm of potential travelers to the country. In early 2003, a Japanese group did tour the country; the first post–September 11 American group is tentatively scheduled for early 2004. In the meantime, the local tourism providers have had to compensate by redirecting the focus of their efforts from international tourism to internal tourism and what is called religious tourism (travel associated with religious rituals). Their businesses, advertisements, and services now cater to those specific markets as they await the reopening of international tourism.[4]

Representations and Narratives: Image and Imagination

The Politics of Place: The Meaning of Opening

Sandwiched in the travel brochure between ads for trips to the Himalayan kingdoms of Nepal and Bhutan, a Kenyan Christmas Family Safari, and a summer in Tuscan, the alluring teaser invites select groups of travelers to the Kingdom for a thrilling opportunity and a truly unique travel adventure. In an age of ecotourism, adventure travel, and culturally sensitive travel, Saudi Arabia is truly one of the last frontiers in international tourism. As a latecomer, Saudi Arabia offers an especially interesting vantage point from which to observe how politics and tourism intersect. The consumption of tourist services cannot be extracted from the social and political relations in which they are embedded.[5]

Tourism has been formally introduced into a country that was previously off limits to private sightseeing travelers not from the contiguous countries. Saudi Arabia has long received masses of visitors, but the only way to access it was through hajj (pilgrimage), visitation of relatives, or employment. For many years, then, Saudi Arabia has hosted internal tourists, Gulf Cooperation Council (GCC) visitors, Yemeni travelers, religious pilgrims, and millions of foreign workers. It is not that travel and foreign visitors are new in the country, but that private international tourism is new. It was extraordinarily difficult for a non-GCC foreigner to gain access to the country. In 1991, while still prohibiting tourism, Saudi Arabia sent abroad a fabulous exhibit of itself, entitled "Saudi Arabia: Yesterday and Today." As Susan Slyomovics observed, it conveyed the statement, "You can't come to Saudi Arabia, so we will come to you."[6]

To appreciate the power and significance of the opening of tourism, one must comprehend the long-standing regulations against mobility and travel in Saudi Arabia. Every foreigner (approximately 6.2 million, just under one-third of the total population) is required to be "sponsored" by a Saudi Arabian citizen, who in turn holds legal, financial, and social responsibility for the behavior of the foreigner. This means that sponsorship is extraordinarily difficult to attain except in the case of simple employment or to conduct the religious rituals of the hajj in Mecca and Medinah. Foreign workers have had restricted mobility; until summer 2001, they could not travel more than 50 kilometers from their place of residence without the written, signed, and dated permission of their sponsor. This extensive system of regulation and supervision ensured appropriate conduct while in the country. It acted in many ways as an extension of the authoritarian state. Tourist visas did not even exist.

The introduction of tourism in Saudi Arabia necessitated a major change in this long-standing system of sponsorship and supervision of foreigners in the country. In an early concession to tourism in September 1999, the state approved a plan that allowed Moslems coming to Saudi Arabia to perform *umrah* (minor pilgrimage) to travel around the country instead of being confined to the holy cities of Mecca and Medina.[7] In April 2000, the state announced it would issue tourist visas that allow foreigners access to the country for reasons other than hajj or employment.[8] While this is a major step in "opening up," it is not as though the Kingdom will be overrun by legions of backpacking college students anytime soon.

The new visa will apparently require tourists to travel in the country through a local company that will take charge of the trip in its entirety and will ensure that all tourists leave the country after their visit. The visa will be valid for one month and will be issued only for group entry rather than for individual travel. The visas are so new that during a January 2000 tour, there was still no "tourist visa" box to check off on the airline form. Yet in the first four months of formal availability, between April and July 2000, 6,546 tourist visas had been issued, mainly to tourists from Europe, Japan, and the United States.[9]

There has been no transition period in which individual travelers or small independent groups negotiated their way through Saudi Arabia. In Egypt, for example, individual travelers choose among their activities. They decide where to stay, what to eat, which sites are worthy of their time, what souvenirs to purchase, and how to negotiate the costs of their experience. In contrast, in Saudi Arabia, several government entities have been established to manage such dilemmas about sites, representation, costs, accommodation, and interaction between locals and tourists. There is less individual experimentation in experiencing Saudi Arabia. This means that questions regarding authenticity are not going to be answered slowly over time in a give-and-take process between tourist and local culture; rather, choices must be made up front because of the formal, structured nature of tourism in Saudi Arabia.[10]

In Saudi Arabia, it is the state that defines tourism (through representatives of the ruling family working with private Saudi Arabian operators) rather than independent, individual private entrepreneurial citizens. Several members of the Al Sa'ud family spearhead the effort to promote tourism. The state favors tourism because it will not only bring in capital, but it may also raise historical consciousness and cultural pride. For now, tourism is tightly controlled and the state is constructing the image to be marketed abroad, to private tourists. The itinerary from which it is impossible to deviate, is highly structured. It is not quite containment tourism or enclave tourism, but it is very much controlled tourism.

The Politics of Pace: Conflict Avoidance

The opening up of tourism is purposefully slow, cautious, and targeted for social and political reasons. A tourism manager for Saudi Airlines said, "The Saudis have received religious traffic and Gulf visitors for hundreds of years. It's not a new thing. But Saudi tourism will not be for the masses. It will be well-targeted."[11] A travel marketer in Jeddah said, "We want to be more open, but not like Dubai," and a director of marketing for a resort hotel was also cautious, ". . . this will happen in small doses in a very controlled way. It should be a gradual transition as we don't want to shock anyone."[12] Dubai, in addition to serving alcohol and allowing freedom in dress and mobility, also has a significant trade in prostitution.

Prince Bandar ibn Khaled, who works with tourism in the Asir region, was straightforward about the political implications of tourism, "Hundreds of thousands of people from different cultures could offend the local population without even knowing it." A public backlash "could delay (foreign) tourism for years."[13] For those advocates of tourism, the challenge is to gently promote tourism (and the hoped for accompanying opening of society) while avoiding a crackdown from socially conservative forces. It is a delicate balancing act. In other Middle East countries, the tourist sector has become a rallying point for opposition forces, most notably in Egypt along the River Nile.

Saudi Arabian officials refer to this as "clean tourism," travel without the negative circumstances that are often attached to the experience, such as gambling, casinos, alcohol, or prostitution. There are, of course, no public entertainment venues, clubs, cinema, or dancing.[14] Tour groups will visit archeological sites, historic locations, lakes, festivals, and museums. There are plans for ecotourism, snorkeling in the coral beds of the Red Sea, and treks in the Empty Quarter desert. Bedouins are "gearing up to take tourists to desert encampments." A new hotel and golf course are planned on the sea with a private beach where Westerners can swim.[15] The latter is relevant because it expands the distinction between behavior in the private and in the public space to encompass the tourist trade. Foreign women could wear bathing suits on such a private beach that was designed and maintained strictly for tourists. Such a resort is similar to enclave tourism, though it is unlike enclave tourist development in much of the developing world, where separation is required by the disparity between the wealth of tourists and the poverty of the countries they visit.[16] Saudi Arabia is relatively prosperous and urban; such separation is prompted by normative preferences.

Why Now and Why Tourism?

In a region of majestic pyramids, winding suqs, Islamic architecture, and pre-Islamic ruins, Saudi Arabia is clearly a latecomer to tourism.[17] There are really two questions to answer: Why tourism, and why in 2000 (finally)? The opening up of tourism is grounded in the reality of the post–Gulf War political economy. There are rational and material reasons for its recent introduction. The promotion of tourism is part of a larger dialogue about national identity. Its introduction in 2000 may reflect a new sense of self-confidence as a modern nation-state and a consolidated national entity. Tourism is promoted as a celebration, not only of the past, but also of the present and of future hopes. It may also reflect the self-assertion of the regime in the wake of Islamist opposition, which had finally begun to lessen at the end of the decade. (Likewise, the downgrading of international tourism as a national priority after the momentous events of September 2001 reflects a renewed sense of political vulnerability and struggle within the country.)

The domestic context of the 1990s was politically and economically difficult for Saudi Arabia and included the turmoil of the Gulf War, Islamist opposition forces on the ascendancy, illnesses for King Fahd, succession struggles in the al Sa'ud family, and new social problems. Guns, drugs, and crime were increasingly reported in Saudi Arabia. The population continued to grow at an astounding rate of about 3.5 percent per year. Unemployment figures among Saudi citizens spiraled. Among recent male college graduates, the unemployment rate was at least 30 percent. Yet there was a continuing dependence on an imported foreign labor force, which constituted about 95 percent of the private sector force. The once-fabulous infrastructure was deteriorating; this was especially true of schools and hospitals. Oil prices hit a ten-year low in 1998. Income per person had tumbled from $16,650 in 1981 to $6,526 in 1998. The ratio of public sector debt to GDP was more than 120 percent in late 1999, the seventeenth straight year of deficit. Clearly, Saudi Arabia needed a new source of revenue to buffer the economy from the volatility of oil prices and it needed a new source of employment. The year 2000–01 was also punctuated by strident international criticism of the Saudi Arabian record on human rights. International organizations like Amnesty International, Human Rights Watch, and even the United Nations all targeted Saudi Arabia for its treatment of women, children, non-Moslems, Shi'a Moslems, and foreign labor. There were anti-Israel (and anti-United States by association) demonstrations in the country; a Saudi airliner was hijacked, and the Imam at the Grand Mosque called for jihad against the forces of oppression. A series of car bombs and explosions unsettled the local and foreign population.

By the end of the 1990s, Crown Prince Abdullah had introduced a series of reform measures designed to build confidence in his leadership and foresight. He continued King Fahd's program of deporting illegal foreign workers, doubled visa fees on foreign labor, slashed subsidies on electricity and petrol, and instituted limits on princely prerogatives (use of phone, planes, and electricity). Abdullah established a Supreme Economic Council in order to regulate the shares market, to revamp the tax code, and to amend property and employment law in order to gain membership of the WTO, for which Saudi Arabia had applied in 1993 (when it was still GATT). Its membership application had been adversely affected because, as representatives of the WTO argued, the Saudi Arabian economy was too heavily subsidized and the market too protected. Troublesome issues included the lack of transparency in public procurement, intellectual property rights, investment rules, and tariff rates.

In response to these problems, Saudi Arabia announced in 2000 a series of sweeping economic changes intended to facilitate its membership of the WTO.[18] For the first time, 100 percent foreign ownership of companies is allowed, foreign companies will have access to favorable loans from the Saudi Industrial Development Fund; foreign investors can invest in the local bourse; the General Investment Authority (GIA) was established as a one-stop shop to issue licenses and to incorporate foreign and joint ventures, and importantly, it appears that the old requirement that all foreigners have a Saudi sponsor will be altered. There is discussion that foreigners will be allowed to own property in Saudi Arabia, that judicial protection will be strengthened and greater public disclosure for investments will be fostered. It is into this ferment and "opening" that busloads of tourists arrived for the first time ever in Saudi Arabia.

Saudi Arabia seeks to achieve several material objectives through the new promotion of tourism. As a demonstration of openness, it will facilitate application to the WTO. The development of the tourist infrastructure will also increase investment opportunities, attract select groups of foreign visitors, and encourage Saudi citizens to remain in the country for their holidays. Unofficial estimates are that Saudi citizens spend more than $16 billion on vacations abroad annually.[19] Indeed, much of the domestic discussion of tourism focuses on internal tourism and on the propagation of Islam. As a growing service sector, tourism is expected to produce acceptable positions for the many unemployed Saudis. Two of the primary attributes required of Saudi Arabians who are employed in the tourism trade are (a) generosity of hospitality and (b) a proud self-image. That is to suggest that the newly-created positions will be compatible with social norms. The decades-old effort to Saudiize the economy remains difficult, as many positions currently held by foreign labor are unattractive to citizens (due to pay, structure, incentives, and norms).

A challenge for Saudi Arabia is to keep money in the country and to circulate the money throughout the various regions and economic sectors. The state and private business community must build backward and forward linkages throughout the economy (in construction, services, agriculture, and transportation) so that Saudi Arabian citizens benefit from the new activity. Tourism must stimulate the local economy, develop capital-producing activity that is independent of oil cycles, and provide acceptable jobs. Unfortunately, experience elsewhere suggests that increasing international integration of the tourist industry decreases the amount of expenditure that stays in the host country. The broad-based relaxation of foreign investment regulations in Saudi Arabia, which has accompanied its application to the WTO, weakens local control over capital. Indeed, four of the six hotels that were utilized by the tour groups were an Intercontinental, a Meridien, a Sheraton, and a Marriott. Under the new WTO-mandated "reforms," such lucrative operations can now be 100 percent foreign owned. It may well be that the economic imperatives of joining the WTO mitigate against the diversification, privatization, and Saudiization of the economy, all long sought after goals in the country.

Many Saudi Arabians want tourism to work, so tremendous resources are being expended. Since 1995, Saudi Arabia has invested $6.66 billion on tourism projects, mostly geared toward internal tourism (Saudis and citizens from neighboring states of the GCC, who do not require visas).[20] The tourist infrastructure is most developed in the southwestern province of the Asir, in the resort town of Taif and in Yanbu on the Red Sea, both favored spots for holidays among Saudis and GCC citizens. It remains to be seen whether the needs of tourists from the Arabian Peninsula are similar to those of tourists from farther-flung origins. The state predicts three million visitors in the next five years and, once the infrastructure is complete, it expects one million tourists per year. There is a new Prince Sultan School for Tourism and Hotel Sciences that opened in Abha to train Saudi Arabian citizens for roles in the tourism sector. At the helm of all of this is Sultan ibn Salman, newly appointed Secretary General of the Higher Organization for Tourism (HOT); Salman al Sudairy assists him. Sultan ibn `Abd al-`Aziz is also supportive of this venture as Saudia Airlines serves as sponsor of tour groups. The HOT is responsible for tourism policy in the Kingdom. It is to evaluate infrastructure, "remove whatever obstacles might hamper tourist activity," and survey and protect tourist sites and folklore items such as handicrafts, markets, and cottage industries.[21]

Cultural Markers that Entice

There is nothing particularly exotic, strange, or mysterious about either Saudi Arabia or tourism. Yet, in the fertile imagination of tourists, a primary lure to tour Saudi Arabia was the sense that it is somehow shrouded, off-limits, and secretive. Though many of the tourists complained often about the constraints that were placed on them (regarding dress, photography, mobility), perhaps the restrictive, slightly taboo quality of the country was also the same reason they paid for the experience. Pre-trip literature clearly states that all female tourists must wear an *abaya* and cover their hair with a scarf for the duration of the trip. All participants are required to sign a waiver that details extreme political restrictions in Saudi Arabia to which they must abide. To my knowledge, no tourist expressed concerns about waiving the right to expression. Image and imagination fertilize each other here. It is not yet clear how long this can be sustained; as more tourists experience Saudi Arabia, the country will indeed be less "shrouded in secrecy."

The "off-limits" character of Saudi Arabia is utilized as a selling point for the tour by the operators (not by Saudi Arabians). The letter of advertisement notes that, even now, no tourist visa exists for entry to the country; each visitor must be sponsored by an influential Saudi and approved by the royal family. Saudi Arabia was introduced in literature that marketed trips as "mysterious and exotic," a "blank spot on the map for most travelers." The pioneering opportunity to be among the first in the door of the country is heralded. The tour "offers a rare chance to explore a country before the imprint of tourism changes it forever." Clearly, the primary draw is to be first, a pioneer traveler to a previously closed Kingdom, which has long resisted outside influence. The image of a pristine country, blessed by oil and urban centers but grounded in the desert and tradition, is articulated. The day-by-day itinerary, with a description of each day's activities, follows the letter of introduction.

Interestingly, some of the same perceived qualities that attracted tourists before September 11 (secrecy, taboo nature, mystery) are those that frighten potential tourists in the wake of September 11.

Producers and Consumers of Place

It is important to note that participation in tourism in Saudi Arabia is quite selective and the producers of knowledge include a wide range of professionals. A foreign tour operator (thus far, American, German, Italian, or Japanese) who manages all logistics and organization leads each tour group. That foreign operator works in conjunction with local tour guides, who are critical to the success of the venture. The Saudi Arabian guides bear responsibility for negotiating, representing, and interpreting their country. They, in turn, work closely with key princes who oversee tourism. Tours also benefit from the participation of representatives of the sponsoring group and study leaders, there to provide expertise.

Who are the early tourists? The participants in the tour were fairly homogeneous in demographic traits, and this makes intuitive sense. Such tourism requires two things: time and money. By and large, the 30 consumers were white, elderly, well-to-do, and retired (or able to turn their business affairs over to someone else for two weeks). As a group, they were well educated and extraordinarily well traveled. The participants had walked on the Great Wall of China, wandered around Moscow's Red Square, hunted on African safaris, and relaxed on Caribbean beaches. Touring Saudi Arabia was one of many travel adventures in their lives. The price of access was $7,700 for 13 days in the country inclusive of all travel, food, accommodation, buses, and tips. No monetary transactions were necessary once in the country (except for personal shopping). A newspaper has already reported that people are complaining about the high price of trips, writing that "a large number of tourists believe that tour operators are charging exorbitant prices to arrange trips to the Kingdom. Tour operators will have to bring down prices to attract more tourists."[22]

The schedule was highly structured and demanding. One could not deviate from the preplanned schedule or strike off on one's own to explore different sites. The only exception to this was within the Aramco compound in Dhahran, where ex-Aracoms, as they refer to themselves, were allowed to search out their old homes from years past. Even there, I was informed that they had a run-in with security guards patroling the compound. Participants were always free to stay behind in the hotel if they chose (but that too was difficult, as there are not swimming pools or gyms available to women travelers yet).

Tour guides always serve an important role in the success of the touring experience. They are ". . . vilified and praised, lampooned and treated with respect and generally emerge as critical figures in the minds of tourists."[23] Tour guides are simultaneously pathfinders, mentors, broker, educators, and interpreters.[24] In countries like Saudi Arabia, where basic information is at a premium, the role can feel overwhelming in its power. Tour guides serve as mediators between foreign consumer and local environment. All information is processed. The Saudi Arabian tour operators were crucial in their ability to relay explanations of behavior in a way that was often humorous and nonthreatening to the tourists. Both local guides were superb in their skills; their personalities were engaging. Interestingly, one guide spoke beautiful English, but did so with an accent. He was perceived by tourists to be not as skilled as the other guide, whom the tourists more openly embraced.

In my role as a study leader, and as an educator by profession, I sought to explain the nuance and complexity of dress, social norms, and behavior. Most of the tourists had little patience for meaningful discussion and preferred instead clear, and vastly oversimplified, answers. The risk is that cultural markers and symbols are de-contextualized. Their meaning and place become secondary to the visual image absorbed through the tourist gaze.[25] For now, at this early moment in tourism, it appears that the primary mediators of knowledge about Saudi Arabia are individuals who bridge the countries in some way; for example, scholars like myself who specialize in the area, a Saudi male married to an American woman, an American woman married to a Saudi man, and an American woman who works for a Prince. Such mediators are occasionally joined by U.S. embassy officials. Aramco, through its facilities and, even more so, through the generous distribution of its publications, serves as a mediator. The local Saudi Arabian tour operators are only now learning about the sites in their country, or how to represent their country to others. They are young, eager, smart, and ambitious, but unfortunately still take a backseat to other more "foreign" mediators.

Representation and the Itinerary

The Saudi Arabian state has been actively involved in the construction of a national memory and identity. Narrative construction and consolidation has been recently evident in the annual *janadriyyah*, in the extensive

Centennial Celebrations of the capture of Mismak Fort, and in the celebration of Riyadh as an Arab Cultural Capital. Such festivals, performances, and rituals sustain and nourish the civic myth that the state propagates through the media, curriculum, and museums. Together they constitute a nation-building project. Tourism is a part of the nationalist project. If, as Anderson informs us, a nation is an imagined community, the Saudi Arabian state now seeks to construct "a shared fact of consciousness"[26] through this project. The task of producing history and consciousness is made easier through oil revenues and control of the discourse. As Jalal demonstrates in Pakistan, there has been an uneven division of labor between state and civil society that has characterized the construction and dissemination of information.[27] Oil wealth has lubricated the state's labor in Saudi Arabia.

A national identity is one that transcends family, particular religious affiliation, and region, and gives content to the idea of self. Identity, and particularly a national identity, is not inherent or primordial. Indeed, it can be strategic and positional.[28] Thus, what become important are the facets of identity that one chooses to emphasize, or de-emphasize in the construction of an image of a nation. Most interesting is understanding the variability in what is included and what is excluded from this representation.[29]

The representation being sold to these pioneering tourists actually covers a wide swath of Saudi Arabia (see the appendix for sites). It will be important over time to observe which sites are added and deleted, as the touring process is refined. Saudi Arabia must find the places and experiences that will, in MacCannell's words, stimulate a "simultaneous caring and concern for another person and for an object that is honored and shared but never fully possessed."[30]

The tour focused on six primary regions, each typified through the compacted lens of tourism. Riyadh, a huge, bustling city, is the foreign affairs center, the national archive, and the center of history and the origins of the state. The portrait of Dhahran in the eastern Province was high technology, petrochemical industry, Aramco, expatriate faces, oil, and consumerism. The days up north in al Jouf, by the border with Jordan, left an impression of the importance of extended family, new central pivot agricultural lands, and the transitions that settled bedouins make. The experience in the marvelous Red Sea city of Jeddah is difficult to typify, but likely was perceived as cosmopolitan and commercial. The image of the Asir was of traditional dance, unique architecture, and ruins. The tour group was actually exposed to a fairly broad spectrum of Saudi Arabia. In the following year, trips to Saudi Arabia were combined with trips to the United Arab Emirates and Oman. Such multinational tourism may promote a greater sense of "GCC-ness" or of being "of the peninsula."

Narrative Privileges

The National Museum in Riyadh, which is spectacular by any stretch of the imagination, opened in 1999. A particular telling of history has long been part of the school curriculum,[31] but only now has history been assembled methodically and displayed in a way that conveys a message through visual, tactile, and aural mediums. A viewer could easily spend days there. The history of Arabia has been distilled into a national narrative.[32]

The exhibit carefully combines religious development, economic activities, technological advancement, climate, and peoples to weave a fabric in which the threads of continuity and traditions of the past are stitched together to produce a spiritual, industrial, and educated place of the future. It offers a construction of identity derived from an exemplary past that will bring the state into the age of (what I think is) modernity with meaning. Reinterpreting the past requires a strong sense of what stories resonate emotionally with populations; to do so where there is a lack of congruence between communal identities and the state requires finesse and subtlety; this is the statecraft to which Davis refers.[33]

The Museum constructs and institutionalizes a particular telling of history, as has been common in national museums.[34] It is a state-produced historical narrative. The National Museum and other regional museums convey a story about the founding of the Kingdom and its development over the decades, which emphasizes the power of Islam, the wisdom of `Abd al-`Aziz and the unity of peoples under the Al Sa`ud. The official narrative presents the historical past, from which it can selectively appropriate, an optimistic vision of the future. The narrative privileges, and meticulously weaves together, the power of Islam and the Al Sa`ud, who protect the moral integrity of the country. It is a national narrative that is "simultaneously ideological and utopic."[35] Important historical reference points include not only the *hijra*, but also the 1744 alliance between Muhammad al-Wahhab and Muhammad Al Sa`ud and the "unification of the tribes" during the early part of the twentieth century. Other tribes and regions were not conquered, but unified. Repeatedly, cities like Taif, Jeddah, and Mecca "opened the gates" to `Abd al-`Aziz. One leaves the National Museum to tour the King `Abd al-`Aziz Memorial Hall. Other than the Prophet Muhammad, he is clearly the central and defining figure in Saudi Arabian history. In fact, the National Museum concludes with `Abd al-`Aziz and the glorious history of state formation under his wise leadership. Curiously, it does not tell the story of Saudi Arabia under the rule of his sons.

The architecture and ambience of the museum are remarkable. In privileging Islam, the pre-Islamic age is constructed as the Period of Conflict marked by security threats, political confusion, and chaos.

The exhibit is visually and aurally disturbing. Strobe lights amid the darkness disorient the viewer; horrible sounds of warring tribes—people screaming, children crying, hooves galloping—make one want to flee the room. The architecture is angular and sharp. As you turn the corner, an escalator awaits to bring you upward to the safety, serenity, and brightness of Islam. (The rooms are bright; the sounds are quietly joyous, the rooms are long and spacious.) Islam moved people into the age of enlightenment, just as contemporary observers move *literally* from the age of ignorance and darkness via escalator into the brightness and illumination of the age of Islam. To foreign tourists, this museum accomplished a great task. I was asked repeatedly about the impending clash between religion and science, and how a "backward" (in the preconception of tourists) faith like Islam could possibly survive in the age of computers. The Museum answered these questions indirectly; the entire complex constitutes a high-technology exhibit of Islam and Saudi Arabia.

The visit to the National Museum was bookended with excursions to the crumbling ruins of al Dir'aiyah, the ancestral home of the Al Sa`ud, and to Mismak Fortress, where the Al Sa`ud celebrate their capture of Riyadh from the Rashidis in 1902. The period from 1744 to the declaration of the modern state is presented in seamless fashion.

Narrative Ambiguities and Confusions

Importantly, the museum does acknowledge a pre-Islamic history. Only a decade ago, this was not openly discussed; when it was cursorily mentioned, pre-Islamic history was thrown together into a morass simply labeled the *jahiliya*. No details were available and discussion was not encouraged. All development prior to the seventh century was portrayed as a turbulent black hole. History did not begin until the time of the Prophet Muhammad. Now however, a large section of the national museum is devoted to this expanse of time and human history. The accelerated pace of significant archeological discoveries in Saudi Arabia may have prompted this change. The state cannot discover, preserve, and trumpet its land as the site of many old societies without situating them in a continuum of time. The state is not yet sure how to represent this period. On the one hand, archeological ruins lend real significance to the role of Arabia in human development. On the other, it confuses the long-standing dominant narrative. So, for now, the museum carefully describes the civilizations and their time, but then suggests through sound, light, and text that the period shortly before Islam (A.D. 400–600) was turbulent.

A second interesting narrative ambiguity concerns an out-of-the-way museum that is devoted to the accomplishments of King Sa`ud. He, of course, has largely been written out of official history. His reign is generally covered in a short paragraph. The bankruptcy of the country is not mentioned. His deposition is not discussed. In commercial and government offices, the standard row of framed portraits of kings often proceeds from `Abd al-`Aziz directly to Faisal, Khalid, and Fahd, with a glaring absence. Yet, an entire, albeit small, museum is dedicated to his rule and his achievements. It is fascinating. He is portrayed as the protégé of his father and in fact once saved the life of his father during hajj when people tried to knife him during a religious ritual (*tawwaf*). There are rare pictures and documents. The museum was deleted from the subsequent tour group itinerary.

Narrative Silences and Exclusions

This official representation of self and history is not always congruent with what one hears in private conversations. The Museum does not reconstruct the many alternative tellings of history that exist throughout the country. It does not recount episodes that were painful for many people during the formative years of the country, such as the massacres in the south or the walls of dead bodies at Taif (called "opening the gates" in the official narrative).[36] Alternative narratives are about conquering rather than unification; violence rather than wisdom, and the abuse of Islam rather than its embrace.[37] Marriage into defeated tribes, long a standard part of the dominant narrative to illustrate the kindness of `Abd al-`Aziz, "was a trinket, like graft. It was un-Islamic." The official narrative does not include diverse regional accounts about social contracts or pacts reached between `Abd al-`Aziz and local notables. It is silent on the pact to separate the public and political from the private and commercial.[38] It does not speak about the negative impacts of the oil boom of the 1970s that reverberated throughout the country, or about obsequious consumption.

Both the Shi'a community and various Sunni Islamist groups have carefully constructed alternative tellings of history. They are every bit as carefully woven as the one in the National Museum. Their histories are coherent narratives, intricate and internally consistent, and woven from a fabric of cultural symbols and language that resonate among people. Khalid al Fawwaz began a long historical telling by explaining, "We must appreciate history, but our history is different from the one being told." Saad Faqih records an alternative history in his publication, "The History of Dissent in Arabia." The Shi'a Reform Movement has recorded its history in opposition publications.[39] Activists commented how very important oral history has been to the Shi'a community. He remembers clearly when, as a young boy, he was called to his uncle's side who said, "ibn akhi (son of my brother), do not believe anything that is written down. History is written by those in power. Do not believe the texts, especially those on religion." Mohamed al-Massori states that "The Wahhabi in contemporary Saudi Arabia do not name the exact ancestors to which we should refer because it would undo their own arguments about authority and obedience. If we really read the early stuff, we would see that the ancestors do not advocate blind obedience to unjust rule, but rebellion . . . Their writing undermines the position of the al Saud, so they have been conveniently dropped from the discourse." For some, then, the dominant narrative is a distortion of social and political history.

The representation of Saudi Arabia portrayed by the itinerary excluded two other important parts of the population. First, tourists did not see the underbelly of Saudi Arabia.[40] This would be expected in any tour of any country; it is just that in Saudi Arabia the underbelly is really quite large, even if hidden from view. There was no discussion of the 7.2 million foreign laborers who comprise about 95 percent of the private sector labor force (and 70 percent of the public sector labor force). Saudi Arabia encounters a difficult dilemma currently—it has about a 40 percent unemployment rate among recent male college graduates, yet remains extraordinarily dependent on the importation of labor. The tourists were not exposed to the self-contained housing compounds, designed to group workers together by nationality and to prevent mobility. They did not see the substandard living conditions of millions. Saudi Arabian guides did explain that now, because of the change in oil markets, Saudi Arabia does have different economic classes for the first time. In fact, Saudi Arabia has always been home to different economic classes; it is just that structurally the underclass has always been composed primarily of foreigners.

Second, except for preplanned excursions, the tour group did not encounter any Saudi Arabian women, fully half of the population. They did visit a school for girls, and had dinner in two Saudi Arabian homes at which women were present. The absence of women on the streets, in the markets, or in the hotels troubled several tourists. To some, the physical absence of women in the public realm was equated with total and complete oppression and servility. Rather than examine the ways in which women creatively negotiate their lives and empower themselves to survive and perhaps prosper in constrained circumstances, some participants sought reinforcement of preexisting images.

Finally, were it not for my lectures, tourists would not have been exposed to the myriad ways in which oil affects society, politics, and economics. The official sites trumpeted the technological glories of oil production; I discussed the ways in which oil affected urbanization, social change, and norms. There are multiple historic traditions in Saudi Arabia, each struggling to assert its truth and relevance.

The Muddy Edges of Controlled Tourism: Globalism and Identity

International group tourism is highly structured, with every minute of every day accounted for by planners. Lacking is spontaneity, flexibility, and indigenous interaction. It seems that distinctions between self and other (Saudi and tourist) are emphasized rather than commonalities. The most revealing moments of tourism occur when the preplanned itinerary does not proceed as scheduled, or when participants refuse to abide by the rules of the game. These "muddy edges" provide rich soil for analysis of the interplay between globalism and identity, or between the needs of tourists and the protection of domestic jurisdiction.

There are three edges at which there is some tension but where national identity clearly has the edge, that is, globalism accommodates identity (tourists abide by rules and norms). These concern prayer times, religious separation in the holy cities, and the death penalty waiver. First, within the constructs of a tour, regular prayer time plays havoc with tour itineraries. As study leader, I sought to explain the power of community prayer, the simplicity of prayer, and to suggest that the call to prayer was part of the fabric of daily business. The tour operator however, had to time to the minute every route and every stop in order to work around prayer times. Two minutes late and the group would miss entering a museum on time; they would have to cool their heels inside a parked bus in a lot. In another instance, a suq was closed for prayer when the bus arrived; the delay in the shopping excursion had repercussions for the remainder of the day since it was then too dark to see the world's largest oasis. My point is that tourism and its operators have to learn to build exciting and feasible tour schedules around prayer; prayer will not, and of course should not, accommodate tourism.

Second, non-Moslems are not allowed into the holy cities of Mecca and Medina. The tour group utilized a nice hotel on the outskirts of Medina as a departure point for a long bus ride north to the magnificent ruins of Madain Saleh. The architecture of the hotel to which we were confined was interesting, designed so that most windows face inward toward a courtyard. The hotel, while comfortable, was silent and solitary; international tourists were not allowed to stroll outside the building. In this way, tourism accommodates identity. Perhaps as more international tour groups go to Saudi Arabia, the atmosphere of the hotel will become more lively and interactive—a way-station for non-Moslem tourists.

Third, the state requires that all tourists sign a penalty waiver before a visa is issued. Being asked to sign a document that you will abide by all laws of a state while you are there is common and acceptable. This particular document, however, stipulates as well that tourists "shall respect the morals, customs, values and feelings of Saudi society . . . I am aware that alcohol, drug narcotics, pornographic materials, and all types of religious, political or cultural leaflets, pamphlets, magazines, books, audio tapes, video tapes, films, or other references of all sorts, contradictory to Islam are prohibited from entering the Kingdom of Saudi Arabia, whether for personal use or otherwise." As currently constructed, this document serves to reinforce pre-existing images of a "mysterious" country rather than enlighten the traveler about law or religion. The ambiguity and broadness of its language serve to confuse rather than elucidate. While it is clear that pork, alcohol, drugs, and pornography are forbidden in the country, it is less obvious how to define the "morals, customs, values and feelings of Saudi society" or what words are "contradictory to Islam." Even if the language is made more explicit, tourists will likely be expected to sign a statement before entry.

Muddy Edges

There are four muddy edges that are the site of maneuvering and contestation between international tourists and national identities. These concern photography, security, social norms/dress, and foreign labor. The way in which these issues play out and the skill with which they are handled will affect the future of tourism in Saudi Arabia. The individuals who champion a very gradual opening are cognizant of the possibility of a "backlash" from socially conservative forces, which could be precipitated by such incidents. These muddy edges represent a struggle over the image of the country, one that has intensified in the wake of September 11.

The Photography Muddy Edge
The participants in the tour were exceedingly well traveled. All were experienced at hosting travel slide shows for their friends and all had beautiful photo albums of their international adventures. It became very difficult (and taxing) to explain repeatedly and often to no avail, why an expenditure of $7,700 for this experience did not entitle them to snap pictures freely. The trip was perceived as a transaction in which the price of admittance entitled them to the privilege of contravening local norms. The truth is that opening the country to tourism is one thing; reproducing images freely is quite another. An effort was made to explain the source of constraints on photography in Saudi Arabia, which stem from considerations of religion (only God can produce a human), social norms (to protect the privacy of women and family), and security (broadly construed). Some tourists could not comprehend this, or simply thought it was silly and

chose to disregard the constraints. No matter how many cautions, prohibitions, and explanations were articulated, many tourists continued to snap photos, often with enormous telephoto lenses. It was a constant bone of contention, and became a serious issue at a museum stop in al Ula, a small town on the way to Madain Saleh. One woman, having just been told that photographs were prohibited in this town, walked to the far side of the bus and began to snap away. The *mutawwa* (loosely and poorly translated as, moral security) approached her. She simply turned and walked away, making the situation even worse. She not only violated the agreements, but also added insult to injury by rebuking local authorities. The Saudi Arabian tour operators were placed in a very uncomfortable position of having to negotiate out of this situation. The process was long and difficult and required the intervention of the local museum director.

In Dhahran, the men and women tourists split into groups so that each could observe a private primary school in operation, the men attending the boys' side, the women going to the girls' section. A male participant asked a female participant to slip a camera under her *abaya* to take a picture of unveiled females. This apparently happened on another tour as well, as recorded in the *Travel & Leisure* article.[41]

In the private home of a local family, after dinner was consumed, cameras came flying out of the bags. The women of the family fled the room. Finally, one older woman consented to photos and kept her face covered as she posed by a fire in the tent. But after countless poses and photos, her scarf would fall from her face and participants would try to sneak a peek of a Saudi Arabian woman. It is not clear how long this kind of cat and mouse game can continue. Will the family put its collective foot down and forbid photos of women while still graciously hosting tour groups? Or, alternatively, was this acceptable and perhaps indicative of the beginning of photos of women outside the family unit?

In Dhahran, we stopped with some fanfare to see the first well in Saudi Arabia from which oil flowed in the 1930s. In the tourist imagination, well #7 serves as a symbol of the fabulous boom of Saudi Arabia—it captures for some a mythology about the transformation of a country from tribal desert beginnings to bustling urban centers, from a nomadic people to a state at the heart of the global economy. We arrived and everybody disembarked to snap this fabled place, only to be told in no uncertain terms that photos of the well were not permitted. I am able to explain constraints on taking pictures of women, the human form, and military installations, but this was difficult to explain. A capped hole in the ground behind a fence does not appear to constitute a security installation, but security is broadly defined in Saudi Arabia.

The real challenge is less over the private memories of individual tourists and more over reproduction on the internet. There are concerns that tourists may post on the internet pictures that were secretly snapped of unveiled Saudi Arabian women. How long Saudi Arabia can invite in foreign tourists and yet restrict their memory banks is not clear. With tourism at the intersection of globalism and national identity, how long can restrictions be placed on paying tourists? The issue is being discussed in Saudi Arabia, as evidenced in an editorial in which the author searches for an explanation of the many restrictions on photography.[42] He argues that forbidding photography serves no real purpose, and in some cases actually creates ill will, bad publicity, and misunderstanding. He made repeated references to incidents involving foreign tourists.

The Security Muddy Edge

The second, and closely related, muddy edge is that of security and permissions. The tour bus arrived at the Hajj Terminal at the Jeddah airport. The structure has won many awards and is striking in its open, stark beauty—rows of white "tent peaks" arrayed against a brilliant blue sky. Tourists walked freely about the open-air terminal, taking pictures even after the local guide asked them to refrain. The discussion went back and forth; tourists simply disregarded his words. Finally, exasperated and uncomfortable, he pleaded with me, "This is serious. We do not have permission. Make them stop." Protracted negotiations took place between the local tour operators and the terminal security guards. There was a good deal of running between offices and there were many permissions to seek. Curiously, the tourists and the U.S. operator were blissfully unconcerned with the delicate position in which we had placed the local guides. The U.S. operator assured me, "We are OK. We have permission." I do not think he understood yet that in Saudi Arabia, not all permissions are equal. And sometimes, you need many permissions. This incident reinforced my observation that it is neither the tourists nor the foreign operators who pay the price for such incidents. It is the local tour guides who are put in precarious positions that require social skills and negotiating abilities.

The Social Norms Muddy Edge

The third muddy edge concerns social norms and proper covering of women. The female tourists chafed constantly about having to wear an abaya and headscarf. Rather than simply assume that it must be worn (as they had agreed prior to the trip), many constantly asked, "Do we have to wear this thing?" I endeavored to explain how different styles and degrees of covering reflect differences in ideology, class, and region. Most never did appreciate the significant variation that exists within the general norm of covering; it was just all black and it was all hot. One foreign tour operator company put a positive spin on the dress requirement in their press coverage of tourism. It suggests that, rather than taking away from the experience of traveling to an exotic place, such rules on covering reinforce the exoticism (which sells tours for them). "There aren't that many places in the world where you have to mesh yourself into the country to see it. It adds an interesting perspective."[43]

Most women grudgingly wore the *abaya*; however, one woman was particularly troublesome. At the old suq in al Hofuf, where group tourism really is a new thing, she paraded through the narrow rows of stalls with her *abaya* unsnapped, so that it flowed open toward the back as she walked. She wore a bright white, tight t-shirt and strolled with her hands in her pockets. Not only did she call attention to herself in this way, she then asked a local guide to assist her in buying a face veil. As if to provide a double insult, she purchased a bedouin burqa (a particular style). Now, her face was fully covered in black, her hair was uncovered, and her *abaya* flapped open as she walked through the rows of merchandise.

Another encounter with social norms became evident after dinner in a private home. One tourist boarded the bus to return to the hotel wearing a striking, new winter coat. She walked out of the home with the personal coat belonging to a family member. She apparently complimented the coat and in turn, the host insisted that she keep it. Saudi Arabians take the social norms of hospitality to new heights. When guests compliment an item, hosts often feel obliged to give the item to the admirer. This was not a wealthy family we visited. How long can families play hosts to tourists if they lose their private possessions? There is a steep learning curve involved for all participants.

The Foreign Labor Muddy Edge

The fourth muddy edge is one that is hidden from the tourist gaze; that is, the living conditions of the foreign labor force. At a road security stop in the Hejaz, it became clear in watching the animated discussion between security and the local guides that our bus driver lacked a proper *igama* (legal work permit). Had our local operator not been so skilled at negotiation, we would have had to turn around and scrap the day's itinerary. On another day, a Filipino bus driver accidentally caught the bus on a large boulder that had tumbled onto the edge of the street during construction. He could not maneuver the bus; we were stuck. As he followed the instructions of the Saudis to disengage from the rock, the side mirror caught on a tree branch. It was hot and humid. The all-important closely timed itinerary was in jeopardy. Tempers flared in a quietly contained manner. The bus would not budge; we sat inside the bus as the men tried to remedy the situation. Several tourists inquired of me, "What will happen to the driver now? What will they do to him?" There was some unease that he would be deported, refused salary, or worse. When I relayed these concerns to the

Saudi Arabian guide, he explained through the microphone that the firm had to fill out insurance forms in triplicate to submit their claims in order to get the repairs done. The tourists sighed with relief.

The muddy edge of foreign labor was again exposed at the end of a long, lovely day touring a farm. We climbed a sand dune, enjoyed tea and dates at the family compound, and watched as hundreds of sheep ran in the pasture. It was a wonderful afternoon. As we prepared to board the bus at the end of the day, it became apparent that the small, windowless cinder block building was the residence of foreign laborers who staffed the farm, probably for all of them. The heat inside must have been searing. Its residential nature was revealed only because of the puppies that played outside and a dried-up okra garden out back. I could have spoken for hours about the conditions of foreign laborers and the restrictions on their mobility. Without entering, I could have accurately described its contents—thin cots for beds, a small butane gas camp stove for food preparation, and no running water. But on private property and having just enjoyed the warmth of this family, it would have been inappropriate. In all fairness, these Filipino workers spoke very highly of their employer. This muddy edge was just barely and accidentally exposed. It cannot be hidden forever.

Tourism and Sociopolitical Discourse: Losing the Monopoly

Nevertheless, this is old-fashioned, private, for-profit tourism. This fundamentally affects control of the discourse. Saudi Arabia has long hosted visiting delegations of specialized groups, for example, nonspecialist scholars.[44] These delegations have traveled under the auspices of cultural and educational exchange; the trips are significantly subsidized, so those travelers are essentially guests of the country. In exchange for the trip, participants are normally expected to contribute different kinds of community outreach upon their return, for example, talks or newspaper articles on the country. Private tourism is quite different; anyone with time and money can sign up for the excursion. Since they paid a hefty price for the tour, no expectations are incumbent upon participants. They may write or evaluate the experience in whatever ways they choose. There is no pretense of scholarly or cultural exchange; these are simply tourists seeing the world. This fundamentally changes the dynamics of travel because the Kingdom can no longer control the discourse about its development.

Within the first year of tourism, the impact was clear. Two full pages of a newspaper were devoted to Saudi Arabia after a writer joined a tour and wrote an account of his experience.[45] Interestingly, these articles are not in the travel section, but comprise the cover story of the "Perspective" (editorial) section, and are headed "Foreign Affairs." The article opens with this rather strong sentence, "Stand the U.S. Constitution on its head, and you have Saudi Arabia," and he continues, "Absent the oil equation, it's a fair surmise that U.S. policy toward this desert kingdom would manifest—at least to some degree—the abhorrence aimed at such repressive regimes as communist North Korea and the Taliban fundamentalists of Afghanistan. Saudi Arabia . . . has ample trappings of a police state." The writer goes on to detail the absence of press freedom, constraints on women, the absence of any free expression, the absence of basic political rights, as well as the lack of movies and concerts.

The first major coverage of tourism in Saudi Arabia appeared in *Travel & Leisure*, a glossy monthly magazine that caters to the industry and to well-heeled tourists. The magazine sent a writer and a photographer to accompany one of the first U.S. tour groups. The table of contents reads, "Shifting Sands: One of the most secretive of the OPEC members, Saudi Arabia has finally decided to open its doors to Westerners. Hitch a ride with the first American tour group to visit a kingdom that still isn't sure that tourists are a good idea."[46] In reference to a brief stay on the outskirts of Medina, the writer asks, "Since the fall of the Soviet Union, how many places are left on earth where you can be restricted to your hotel?"

Newsweek, too, carried a very brief blurb on "Touring Muslim Style," in which the author suggested rules of the road for visits to Islamic countries. The only mention of Saudi Arabia was that all female tourists would be issued a black *abaya*, the voluminous cloak Saudi Arabian women wear.[47] It is apparent that the state will lose its monopoly on the discourse; permitting tourism and the construction of tourist memories, then, is actually a rather bold and risky move on the part of its sponsors.

Identity and Tourism: On Being and Belonging in Saudi Arabia

The complexity of the political economy of tourism in Saudi Arabia is demonstrated in its muddy edges; in the loss of the state monopoly of discourse, in the inclusions and exclusions in representation, and in the motivations of tourists to travel there. The tourist experience also demonstrated how quickly things are changing in Saudi Arabia. Sites that were pristine ten years ago are now ringed by tourist villas and amusement parks. Ruins that were poignant in their worn majesty have been restored to gleaming newness and are easily accessible by cable car. Suqs that were off the beaten track are now on international itineraries.

It is also evident, however, that new spaces for public discourse are cautiously opening in Saudi Arabia. There simply is more discussion about more subjects in public than previously. For the first time in recent memory, there is acknowledgment of difference among Saudi Arabians. That is, different regions, costumes, and customs are acknowledged and sometimes celebrated in museums and shows. Together with a dominant narrative of Islam and `Abd al-`Aziz, there exists acknowledgment of diversity. In addition, there is for the first time a new comfort level in acknowledging the pre-Islamic past. Rather than denying it, it is analyzed in museums.

There is a tremendous upside to the fact that Saudi Arabia is such a latecomer to international tourism and to archeology. Rich ruins that lay beneath the desert are so late in being discovered—archeology is just unfolding—that the sites are protected. Shards and monuments will remain in Saudi Arabia and be documented by a new generation of Saudi Arabian archeologists. They will not be looted and taken to capital cities on other continents. The sense of self and domestic jurisdiction (vis à vis foreigners) is strongly enough embedded to protect national resources. Furthermore, tourism was only initiated in the year 2000, long after the jargon of "sustainable development" became a part of our lexicon.[48] Very late incorporation into the global tourism economy may prove to be a benefit and allow Saudi Arabia to avoid pitfalls that marred tourist development in the years prior to cognizance of sustainability.[49]

"Being a Saudi" has been defined in recent years vis à vis the other, the other being the millions of foreign laborers who staff the economy. Identity and citizenship were about belonging to a community that was distinguished from foreign laborers by particular social norms and by economic privilege. The rights and obligations of citizenship have been defined in social and economic ways to encompass Islamic values, conformist social behavior, and the centrality of the family unit. Tourism is very much about this evolving national narrative on being and belonging. The muddy edges of cultural representation reflect contested voices within Saudi Arabia (about gender, ethnicity, social norms, authoritarianism, and Islam). International tourism—as a manifestation of globalization—will certainly be caught in the unfolding, and intense, struggle within Saudi Arabia between religious conservatives and liberals, all of whom perceive themselves as the true reformists. Analyzing tourism provides a rich research agenda on the interplay of global economic imperatives and national identity as it relates to gender, region, religion, and ethnicity.

Appendix: A Description
of the Tour Itinerary

In Riyadh, located in the central Province, participants visited the stunning new National Museum, the fortress-like Diplomatic Quarter, Qasr al Tuwaiq, al Dir'aiyah (the ancestral home of the Al Sa`ud family), Mismak Fort (where `Abd al-`Aziz and his band of 40 men captured the Najd back from the Rashidis), and a camel market. In Dhahran in the Eastern Province, participants visited the hi-tech exhibit at Aramco, well #7 where oil was discovered in 1938, the infrastructural wonder of the causeway that links Saudi Arabia to the island state of Bahrain, and a private school (where male tourists observed the boys' section and female tourists observed the girls' section). An excursion to the old suq in al-Hofuf was also on the itinerary, as was a stop at a date market. The stay in al-Jouf was shaped by our experiences with the family of the Saudi Arabian tour guide. Also there, tourists saw many ruins including Domat al-Jandal, Sakaka, Qasr Zabel, Qasr Marid, the mosque of Omar, and Rajajil, a small Stonehenge-like monument of standing rocks. The group then used a hotel on the outskirts of Medina proper (into which non-Moslems cannot go) as a point of departure for a trip up north to see the remnants of the Hejaz Railway and the tombs cut into rock in the dramatic landscape of Madain Saleh. In the beautiful port city of Jeddah, tourists visited the Abdul Raouf Khalil Museum (a private collection of artwork of varied quality and origin), the Greek Island Restaurant (to which Saudis would never go), the Hajj Terminal, the historic home of the Naseef family, and the old Jeddah suq. The highlight of the city was a dinner in the backyard of a private villa, complete with laser and sound show and a fashion show. Finally, the days in the Asir included stops at the National Park, Habala Village, Rigal al-Ma, and the market of Khamis Mushayt.

Notes

1. Colin Michael Hall, *Tourism and Politics: Policy, Power and Place* (Chichester: John Wiley and Sons, 1994), 194.
2. Susan Ossman, "Boom Box in Ouarzazate: The Search for the Similarly Strange," *Middle East Report*, September–October 1995, 12–14.
3. The empirical part of this analysis is based on my participation in some of the first study tours of Saudi Arabia in January and October 2000. I served as the study leader for a private tour group from the United States that traveled under the auspices of a national museum. In that capacity, I accompanied the groups,

served as a resource person, and presented a lecture in each city (on topics rang-ing from history, oil, economics, politics, and society). This analysis is in no way associated with the tour operators, nor does it reflect upon their performance, which was superb. This is an attempt to grapple with new and complex sociopo-litical issues that emanate from tourism. The author is solely responsible for the views expressed.

4. This chapter is about private international tourism. It does not directly address internal tourism, GCC tourism, or religious travel, all of which are related but likely have different dynamics.

5. J. Urry, "The 'Consumption' of Tourism," *Sociology*, 24, 1, 1990, 23–5.

6. Susan Slyomovics, "Tourist Containment," *Middle East Report*, September–October 1995, 6.

7. "Hotel Operators Eye Opportunities in Saudi Arabia," *Reuters*, May 16, 2000.

8. "Saudi Tourism Will Have Slow Start," *Gulf News*, April 6, 2000, and "Saudi Minister Says Sponsorship to be Scrapped," *Reuters*, April 27, 2000.

9. "6500 Tourists Get Saudi Visas," *Agence France-Presse*, July 31, 2000.

10. On authenticity, which I think will be an important question in Saudi Arabia, see Donald Getz, "Event Tourism and the Authenticity Dilemma," in *Global Tourism: The Next Decade*, William Theobald, ed. (Oxford: Butterworth–Heinemann, 1996); S. Lash and J. Urry, *Economies of Sign and Space* (London: Sage Publications, 1994); Erik Cohen, "Contemporary Tourism—Trends and Challenges: Sustainable Authenticity or Contrived Post-Modernity," in *Change in Tourism: People, Places, Processes*, Richard Butler and Douglas Pearce, eds. (London: Routledge, 1995); John Hutnyk, "Magical Mystery Tourism," in *Travel Worlds: Journeys in Contemporary Cultural Politics*, Raminder Kaur and John Hutnyk, eds. (London: Zed Books, 1999), and Hazel Tucker, "Tourism and the Ideal Village," in Abram et al.

11. "Saudis Seeking Tourists, Preferably the Well-Off," *Agence France-Presse*, Dubai, May 11, 2000.

12. "Hotel Operators . . ." *Reuters*, May 16, 2000.

13. Eileen Alt Powell, "Saudi Tourism: Conservative kingdom is finally opening its door to foreign visitors," AP, Abha, *Northwest Arkansas Times*, May 16, 1999.

14. Though a Disneyland-style project, the first in the Middle East, has recently been announced in Riyadh. It will feature Star Wars, Hollywood Studio, and a Wild Wadi boat ride through turbulent waters. *Saudi Press Agency*, January 2, 2001.

15. Ibid.

16. Tim Mitchell, "Worlds Apart: An Egyptian Village and the International Tourism Industry," *Middle East Report*, September–October 1995, 8–11.

17. For a critical analysis of tourism in the Middle East, see "Tourism and the Business of Pleasure," an issue of *Middle East Report* devoted to the subject, September–October 1995, no. 196.

18. James Gavin, "Saudi Arabia: All Change," *Middle East Economic Digest*, June 25, 2000.

19. Abdullah al Shihri, "Saudis Establish Tourism Body," *AP*, Riyadh, April 17, 2000. Such figures suggest that Saudi Arabia is not simply a receptor

destination as is the case for much of the developing world; rather, Saudi Arabians themselves are active travelers elsewhere.

20. *Gulf News* Editorial, "New Challenge for Riyadh," April 8, 2000.

21. "New Council to Promote Tourism," *Saudi Arabian Embassy Newsletter*, May 2000.

22. *Arab News*, July 30, 2000.

23. Philip L. Pearce, *The Social Psychology of Tourist Behavior* (Oxford: Pergamon Press, 1982), 137.

24. Ghana Gurung, David Simmons, and Patrick Devlin, "The Evolving Role of Tourist Guides: The Nepali Experience," in *Tourism and Indigenous Peoples*, Thomas Hinch and Richard Butler, eds., (London: International Thomson Business Press, 1996), 107–28.

25. The phrase was coined by John Urry, *The Tourist Gaze: Leisure and Travel in Contemporary Societies* (London: Sage, 2001).

26. See Uri Davis in Butenschon, Davis, and Hasassian, *Citizenship and the State in the Middle East* (New York: Syracuse University Press, 2000), 59.

27. Ayesha Jalal, "Conjuring Pakistan: History as Official Imagining," *International Journal of Middle Eastern Studies*, 27 (1995), 77.

28. Stuart Hall, "Introduction: Who Needs Identity?" in S. Hall and P. duGay, eds., *Questions of Cultural Identity*, 1996.

29. See Simone Abram, Jaqueline Waldren and Donald McCleod, *Tourists and Tourism: Identifying with People and Places* (Oxford: Berg, 1997) for discussion of identity and tourism.

30. Dean MacCannell, *The Tourist: A New Theory of the Leisure Class* (Berkeley: University of California Press, 1999), 203.

31. See Madawi Al-Rasheed, "Political Legitimacy and the Production of History: The Case of Saudi Arabia," in *New Frontiers in Middle East Security*, L. Martin, ed. (New York: St. Martins Press, 1999), 25–6.

32. As well, a 12-volume Arabic language "Encyclopedia of Folklore of the Kingdom of Saudi Arabia" was just published last year. See Judith Miller, "Encyclopedia Raises Veil on Ancient Saudi culture," *New York Times*, June 20, 2000.

33. Eric Davis, "Theorizing Statecraft and Social Change in Arab Oil-Producing Countries, in *Statecraft in the Middle East: Oil, Historical Memory and Popular Culture*, Eric Davis and Nicolas Gavrieldes, eds. (Miami: Florida International University Press, 1991), 13.

34. On museums, see Michael Hitchcock, Nick Stanley, and Siu, King Chung, "The South-east Asian 'living museum' and its Antecedents," in Abram et al., *Tourists and Tourism*.

35. Layoun notes this combination in her discussion of nationalism-as-narrative in Lebanon. In Mary Layoun "A Guest at the Wedding," in Caren Kaplan, Norma Alarcon, and Minoo Moallem *Between Woman and Nation* (Durham: Duke University Press, 1999), 94.

36. In the official narrative, it is written that several conquered cities "opened their gates" to `Abd al-`Aziz and his unifying forces. In alternative narratives, less benign language is utilized to describe the same events. The title of this chapter is intended to capture the struggle over narratives on tourism.

37. Alternative Islamist tellings are derived from in-depth interviews with Saad al-Faqih (MIRA), Mohamed al-Massari (CDLR), and Khaled al-Fawwaz (CAR) in 1997 and 1999, and from several interviews with Shi'a activists between 1992 and 1998.

38. Alternative regional tellings are derived from extensive interviews across in Saudi Arabia in 1989–90.

39. See Madawi Al-Rasheed, *Political Legitimacy and the Production of History*.

40. Though there now appears to be a new mode of voyeur tourism, in which the itineraries of foreign tourists are purposely designed to bring busloads into the ghettos and shantytowns of the developing world.

41. Ted Conover (writer) and Brown W Cannon III (photographer), "Shifting Sands," *Travel & Leisure*, March 2000, 228.

42. Khalid al Maeena, "Clicking Off the Curbs of Out-dated Practices," *Gulf News*, May 24, 2000.

43. Powell, "Saudi Tourism . . ." *Northwest Arkansas Times*.

44. Gwenn Okruhlik, "Bringing the Peninsula in From the Periphery: From Imagined Scholarship to Gendered Discourse," *Middle East Report*, July–September 1997, no. 204, 36–7.

45. Jack Schnedler, "Saudi Arabia: Our Strange Bedfellow," *Arkansas Democrat Gazette*, April 16, 2000.

46. Conover and Cannon, "Shifting Sands," 154.

47. Carla Power, "Touring Muslim Style," *Newsweek*, July 10, 2000, 70.

48. Peter E. Murphy, "Tourism and Sustainable Development," in Theobald, 274–90.

49. In a tangential but parallel vein, the massive encyclopedia of Saudi Arabian folklore that was recently published is described as "a truly nationalist project." The contributors said that such an endeavor could not be undertaken until the last decade because tribal and regional divisions continued to plague the country. "Until Saudis spoke the same Arabic dialect and tribal and regional cultural differences diminished, a project examining the country's heritage would have been too contentious to be approved by the censors." (Sa'ad al Sowayan, in Judith Miller, "Encyclopedia Raises . . ." *New York Times*.) Again, the country was late in formally preserving heritage, but the long delay also made preservation feasible. Alas, there are reports that social and regional divisions are in the ascendant again.

Chapter 9

Evacuating Memory in Postrevolutionary Yemen

Gabriele vom Bruck

*Let me state my problem from the outset. It is
how to keep the self without being nostalgic.*

—Marilyn Strathern

There has been a considerable literature investigating various dimensions of
remembering and forgetting tragic events in diverse social contexts. It has
focused on issues such as the manifest and repressive mediations of memory
and the hegemonic and often contradictory processes of producing, distributing, and consuming knowledge about the past as they take place in institutions and at historical sites.[1] Focusing on autobiographical memory, my
concern is to examine how members of a former Yemeni ruling elite, who
became the main target of a revolution, remember and forget the past. This
is particularly poignant because it is in the nature of hereditary elites that in
many ways they define themselves through the past. What often amounts to
trauma is the contradiction between their sense of self—derived from a
genealogical and historical past that is a source of pride—and the stigmati-
zation suffered as a result of being identified with that history. For the most
part, there is an official discouragement of invoking a past seen as unworthy
of remembering in terms other than debasement. According to Caruth,
"trauma is a repeated suffering of the event, but it is also a continual leaving
of its site."[2] Some of the life stories I relate demonstrate the conflictual
departing from and revisiting of trauma. The traumatic engagement with
the past consists in this elite's endeavor to depart from a history that might

cause their descendants pain, and to negotiate the terms of inclusion and exclusion in the state, which was founded after their fall from power.

Learned members of this elite—locally referred to as *sadah* (sg. *sayyid*) or *hashimiyin* (sg. *hashimi*)—tend to consider themselves to be "people of memory." Indeed, by reason of their putative descent from the Prophet, memory of the sayings and deeds of their forebears who were great `ulama and Imams forms a substantial part of their identity. As self-styled carriers of the Prophet's message, the *sadah* conceive of history as a narrative of the creation of *sayyid* kinship, which begins with the birth of the Prophet. History is embodied in the activities of their ancestors and thus in kinship relations.[3]

Idealized versions of Zaydi history as the implementation of principles of social justice coexist with contestatory memories of the pursuit of power through the exercise of punitive violence. An appraisal of the modalities of the writing of this history (or histories) awaits further research.[4] My own objective is much more modest: I wish to reflect on the personal predicament of people who experienced a revolution in the course of which they served as the foil for the new regime's moral and political ascendancy. What is their sense of "past" and "self" in a transformed political setting where their existence is at once denied and referred to in many implicit, sometimes derisive ways?

Until 1962, when the Zaydi-Shi`i Imamate was overthrown and a republic declared, *sayyid* rule was based on a combination of factors: most notably descent from the Prophet, the exercise of force, and widespread belief in their exceptional capacity to interpret divine knowledge. During the Imamate, the only Shi`i power that lasted for over a millennium,[5] the *sadah* monopolized leading positions in the government and contributed to the promotion of Muslim scholarship, but many lived as farmers in modest conditions. By virtue of their kinship with the former rulers, the revolution targeted the *sadah* more than other representatives of the old regime.

In the Imamate, *sayyid* identity was unproblematic in so far as its laws and institutions defined the *sadah* according to religious criteria and reserved a special place for them in the body politic.[6] One of the central features of republican state formation in 1962 was the separation of political office and religious status. Since the republic has committed itself to the elimination of religiously sanctioned social distinctions, there has been a Tocquevillian shift from a society formally ordered by claimed descent to one in which all citizens are nominally equal.

By introducing the notion of "citizen" (*muwatin*), republican leaders have aspired to create a homogeneous society that transcends particularist identities. Republican legislation no longer recognizes the *sadah* as a distinct social category. This, however, does not sufficiently explain the precarious nature of *sayyid* identity in present-day Yemen. It remains politicized because doubts are cast on the *sadah*'s loyalty to the republic. The media demonize the Imams, depicting them as oppressors who monopolized the country's resources for their own good. The *sadah*, who are related to the Imams, have experienced the defamation as a personal affront that has contributed to highlighting and perpetuating their sense of distinctness, even while many have attempted to play down this feature of their identity. They must reconcile notions of descent from the founder of Islam with anti-*sayyid* stereotypes that portray them as people guided merely by political ambitions. Having considered themselves Yemeni for centuries, in 1962 they learnt that they were not, or at least less so than other Yemenis.[7]

In what follows, I examine how *sadah* from both privileged and disadvantaged backgrounds make sense of their lives in the light of their memories of the history of the *ahl al-bayt*[8] and their most recent past. In relation to the manner in which the revolution has been officially memorialized, their experiences of this period are both marginalized and silenced. This partly explains efforts at suspending memory. Traditional *sayyid* education places emphasis on the memory of genealogies, the lives of Imams, and their rulings (*ikhtiyarat*). The official ideology of the Imamate fostered a culture of remembrance based on the *taqlid ahl al-bayt* (tradition of the Prophet's kin) and the memory of the martyrdom of Imams. Even though remembering plays a pivotal role in the production of *sayyid* identity, some *sadah* induce "forgetting" as a way of remaking the self. Some manipulate links with their biographic past by retrospectively deconstructing the virtue that used to be associated with being of *sayyid* descent. For example, self-imposed suppression of memory takes the form of failing to pronounce names or titles whose articulation enforces remembering, which has inevitable political implications. Another salient feature is declining to transmit to the next generation the very knowledge that initiates historical self-consciousness among the *sadah*. It is argued that the suppression of historical memory aims at neutralizing the *sadah's* sense of marginality and at achieving recognition as full Yemeni citizens by those who question their right to that status. Some *sadah* conceive of the self-imposed suppression of memory as enabling survival in a transformed environment where, in certain respects, the mark of distinction has become a stigma. The present circumstances, which render their lives precarious, encourage exploration of the ways in which power and Kinship ideology operate in the formation of memory regimes.

Sadah memories of the revolutionary years have not lost their sharpness not least because official denial of their victimization and defamation has precluded the legitimation of these memories. The politics of memory in contemporary Yemen has inspired declarations about heroic commitment to the revolution, but has discouraged the victims from speaking out—even in the company of their children. This, as David Cohen makes us consider, is not the consequence of forgetting, but of continuous acts of control in both public and private places.[9] They produce a self-awareness of surveillance whereby silence points to embodied and historically situated knowledge, which remains tacit. Silence becomes a formative event in these uncertain and provisional projects of self making; it also throws a new and different light on those known as principal producers and interpreters of knowledge. The fusion of memories of the history of the *ahl al-bayt* and of persecution in the 1960s may be conceived of as a partial mental escape due to (self-)censoring mechanisms. Memories of the history of the *ahl al-bayt*, which were of course cultivated by the Imamic state, have acquired different meanings and functions in the republican era.

Ahmad al-Husaynat

I begin with the story of Ahmad, a man in his forties, who was born into a prominent family.[10] His father served in the government of Imam Ahmad. Ahmad has been searching for alternative ways of being a Zaydi and a *sayyid* that are compatible with both his self-image and official ideology. He has followed directions in his life that diverge significantly from those of his forebears. Rather than embarking on a career based on religious learning, he studied economics. He accepted his sister's marriage to a man of modest means who was not a *sayyid*. He felt the bias against the *sadah* since his early childhood, and tried to shape relations with others so that his children would not experience the same kind of prejudice. Ahmad was five years old when his brother, his sister, and he had a fight with the neighbors' children.

> We threw stones and swore at each other. The other children abused us, and one of the words they used was "sayyid." I did not understand the meaning of the word. When we returned home our mother explained it to us, telling us not to use it and to keep this knowledge to ourselves. The incident left me very confused. How could I be a *sayyid* and be treated like that? When I later learnt that some people do not like Imam `Ali, I felt betrayed and sad. When I attended elementary school, I felt that the other students were reluctant to befriend me. Some boys had been told by their parents to beware of me because I was a *sayyid*. I was unable to resolve the tension between the teachings of Islam which call on believers to love the Prophet, and people's hatred of his progeny. I was so affected by those experiences that I could not concentrate well in school.

Ahmad witnessed the humiliation of *sadah* in the streets and was belittled by his Egyptian teachers who arrived in Yemen after President Nasir had sent his troops to support the republic. At school, the certificates of children of *sayyid* descent recorded their names with the specification *mulaqqab sayyid* (*"soi-disant sayyid"*). The honorific title and generic label "sayyid" was treated like a nickname and the genuineness of descent from the Prophet disputed.

Once Ahmad became a father, he refrained from telling his son about his identity because "once he knows he will also feel the pain. He will feel that people do not like him because he is a *sayyid*. I want to protect him from the harassment we have experienced ourselves." When his son, `Ali, had reached the age of 11, his father told him that he had to start praying. `Ali asked why he had to assume his religious duties earlier than Muhammad, his close friend whose father is one of Ahmad's colleagues. His father explained to him that he had to conduct himself in the best possible manner. Dissatisfied with the reply, `Ali repeated his question. "Because you are a descendant of the Prophet (*ibn al-nabi*)" he was told. "Am I?" `Ali was astonished and proud. In the end, perhaps spurred by his own pride, Ahmad told his son about their social background and drew his attention to the fact that as a *sayyid*, he was expected to perform especially well in society and had to be serious about his religious duties.

Reflecting on that encounter, Ahmad told me that his son had probably suspected that he was from the Prophet's progeny. Ahmad's children have asked questions that had troubled him during his childhood. "Why do people dislike Imam `Ali? Why don't they love his descendants (*awladuhu*)?" Their father explained to them that people are resentful toward those whom they cannot emulate. "`Ali was very honest, he was too generous and kind; he was close to God, and immensely courageous. He put people on trial; they had to learn to love him. `Ali taught us to be kind and humble." It was Imam `Ali's heroism that most impressed the young `Ali, and he asked his father to let him read his biography. On the eve of the twenty-first century, however, Ahmad felt that the Sunni Islamists had strengthened to the extent that the Zaydis should no longer declare themselves.[11] "If my son asks me any questions about the *zaydiyyah*, I no longer answer him. I do not want him to be in trouble."

Ahmad's daughter, Zaynab, has a girlfriend who belongs to a family that holds decidedly anti-*sayyid* sentiments. Ahmad thinks that the girl has been vaunting her own family at the expense of his daughter's.

> They give her more sweets than we give our daughter. That way they try to outperform us. My daughter is aware of this. Once her friend told her "You are not a *sharifah*" to which my daughter replied, "How do you know?" The girl said "I know you are not." Later that day my daughter told me that it was wrong to challenge her friend. She felt she should have just kept quiet.

Ahmad reappropriated his family history through his reading of Zaydi history. He took pride in his descent, but was troubled by the ruthless ways in which some members of the Prophet's House had pursued power. He noted that even though Zaydi doctrine required the believers and above all the *ulama* to criticize violations of religious principles, some of his ancestors were known for their cruelty and had imprisoned and killed those who had censured their style of governance.

> Imam `Abdullah b. Hamza (d. A.D. 1217) killed many *ulama* because they opposed him, and so did several others. One of my ancestors, who was an Imam, read the Qur'an each night and spent long hours praying. He bravely fought foreign invaders which is why many *ulama* praise him. They think that he was an Imam of both the pen and the sword. But he treated his enemies with cruelty. After a revolt, the men captured by his soldiers had to carry the impaled heads of their slain comrades from one town to another. Some had their feet tied and were dragged across the rubble by horses.

Ahmad's critical appraisal of Zaydi history may be interpreted as a demythologizing of the past which is conducive to coming to terms with the present.[12] However, in the present political circumstances some elderly *sadah* are uncomfortable with the exposure of Imam `Abdullah b. Hamza's style of rule. A couple of years ago, a Yemeni historian published an article about the Imam's destruction of a village inhabited by people who adhered to a movement the Imam had declared as heretical. The author uncovers memories of the raids and the raping of women by the Imam's soldiers. Some scholars reacted angrily, accusing him of playing into the hands of their republican enemies who paint a dark picture of Zaydi history. These scholars argued that disclosure of these facts could only harm the *sadah*.

Qasim al-Taghi

Qasim, whose father played a prominent role in the revolution, belongs to one of the formerly underprivileged branches of a renowned *sayyid* house. His location *between* the high-ranking *sadah* and non-*sadah* (*Qahtaniyyin*) has produced a sense of self constituted in ambivalent displacement and belonging. This condition, it must be kept in mind, is not entirely contradistinctive to the past. Indeed, memory inscribes a time–space, which does *not* privilege the revolution; rather it produces continuities between the past and the postrevolutionary present. Qasim's case highlights the range of possible self-definitions within the category "sayyid." He was not brought up to conduct himself like his peers from more distinguished backgrounds, nor does he believe that kinship with the Prophet obliges him to be pious.

Qasim's family traces descent to a famous Imam who ruled in the seventeenth century. However, in the last two centuries none of his family has been eligible for the supreme office because they no longer fulfilled the requirement of excellent scholarship.[13] The lack of education and poverty reflected broad divisions in Imamate society that also accounted for the social heterogeneity among the *sadah*. People like Qasim's family experienced the cleavages of descent-based dominance and internal diversity differently from other *sadah* because of their intermediate position, as representatives of the Imamate in their own right by reason of their kinship with the ruler, yet subordinate within the Prophet's House. Qasim's father's perception of the *sadah* who held the reins of power was not fundamentally different from that of *Qahtaniyyin* who contested Imamate rule. His memories place emphasis on the misery suffered even by members of the *sayyid* nobility, revealing that master narratives of *sayyid* rule with their utopian rhetoric of a just social order did not prevent profound moral scrutiny and desire for a change of regime. In spite of his participation in the revolution and his subsequent assumption of a governorship in the area formerly ruled by his more fortunate relatives, Qasim's father has not suffered less discrimination than them. The experience of identification with a vilified regime echoed his earlier debasement as a low-ranking *sayyid*. Underprivileged *sadah* like him, who risked their lives for the republic, have come to realize that in the aftermath of the revolution, no distinctions were made between them and the Imams' loyal servants. These *sadah* both identify with and feel disillusioned with the revolution. During the 1950s, Qasim's father questioned his loyalty to a state that purported to represent the *sadah*, but had little to offer to men like him. Collaboration with other revolutionary officers meant that he abandoned `Alid ideology and risked denunciation by other *sadah* without gaining full recognition as a republican in the newly created state. Therefore, he dissociates the memory of the revolution from the republican regime by which he feels betrayed.

Unlike some boys from learned houses (*buyut al-`ilm*) who thought about becoming Imams, Qasim never cultivated such dreams. When he was still young, he experienced the prejudice held against the *sadah* by his schoolmates, and still feels ambivalent about his identity even today. However, it would be wrong to assume that his identity lies in nothing more than *not being Qahtani*. He held the view that the *sadah* were different from other people by virtue of their history and their exclusion from certain impure occupations such as butchering and tanning, but not that they should be granted any privileges.[14]

> When I was a child, my parents did not talk to me about our virtues as *sadah* or about the history of the *ahl al-bayt* and the Imams. We possess genealogical

records but they were never shown to me. I and my brothers learnt about ourselves from other children who called us "sayyid" in a derisive way. When I attended elementary school in the 1960s, the other boys informed me that they belonged to *qabilat* so-and-so. This made me wonder who I belonged to. They told me in a negative way what I was. Our teachers told us about the Imams' struggle against the colonizers [the Ottomans], but most of the time they portrayed the Imams as evil. They told us that the revolution would lead the nation into a bright future. The students were brought up to hate the Imams. I learned more about my background when I began reading about the history of the *ahl al-bayt* and the Yemen in my twenties.

In those days [after the revolution], many *sadah* changed their names. Titles like `Imad al-Din ("the pillar of religion") were no longer used. For several years I did not even know that my cousin's name was Sharaf al-Din ("the honour of religion"). I only heard him being addressed as Sharaf. A few years after the revolution, my aunt suddenly called him Sharaf al-Din. I was confused and told her that his name was Sharaf. Then I understood.

My father supported the republicans. During President Nasir's heyday, he listened to the radio programs from Cairo all night, and then talked to people about them when he went to the suq the next day. He stopped wearing the `imamah* (headgear worn by men of the religious elite) and dressed in a suit. He was seen as a traitor by other *sadah*. I grew up in a revolutionary milieu, and I almost hated the *sadah*. We were very poor; we did not benefit from the system at all. Yet all *sadah* were held responsible for what the Imams did. After the revolution my father became a governor. However, he became estranged from the new regime when it began to attack the *sadah* collectively. He felt he was living in a hostile environment. When my brother married the daughter of a royalist, he was delighted, though other members of the family were less approving.

After the wedding, one of his wife's kin told me "they do not share more than blood." Qasim was conscious of the difference between his family and the high-ranking *sadah* who had a classical education. Although he and his brother obtained university degrees and have succeeded in their careers, they felt that the *sayyid buyut al-`ilm* did not recognize them as equals. Qasim's brother, who often appeared careless to his wife, was told by her that "he was a *qabili*", and should avoid acting as a role model for their child.

On the other hand, Qasim shared a sense of insecurity with other *sadah* and resented the prejudice held against them by some of the *Qahtaniyyin*.

The others [the *Qahtaniyyin*] think that we should be expelled from the country, that we have no right being here. They think that none of us should be in a good position. My half-brothers are different from me and my brother because their mother is not of *sayyid* descent. They are more relaxed and happy, they do not worry about life like us.

Qasim's ambivalence about his identification with the normative expectations that "sayyid" entails might also explain why he does not feel obliged to express filial piety in public. For most *sadah*, religious practice is a commemoration of the past, which is imbued with values of kinship, a past which for men like Qasim is both identity constituting and alienating.

> I no longer know how to pray. When friends ask me to lead the prayer I apologize.

Qasim's wife told me what happened when the couple lived in New York and the martyrdom of al-Husayn was commemorated at the local mosque. This ritual (`Ashura) is an occasion for expressing personal allegiance to the Prophet and his family.

> Of course I was eager to attend and I encouraged my husband to join me. He asked me "Why mourn someone who died so long ago?" My mother then told me to stay home with my husband and I didn't go either.

Qasim's failure to attend the emotionally charged rituals, which are chief agents of "memory bonding"[15] and which interpret the past on behalf of believers, helps him to distance himself from a subjectivity that is structured around discourses of persecution and martyrdom. By declining to attend the ritual, Qasim repudiates the melancholic turning inward that characterizes these occasions. On the other hand, his biographical memory has produced a sense of victimization, a classical Shi`i theme related by *sadah* who perceive a continuity between the history of persecution suffered by the *ahl al-bayt* and the recent past. Against the background of Qasim's experience of marginality, poverty, and stigmatization by reason of his remote kinship with the ruling dynasty, his refusal to fully inhabit the past is a poignant reminder of the potential social and psychic cost of living under the sign *sayyid*. Why should he identify with a personalized history of death and tragedy, a history that was enacted by the powerful "others" among his kin? The question of how Imamate history since the days of Imam `Ali is to be remembered will occupy young *sadah* in the following decades. Qasim, for one, insists that remembrance is better directed to the living and to the future than to the past.

Name Calling

Ahmad developed his sense of identity through negative identification after experiencing verbal abuse by his playmates. After the suppression of the Imamate's political culture that had drawn on symbolism associated with the *ahl al-bayt*, it was possible for *sayyid* children to grow up ignorant of their background. When the young Ahmad was labeled "sayyid" by his peers, the term was intended to be demeaning, yet he did not understand it. When he finally found out, he was asked to keep quiet about it. Experiences of this kind have undermined both Ahmad's and Qasim's confidence. As Judith Butler notes, speech that injures lays one "open to an unknown future"; it highlights "the volatility of one's 'place' within the community of speakers." The force of a contemptuous name "depends not only on its iterability, but on a form of repetition that is linked to trauma, on what is, strictly speaking, not remembered, but relived, and relived in and through the linguistic substitution for the traumatic event."[16] As demonstrated by Ahmad's case, a person's sense of distinctness can be potent, or perhaps more potent, when it is not deliberately taught. The circumstances in which he acquired a memory of the word his mother told him to forget served to increase its mnemonic power. For Ahmad, it was the sound of the unknown word shouted at him, the word that took the same trajectory as the stone thrown at him that gave the event historical weight. In the 1960s, for some *sadah* the honorific title "sayyid" that had been so central to Imamate rule became a private memory even while they suffered discrimination in its name.

People who are reluctant to pass the memory of being of *sayyid* descent to the next generation are forced to engage with the past even while attempting to shed it. One day I was talking to a scholar when his six-year-old daughter returned home in a confused state of mind. Nabila, one of her playmates, had told her "You are a Hashimi, you are bad (*anti hashimiyyah, anti shu'ah*)." "You had better stop playing with her," her father told her, declining to explain the meaning of "hashimiyyah" to her. After she had left the room, he explained to me "I do not want her to know, I do not want her to feel different from the other girls. If I tell her that she descended from the Prophet, I have to tell her about our family. I never told her that her uncle was executed [in 1962] and that we lost our property. She would start to feel resentful."

However, when she had grown up, he agreed to her marriage to a member of the former ruling house. This marriage counteracted his earlier attempt to avoid raising her awareness of her distinctive status and the *sadah*'s persecutions during the 1960s. Her husband is denied both Yemeni citizenship and compensation for confiscated property. Like Qasim's father who had been an ardent revolutionary but welcomed his son's marriage to a girl of royalist background, this man was saddened by the ongoing discrimination against the *sadah*. "Even if you lived abroad and changed your ideas about the Imamate," he said, "it will not be forgotten that you come from a certain family. You will always remain a reactionary (*raj'i*)."

Name calling may produce confusion and apprehension. However, uttering that name that is intended to be stigmatizing or left unpronounced may help in reasserting oneself. In one case, a 17-year-old girl who had an argument with a servant resisted the indignity she suffered by proclaiming her *sayyid* descent.

> For some time Taqiyyah had suspected the Somali servant of stealing things; some underwear and even cooking oil and flour had disappeared from the house. She told the servant that she had not been cleaning well and that things had gone missing. The servant became angry, countering that although she was working for peanuts, she had done rather well in her job. As they were shouting at each other, the servant asked the girl "And who are you anyway?" Taqiyyah was deeply insulted; as she threw herself backwards onto the cushions, she whimpered tearfully "I am a descendant of the Prophet! (*Ana bint al-nabi!*)"

By proclaiming herself to be a descendant of the Prophet, Taqiyyah carries the name "sayyid" like a badge of honor. Her behavior speaks of both vulnerability and self-possession. Not only had republican youth insulted her father by throwing his `imamah* (headgear) into the dirt while he was walking in the street in the early 1960s, but now even her servant tried to put her in her place. Butler raises the question of whether hate speech and even subtle disparagement always work and whether linguistic injury indeed produces social subordination.[17] The *sadah* resist identity formation through injury by refusing to accept the negative stereotyping that is often implied in references to the *sadah*. One *sayyid* told me that whenever he heard speech that stigmatized the *sadah*, he would challenge the speaker by asking him "I am a *sayyid*, what do you mean?" Thus, he at once exposes and counters the impudent exercise of this type of speech, leaving the meaning of the term unspecified and open to interpretation. This talking back, a kind of counterappropriation of offensive speech, screens the person from injury or at least mitigates it. This man appropriates the very name by which the *sadah* are abused in order to deplete it of its degradation, revaluing affirmatively the category label "sayyid."[18]

Name Dropping

One response to anti-*sayyid* prejudice is "self-willed amnesia" enacted through name dropping and renaming.[19] This is significant because patronymics and certain first names possess mnemonic agency, thus motivating people to think about or to remember certain events or people.

> I was sitting in the office of a high government official when his secretary brought him a note. "Ah!" he exclaimed, "Yahya Muhammad al-Nasir!

Why didn't he tell us straight away?" He had had two messages from a man called Yahya Muhammad, asking him to return his calls. Turning to me, interrupting our conversation, he said with a smile, "this man tries to be more republican than the republicans. When the army called upon professionals like him to undergo a few months of training, he signed up enthusiastically in order to demonstrate his patriotism. He wants it to be known that he no longer cares about his background. But he only makes things difficult for people like me. See how long it took me to find out who he is?"

Those who carry the patronymic know that people's response to their names is an ethical and political act.[20] Yahya's decision to abandon his name is a kind of self-disciplining aiming to foreclose "othering." As Moraru notes, "When names come . . . under attack something very disturbing is about to happen: the . . . obliteration of the other, expelling the other from a certain shared space, from culture, memory, and history."[21]

Yahya al-Nasir grew up in a northern province where his father was governor. Yahya's father died before the revolution, while his brother was executed. In his youth, Yahya had been influenced by the ideas of the 1948 reformers who demanded a constitutional government. He was dissatisfied with the education system, and when he reached adolescence he left Yemen in order to study in another Arab country. His brother's execution motivated him to join the royalist resistance to the new republican regime. On returning to Yemen, he no longer used his famous patronymic, which had been carried by several Imams and Muslim rulers before him.[22] Patronymics like Yahya's, which mark the body as *sayyid*, do not just confer recognizability and legitimacy over time. They bring the whole family history, the history of the Imamate, and even transnational histories to bear on the newborn who is thus named. During the Imamate, names such as these instituted a political reality and invoked relations of power and command, thus assuming a "*historicity*" in their own right. Moreover, "what might be understood as the history which has become internal to a name, has come to constitute the contemporary meaning of a name; a sedimentation that gives the name its force."[23]

Prominent patronymics, then, are narrative fragments that commemorate people, historical events, and relations of power—a connection that did not escape opponents of the Imamate such as Muhsin al-`Ayni, who became prime minister in 1972. Several years before the revolution, he wrote: "We want a ruler stripped of his holiness—we want a ruler called Salih, Sa`id, `Ali, just like you, me and other people. We have tried these (Imamic titles) al-Mutawakkil `ala 'llah, for 1,000 years, and the result is plain to see."[24]

Those *sadah* who omit their patronymics induce forgetting in themselves and others, thus suspending memory and dehistoricizing the body. This produces rupture but opens up avenues towards recreating the self and reconstructing relationships with others. It is the untold, "dropped" name that provides a stimulus for the redirection of life; as the object of genealogical and political history, it contrasts with names on gravestones that inscribe the dead person's kinship with the Prophet. Name dropping here is an "act of strategic ambiguity," producing the effect of an identity at play, a situational disengagement from stereotypical notions of *sayyid* identity.[25] Battaglia stresses the detachability of names from both the physical person and political value, which indicates the importance of the contextual and relational nature of acts of naming.[26] By repositioning himself as a person without a patronymic, Yahya obliterates a crucial aspect of selfhood, seeking to enjoy unequivocal recognition as a Yemeni like the *qaba'il*, the majority of whom do not carry patronymics. He wishes to counteract stereotypes of the *sadah* as people driven by a will to power. However, like those who pledge indifference to religious duties, he discovers the limits of his capacity to subvert the stereotypes commonly held by the new elite.

In another case, a man of a renowned *sayyid* house called his son ʿUmar after the second caliph. This man proclaims adherence to a marginal Zaydi school that recognizes the rule of the first caliphs and the supreme leadership of a non-ʿAlid.[27] The name ʿUmar had never been given to any member of his house. His brother, who is more attached to Shiʿi orthodoxy, admitted that he could not have given such a name to his son. The third brother called his sons al-Hadi (the guide) and al-Mahdi (saviour). Al-Hadi's name was carried by an Imam and by one of the boy's forebears who lived in the fifteenth century and was renowned for his piety. The young al-Hadi, who grew up knowing that both his grandfathers had been executed, studied science. When his first son was born, his father invoked the repertoire of names established by his forebears. However, he called his son after a ninth-century Iraqi Shiʿi poet. Nobody criticized him openly, but his father's teacher told me "I do not like this name. No one from the *ahl al-bayt* ever carried it." Rather than resurrecting the image of the poet, the name tells the story of the boy's father's journeys across old and new memory worlds. In spite of the name's association with a historic Shiʿi thinker, its trajectory is a mental space outside Yemen. By refraining from using his son's name as an interlocutor between the infant and the ancestors, the boy's father constitutes himself in terms of the discontinuity between a present and a past that he no longer fully inhabits yet has not lost.

Conclusion

In a thoughtful introduction to a collection of essays dealing with the tension between memory and history, Laqueur argues that in today's world, a bit less memory and a bit more history "would not be such a bad thing."[28] But are memory and history necessarily far apart? Reflections on this subject raise questions about the relation of memory to historical knowledge, and between narratives and the production of history, which I cannot tackle here. It would appear that *sadah* memorization—at once an interpretation of the past and in need of interpretation—is potentially a form of history making and even critical history. Memory, willfully or forcefully evacuated, is a kind of 'history in waiting;' because it is contested, it is political. Over the centuries, the *sadah*, among others, have been producers of "official history," and have testified to the fact that even personalized memory may translate into (or at least stimulate) explorations of the political and moral failures of Imamate rule.[29] In other words, memory of the recent past is a discourse of both victimization and of self-victimization.

It emerged from personal reminiscences that the former politically charged culture of remembrance offers little self-assurance and has occasionally given way to purposeful erasure and concealment caused by the fear of discrimination. Acts of willful "forgetting" (*not* naming oneself after the ancestors, *not* commemorating them) are about detachment from that culture so as to visualize a future and achieve full integration into republican society. Renaming, name dropping, and failing to name children after renowned *ahl al-bayt* produce a historically situated moral discourse for relocating the self. Many *sadah* are caught up in the conflict between denial and remembrance as when children are no longer brought up as *awlad al-nabi* (descendants of the Prophet).[30] However, as the case of Ahmad al-Husaynat illustrates, attempts at disconnecting themselves from this knowledge are constrained by the imperatives of the past, with its psychological sedimentation of specific memory regimes. This raises questions about the extent to which the self comes to fully believe what the body is made to perform. In many respects, memory of the *ahl al-bayt*, once central to public and political culture, has been scrutinized and suspended.[31] Intentional suspension of memory, despite its potentially liberating effects, is also "a form of bruising or scarring that necessarily entails loss of the word"—that self-imposed silence, *not* speaking one's name.[32] And yet the very act of refraining from doing, of relinquishing, shapes these people's sense of self, and is a kind of remembrance of what they once were and how they have made their contemporary lives.[33] The majority of *sadah* are not eager to recuperate an identity that is linked to exclusive claims to power, but ask for the right to remember their past without fear of being declared "foreigners."

However, the repression of memory is not just self-willed. In spite of the growing recognition of the cultural constitution of memory among psychologists and theorists of literature, these scholars have paid little attention to the politically imposed discouragement that is conducive to its repression.[34] The repression of memory (e.g., by genocide survivors) is treated as the subject's inability to deal with trauma and to communicate it in the form of narrative memory, partly as a result of the features of the forms of representation available to them.[35] As argued here, the (self) imposed silence about the revolution and emphasis on the loss congenial aspects of *sayyid* rule have led many Yemeni *sadah* to evacuate their memories of the past, a past they no longer authorize. However, the articulation of nonconforming memories of the revolution might provide healing integration for both individuals and the wounded national body.

Notes

I wish to thank Iris Jean-Klein for her insightful remarks on an earlier version of this chapter and Harold Schickler for editorial advice. A previous version was presented at a workshop on *Les identités dans le monde musulman aujourd'hui: Repli et dialogismes* organized by the Centre d'Histoire Sociale de l'Islam Méditerranéen (Ecole des Hautes Etudes en Sciences Sociales), November 2002. I benefited from the thoughtful remarks made by the participants and should like to thank Jocelyne Dakhlia and François Pouillon for inviting me.

1. Lisa Yoneyama, *Hiroshima Traces: Time, Space, and the Dialectics of Memory* (Berkeley: University of California Press, 1999), 26–7.
2. Cathy Caruth, "Introduction" *American Imago*, 48 (1991): 1–12. Special Issue: Psychoanalysis, Culture, and Trauma, 10.
3. On this issue, see Gabriele vom Bruck "Kinship and the Embodiment of History." *History and Anthropology*, 10 (1998): 263–98.
4. See, e.g., Paul Dresch "Imams and Tribes: The Writing and Acting of History in Upper Yemen." In *Tribes and State Formation in the Middle East*. Philip S. Khoury and Joseph Kostiner, eds. London: I.B. Tauris, 1991.
5. The Yemeni Imamate was founded by al-Hadi Yahya b. al-Husayn (d. A.D. 911), the leader of a Zaydi community in Madina, in the ninth/tenth century. The Zaydi-Shi`i doctrine that lent legitimacy to the Imamate distinguishes itself from the Twelver Shia by recognizing Zayd b.`Ali, the great grandson of Imam `Ali, as its founder. Rather than focusing attention on a hereditary line of Imams, the Zaydis are prepared to pay allegiance to any male descendant of `Ali and Fatima who has an excellent proficiency in the Islamic sciences and claims leadership by "rising" against tyrants (*khuruj*).
6. The supreme leader (Imam) was *de jure* chosen from among them.
7. A central ideological feature of this conflict are ancient divisions between the *Qahtaniyyin* ("southern Arabs"), who form the majority of Yemenis, and the `*Adnaniyyin* ("northern Arabs"). The *sadah* consider themselves to be `*Adnaniyyin*. These divisions formed part of revolutionary rhetoric during the 1960s and have been alluded to ever since.

8. Literally "People of the House." The term occurs in the Qur'an 33, 33 "God will remove the stains from you, oh people of the House, and purify you completely." It was interpreted especially among the Shia as referring to the Prophet's cousin `Ali, his daughter Fatima, and their sons al-Hasan and al-Husayn who are also mentioned in the famous "Mantle hadith."

9. D.Cohen cited in Ann Stoler and Karen Strassler "Castings for the Colonial: Memory Work in 'New Order' Java." *Comparative Study of Society and History*, 42 (2000): 17.

10. Names used in this chapter are fictitious.

11. In brief, they postulate a literal interpretation of the Qur'an and oppose *ijtihad* (independent judgment). Many consider the Zaydis—like the Shia in general—as *ahl al-bid'ah* or "innovators."

12. Yael Zerubavel, "New Beginning, Old Past: The Collective Memory of Pioneering in Israeli Culture," in Laurence J. Silberstein, ed., *New Perspectives on Israeli History: The Early Years of the State* (New York University Press, 1991), 208.

13. The predominant school of the Zaydi *madhhab*, the *hadawiyyah*, insists that the Imam be of `Alid descent and be erudite.

14. By virtue of their descent, most *sadah* used to consider the pursuit of these occupations to be dishonorable. However, according to Meissner, in Sharafayn in northern Yemen where he conducted fieldwork, some *sadah* worked as butchers. (See Tribes at the core: Legitimacy, structure and Power in Zaydi Yemen, continuation of edit) Ph.D. diss., Columbia University, 1987, 201.

15. Thomas Butler, "Memory: A Mixed Blessing," in *Memory: History, Culture, and the Mind* (Oxford: Basil Blackwell, Wolfson College Lectures, 1989), 20.

16. Judith Butler, *Excitable Speech: A Politics of the Performative* (New York and London: Routledge, 1997), 4, 36.

17. Ibid., 19.

18. Ibid., 13–15; Judith Butler, *The Psychic Life of Power: Theories in Subjection* (Stanford: Stanford University Press, 1997), 104.

19. Lawrence Rirmayer, "Landscopes of Memory: Trauma, Narrative, and Disassociation," in *Tense Past: Cultural Essays in Trauma and Memory*, Paul Antze and Michael Lambek, eds. (London: Routledge, 1996), 193.

20. Christian Moraru, " 'We embraced each other by our names': Levinas, Derrida, and the Ethics of Naming" *Names*, 48 (2000), 49.

21. Ibid., 58.

22. Unlike patronymics such as al-Nasir, first names do not always evoke the memory of persons but may still indicate noble status. Personal names associated with the Islamic tradition are commonly used all over Yemen. However, those female names equivalent to male two-part, theophoric names e.g., `Abd al-Rahman, "Servant of the merciful," were used exclusively by women of the elite e.g., Amat al-Salam, "Servant of peace" and Amat Allah, "Servant of God." Since the revolution these names have rarely been given to girls. Yahya al-Nasir had already changed the names of his daughters during the civil war. Both girls had names with the prefix "Amat." One of the girls, Amat al-Malik, "Servant of the king," was renamed Farida "precious pearl."

23. J. Butler, *Excitable Speech*, 36.

24. Quoted in Robert Serjeant, "The Yemeni Poet Al-Zubayri and his Polemic against the Zaydi Imams" *Arabian Studies*, 5, 1979, 96.
25. Debbora Battaglia, "Toward an Ethics of the Open Subject: Writing Culture in Good Conscience," in Henrietta Moore, ed., *Anthropological Theory Today* (Oxford: Polity Press, 1999), p. 126.
26. Ibid., p. 124.
27. The branch of the *zaydiyyah* that proclaims these ideas is the *salihiyyah*.
28. Thomas Laqueur, "Introduction" *Representations* 69 (2000): 1–8. Special Issue: Grounds for Remembering.
29. In this chapter, I have only touched upon this issue; see Gabriele vom Bruck "Disputing Descent-Based Authority in the Idiom of Religion: The Case of the Republic of Yemen." *Die Welt des Islams*, 38 (1998): 149–91; see 175–87.
30. Susan Slyomovics, *The Object of Memory: Arab and Jew Narrate the Palestinian Village* (Philadelphia: University of Pennsylvania Press, 1998) xiii.
31. Nowadays organizations such as the *mu'assasat ahl al-bayt*, which were established after unification in 1990, exist only in name, though one can of course find historical works about the *ahl al-bayt* in the bookshops.
32. Jocelyne Dakhlia, "New Approaches in the History of Memory? A French Model," paper delivered at the Marc Bloch Centre in Berlin, 1999.
33. On this aspect of forgetting, see Homi K. Bhabha, *The Location of Culture* (London: Routledge, 1994), 160–1; Ian Hacking "Memory Sciences, Memory Politics," in *Tense Past: Cultural Essays in Trauma and Memory*, Paul Antze and Michael Lambek, eds. (London: Routledge, 1996), 70; Karen Middleton "Circumcision, Death, and Strangers," in *Ancestors, Power and History in Madagascar*, Karen Middleton, ed. (Leiden: Brill, 1999), in 221.
34. Mieke Bal, "Introduction," in Mieke Bal, Jonathan Crewe, and Leo Spitzer, eds., *Acts of Memory* (Hanover and London: Dartmouth College 1999), x. Also see, e.g., Ted Swedenburg, *Memories of Revolt: The 1936–1939 Rebellion and the Palestinian National Past*. (Minneapolis: University of Minnesota Press, 1995); Stanley Cohen, *States of Denial: Knowing About Atrocities and Suffering* (Cambridge: Polity Press, 2001).
35. Craig Barclay, "Autobiographical Remembering: Narrative Constraints on Objectified Selves," in David Rubin, ed., *Remembering Our Past: Studies in Autobiographical Memory* (Cambridge: Cambridge University Press), 122; Ernst Van Alphen, "Symptoms of Discursivity: Experience, Memory and Trauma," in *Acts of Memory: Cultural Recall in the Present*. Mieke Bal, Jonathan Crewe, and Leo Spitzer, eds. (Hanover and London: Dartmouth College, 1999).

Chapter 10

Seeing Like a Citizen, Acting Like a State: Exemplary Events in Unified Yemen

Lisa Wedeen

Introduction

This chapter uses a discussion of three recent events in Yemen to dramatize the relationship between state power and the experience of citizenship in the aftermath of national unification in 1990.[1] The first event is a "direct," purportedly competitive presidential election on September 23, 1999, the first since unification and unprecedented in the histories of the former countries of North and South Yemen. The second is the celebration of the tenth anniversary of national unification on May 22, 2000, including the extraordinary preparations leading up to the event. The third is the public sensation following the arrest and prosecution of a man touted as Yemen's first bona fide "serial killer," which occurred during the lead-up to the decennial celebration.

As a period in the short history of unified Yemen, these years can be characterized as years of renewed political jockeying between a durable regime with meager institutional capacities, on the one hand, and a mobilized citizenry, on the other. These events are exemplary in the sense that each exposes aspects of lived political experience in Yemen—a country where lively, critical public discussion, a weak but multiparty system, a free press relative to other parts of the Arab world, and active civic associations indicate vibrant, participatory political practices in the absence of fair and free elections.[2] Viewing these episodes together makes it possible to draw more general comparative lessons about the anatomy of citizen contestation and regime control in newly forming nation-states.

Each of the events betrays a note of irony. The election was widely heralded as "the first free direct presidential election" ever held in Yemen, and there was never any doubt about the ability of the incumbent to capture the majority of the vote. Yet the ruling party, on dubious legal grounds, barred the opposition's jointly chosen challenger from the race and then appointed its own opponent. President `Ali `Abd Allah Salih had a chance to win what the world would have regarded as a fair and free election, but chose instead to undermine the process, using the apparently democratic form to foreclose democratic possibilities. In the case of the unification anniversary, both the preparations and the event itself required the regime to introduce state-like interventions in domains where they had never been seen before. In areas of everyday practice, such as garbage collection and street cleaning, the state made itself apparent to citizens in ways that could only serve to remind them of how absent it usually was. Finally, the revelation that a shocking series of murders had taken place inside the state-run university produced communities of criticism in which people found themselves sharing a sense of belonging to a nation the existence of which was merely imputed by the failure of the state to exercise its expected role of protecting its citizens.

The first two events pose a puzzle. In the case of the presidential election, why would a regime that was guaranteed to win a real election undermine its credibility unnecessarily? The case of the unification ceremonies repeats the puzzle in a different form (one common to many poor dictatorships). Why spend a reported $180 million on a celebration in a country with a per capita annual income of less than $300, when state coffers are drained and the IMF is pressing for austerity? The third event differs from the first two in that it occurred independently of state officials' intentions, if not, as critics were quick to point out, of state practices. Like the other two, however, the publicity surrounding the arrest and the discussion that animated public life in the aftermath of the grisly revelations exemplified the ways in which a political community is formed by the shared experience of events. In this case, unlike the other two, the publicity attending the arrest, rather than exaggerating the presence of state institutions, advertised their absence. Registered in reactions to this event is the "moral panic"[3] of citizens longing for a state capable of protecting them. By being aware of the simultaneous and common character of their anxieties, moral entitlements, and desires, even in the absence of state institutions, inhabitants of a common territory were able to experience a shared sense of connection to it.

This chapter explores three counterintuitive understandings of the relationships among state sovereignty, democracy, and nation-formation. First, whereas contested elections may require "strong" states and national coherence,[4] other forms of democratic activity, such as widespread political activism and lively public debates may exist *because* state institutions are fragile and affective connection to nationness only mildly constraining. As we shall see, the fragility of the state and the vibrancy of civic life mean that the regime's exercise of power is both blatant and intermittent. Second, common experiences of moral panic may be just as effective as, or even more capable than, state spectacles in generating a sense of passionate belonging to the imagined community of the nation. Third and relatedly, experiences of national belonging may actually be shared in the breach of state authority—in the moments when large numbers of people, unknown to each other, long for its protection. Or put differently, Yemen demonstrates how events of collective vulnerability can bring about *episodic* expressions of national identification. This chapter is devoted to elaborating these arguments while narrating the events that bring them to the fore.

The First Presidential Elections:
Acting Like a State, Part One

President `Ali `Abd Allah Salih has been in power for 25 years, as the leader of North Yemen since 1978 and of unified Yemen since its inception in 1990. Yet in spite of the regime's durability, the Weberian fantasy of a state that enjoys a monopoly on violence—legitimate or otherwise—is not remotely evident. In a country of 18.5 million people, there are an estimated 61 million weapons in private hands.[5] The state is incapable, moreover, of providing welfare, protection, or education to the population. Complaints are heard with incantation-like regularity all over Yemen about the absence of "security" (*aman*) and "stability" (*istiqrar*), the inability of the state to guarantee safe passage from one region to another, to put a stop to practices of local justice, and to disarm the citizenry. There is also little evidence to suggest that the incumbent regime has succeeded in constructing a sense of membership that is coherent and powerful enough to tie people's political allegiances to the nation-state. Yet, Yemen cannot be placed in the category of countries like Yugoslavia or Rwanda, where violence has destroyed communities and shattered the fragile political arrangements previously in existence. In an era when some nation-states are being challenged by ethnic conflict and the fragmentation of previously unified multinational political communities, while others are undermined by transnational patterns of migration and of capital accumulation, a never-before-united Yemen has managed to survive despite markedly weak institutional capacities and a peripheral location in the global economy.[6]

Unified Yemen came into being at the end of the cold war when a non-democratic state dependent on labor remittances and donor aid combined with an unsuccessful, authoritarian socialist one. The idea of Yemen as a single political entity preceded actual unification, as evidenced by constitutionally mandated goals in the two separate states calling for unity, by failed unity agreements, and by stories, songs, and poetry dating back to the early 1920s. Moreover, key figures in the socialist People's Democratic Republic of Yemen in the South were from the North, and politicians in the North's Yemen Arab Republic hailed from the South. Yet, importantly, unlike other recent examples of unification such as Vietnam and Germany, North and South Yemen had never united into a single nation-state before 1990.[7] In this sense, the Republic of Yemen is not an instance of "re-unification," but a new experiment in nation-state formation. Or put differently, although nationalist identification with the state requires ongoing work in any country, there were no prior political arrangements that regulated membership in a territorially determinate association of Yemeni citizens, who, as "a people," could identify themselves with an existing common political authority.

Unification between North and South occurred under the condition that a transition to democracy would take place. And in the early 1990s, openly contested elections for parliament, a wide array of critical newspapers, and a plethora of political parties made Yemen one of the only Middle Eastern countries to tolerate peaceful, adversarial politics. Then the brief, two-month Civil War of 1994 altered the conditions of democratic possibility, producing an annexationist politics that continues to reinforce northern dominance.[8] The parliamentary elections of April 1997, which the Yemeni Socialist Party (YSP) and two other small, southern based opposition parties boycotted, were widely understood to be less democratic than those in 1993.[9] Voter turnout in the South was low, the ruling party won a clear majority of seats (187 out of 301), and the seats of the main Islamicist party, *al-Tajammu` al-Yamani lil-Islah*, decreased from 62 to 53.[10] Indeed, although the ruling General People's Congress (GPC) party and the main Islamicist party had forged an informal coalition for the 1997 elections, thereby agreeing not to oppose each other in specific districts, many "independents" in those districts turned out to be identified with the ruling GPC party. As a consequence, the ruling party's control of parliament was overwhelming in 1997—close to 266 seats, or 75 percent of the assembly.[11] In some districts, outcomes were decided in advance, failing to fulfill even a "minimalist's" view of a democracy in which electoral outcomes are uncertain.[12] The 1999 presidential "election" both demonstrated and contributed to the assertion of northern control and the corresponding constriction of permitted, institutionalized political contestation.

Although the regime represented itself to foreign donors and citizens alike as an "emerging democracy,"[13] the staged elections could not possibly have been intended to reassure Yemeni democrats or foreign observers of the regime's commitment to institutionalizing competitive, free elections. Opposition leaders wondered aloud when an "ornamental democracy" (*dimuqratiyya shakliyya*) might become a genuine one. In newspaper articles and other public venues, people identified with the opposition denounced the elections as mere "trappings" (*libas*)—another example of a "theatrical comedy" on the part of the regime, which was gradually narrowing the prospects for democratic politics in Yemen.[14] The political scientist, Muhammad 'Abd al-Malik al-Mutawakkil, even likened the event to "a Hindi film—long, boring, and exorbitantly expensive."[15]

Two months before the election a unified opposition had chosen its candidate for president, 'Ali Salih 'Ubbad, or "Muqbil," the Secretary General of the YSP, a southerner who, everyone acknowledged (even Muqbil), had no chance of winning, but who could put forth an alternative agenda, increase people's awareness of democratic practices by competing, and open up possibilities for future electoral successes. In order to begin his campaign, however, Muqbil had to be approved by 10 percent of parliament's members. This system, borrowed from Tunisian judicial codes, enabled the regime to weed out undesirable nominees, and Muqbil's candidacy was thereby rejected. Thus the regime, rather than sailing to victory in an openly contested election, chose to disqualify the opposition candidate, turning the event into the phony referendum familiar to many postrevolutionary and postcolonial polities. Nor did the ruling party stop there. To replace the opposition's candidate, the regime nominated one of its own southern members, Nagib Qahtan al-Sha'bi. The son of its first president, who was deposed and imprisoned in 1969 during a coup d'état carried out by socialists, Nagib and his family had fled to Cairo where they had received support and protection for years from the antisocialist North. Election day, then, offered people the choice between two candidates from the same party, the ruling president from the North, and the puppet-like contender whose origins were identifiably southern. One published cartoon depicted Nagib as a windup toy. A joke echoed this sentiment: "Nagib is elected and is then asked, 'what is the first thing you are going to do?' He replies: 'Make 'Ali 'Abd Allah Salih president.' "

Yet, even by producing a bogus alternative candidate, the regime enabled some form of limited choice. A few people voted for Nagib Qahtan despite his compromised candidacy. As a taxi driver from Ta`izz argued: "even though I don't know Nagib, he's got to be better than `Ali `Abd Allah. The president steals and he allows others to steal. And when a good prime minister like Faraj Bin Ghanim tries to intervene, he is sacked."[16] People were broadly aware that they could register their protest in at least four ways: they could boycott the election; they could vote for Nagib; they could cross out both candidates' pictures; or they could write in a candidate, as some people claim to have done. For instance, several state employees and opposition politicians reported people writing in the name of Sa`d Zaghlul, a famous Egyptian nationalist who died in 1927. Rumors circulated that another voter wrote "stupid" (*ahbal*) below Nagib's picture and "robber" (*sariq*) under the president's.

According to official reports, more than 66 percent of the electorate took part in the presidential election, with President `Ali `Abd Allah Salih garnering 96.3 percent of the vote. Independent observers and opposition party members alike, however, estimated that only 30 percent of registered voters bothered to go to the polls. In the aftermath of the election, stories abounded about poor voter turnout, 3,000 stuffed ballot boxes hidden in reserve, army personnel dressed in civilian clothing casting additional ballots, and minors voting—some more than once.[17] The act of voting required people to put their thumbprint on the computer generated list of registered voters, and afterward regime supporters and fearful citizens were eager to signal loyalty by displaying their inked thumbs in public. Stories were told of people who had failed to vote purchasing inkpads from local stores in order to dissemble having participated. People reported being visited by friends checking to see whether they had voted. The inked thumb became a particularly fraught signifier registering either participation in the elections or the fear of having not done so. Or to put it differently, an inked thumb could mean that a person had participated out of duty, love, or fear, or that a person had not participated but could act "as if" he had.[18] The following joke speaks to the latter condition: "A guy goes to a qat chew and shakes hands with his thumb up to prove that he has voted [a practice many adopted the day after the elections].[19] His friend says, 'why is your thumb red?' He replies, 'they ran out of blue inkpads at the store.'"

The ballot sheets themselves, however, signaled the solemnity of official state practice. Colored photographs and the names of the two candidates appeared on each ballot. `Ali `Abd Allah Salih was pictured in suit and tie. Below him were the hallmarks of his campaign, three encircled images, the logos of the three main groups that had ostensibly supported the president: The *al-majlis al-watani* (a loosely knit group of parties, including Ba`thists and some Nasirists) depicts three hands clasping a torch to symbolize unity; the main Islamicist party, *al-Tajammu` al-Yamani lil-Islah*, portrays the sun shining brilliantly on the horizon to connote a "bright future"; and the ruling GPC party's insignia is the horse—symbol of power and bravery (*shumukh*) or of a shared Arabian genealogy (depending on whom one asks). Nagib Qahtan's portrait was set against the backdrop of a sky, the scales of justice to the right, a rather innocuous reference to (both candidates') declared commitments to procedural justice and judicial reform.

Political posters of the president also covered the walls of buildings and the windows of shops.[20] The Delacroix-like portrait of `Ali `Abd Allah Salih astride a stallion and draped in a billowing Yemeni flag conjured up for some Yemenis images of `Ali ibn Abi Talib, the son-in-law of the prophet and a symbol of legitimate rule for Zaydi (Shi`i) Islam. The original poster, which towers over a main commercial thoroughfare, allegedly cost the regime $13,000, an exorbitant sum for ordinary citizens.[21] Other posters combined `Ali `Abd Allah Salih's portrait with advertisements for companies such as Canada Dry and Daewoo, thereby blending domestic kitsch with global capitalism in ways that probably saved the regime some money. Corporate endorsements signified that the president enjoyed the backing of capital, and that investor confidence was indifferent to, if not supportive of, phony electoral processes.

No one disputed that the Yemeni president would have won an openly contested election against Muqbil, if not by the margin by which he allegedly actually won. As the political scientist François Burgat points out, had leaders of the Islamicist party, *al-Islah*, decided to put forward their own nominee, there might have been some cause for concern among regime officials, but the party's decision to support the president eliminated any prospects for competition, even before the regime's denial of Muqbil's candidacy.[22] Salih's assured victory raises the question of why the regime would bar the opposition's candidate, guaranteed to lose a fair and free election, from running. Members of the opposition and the ruling party speculated that Muqbil's personality was to blame; he was difficult and refused to ingratiate himself with members of Parliament who might have voted to allow his candidacy. In the words of one opposition politician, "Muqbil doesn't hold his tongue—he'll say anything, and the impact on public opinion of criticizing the president's personality directly inclined the president to make that decision." Politicians close to the president and in the opposition argued that `Ali `Abd Allah Salih had personally ordered Parliament's members to deny Muqbil's nomination. The president was worried, in this view, that a YSP candidate would polarize North and South, thereby solidifying deep, regional divisions that had emerged after union and had worsened in the aftermath of the civil war. "Victory" required more than winning the elections; it demanded a vision of unity in

which 'Ali 'Abd Allah Salih could represent both regions. Being a "tacti-
cian" rather than a "strategist" or statesman, argued one presidential advisor, meant that the president missed a historical opportunity, thereby
revealing himself to be like other dictators who prefer garnering a literally
unbelievable number of votes, rather than risk the political uncertainty that
a less decisive but more credible victory would have entailed. One key
opposition figure likened the president to "a guy who sells groceries at a
road stand" (*sahib al-sandaqa*): "he's busy with the little things and can
profit from the details, but he loses sight of the big picture. He has small
ideas." Slogans congratulating the "father of Ahmad" (*Abu Ahmad*) also
suggested the regime's dynastic ambitions, thereby implying that although
the president knew that he would win, he did not want to set precedents
that might endanger his son's succession. In contrast, some educated professionals who defended the regime justified Salih's move by arguing that
democracy must proceed gradually. This referendum was a first step in
getting people used to the process, and future presidential elections would
be more democratic than this one. Within a roughly familiar "civilizing
process" narrative, arguments about ill-prepared citizens suggested that
some elites in Yemen viewed citizens as not yet ready to engage in the
mature electoral processes of the developed world. No one, however, could
answer why the regime would put forth another candidate from its own
party in Muqbil's stead—a variation on the sham election that, to my
knowledge, has no historical precedent.

I want to argue that the orchestrated event not only ensured an electoral
outcome that was already obvious, but also provided an occasion for the
regime to announce and enact its political power. This political power, in
turn, resides and was made manifest in the regime's use of democratic procedures in order to empty democracy of what liberals take to be its content:
fair, competitive elections. The elections signaled that "support" for the
president, by those who admire, fear, and loathe him, was becoming tied to
public performances of democratic openness *and* to the sense of lost opportunities such public performances reiterated. For example, in response to a
questionnaire asking whether she "supported the government's policies," a
housekeeper from the distant, northern mountainous region of Haraz said
that she did. When I asked her later how she could give this response when
she complained constantly about government actions, she explained, "I'm
with them because what's the point of being against them . . . right? They're
the ones in power." The elections communicated this absence of actual
alternatives by presenting a bogus one.

This excessive bogusness operated as both a signaling device and a
mechanism for constituting the political power it signaled. The "elections"
conveyed to politicians in the opposition and to disaffected ordinary

citizens that the regime would actively intervene to foreclose democratic possibilities. The elections were constitutive because they provided the occasions through which the regime could impose this authoritarian impulse onto citizens—at least temporarily. Even when such disciplinary strategies are contested, they are still partially effective—organizing men and women to participate and consume the regime's idealized version of the real. Men and women worked to register voters and to ensure that polls functioned in an orderly fashion. Soldiers were bussed in to vote and ensure stability. Official institutions, including foreign donor organizations,[23] devoted time and money to organizing and orchestrating an event everyone knew to be fraudulent. People gathered together in crowds to hear both candidates avow their commitments to institutional reform, stability, security, the material well-being of ordinary citizens, and to democracy itself. The event had the effect of exercising power by announcing it publicly, thereby forefending against the deleterious effects of weak state institutions and IMF pressures by reminding citizens that even regimes without a monopoly over violence have some measure of control.

Some part of the control a regime exercises derives from its efforts to act like a state. Such enactments always rely on preexisting mechanisms of coercive, utilitarian, and normative compliance. As this chapter shows, in the case of Yemen, where the preexisting forms are especially meager, the way the regime of `Ali `Abd Allah Salih attempts to bring itself into being as a state can be seen especially clearly. No regime actually enjoys an undisputed monopoly over force, if crime statistics are any indication, but the Yemeni regime's coercive control is exceptionally limited, especially outside the capital. Nevertheless, Yemen does have an army, many of whose key officers derive from the president's region and family grouping of Sanhan in the Northern Highlands. The army has been used to quell resistance in the northeastern areas of Ma'rib and al-Jawf, as well as in the southern areas, such as Kud Qarw village (near Aden) and in al-Dali`. *Human Rights Watch* reports the detention of political prisoners, torture, and death sentences.[24] In the past, the regime has also threatened to dissolve a main opposition party, the YSP, and has harassed the independent press on a number of occasions. Security officials infiltrate opposition organizations in order to intimidate and divide would-be dissidents while also providing information about subversive activity to the president.

Even so, a key aspect of the Yemeni example is that such forms of social control do not generate the sorts of fear characteristic of many dictatorships. The government's deployment of military and paramilitary units has usually been a *response* to an overt challenge to the regime's authority rather than a prophylactic, protective form of preempting dissent. Yemen, moreover, possesses a dense network of associations and a degree of local civic participation unparalleled in other parts of the Arab world.[25] In the (qualified) public spheres of opposition-oriented conferences, political party rallies and meetings, Friday sermons, newspaper debates, and qat chew conversations—even in the daily television broadcasts of parliamentary sessions—Yemenis from a variety of regional and class backgrounds routinely criticize the regime without fear of repercussions found in regimes classified as "authoritarian."

The regime also exploits its utilitarian mechanisms of social control by purchasing the loyalty of would-be subversives. Automobiles, homes, vacations, and foreign bank accounts are perquisites of allegiance. Politicians who do not support the regime may also periodically benefit from its largesse. Influential opposition figures sometimes have to make difficult choices about whether to accept such amenities as a bodyguard or a car for the family or money for medical treatment abroad—decisions that may ease life's burdens but may require compromises or generate unsettling questions about political commitments. In the absence of a state capable of delivering public goods and services through common administrative institutions, political figures who have no sources of independent wealth may have to rely on the personal largesse of regime members.

Finally, the northern, Sanhan-dominated regime seems genuinely popular in key areas of the North and in isolated parts of the South. The North is not a unified region, but many inhabitants—especially in the capital and the Northern Highlands—actively support the president even when they do not have to. The working class area of Hudayda in the Tihama, the city of Ta`izz and much of *al-mintaqa al-wusta* or "middle region," as well as parts of the northeastern desert regions of al-Jawf and Ma'rib, do not overwhelmingly support the regime—if riots and organized, armed resistance are any indication. Even in these areas, however, some would have voted for the president. Although the minority of Yemenis living in the South would probably have voted for a southern candidate, had a genuine representative of the region run for the presidency, the South's small population (of anywhere from 2.5 to 4.5 million inhabitants) would not have significantly affected the president's electoral majority.[26] Moreover, dissatisfaction with the former rule of the socialist party among groups who self-identify as "tribal" in the interior, or *wadi,* region of Hadramawt would have given the president some support there. The ruling GPC party has enjoyed backing among southern groups whose organizations were prohibited during the socialists' rule there. Despite electoral infractions during parliamentary elections of 2003, the YSP's poor performance—the party won seven seats out of 301—further supports the claim that the president would have won a fair and free election. The common assumption that nondemocratic regimes have no popular support is

belied by the president's observable popularity in many areas. Even ambivalent voters argued on more than one occasion that "the devil you know is
better than the devil you don't."[27] Given the president's ability to win a
credible election (or, for that matter, to rig one covertly), the regime's decision to produce an overtly phony one implies that the event did more than
exemplify political power; it was also doing the work of creating it by
demonstrating to officials and citizens alike that the regime could get away
with the charade.

Arguably, postelection politics have continued to narrow possibilities for
institutionalizing liberal democracy. In an August 2000 letter to the speaker
and members of parliament, President `Ali `Abd Allah Salih and 144 members of parliament recommended constitutional amendments that would
lengthen parliamentary members' tenure in office from four to six years,
thereby postponing elections scheduled for April 2001. A nationwide referendum in February 2001 approved this extension and also lengthened the
presidential term from five to seven years, thereby enabling Salih to remain
in office until 2013 when opposition leaders anticipate that Salih's son,
Ahmad, will make a bid to take over. The referendum also authorized the
president to appoint a 111-member "Consultative Council," which
activists charge will allow the president to offset the role of the elected parliament and promote indirect executive control over legislation. Moreover,
elections for local councils, held at the same time as the referendum, were
marred by opposition charges that voter registration lists had been rigged.
Violence also undermined free elections. Forty persons reportedly died and
more than a 100 were injured in clashes between supporters of different
parties and security forces; official sources claimed that 11 died and 23 were
injured. Disputes over irregularities in at least 20 percent of the poll centers
meant that final results in those areas were never announced. The ruling
GPC party celebrated a comfortable majority in the councils, but opposition leaders charged that results were fraudulent. Even were outcomes to be
fair, the local councils' resources and decision-making powers remain circumscribed by the fact that the president appoints the heads of the councils.[28] Preparations for the parliamentary elections of April 27, 2003 were
similarly tainted with charges of irregularities in registration, and postelection conflicts also raised doubts about the process. The unresolved assassination on December 28, 2002 of a key spokesman for liberal democracy,
Jar Allah `Umar, moreover, threatened to undermine a united opposition
and may have additional chilling effects on future institutionalized electoral
contestation.[29]

The ability to foreclose alternative possibilities to the regime's dominance is, in part, a result of "theatrical" occasions, such as the presidential
election, that the regime invents to reproduce its political power.[30] It is also

the product of a balancing act, which entails meting out punishments and distributing payoffs, as well as cultivating some belief in the regime's appropriateness. But the elections also suggest a "muddling through" approach to anxieties about citizen disorder and regional polarization in a world where civil society and the agonistic public conversations it generates are backed by the violent potentialities that an armed population makes apparent.

The Decennial Celebration: Acting Like a State, Part Two

The decennial celebration, like the presidential election, exemplifies the ways in which the regime attempts to redefine the terms of electoral politics and national unity, producing performances in which an identifiably northern regime specified its dominance (and southern subordination) simply because it could. The regime harnessed national spectacles to the task of constraining democratic practices by staging scenes of consensual unity and popular sovereignty. The posters of the president hoisting up the Yemeni flag, which were distributed in the weeks prior to the actual spectacle celebrating the tenth anniversary of unification, summarized the regime's approach to the founding of the nation-state. The same picture had originally depicted the presidents of North and South together in 1990; the northern president raised the flag while his southern counterpart stood behind him. In an effort to obscure the history of partnership that had initially animated union, the southern president's image had been deleted from the photograph of 2000.[31]

The festivities around the tenth anniversary of unification culminating in celebrations on May 22, 2000 illustrated the regime's idealized representation of national belonging. They also registered a paradox at the heart of the regime's state- and nation-building projects. On the one hand, unified Yemen was founded on what anthropologists Jean and John Comaroff have termed "the modernist ideal of the nation-state," a "polity held together by the rule of law, by the claim of government to exercise a monopoly over legitimate force, by a sense of horizontal connection, and by universal citizenship which transcends difference."[32] The celebrations around unification, orchestrated for both foreign and domestic consumption, were an attempt to project this image of the nation-state. On the other hand, the production of this ideal required the violation of some of its principles and the concealment of countertendencies, which include appeals to local justice or other assertions by regional communities—often termed "tribal"— against the jurisdiction of the state.[33]

In other words, in order to generate an image of a modernist nation-state, the regime had to do *whatever* was necessary to make the projection happen, or seem to happen, in actuality. For example, the unification festivities burdened the regime with a host of security concerns that, in turn, generated new forms of intervention and new efforts to monopolize force. The regime set up roadblocks, multiplied checkpoints, and ordered all mobile phones and pagers shut off at midnight on May 16. The regime also barred tourists from entering the country until June 1 to prevent the public relations fiasco that a kidnapping might cause. Unification celebrations made travel from one region to another particularly difficult. Rumors of curfews and of not being allowed to leave San`a' kept many people off the roads and in their homes.

The regime also made an extraordinary effort to be an effective state by delivering public services. The main streets sparkled with lights and were unusually clean. Garbage was collected more regularly than usual. Rumors suggested that workers actually moved refuse from areas of the city where the foreign delegations were visiting to areas of the city off the beaten path. Blue paint was distributed so that shop doors could be freshly coated. And residents of spacious homes in the posh area of Hadda were given money to vacate them so that visiting dignitaries could be comfortably housed in places outfitted with imported furniture. One educated woman in San`a' noted that the occasion demonstrated the regime's ability to provide state services, at least temporarily. In this light, her sisters raised questions about the regime's seeming lack of "political will" (*irada siyasiyya*) to build durable state institutions capable of ensuring citizens' protection and stability, and of providing the services for everyday life on a more regular basis than an official occasion demands.

Preparations also generated considerable ire among ordinary citizens. The celebrations cost anywhere from 20 to 50 billion riyals. In fact, teachers did not receive their paltry salaries and civil servants had their salaries halved in the month of April so that the regime could pay for the festivities. Regime officials were so concerned that the 1,600 youths mobilized to participate in the festival would fail to show up that they postponed the announcement of examination results to induce participation.[34] Those students who did not attend would automatically receive a failing grade. Air force planes had been flying in formation above the capital every morning for weeks, the deafening sounds from low flying aircraft a consistent reminder and, indeed, an instance of the excess associated with the ceremonies. Rumors that prices would rise once the celebrations were over also made people nervous and angry. In the working-class neighborhood of Hasaba, people hoarded food in preparation for imagined disasters. Even families identified with the ruling GPC party were anxious. One woman whose husband worked as a policeman asked why the regime would put on such a spectacle at a time when people have no money and the government is giving civil servants less of their salaries, or withholding salaries altogether in order to pay for the event. Another lower middle-class woman said, "many of my friends are stocking up on food because they are worried about a coup or something" during the ceremony. Another woman giggled, "we were afraid of the solar eclipse, and now we are afraid of the holiday." Another worried that the ceremony might result in an assassination, "like Sadat's." Apprehension around the event spoke to the regime's inability to ensure order routinely. As the above statements indicate, the fact that the regime could perform like a state raised questions about why it failed to do so regularly. People also reminded each other of the state's fragilities, so that activities in which the regime was required to be a state were fraught with anxiety.

The actual event began with `Ali `Abd Allah Salih's arrival in a motorcade to the official parade grounds where foreign dignitaries and Yemeni politicians were already seated. Only invited guests were permitted to view the festivities from the parade grounds, and invitations specified that would-be spectators had to gather at six in the morning at the Police College in order to be bussed to the stands where they would watch the festivities. For those viewing the event on television, the beginning of the broadcast showed an edited sequence of clips of the president in a variety of official contexts: crowds cheer him; he responds to questions at a press conference; and planes fly overhead in a display of Yemen's military might.

The president took his seat next to Saudi Arabia's Crown Prince `Abd Allah, perhaps the most important official to attend the ceremony. A panegyric to `Ali `Abd Allah Salih and the union could be heard over the loud speaker extolling the leader as the "symbol of the nation" (*ramz al-watan*) and the "creator of the glorious union" (*sani` al-wahda al-majida*). Like the posters that omitted the cofounder of the union, `Ali Salim al-Bid, the speeches, poems, and visual displays of the unification's anniversary attributed the union to a single founder. The former ruling party of the South proved a specter that haunted the proceedings for those whose memories of history or whose political commitments made them want some acknowledgment of the original founding. When the camera mistakenly aimed its lenses at rows of empty seats, knowing viewers could see the visible absence of socialist members who had decided not to attend.[35]

YSP members were divided about whether to accept invitations to the gala event. Some members argued that the holiday commemorated unification and therefore was every citizen's holiday. The victory of the North in the war was a separate event and should be treated as such. Other members argued that although they were for the union, the 1994 war was a big loss. Attending the celebrations would endorse the regime's version of unity and lend unwitting support to northern dominance. In one qat chew conversation held at this time, Jar Allah ʿUmar, the late Assistant Secretary General of the party, argued that "the absence of equality between North and South made the initial hopes of unification seem hollow, and its democratic possibilities elusive." For him, even the word "*infisal*" (secession) had lost its dangerously titillating charge. "People are likely to use the word or to threaten its invocation as a way of policing public space, but it has lost some of its meaning. Words like 'revolution' have also been emptied of their political significance, subject to the banalities of repetition." Some members favored a separate YSP celebration in Aden; while others maintained that the capital of Yemen was Sanʿaʾ and any national event should be held there. After multiple discussions, leaders decided to let individual party members decide for themselves whether to accept the regime's invitation. Some went to the event and others did not.

In terms of the modernist ideal of the nation-state, the celebration represented the image of universal citizenship that is part of that ideal, but in the Yemeni context the image required a hybrid of particular regional practices subsumed under an assertion of northern dominance that was intended to unify but proved divisive. This hybridity was most evident during the folklore sequences, when a clunky float of terraced mountains and the façade of *Bab al-Yaman* (the main entrance to the capital's traditional market) with ten candles on top and a big number 22 (for the original founding, May 22) on the front appeared on the grounds like a gigantic, mobile birthday cake. As the float moved to the center of the parade grounds, the names of the different regions of Yemen were recited over a loudspeaker system. Men on horseback and others with rifles dressed in Northern Highlands tribal dress and brandishing the conventional daggers (*janabi*, sing. *janbiyya*) filled the parade grounds. At times, the television zeroed in on participants who looked confused or whose horses were misbehaving, but as the spectacle progressed, television cameramen filmed an impressive array of men who combined dance steps from the Northern Highlands with those from the northeastern desert.[36] As the dancers moved in unison, the event began to take on the regimented character of a Busby Berkley extravaganza, with the synchronized moves and geometric shapes common to most mass spectacles. The choreographed folk dance part of the spectacle was the regime's effort to make Yemeni "culture" into an explicitly national object—one that hybridized North and South, coastal and interior regions of the country.[37] In one recognizably coastal dance, for example, a Northern Highlands dagger was used rather than the typical stick. In another dance, men performed stunning southern sword work while dressed in identifiably Northern Highlands clothing.

These spectacles undoubtedly put forth *images* of unity,[38] but there is little evidence to suggest that they either signaled existing unity or actually worked to *create* it. Thus the significance of these public exhibitions was not their ability to weld an inchoate national community together, although the festival may have generated feelings of communal pride for some. Rather, the festival defined national community in ways that required and advertised a substantial array of regulatory and intrusive capabilities associated with a state.

On the level of visual representation, such displays were open to multiple interpretations and invited resignification. For some self-identified northern and southern spectators, despite the projection of an explicitly unified national culture, each region's practices were both referenced and relativized in relation to northern, and more particularly Highlands, visual dominance. Others, particularly southerners, interpreted the spectacle neither as expressive of unity nor as an instance of northern dominance, but rather as the failure of an explicitly northern imagination to produce dances that did not borrow from the creative movements of the South.[39]

Although the spectacle's preparations required the careful consideration of the foreign delegates' comforts and distractions, the spectacle's images seemed primarily intended for domestic consumption. Few foreign spectators would be able to distinguish among various regional practices, but most Yemenis could. Similarly, the regimented military parade that followed the folkloric sequences implied the importance of the spectacle's domestic messages: ordered lines of soldiers in a modified goose step and varying colors of camouflage fatigues represented troops' respective institutional affiliations. The occasion also entailed displaying the latest addition to the Yemeni army's military technology with an air show and presentation of an "all-terrain armoured vehicle built exclusively in Yemen."[40] Although such displays of military power are typical of most national spectacles, it is inconceivable that Yemen's military hardware would frighten spectators from countries such as Saudi Arabia or the United States. Indeed as two firsthand Yemeni observers with experience in military affairs told me after the spectacle, the display of weapons was unlikely to impress foreign viewers, but was rather intended for domestic consumption. The description of the tank manufactured in Yemen suggests that Yemen's defense forces might have domestic uses for the tank: "the vehicle has bullet-proof armour plating and a high-velocity machine gun with the ability to turn 360 degrees mounted on top. With Yemen's varied landscape a key factor in its design, the vehicle has been adapted to perform in all conditions, particularly in mountain regions. Its flexibility and ability to operate at high speeds have impressed military observers, who expect it to be a vital part of Yemen's defence forces."[41]

The ordered, mass-mobilization event was the largest and most regimented of its kind in Yemen's history of spectacular displays. Yet the representations of consensual unity could not mask the underlying tensions that preparations for the event had made public. Even members of the ruling party disagreed on how the nation should be represented. Not unusually for any polity, gender was one site of contestation. Among the 100,000 participants, about 1,600 were ten-year-old boys and girls who represented the generation born after unification. Several Yemeni scholars, headed by Shaykh `Umar Muhammad Sayf, member of the GPC, issued a religious opinion (*fatwa*) prohibiting the participation of females in the parades, but their efforts came to nought. Why would the regime spend scarce resources and risk alienating important allies and ordinary citizens by producing such an event?

In part, the answer rests on insights drawn from the first event discussed in this essay. The example of the presidential "election," in which the regime put forth an opposing candidate from its own party and converted what had promised to be the first free, competitive race into a phony semblance of democratic politics, is an example of a regime acting to express political power for its own sake—to demonstrate its ability to induce modest participation in, and contain the disappointment of, bogus elections. Similarly, the unification ceremonies not only offered something of a preview image of a modernist nation-state, but they also enacted the conditions of its possible emergence by giving the regime an opportunity to act like a state. State intervention entailed putting into practice mechanisms of enforcement that helped ensure the regime's temporary monopoly over violence, as well as producing public services to which most citizens remain unaccustomed.

In both events we see the regime attempting to reproduce power by developing competencies that allow the regime to monitor and control citizens. These attempts are all the more remarkable in the context of the regime's fragile institutional capacities. The regime's efforts to reproduce its power have therefore tended to rely not on generating durable institutions (although there are some), but rather on the sporadic, intermittent assertions of power that strategies like spectacular displays allow. These spectacles may also be attempts to construct a national community in the absence of adequate state institutions, such as schools, generally entrusted with that role. It remains unclear, however, how successful such festivities are at actually generating, as opposed to projecting abstractly, national belonging.

Images of national unity do not paper over the divisions that generate lively worlds of debate in Yemen. Both the elections and the unity celebrations provided discursive contexts within which alternative forms of "groupness" and politics could take place. Indeed, in the absence of a repressive apparatus capable of controlling (let alone monopolizing) force, spectacles inspire public communities of political argument that are often at odds with the regime's vision of political dominance. The disclosure of serial killings on state property during preparations for the nation's anniversary celebration reinforced this disarticulation of state and nation, in which citizens could experience themselves as part of the nation without a state capable of ensuring communal safety.

Murders in the Morgue: Seeing Like a State, Part Three

The "murders in the morgue" case became public knowledge on May 10, 2000, when two mutilated female bodies were discovered at San`a' University. Two days later, police arrested a Sudanese mortuary technician at the medical school, claiming that he had confessed to raping and killing five women. Adam, also Muhammad Adam `Umar Ishaq (whose full name was rarely reported), was a 45-year-old Sudanese citizen who allegedly admitted to an increasing number of murders—16 in Yemen and at least 24 in Sudan, Kuwait, Chad, and the Central African Republic.[42] The Nasirist newspaper reported stories that he had killed up to 50 women.[43] It was said that Adam implicated members of the university's teaching staff who, he said, were involved in the sale of body parts. According to Brian Whitaker's account in *The Observer* one month later, Adam "had enticed women students to the mortuary with promises of help in their studies, then raped and killed them, videotaping all his actions. He kept bones as mementos, disposed of some body parts in sewers and on university grounds, and sold others together with his victims' belongings."[44]

A purported and obviously contrived interview with Adam published in the Yemeni armed forces newspaper, *26 September*, provided supposed details of the grisly killings, which registered the interviewer's fascination with the particulars and a desire for precision worthy of a detective, as in the following example:

> Interviewer: How did you kill and dispose of the corpse of your victim?
> Adam: I strangled her or I banged her head on the ground of the tiled floor.
> Interviewer: Immediately when she entered the morgue?
> Adam: As soon as the victim entered the morgue I hit her head on the wall or on the ground.
> Interviewer: And why did you cut up or slice your victim after that?

Adam: In order to obscure her features. I'd already started to cut up the victim and this cutting wasn't a process of slicing . . . I would cut her in half and I cut her body in parts and then I would hide it for two days or three days, and then I'd skin it and chop the rest into small pieces and I'd clean the bones and put them in the sink after dissolving the flesh in acid.[45]

When asked why he had "chosen" these specific women to kill, he answered: "The impulse (al-dafi`) is for some unknown reason (huwa hajjatan fi nafs ya`qub). When I see girls, specifically beautiful ones, in my mind something happens. I can never resist it."[46] Adam claims to have begun killing early, before he married, when he was 22 or 23 years old. He was supposedly influenced by Satanic books, especially those written by foreigners and translated into Arabic, such as an alleged book with the title, The Killer of Women (Qatil al-Nisa'). He also acknowledged that he was pained by his actions, but he could not explain what comes over him. When pressed to clarify what his motivation or impulse for killing was, he replied, "I kill her in order to let her enter heaven without her realizing, and I go to hell." When asked why he had spared his wife, he replied laughingly, "Is she a woman?" He flatly denied marketing the organs, and refused to say how many women he had killed in Yemen and abroad. (All of Adam's statements are from the same interview.)

In a broad spectrum of Yemeni newspapers, one or two pictures of the accused appeared. They showed either a wild-eyed man of color behind the bars of his cell, or an impish man in Sudanese dress, handcuffed. All newspapers uncovered the unfolding drama by reporting rumors, speculations, and questions that both reflected and generated anew a community of argument about the nature, causes, and disputed facts of the case. The progressive independent (then) tri-weekly al-Ayyam reported that the Council of the University of San`a' had fired Adam from his job in December 1999 after he was found guilty of bribery. The paper asked, "How was the killer reinstated in his job after being expelled for bribery?"[47] The independent weekly al-Haqq, said in a front page story that the Sudanese serial killer began his life in Yemen as a gardener at the residence of the San`a' Bank director, but was dismissed because he made the director feel "uneasy." The director's son was surprised to learn later that Adam had become an anatomy technician at the Faculty of Medicine, because he knew that Adam had no qualifications for the job.[48] The English language newspaper, Yemen Times, wondered whether the "mystery of the serial killer's accomplices" would be "revealed."[49] The independent weekly al-Shumu` asked: "who is responsible for these crimes of the murderer (saffah) of the College of Medicine? The College of Medicine is lax (sa'iba) and its security administration doesn't fulfill its duties."[50] The newspaper of the Sons of Yemen

League, *Ra'y*, devoted its headlines to the "faculty butcher" who "kills 16 and sells their organs."[51] *Al-Umma*, the weekly paper of *al-Haqq* (the Zaydi Islamicist party) reported that "the luggage of the accused Sudanese was brought back from Khartum Airport. Only the identity cards of the Iraqi student Zaynab and the Yemeni, Husn, were found. No other documents were discovered except a videocassette that is said to contain recordings of two or three of the victims. A common feature among the corpses recovered is that they did not contain livers, hearts, or kidneys, which confirms suspicion that [the crime] involves a trade of human organs."[52] The YSP's *al-Thawri* cited police sources claiming that "several security men have been detained" in connection with the crimes at the Faculty of Medicine.[53] *Al-Sahwa*, the major Islamicist party's paper, covered the "demonstrations of anger," when over 5,000 students took to the streets demanding broad investigations of the "butchery" (*majzara*) at the Faculty of Medicine.[54] Literate people read newspaper reports aloud to others who could not read. Television and radio reports also informed illiterate Yemenis, and well-known mosque leaders, such as `Abd al-Majid `Aziz al-Zindani, recorded scathing condemnations of state impropriety and moral laxity that were then distributed on cassette tapes. Children made extra money by selling additional photocopies of newspaper pages reporting details of the horror. Unprecedented stories of regime complicity and citizen vulnerability animated public discussions.

Debates in newspapers, in the streets, during Friday mosque sermons and qat chews, and in government offices laid bare how easily civic terror can be generated by perceptions of ineffective state institutions, and how public appeals can be made on the basis of the moral and material entitlements that citizens of even the most nominal of nation-states felt were due to them.[55] People were outraged that the university had not done more to protect its students or to investigate the disappearances. Criticisms focused on the incapacities of the state, the corruption and potential complicity of the regime, and the need for the seemingly elusive but desirable "state institutions" (*mu'assasat al-dawla*). In one qat chew I attended, someone went as far as to claim that serial killings could never happen in the developed United States—a point I hastened to correct.

Students of nationalism might be tempted to interpret the narratives about the Sudanese serial killer as an instance of "othering," in which understandings of the nation are brought into being by contrasting Yemenis with Sudanese. In a country with high unemployment, Adam's status as a Sudanese immigrant with a job did bring to the fore prejudices rarely expressed in public.[56] A union leader, for example, charged that "the employment of a foreigner as a university technician contravened a presidential decree."[57] The Sudanese community, which is several thousand strong, immediately condemned Adam's crime and many said they feared a backlash. Yet, interestingly, although there were some expressions of anti-Sudanese sentiment, especially among the working-class poor, many Yemenis went to great lengths to disavow the chauvinist statements of others. Indeed, if homogeneity is a typical "national fantasy,"[58] Adam's imprisonment and the subsequent talk about it suggested that not all national citizens shared this desire for homogeneity or thought that it required demonizing Sudanese others. In this vein, one Yemeni intellectual argued that within a broadly Arab nationalist framework, Sudanese were not considered others at all, but were rather seen as a subgroup of Arabs whose "habits and ways of thinking were especially similar" to Yemeni ones.[59] What made a Yemeni a Yemeni *in this instance* was therefore the common moral panic that gripped citizens and enabled them to experience themselves as a community—as a group of people who shared a sense of belonging with anonymous others in what Benedict Anderson has called, borrowing from Walter Benjamin, "homogeneous, empty time."[60] In this view, what gave these citizens a sense of their shared experience was not only the common practice of conversing about the crimes, but the recognition that all over Yemen strangers were conducting similar conversations about this unparalleled event. Etienne Balibar argues that "a social formation only reproduces itself as a nation to the extent that through a network of apparatuses and daily practices, the individual is instituted as *homo nationalis* from cradle to grave, at the same time that he or she is instituted as *homo oeconomicus, politicus, religious.*"[61] In other words, people are not born with feelings of national attachment; national citizens have to be made and remade. In the absence of state institutions capable of generating *homo nationalis*, the shared fascination with Yemen's purportedly first serial killings could nevertheless produce conditions in which a putative "nation" of Yemenis longed for a state capable of protecting them.

Admittedly, the existence of shared arguments and the knowledge that anonymous others are similarly engaged in conversation may be a necessary condition for national connectedness, but it is certainly not a sufficient one. For one, the debates were not confined to Yemenis. Non-Yemenis living in Yemen were also engaged in similar discussions. And the tabloid presses throughout the Arab world covered the event in all of its ghastly detail. Nevertheless, claims of moral and material entitlement, the outrage that attended the event, and the stated hopes that a representative state could be made accountable and ensure safety—these were conversations in which Yemenis often appealed *as a people*,[62] wondering aloud too how such a crime could happen *in Yemen*.[63] In other words, people often framed their complaints in terms of a territorially determinate group of Yemeni citizens, who, as "a people," could criticize the regime for failing to act as an effective political authority.

One might also argue that the murders in the morgue simply prompted people to gossip or to discuss a new topic—mostly with their familiar inter-locutors and sometimes with strangers they were unlikely to see again. But technologies of communication, such as print media and tape recordings of Friday mosque sermons, worked in tandem with social practices, such as qat chew conversations, to generate public knowledge both of the event itself and of anonymous others simultaneously engaged in discussions of it: people talked about the event *and* its circulation (about the boys selling photocopies on the streets; about relatives who telephoned to express con-cern for the well-being and safety of their kin; about the distribution of Friday mosque sermon cassettes; and about previous qat chew conversa-tions in which aspects of the event were probed with painstaking detail). To be sure, other events have generated lively discussion in public places, but the scope of debate about the murders in the morgue was by all accounts unprecedented. For example, one of the editors of *al-Ayyam* claimed that newspaper issues featuring stories about the murders in the morgue sold 75,000 copies, more than double the number of copies usually circulated. The murders in the morgue conversations constituted a self-organized "public sphere"[64] in which citizens, many of whom were strangers to one another, deliberated on the radio, in newspapers, and in qat chew conver-sations.[65] These debates represented the practice of "nationness"[66]—not evidence of a real or enduring collectivity, but of a contingent event whose significance lies in its ability to reproduce the vocabularies of imagined community and popular sovereignty, occasioning the temporary manifesta-tion of community in the warp and weft of everyday political experience.

In contrast to much of the mainstream literature on nationalism, the murders in the morgue case suggests that experiences of national belonging can be generated by transient events of collective vulnerability rather than by state institutions,[67] industrialization,[68] or even the ongoing effects of print capitalism.[69] In this view, nationness need not develop; it can also happen, "suddenly crystallizing as a basis for individual and collective action" within a "political field" conducive to such consolidation.[70] In the broader political context in which nation-state-ness is the privileged form of political organization, the "nation" then becomes the intelligible category through which people imagine political community. In Wittgensteinian terms, what makes this community "national" has to do with the ways in which, in the age of nation-states, imagining a nation is simply what it means to imagine an abstract sovereign "people" (*sha`b*) whose political community is comprised of anonymous others. Doing so effectively may require a plausible rhetorical appeal to language, culture, and/or history—but it does not imply that those characteristics be historically correct and universally shared in the way imaginations represent them.[71] Rather, "protean" communities of argument, prompted by identifiable events, help generate conditions of possibility, idioms of affective connection, and practices of reproduction through which experiences of common belonging to a territory might be institutionalized, or just made available as an organizing principle for making some demands and registering grievances.[72] Nation-ness can wax and wane because the nation is not a "thing," but a set of dispositions inscribed in material practices. National solidarities (and other forms of local or regional attachment) exist through the ongoing work of political entrepreneurs, but also, as in this case, through the acephalous transmission of identifications in ordinary activities of communication.

In the context of heightened and sustained public debate, the gender politics of the crime elicited multiple interpretations, which tended to coincide with the variety of prevailing attitudes about women's place in the putative nation. Yemen's medical school, established nearly 20 years earlier with $35 million in donations from the Emir of Kuwait, produced the first female doctors in the 1990s. Nearly half of the 3,500 students enrolled in the college are women, and many women from other countries without medical schools, or without medical schools that admit women, traveled to study at the $3,000-a-year institution.[73] When the killings were first disclosed, parents talked of pulling their daughters from the university. Some local bus (*dabbab*) drivers and their money collectors teased women who rode the bus to the university about their destination, often calling out ominously "the Sudanese, the Sudanese." Some members of the Islamicist *al-Islah* party used the case to justify their position that educating women leads to trouble. Others within *al-Islah* suggested that appropriate safeguards had to be established so that women could be educated safely, and perhaps separately. Among socialists and their allies, discussions ensued about the normative attitudes that underpinned security police responses to reports of women missing. The mother of the 24-year-old Iraqi woman, Zaynab Sa`ud `Aziz, whose remains were positively identified, was purportedly told to "search the dance floors" when she reported her daughter's disappearance.[74] Other families did not report their daughters missing, supposedly because they worried that their daughters had engaged in illicit sex or run off with a lover. In Arabic language tabloids circulating in Yemen and elsewhere, Adam was even referred to as "the San`a' Ripper."

The tabloids' analogy of San`a''s serial killer to the legendary Jack the Ripper of late Victorian London may be, in some respects, apt: both were what historian Judith Walkowitz calls "catalyzing" events in which the felt absence of law and order combined with fears of sexual danger to galvanize "a range of constituencies to take sides and to assert their presence in a heterogeneous public sphere."[75] The narrative's potency—its ability to stimulate conversation outside the capital where the events took place—may also have to do with the ways in which the capital city is presumed to be the place where state power and services, including security, reside. The point to be made here is not that bad things happen in all countries, but rather that Yemenis from a variety of class and regional backgrounds, through divergent media, tended to coalesce as a community through the circulation of explanations that privileged state incompetence and linked it to both moral and political corruption. Citizens located their sense of entitlement as a people in a fantasy of impersonal, effective state institutions and the consequent protection they might offer.

The regime's responses to the "murders in the morgue" were paradoxical. On the one hand, officials put forward the images of Adam for public consumption. In the official view, Adam was a depraved man who drank alcohol. In the unfolding of the official account, Adam confessed to 16 murders and provided explicit details of his crimes. In the first killing of 1995, according to his alleged statement to the police, he met Fatima, a Somali woman, in downtown San'a'. He convinced her that he was a well-known professor at the medical school and he enticed her with money to visit him repeatedly at the morgue. There they would have sex; Adam claimed to have had sex with her more than 12 times before killing her. Another woman came to the morgue to collect body parts for a medical experiment. As she entered, he sprayed a chemical on her face, thereby rendering her unconscious. It was at this point that he remembered that her friend was outside. He invited her in, sprayed her in the face as well, and disposed of both bodies in acid.[76] The confessions continued, and the state, if slow to react at first, seemed to present an airtight case in which prosecution would be swift, justice enacted, and the rule of law upheld. True, some regime officials seemed incompetent or corrupt, but the state could operate to protect and unite its citizens in the aftermath of the tragedy. The Prime Minister suspended the dean of the medical school and his deputy, and he fired the university's head of security in attempts to respond to citizen unrest. The judge, Yahya al-Islami, ruled that Adam be taken to the "forecourt of the morgue" in plain view of students and faculty, where he would be "tied to a wooden board, lashed 80 times for his admitted use of alcohol, then executed, either by beheading with a sword or by lying face down and being shot three times through the heart."[77]

On the other hand, the regime's attempts to manage the Adam affair seemed partial and ambivalent. Both police officers' slow response to initial inquiries by Zaynab's mother and the suspicion that regime officials were implicated in the killings were also part of the public discourses circulating vigorously in the aftermath of May 10, and the regime could do nothing to prevent criticisms from occupying much of public discussion. Moreover, when newspapers published the names of the victims in the beginning of June, several of the women Adam had confessed to killing turned up alive and in court for the trial of June 3. A woman claiming to be Nada Yasin, a 21-year-old whose rape and mutilation Adam had described in detail, apparently appeared in court with her sister who verified her identity—although there was some disagreement about whether she was, in fact, Nada. Indeed, as Adam's confessions became obviously less reliable, stories began to disseminate about high-ranking government officials' complicity in an alleged prostitution ring. According to these accounts, Adam was the "fall guy" for a great government conspiracy. None of the evidence at the trial supported these claims, but the fact that such rumors circulated revealed worries about a regime that not only failed to build proper state institutions but also contributed to the nation's moral deterioration. As the school's founding dean said, "We have had to ask ourselves some hard questions, such as 'Is there a moral decay?' and 'What happened to our standards?' "[78] The regime's decision to bring in a team of German forensic experts also proved embarrassing. They found pieces of more than 100 bodies in the morgue, mostly men's that had never been entered in the morgue records. Professors claimed, according to the same article in the *New York Times*, that "deliberately loose controls were adopted in the medical school's early years, when illicit importation of bodies and body parts was necessary to circumvent Islamic injunctions in Yemen against dissection." Certainly loose controls at the university were not merely the product of injunctions—Islamic or otherwise. Indeed, the criticisms that circulated in public were simultaneously about the unusual horror of the event and the all-too-familiar experience of loose controls. The regime's attempts to manage moral panic, then, also registered its incompetence and laid bare the limits of state power. Legal scholars and ordinary citizens appealed to the constitution and bemoaned the absence of institutions that could make officials accountable and people safe. Even the harsh sentence made evident some of the inadequacies of a regime and the vulnerabilities of supposed commitments to the rule of law. Adam was eventually convicted of only two murders—Zaynab's and that of Husn Ahmad `Attiya, a 23-year-old woman from Hamdan whose remains were found in the morgue's drains—and sentenced to death. The judge's insistence that the execution be carried out on university property drew criticism from students and faculty at the college, as well as from local human rights lawyers. Adam's defense lawyer also complained that he had been permitted only one five-minute meeting with his client in the entire six months between arrest and conviction.

The sentence, too, exemplified the tensions between various aspects of a distinctly modernist ideal of the nation-state. Muhammad

Adam 'Umar Ishaq was finally executed, near but not on university grounds, in a public square in the neighborhood of al-Madhbah on June 20, 2001. With security forces cordoning off the square, in front of the victims' families and a crowd estimated to be in the thousands, a single policeman fired five bullets into Adam's back. The regime could mobilize its security apparatus and enforcement capabilities in retrospect. It could even exercise its "legitimate" or moral right to dispense violence. But faith in constitutionality and desire for the rule of law, which were expressed in newspaper accounts, in ordinary conversations, and in the fact of the trial, were at odds with the prosecution's story and the judge's initial rush to judgment. The nation as a group of anonymous citizens who occupy a shared sense of attachment by virtue of undergoing common experiences was being formed in the breach of state authority. The publicity around the serial killings demonstrated the fragility of state power at the same time that it made manifest a process of nationness predicated on moral panic and the desire for protection.

Protection, as Charles Tilly points out, has two contrasting connotations. The comforting sense of the term "calls up images of the shelter against danger provided by a powerful friend, a large insurance policy, or a sturdy roof."[79] The other sense of the term connotes "the racket in which a local strong man forces merchants to pay tribute in order to avoid damage—damage the strong man himself threatens to deliver. The difference [between the two senses], to be sure, is a matter of degree."[80] Tilly likens state making to organized crime in the sense that states tend to stimulate the very dangers against which protection is then required. Of course the analogy between a state and the mafia has limits, as Diego Gambetta has pointed out.[81] Plausible arguments can be advanced, moreover, that Yemen's regime operates more like a mafia than like a state. The points to be made in the context of the three events analyzed above are simply that: (1) Regimes that do not fulfill the conditions of a "minimal state"[82] by enjoying sufficient control over violence to be perceived by citizens as protecting them "whether they like it or not"[83] may end up being more "democratic"—more encouraging of civic associations, vibrant political debate, and substantive thinking about politics—than regimes with efficacious state institutions and/or passionate attachments to a nation. The fictitious elections dramatized the regime's power to foreclose democratic possibilities, but official power remains limited by the vigorous, qualified public sphere activities that coexist with, and offer public criticisms of, these phony rituals. (2) Public spectacles generate the sorts of security dangers that then prompt, and sometimes justify, state protection. The Yemeni regime can at times act like an effective state, and public spectacles such as the presidential election or the unification ceremonies place these acts on display for citizens' consumption. (3) Public criticisms of regime practices, however, reveal that many citizens want protection in Tilly's first, optimistic sense of that term. Incidents such as the serial killing drama suggest that "nationness" might nevertheless be constituted in the absence of a sovereign state, through the shared experiences of belonging to a community imagined in the breach of institutional authority.

Concluding Remarks

By way of a conclusion, further reflections on three points: First, many scholars of political transitions have taken national unity and the existence of a sovereign state as prerequisites for the development of democracy. Dankwart Rustow, for example, views national unity as a necessary condition for a transition to democracy: "the vast majority of citizens in a democracy-to-be must have no doubt or mental reservations as to which political community they belong to."[84] Juan Linz and Alfred Stepan argue that a transition to democracy is exceedingly difficult in a country that has a "stateness problem." According to these authors, "modern democratic governance is inevitably linked to stateness. Without a state, there can be no citizenship, without citizenship, there can be no democracy."[85] The Yemeni example, by contrast, suggests that lively political activity and experiences of citizenship may actually thrive because the state is fragile and national identification tenuous. Admittedly, my account has not produced adequate evidence to establish a strong causal claim, but it does support hypotheses to be tested. State-formation seems to entail modes of regimentation and pacification that are antithetical to democratic activities, if by "democratic activities" we include the presence of civic associations and also the informal political practices of vigorously debating with others in public questions about action—about what should be done. In Western Europe, the birth of electoral forms of government occurred after "absolutizing" monarchies created unified institutions of power, controlled directly by the ruler, who gradually came to preside over the decentralized, feudal aristocracy.[86] According to Norbert Elias's account, state-formation also entailed the pacification of restive populations through the introduction of codes of conduct, manners, norms, prohibitions, and constraints that worked to co-opt elites and "civilize" the population—a pacification that conditioned the form that liberal democratic institutions assumed historically, and that may have helped to ensure their durability.[87] Similarly, in *Discipline and Punish*, Michel Foucault suggests that Western European states became increasingly capable of regulating their subjects, devising a "specific technology of power . . . called 'discipline,'" which replaced the external sovereign authority.[88] The disciplinary power of modern liberal states works by virtue of the internalization of patterns of authority previously experienced as external constraints. It operates by producing persons whose "subjectivity" or "individuality" is formed by a multitude of specialized institutions and disciplines.[89] Disciplinary power produces "docile bodies," according to Foucault, which both participate in and are the results of these new mechanisms of social control.[90] The argument is by now familiar, and the coherence of these "technologies" may be exaggerated. The point to be registered here is that the institutions through which states generate power, such as armies, schools, and factories, may help to ensure the durability of electoral institutions while also destroying vigorous forms of public life that are participatory and discursively vibrant, but also inherently less stable and institutionalized than liberal democracy has come to be. Citizens in fragile states may thus enjoy lived experiences of participation and contestation that are eliminated when states regularize their monopoly over force and their control over populations. The Yemeni case suggests not only that civic participation can exist under conditions of tenuous state control, but also that it may be an effect of such conditions.[91] Similarly, the contested character of national unity may encourage civic participation rather than undermine it. A national politics that puts too much emphasis on unity and consensus often comes at the expense of not tolerating difference. When late centralizing regimes make efforts to be state-like or define the terms of national unity, they often narrow democratic possibilities rather than broaden them. The Yemeni case also invites scholars to think of civic engagement, not as an instrumental good leading to formal democratic institutions,[92] but as the very activity of energetic political participation in its own right.

Second, if spectacles operate to teach or signal the reality of the regime's domination, they are also strikingly visible instances of that domination and of its precariousness. Spectacles provide the occasions for regimes to mobilize citizens to enact the conditions of their membership and to exaggerate the existence of their state-like qualities. In Yemen, as opposed to an authoritarian context such as Syria, these spectacles can be occasions for temporarily dominating without saturating social, or even political, life. The regime has a monopoly over official pageantry; and it has some control over its self-representation as a nation-state. But the images a fragile state is able to convey are intermittent and transient—hints of political possibility rather than established facts. Some citizens were aware of the ways in which the elections and subsequent spectacles were simultaneously announcements, generators, and barometers of the regime's power. The regime had to mobilize people, channel goods and services, and produce the messages that would become the subject of newspaper reports, street and qat chew conversations, and intellectuals' conferences. The regime could navigate various contestations in political life by ignoring most, co-opting some, punishing others—and doing it all publicly. By acting like a state, the regime was not dissimulating stateness; it was being one.

Third and relatedly, cases of early state-formation in Western Europe suggest that the state evolved into a powerful set of institutions before nationalism developed as the articulated, ideological expression of common political identification.[93] National identity emerged from the state in the form of a legal framework for citizens as rights-bearing individuals.[94] Scholarly accounts of a number of postcolonial states, as well as of Central Europe, suggest a second, different relationship between state- and nation-building. In these cases, regimes have had to construct an effective institutional apparatus while concomitantly cultivating national consciousness. The need to consolidate state power while generating national identification affects the kinds of institutions, practices, and loyalties these regimes can produce. In the examples of many postcolonial states, such exigencies have produced authoritarian regimes that deliver goods and services in return for a modicum of national allegiance and a lot of obedience.

The case of Yemen suggests a third model of political development involving the emergence of vague, mildly constraining forms of national identification in the absence of an effective sovereign state. The state is generally incapable of playing a compelling educative or formative role in fashioning national persons. The serial killing incident points to a possible grassroots source of nation-building in the absence of a strong or effective state. It suggests that discursive practices, such as newspaper and television reports, mosque sermons, street and qat chew conversations help to construct national persons by producing the shared conditions under which a community of anonymous fellow citizens can be imagined into existence. In Anderson's terms, a nation entails citizens becoming aware that their concerns are "being replicated by thousands (or millions) of others of whose existence [they are] confident, yet of whose identity [they have] not the slightest notion."[95] Yemen shows how shared entitlements to state protection can bring into being *episodic* instances of a national life.

Notes

This chapter is based on open-ended interviews and ethnographic research conducted during 14 months of fieldwork (summer 1998; summer and fall 1999;

spring 2000; September 2000; fall 2001; winter 2002; fall 2003). The title is, of course, beholden to James C. Scott's *Seeing Like a State*. An early version of this chapter was presented at the Second Mediterranean Social and Political Research Meeting, Florence, March 21–25, 2001, Mediterranean Programme, Robert Schuman Centre for Advanced Studies, European University Institute. Subsequent drafts were presented to audiences at The University of Pennsylvania (2002), The University of Chicago (2002; 2003), and The University of Wisconsin, Madison (2003). In particular, I would like to thank Nadia Abu El-Haj, Madawi Al-Rasheed, Isa Blumi, H. Zeynep Bulutgil, Craig Calhoun, Sheila Carapico, Dipesh Chakrabarty, Jim Chandler, Michael Dawson, Dilip Gaonkar, Ellis Goldberg, Debbie Gould, Yusuf Has, Engseng Ho, Leigh Jenco, Matthew Kocher, Ben Lee, Zachary Lockman, Claudio Lomnitz, Patchen Markell, W. Flagg Miller, Harris Mylonas, Anne Norton, Stacey Sheridan Philbrick, Hanna Pitkin, Don Reneau, Jillian Schwedler, William H. Sewell, Jr., Susan Stokes, Ronald Suny, Charles Taylor, Ed Webb, John Willis, Anna Wuerth, and Iris Marion Young. I dedicate this chapter to the memory of Jar Allah `Umar.

1. My analysis depends on readers understanding the differences I am registering among the terms "state," "nation," and "regime." By "state" I mean a common set of institutions capable of distributing goods and services and controlling violence within a demarcated, internationally recognized territory. By "nation" I refer to a shared sense of belonging simultaneously with anonymous others to an imagined community. By "regime" I mean the political order of a particular leader or administration. For example, we tend to say "the regime of `Ali `Abd Allah Salih," but not "the state of `Ali `Abd Allah Salih."

2. Sheila Carapico, *Civil Society in Yemen: The Political Economy of Activism in Modern Arabia* (Cambridge: Cambridge University Press, 1998); Jurgen Habermas, *The Structural Transformation of the Public Sphere: An Inquiry into a Category of Bourgeois Society* (Cambridge, MA: MIT Press, [1962], 1996).

3. Jean Comaroff and John L. Comaroff, "Occult Economies and the Violence of Abstraction: Notes from the South African Post-Colony," *American Ethnologist*, vol. 26, no. 3, 1999, 279–301.

4. See, e.g., Dankwart A. Rustow, "Transitions to Democracy: Toward a Dynamic Model," *Comparative Politics*, vol. 2, no. 3 (April 1970), 352; Juan Linz and Alfred Stephan, *Problems of Democratic Transition and Consolidation* (Baltimore and London: The Johns Hopkins University Press, 1996).

5. The population figure is from the World Bank Memorandum of the president of the International Development Association and the International Finance Corporation to the Executive Directors on a Country Assistance Strategy for the Republic of Yemen, August 6, 2002. The oft-cited figure on arms is close to the Ministry of Interior's estimate of 60 million weapons in the country (*Yemen Times*, January 28, 2002). In the period 1999–2000, the population was estimated at 16 million people with 51 million arms.

6. This characterization of the contemporary world is taken from Ronald Beiner's introductory essay, "Why Citizenship Constitutes a Theoretical Problem in the Last Decade of the Twentieth Century," in *Theorizing Citizenship* (Albany: State University of New York Press, 1995).

7. The term Yemen is considerably older than are aspirations for a modern nation-state, however. Important historical antecedents for Yemen's twentieth-century "imagined unities" include repeated invocations of the term "Yemen" in the *Traditions of the Prophet* to indicate the territory south of Mecca and the centuries old identification of various local literatures and practices as explicitly "Yemeni"; Paul Dresch, *A History of Modern Yemen* (Cambridge: Cambridge University Press, 2000), 1, 6, 11, 49–50, 184, 209–10. The border between North and South was drawn in 1905, but there is no evidence to suggest that "Yemen" referred to a coherent political entity or enjoyed the imaginative status of nationhood before the interwar period. Even in this latter period, such imaginings overlapped with, and were often less important than, appeals to local, regional attachments. For a discussion of the varying ways in which Yemen was understood, see, in addition to Dresch, Franck Mermier, "Yemen, les héritages d'une histoire morcellée," in *Le Yémen contemporain* Remy Leveau, Franck Mermier, and Udo Steinbach, eds. (Paris: Éditions Karthala, 1999), 7–35; Yémen: "L'État face à la démocratie," *Monde arabe Maghreb-Machrek* 155, 3–5; "L'islam politique au Yémen ou la 'Tradition' contre les traditions?" *Monde arabe Maghreb-Machrek* 155, 6–19; and my *Peripheral Visions: Political Identifications in Unified Yemen* (in preparation). For a discussion of aspirations towards unity prior to unification, see also F. Gregory Gause III, "The Idea of Yemeni Unity," in *Journal of Arab Affairs*, vol. 6, no. 1 (1987), 55–81; and Fred Halliday, "The Formation of Yemeni Nationalism: Initial Reflections," in *Rethinking Nationalism in the Arab Middle East,* Israel Gershoni and James Jankowski, eds. (New York: Columbia University Press, 1997).

8. Abu Bakr al-Saqqaf terms this annexationist politics "internal colonialism" in his pamphlet *Al-wahda al-yamaniyya: min al-indimaj al-fawri ila isti`mar al-dakhili* (London: Barid al-Janub, 1996). See also his essay, "The Yemeni Unity: Crisis in Integration," in *Le Yémen contemporain* (Paris: Éditions Karthala, 1999), 141–59. For a brief but helpful discussion of the war, see Sheila Carapico, "From Ballotbox to Battlefield: The War of the Two `Alis," *Middle East Report*, 190, 25, 1 September/October 1994, 27.

9. Iris Glosemeyer, "The First Yemeni Parliamentary Elections in 1993: Practising Democracy," *Orient* 34 (1993), 439–51.

10. Renaud Detalle, "The Yemeni Elections Up Close," MERIP 185, 1993, 8–12; Les élections legislatives du 27 avril 1993, *Monde arabe Maghreb-Machrek* 141, 3–36; Abdo Baaklini, Guilain Denoeux, and Robert Springborg, *Legislative Politics in the Arab World: The Resurgence of Democratic Institutions* (Boulder and London: Lynne Reiner, 1999); Jillian Schwedler, "Democratization in the Arab World? Yemen's Aborted Opening," *Journal of Democracy* 13.4 (2002), 48–55.

11. Schwedler, "Democratization in the Arab World?"; Dresch, *A History of Modern Yemen*, 209.

12. Adam Przeworski, *Democracy and the Market: Political and Economic Reforms in Eastern Europe and Latin America* (Cambridge: Cambridge University Press, 1991).

13. The National Democratic Institute, an organization associated with the United States' Democratic Party, helped the regime to host the "Emerging Democracies" conference, in which 15 countries participated in June 1999.

14. Muhammad 'Abd al Malik Al-Mutawakkil, "Al-shar'iya al-mafquda.. wa al-shar'iya al-muhtamala." *al-Wahdawi*, October 5, 1999; Muhammad 'Ali Al-Saqqaf, "Al-hanin ila shumuliyya." *al-Ayyam*, September 27, 1999; Muslih Ahmad Muthana, "Hunak thalatha milayin marid bi fayrus al-kabid lan yusharik fi al-intikhabat." *al-Wahdawi*, September 21, 1999.

15. Al-Mutawakkil, "Al-shar'iya al-mafquda..wa al-shar'iya al-muhtamala," 1999.

16. Faraj Bin Ghanim served as prime minister of Yemen from May 17, 1997 until his resignation on April 29, 1998.

17. According to one source, there were 20,100 ballot boxes made, but only 17,148 distributed. The source took this to mean that the undistributed ones were to be used in an "emergency situation" so that the regime could show that it had not only amassed the required majority, but also generated enthusiasm for the elections.

18. Lisa Wedeen, *Ambiguities of Domination: Politics, Rhetoric, and Symbols in Contemporary Syria* (Chicago: University of Chicago Press, 1999).

19. Qat is a leafy stimulant that Yemenis chew in the afternoons—frequently at public gatherings. Marriages are often arranged, commercial transactions accomplished, and political deals solidified over qat. Qat chews are also occasions to discuss with friends, familiars, and some strangers political topics of general concern. Conversations range from the abstract to the concrete, from the meanings of Yemeni-ness to date palm cultivation problems in the Hadramawt. Chapter 4 of my forthcoming *Peripheral Visions: Political Identifications in Unified Yemen* deals with the political significance of qat chews in detail. See also Shelagh Weir's informative *Qat in Yemen: Consumption and Social Change* (British Museum Publications, Ltd., 1985) and the eloquent descriptions in Brinkley Messick, *The Calligraphic State: Textual Domination and History in a Muslim Society* (Berkeley and Los Angeles: University of California Press, 1996).

20. There were relatively few political posters of Nagib Qahtan, and those that did exist were hand placed by party members on public walls. No such posters were available for purchase, nor could they be found in shop windows.

21. Estimates of the average annual per capita income vary for this period from approximately $270 to $347, depending on the source and year. See, e.g., the World Bank report (1999) and the *Yemen Times*, November 13–19, 2000.

22. François Burgat, "Les élections présidentielles de septembre 1999 au Yémen: du 'pluralisme armé' au retour à la 'norme arabe,'" in *Monde arabe Maghreb-Machrek*, no. 168, avril–juin 2000, 70.

23. Ibid., 70.

24. *Human Rights Watch*, Yemen, 2000, 420 (references are to an early draft of the report).

25. Carapico, *Civil Society In Yemen*; Sheila Carapico, "Yemen between Civility and Civil War," in *Civil Society in the Middle East*, vol. II, ed. Augustus Richard Norton (Leiden and New York: E.J. Brill, 1996), 287–316.

26. It is difficult to obtain population breakdowns by region in Yemen. *The World Gazetteer's* estimates of approximately 4.5 million inhabitants of the South in 1994 and 4.2 million in 2003 strike me as inflated; the overall population

figures cited are high by any other source's standards (close to 16 million in 1994; close to 23 million in 2003). The suggestion of migration away from the South is intriguing in its own right, however. Officials in the ruling GPC and members of the opposition quoted me the figure of 2.5 million inhabitants of the South in 1999.

27. I have chosen to render this expression idiomatic in English. In Arabic, the literal translation would be, "the devil you know is better than the human you don't."

28. *al-Ayyam*, August 21, 2000; *Human Rights Watch* 2000, 420–4.

29. For a discussion of how Yemen's ruling party managed to enjoy an electoral landslide in the April parliamentary elections, see Sheila Carapico, "How Yemen's Ruling Party Secured an Electoral Landslide," *Middle East Report Online* (May 16, 2003). Even were such elections to be fairly contested, parliament's actual political powers remain extraordinarily limited. Some Yemenis believe that the president, the ruling party, and/or the security forces encouraged the assassination of Jar Allah `Umar in order to prevent an effective opposition coalition from forming. Others argue that "*jihadi*" or "*salafi*" extremists outside the political mainstream, with possible links to al-Qa`ida, may have begun targeting secular and liberal intellectuals, along with foreign interests and security forces. It may never be clear whether the assassin, `Ali Ahmad Muhammad Jar Allah, acted alone—or, if he acted in cooperation with co-conspirators, who they were. The regime has rounded up suspects in association with `Umar's murder, but many details of the interrogations have not been made public. See Sheila Carapico, Lisa Wedeen, and Anna Wuerth, "The Death and Life of Jarallah Omar," *Middle East Report Online*, December 31, 2002.

30. For a discussion of the ways in which rhetoric and symbols not only exemplify but also produce power for a regime, see my *Ambiguities of Domination*.

31. Such an act was not without precedent, of course. Stalin deleted Trotsky from the historical record, for example. The fictional account from Milan Kundera's *The Book of Laughter and Forgetting* is also noteworthy. Importantly, several YSP members recall that the two presidents jointly raised the flag, but I could find no picture to substantiate that memory. Instead, in the capital's Military Museum a photograph taken in 1990 does depict al-Bid, the former president of the South, gazing up from behind as `Ali `Abd Allah Salih raises the flag. Museum curators argued that although political posters had excised al-Bid's image, they displayed the photo of the "traitors" because they were "protecting the historical record" (author's interview, Fall 2002).

32. Jean Comaroff and John L. Comaroff, "Policing the Occult in the Postcolony: Law and the Regulation of 'Dangerous' Cultural Practices in South Africa and Elsewhere." Unpublished paper, 1998; See also Comaroff and Comaroff. "Policing Culture, Cultural Policing: Law and Social Order in Postcolonial South Africa," *Law and Social Inquiry*, 29 (1), forthcoming 2004.

33. The words "tribe" and "tribal" are deeply problematic, fraught terms in the Middle East studies literature. My use of them here is not meant to disregard debates about usage, or to ride roughshod over the complex issues invocations

of the concept bring to the fore. Yemenis use the terms often and in varying ways, sometimes referring to the organization of real and fictive kin, and sometimes as a pejorative term to mean "country bumpkin" (Carapico, "Yemen between Civility and Civil War") or uncivilized. As Paul Dresch points out, Yemen's "tribes" do not fit anthropological characterizations of "corporate" groups: "Tribes do not cohere as wholes around people at odds, and a tribesman who feels himself wronged but does not receive support from his tribe may leave and take refuge with another tribe. He may even become permanently part of the group he joins" (Dresch, "Imams and Tribes," 225). My current book project addresses the term's scholarly and local connotations in depth.

34. Author's interview with the Minister of Education, May 2000.
35. In the video version of the festival, the scene of empty seats is edited out.
36. Najwa Adra's work on "tribal dancing" links the *bara`* (a Yemeni group dance performed by men outdoors in the Northern Highlands) to the growth of Yemeni nationalism in the essay, "Tribal Dancing and Yemeni Nationalism: Steps to Unity," in RE.M.M.M. 67, 1, 1993. In "Dance and Glance: Visualizing Tribal Identity in Highland Yemen" she connects dancing to conceptions of tribal affiliation or groupness. See *Visual Anthropology*, vol. 11 (1998), 55–102.
37. See Richard Handler, *Nationalism and the Politics of Culture in Quebec* (Madison and London: University of Wisconsin Press, 1988), 14.
38. Najwa Adra, "Tribal Dancing and Yemeni Nationalism" (1993), 166; Benedict Anderson, *Imagined Communities* (London: Verso, 1991), 22, 145.
39. I watched this spectacle with northern and southern Yemenis on May 22, 2000. I thank W. Flagg Miller for bringing my attention to additional alternative readings.
40. *Yemen Observer*, May 31, 2000, front page.
41. Ibid.
42. *The Observer*, June 11, 2000.
43. *al-Wahdawi*, May 16, 2000.
44. *The Observer*, June 11, 2000.
45. *26 September*, May 18, 2000, 4.
46. Ibid. I am indebted to Maurice Pomerantz and Muhannad Salhi for bringing my attention to the fact that this expression matches the phrase in Quranic verse 12: 68. The phrase refers to Jacob's unexplained desire to have his sons enter into Joseph's palace through different doors: "And when they entered after the manner their father commanded them, it availed them nothing against God; but it was a need in Jacob's soul that he so satisfied. Verily he was possessed of a knowledge for that We had taught him; but most men know not" (from A.J. Arberry's translation, George Allen and Unwin Ltd., 1955). Adam's alleged usage of the phrase suggests that the expression has become a common way of referring to an unexplained desire unknown to others.
47. *al-Ayyam*, May 20, 2000.
48. *al-Haqq*, May 21, 2000.
49. *Yemen Times*, May 29, 2000.

50. *al-Shumu`*, May 20, 2000, 2.
51. *Ra'y*, May 16, 2000.
52. *al-Umma*, May 18, 2000.
53. *al-Thawri*, May 18, 2000.
54. *al-Sahwa*, June 1, 2000, headlines.
55. Comaroff and Comaroff, "Occult economies and the violence of abstraction."
56. *The Observer*, June 11, 2000, 3.
57. Ibid.
58. See Lauren Berlant, *The Anatomy of National Fantasy: Hawthorne, Utopia, and Everyday Life* (Chicago: University of Chicago Press, 1991).
59. Author's interview, May 2000.
60. Benedict Anderson, *Imagined Communities* (London: Verso, 1991), 24; Walter Benjamin. *Illuminations* (London: Fontana, 1973), 265.
61. Etienne Balibar and Immanuel Wallerstein, *Race, Nation, Class: Ambiguous Identities* (London: Verso, 1991) 93.
62. Lauren Berlant, "The Subject of True Feeling: Pain, Privacy, and Politics," in *Cultural Studies and Political Theory* (Ithaca: Cornell University Press, 2000), 45.
63. There is a growing literature on the sale of body parts that interprets actual marketing practices and the stories circulating about purported trafficking as products of "globalization" or neoliberal capitalist policies. See, e.g., the provocative account by Comaroff and Comaroff, "Occult Economies and the Violence of Abstraction."
64. Habermas, *The Structural Transformation of the Public Sphere.*
65. The theme of public sphere practices is discussed in detail in chapter 4 of my *Peripheral Visions: Political Identifications in Unified Yemen*, in preparation. See also my "Concepts and Commitments in the Study of Democracy," in Ian Shapiro, Rogers Smith, and Tarek Masoud, eds., *Problems and Methods in the Study of Politics* (Cambridge: Cambridge University Press, 2004), forthcoming.
66. Rogers Brubaker, *Nationalism Reframed: Nationhood and the National Question in the New Europe* (Cambridge: Cambridge University Press, 1996), 19.
67. Eric Hobsbawm, *Nations and Nationalism since 1780* (Cambridge: Cambridge University Press, 1990); Charles Tilly, ed., *The Formation of National States in Western Europe* (Princeton: Princeton University Press, 1975); Charles Tilly, *Coercion, Capital, and European States, AD 990–1990* (Cambridge: Blackwell 1990); Michael Mann, *Sources of Political Power*, vol. 2 (Cambridge: Cambridge University Press, 1993); Michael Mann, "A Political Theory of Nationalism and Its Excesses," in Sukumur Periwal, ed., *Notions of Nationalism* (Budapest: Central European University Press, 1995), 44–64; Eugen Weber, *Peasants into Frenchmen* (Stanford: Stanford University Press, 1976); Ernest Gellner, *Nations and Nationalism* (Oxford: Basil Blackwell, 1983).
68. Gellner, *Nations and Nationalism.*
69. Anderson, *Imagined Communities.* The example of September 11 provides a case in point of collective vulnerability.
70. Brubaker, *Nationalism Reframed*, 19; See also William H. Sewell, Jr., "Three Temporalities: Toward an Eventful Sociology," in Terrence J. McDonald, ed., *The Historic Turn in the Human Sciences* (Ann Arbor: University of Michigan

Press, 1997); Craig Calhoun, "The Problem of Identity in Collective Action," in *Macro-Micro Linkages in Sociology*, ed. Joan Huber (Newbury Park, Calif.: Sage, 1991), 51–75.

71. I am indebted to Patchen Markell and Craig Calhoun for this formulation.

72. Brubaker, *Nationalism Reframed*, 10.

73. *New York Times*, December 3, 2000.

74. *The Observer*, June 11, 2000.

75. Judith Walkowitz, *City of Dreadful Delight: Narratives of Sexual Danger in Late-Victorian London* (Chicago: University of Chicago Press, 1992), 5.

76. *The Observer*, June 11, 2000.

77. *New York Times*, December 3, 2000.

78. Ibid.

79. Charles Tilly, "War Making and State Making as Organized Crime," in *Bringing the State Back In* (Cambridge: Cambridge University Press, 1985), 170.

80. Ibid.

81. Diego Gambetta, *The Sicilian Mafia: The Business of Private Protection* (Cambridge and London: Harvard, 1993), 7.

82. Robert Nozick, *Anarchy, State, and Utopia* (Oxford: Basil Blackwell, 1974).

83. Gambetta, *The Sicilian Mafia*, 7.

84. Rustow, "Transitions to Democracy," 352.

85. Linz and Stepan, *Problems of Democratic Transition and Consolidation*, 27.

86. Anderson, *Imagined Communities*, 55.

87. Norbert Elias, *Power and Civility: The Civilizing Process*, vol. 2 (New York: Pantheon Books, 1982).

88. Michel Foucalt, *Discipline and Punish: The Birth of the Prison* (New York: Vintage Books, 1979), 194.

89. Timothy Mitchell on Foucault, "The Limits of the State: Beyond Statist Approaches and Their Critics," *American Political Science Review*, 85, 1 (March, 1991), 93; see also Louis Althusser, "Ideology and Ideological State Apparatuses Notes toward and Investigation," in *Lenin and Philosophy and Other Essays* (New York: Monthly Review Press, 1971).

90. Foucault, *Discipline and Punish*, 135–69.

91. The history of the early United States suggests the same phenomenon—as do many pre-revolutionary situations. Sheila Carapico makes a compatible but not identical argument; her emphasis is on the ways in which "Yemeni states, lacking major outside benefactors or domestic wealth, may be unique in the region in their need for civil society" (Carapico, *Civil Society in Yemen*, 17; see also chapter 5; and "Yemen between Civility and Civil War"). Her aim is to challenge prevailing stereotypes of conservatism and passivity often attributed to tribalism and to Islam by charting the history of activism within the context of local civic associations and self-help projects. My point here might also be likened to Joel Migdal's insights from *Strong Societies and Weak States: State–Society Relations and State Capabilities in the Third World* (Princeton: Princeton University Press 1988), but it differs in two ways. First, I am not claiming that there is a zero-sum relationship between weak states and strong societies, or

that we can even measure weakness and strength in ways that make consistent sense. I am suggesting that the Yemeni example—in which the state is "weak" *by anyone's definition* and political participation is vibrant and backed by significant coercive power—provides a corrective to some of the prevailing assumptions in the literature on democracy or "democratization." Some of these assumptions are dealt with at greater length in chapter 4 of my *Peripheral Visions* (in preparation). Second, my argument is concerned with the phenomenology of citizenship, the ways in which people talk about and practice their experiences of, and desires for, state authority and political community.

92. Robert D. Putnam, with Robert Leonardi and Raffaella Y. Nanetti, *Making Democracy Work: Civic Traditions in Modern Italy* (Princeton: Princeton University Press, 1993).

93. Hobsbawm, *Nations and Nationalism since 1780*; Gellner, *Nations and Nationalism*; Mann, *Sources of Social Power*, vol. 2, and "A Political Theory of Nationalism and Its Excesses"; Weber, *Peasants into Frenchmen*. For a contrary account of nationalism in England, see Steven Pincus, "Nationalism, Universal Monarchy, and the Glorious Revolution," in *State/Culture: State-Formation after the Cultural Turn*, ed. George Steinmetz (Ithaca: Cornell University Press, 1999), 182–210.

94. Gershom Shafir, "Introduction: The Evolving Tradition of Citizenship" in *The Citizenship Debates: A Reader* (Minnesota: University of Minnesota Press, 1998).

95. Anderson, *Imagined Communities*, 35.

Bibliography

Newspapers

al-Ayyam
al-Haqq
al-Majala
al-Mithaq
al-Quds al-Arabi
al-Sahwa
al-Sharq al-Awsat
al-Shumu
al-Thawra
al-Thawri
al-Ummah
al-Wahdawi
Financial Times
New York Times
Ra'y
The Observer
Yemen Observer
Yemen Times
26 September

Books and Articles

Abu-Butayn, `Abd Allah ibn `Abd al-Rahman. *Al-intsar lil hizb al-muwahddin.* Al-Hasa: Maktabat ibn al-Jawzi, 1987.
——. *Rasa'il wa fatawa.* Ibrahim al-Hazimi, ed. Riyadh: Dar al-Sharif, 1995.
——. *Ta'sis al-taqdis fi kashf talbis daud ibn jarjis.* Beirut: Mu'assasat al-Risalah, 2001.
`Abd al-Muhsin, Ibrahim ibn `Ubayd ibn. *Tadhkirat uli al-nuha wa al-`irfan bi ayyam al-wahid al-dayyan wa dhikr hawadith al-zaman.* 5 vols. Riyadh: Mu'assasat al-Nur, n.d.
ibn `Abd al-Wahhab, Muhammad *Mu'allafat al-shay kh al-imam muhammad ibn `abd al-wahhab.* 11 vols. Ed. by various. Riyadh: n.p., n.d.

Abram, Simone, Jaqueline Waldren, and Donald McCleod. *Tourists and Tourism: Identifying With People and Places*. Oxford: Berg, 1997.

Abu-Lughod, Janet. *Rabat: Urban Apartheid in Morocco*. Princeton: Princeton University Press, 1980.

Adas, Michael. *"High" Imperialism and the "New" History*. Washington, DC: American Historical Association, 1994.

Adra, Najwa. "Tribal Dancing and Yemeni Nationalism, Steps to Unity." *RE.M.M.M.* 67, 1 (1993): 161–7.

———. "Dance and Glance: Visualizing Tribal Identity in Highland Yemen." *Visual Anthropology* 11 (1998): 55–102.

al-Akwa`, Muhammad `Ali. *Hayat `alim wa amir*. 2 vols. San`a': printed by the author, 1996.

Al `Abd al-Latif, `Abd al-`Aziz ibn Muhammad. *Da`awa al-munaw'in lil da`wat al-shaykh muhammad ibn `abd al-wahhab*. Riyadh: Dar al-Watan, 1992.

Al `Abd al-Muhsin, Ibrahim ibn `Ubaid. *Tadhkirat uli al-nuha wa al-`irfan bi ayyam allah al-wahid wa al-dayyan wa dhikr hawadith al-zaman*. 4 vols. Riyadh: al-Nur, n.d. Vol. 5, Buraida: al-Salman, 1406.

Al al-Shaikh, `Abd al-Rahman ibn `Abd al-Latif ibn `Abdallah. *Mashahir `ulama' najd wa ghayrihim*. Riyadh: Dar al-Yamama, 1974.

van Alphen, Ernst. "Symptoms of Discursivity: Experience, Memory, and Trauma." In *Acts of Memory: Cultural Recall in the Present*. Mieke Bal, Jonathan Crewe, and Leo Spitzer, eds. Hanover and London: Dartmouth College, 1999.

Althusser, Louis. "Ideology and Ideological State Apparatuses (Notes Towards an Investigation)." In *Lenin and Philosophy and Other Essays by Louis Althusser*. New York: Monthly Review Press, 1971.

Altorki, Soraya and Donald P. Cole. "`Unaizah, le 'Paris du Najd': le changement en Arabie saoudite." *Monde Arabe: Maghreb-Machrek* 156 (Avril–Juin 1997): 3–22.

Anderson, Benedict. *Imagined Communities*. London: Verso, 1991.

Anderson, Gary. "Differential Urban Growth in The Eastern Province of Saudi Arabia: A Study of the Historical Interaction of Economic Development and Socio-Political Change." Ph.D. diss., Johns Hopkins University, 1985.

Anderson, Irvine. *Aramco, the United States and Saudi Arabia: A Study of the Dynamics of Foreign Oil Policy 1933–1950*. Princeton: Princeton University Press, 1981.

ibn `Aqil, Abu 'Abd al-Rahman. *Diwan al-shi`r al-`ammi bi lahjat ahl najd*. 5 vols. Riyadh: Dar al-`Ulum, 1982–86.

———. *Ansab al-usar al-hakimah fi al-ahsa*. 2 vols. Riyadh: Dar al-Yamama lil Tiba`a wa al-Nashr, 1983.

———. *Al-Jarba fi al-tarikh wa al-adab*. Riyadh: Dar al-Yamama lil Tiba`a wa-al-Nashr, 1983.

———. *Al-`ijman wa za`imuhum rakan ibn hithlayn*. Riyadh: Dar al-Yamama lil-Tiba`a wa al-Nashr, 1983.

———. *Masa'il min tarikh al-jazirah al-`arabiyyah*. Riyadh: Mu'assasat dar al-Asalah, 1994.

———. *Amir shu`ara al-nabat, muhammad ibn lu`bun*. Riyadh: Dar ibn Lu`bun, 1997.

Asad, Talal. "Conscripts of Western Civilization." In *Dialectical Anthropology: Essays in Honor of Stanley Diamond.* Vol. 1. Gainesville, FL: University Press of Florida, 1992.

'Atiq, Hamad ibn 'Ali. *Al-Difa' an ahl al-sunnah w'l-ittiba'.* Riyadh: Dar al-Hidayah, 1990.

———. *Majmuat rasa'il hamad ibn 'ali ibn 'atiq.* Riyadh: Dar al-Hidayah, n.d.

al-Azmeh, Aziz. *Islamic Modernities.* London: Verso, 1996.

al-'Azzawi, 'Abbas. *Tarikh al-'iraq bayn 'ihtilalayn.* Qum: Amir, 1990.

Baaklini, Abdo, Guilain Denoeux, and Robert Springborg. *Legislative Politics in the Arab World: The Resurgence of Democratic Institutions.* Boulder and London: Lynne Reiner, 1999.

Bal, Mieke. "Introduction." In *Acts of Memory.* Mieke Bal, Jonathan Crewe, and Leo Spitzer, eds. Hanover and London: Dartmouth College, 1999.

Balibar, Etienne and Immanuel Wallerstein. *Race, Nation, Class: Ambiguous Identities.* London: Verso, 1991.

Bamberg, J.H. *The History of the British Petroleum Company.* Vol. 2. *The Anglo-Iranian Years, 1928–1954.* Cambridge: Cambridge University Press, 1994.

Barclay, Clay. "Autobiographical Remembering: Narrative Constraints on Objectified Selves." In *Remembering Our Past: Studies in Autobiographical Memory.* David Rubin, ed. Cambridge: Cambridge University Press, 1996.

al-Barrak, S. and G. Hussain. 'A Study into the Agro-Climatic Conditions in the Central and Eastern Regions of Saudi Arabia. '*Arabian Gulf Journal of Scientific Research* 1, 2 (1983): 551–67.

al-Bassam, 'Abd Allah 'Abd al-Rahman. '*Ulama najd khilal thamaniyat qurun.* 2nd ed. 6 vols. Riyadh: Dar al-'Asimah, 1419, 1998.

———. *Khizanat al-tawarikh al-najdiyyah.* 10 vols. N.p., 1999.

al-Bassam, 'Abd Allah 'Abd al-Rahman ibn Salih, '*Ulama' najd khilal thamaniyat qurun.* 3 vols. Mecca: al-Nahda al-Haditha, 1398/1978–79.

al-Bassam, 'Abd Allah ibn Muhammad. *Tuhfat al-mushtaq min akhbar najd wa al-hijaz wa al-'iraq.* [Transcription of original manuscript by Nur al-Din Shuraybah, 1956.]

al-Bassam, Yusuf ibn Hamad. *Al-Zubair qabla khamsin 'amman ma'a nubdha tarikhiyya 'an najd wa al-Kuwait.* Riyadh: al-Farazdaq, 1391/1971.

Battaglia, Debbora. "Toward an Ethics of the Open Subject: Writing Culture in Good Conscience." In *Anthropological Theory Today.* Henrietta Moore, ed. Oxford: Polity Press, 1999.

Beiner, Ronald. "Why Citizenship Constitutes a Theoretical Problem in the Last Decade of the Twentieth Century." In *Theorizing Citizenship.* Albany: State University of New York Press, 1995.

Benjamin, Walter. *Illuminations.* London: Fontana, 1973.

Berkey, Jonathan P. *The Transmission of Knowledge in Medieval Cairo. A Social History of Islamic Education.* Princeton: Princeton University Press, 1992.

Berlant, Lauren. *The Anatomy of National Fantasy: Hawthorne, Utopia, and Everyday Life.* Chicago: University of Chicago Press, 1991.

———. "The Subject of True Feeling: Pain, Privacy, and Politics." In *Cultural Studies and Political Theory.* Cornell: Cornell University Press, 2000.

Betancourt, Rómulo. *Venezuela: Oil and Politics.* Boston: Houghton Mifflin, 1978.

Bhabha, Homi K. *The Location of Culture*. London: Routledge, 1994.

ibn Bishr, 'Uthman. `Unwan al-majd fi tarikh najd*. 2 vols. Riyadh: Darat al-Malik 'Abd al-'Aziz, 1982.

Blumi, Isa. "Looking Beyond the Tribe: Abandoning Paradigms to Write Social History in Yemen during World War I." *New Perspectives on Turkey* (Spring 2000): 117–43.

———. "To Be Imam: Empire and the Quest for Power in Ottoman Yemen during World War I." In *The Great Ottoman-Turkish Civilization*. Vol. 1. Kemal Çiçek, Ilber Ortayli, and Ercüment Kuran, eds. Istanbul: Yeni Türkiye Odasi, 2000. 731–42.

———. "The Ottoman Empire and Yemeni Politics in the Sancaq of Ta'izz, 1911–1918." In *Arab Provincial Capitals in the Late Ottoman Empire*. Hanssen, Weber, and Philipp, eds. Beirub: Beiruter Texte Und Studien, 2003.

Bosworth, C.E. A Note on *Ta`arrub* in Early Islam. *Journal of Semitic Studies* 34, 2 (1989): 355–62.

Bourqia, Rahma and Miller, Susan G., eds. *In the Shadow of the Sultan: Culture, Power, and Politics in Morocco*. Cambridge, MA: Cambridge University Press, 1999.

Brubaker, Rogers. *Nationalism Reframed: Nationhood and the National Question in the New Europe*. Cambridge: Cambridge University Press, 1996.

vom Bruck, Gabriele. "Kinship and the Embodiment of History." *History and Anthropology* 10 (1998): 263–98.

———. "Disputing Descent-Based Authority in the Idiom of Religion: The Case of the Republic of Yemen." *Die Welt des Islams* 38 (1998): 149–91.

Burckhardt, John Lewis. *Travels in Arabia*. London: Frank Cass, 1968.

Burgat, François. "Les élections présidentielles de septembre 1999 au Yémen: du 'pluralisme armé' au retour à la 'norme arabe.'" *Monde arabe Maghreb-Machrek* 168 (Avril–Juin 2000): 67–75.

Burke, Edmund. *Edmund Burke: Selected Writings and Speeches*. Peter J. Stanlis, ed. Garden City, NY: Anchor Books, 1963.

Butler, Judith. *Excitable Speech: A Politics of the Performative*. New York and London: Routledge, 1997.

———. *The Psychic Life of Power: Theories in Subjection*. Stanford: Stanford University Press, 1997.

Butler, Thomas. "Memory: A Mixed Blessing." In *Memory: History, Culture and the Mind*. Oxford: Basil Blackwell. Wolfson College Lectures, 1989.

Calhoun, Craig. "The Problem of Identity in Collective Action." In *Macro-Micro Linkages in Sociology*. Joan Huber, ed. Newbury Park, CA: Sage, 1991. 51–75.

Cannadine, David and Price, Simon. *Rituals of Royalty: Power and Ceremonial in Traditional Society*. Cambridge: Cambridge University Press, 1987.

Carapico, Sheila. "From Ballotbox to Battlefield: The War of the Two `Alis." *Middle East Report*, 190, 25, 1 (September/October 1994): 27.

———. "Yemen between Civility and Civil War." In *Civil Society in the Middle East*. Vol. II. Augustus Richard Norton, ed. Leiden and New York: E.J. Brill, 1996.

——. *Civil Society in Yemen: The Political Economy of Activism in Modern Arabia*. Cambridge: Cambridge University Press, 1998.

Carapico, Sheila, Lisa Wedeen, and Anna Wuerth. "The Death and Life of Jarallah Omar." *Middle East Report Online* (December 31, 2002), http://www.merip. org/mero/mero123102.html.

Carr, E.H. *What is History*. London: Penguin, 1961.

Caruth, Cathy. "Introduction." *American Imago* 48 (1991): 1–12. Special issue: Psychoanalysis, Culture and Trauma.

Chaudhry, Kiren Aziz. "The Price of Wealth: Business and State in Labor Remittance and Oil Economies." *International Organization* 43 (Winter 1989): 101–45.

Cheney, Michael Sheldon. *Big Oil Man From Arabia: From Camel Back to Cadillac—Or the Amazing Adventures of Aramco, the American Overseas Oil Company that is Transforming Saudi Arabia*. New York: Ballantine, 1958.

Cohen, Erik. "Contemporary Tourism—Trends and Challenges: Sustainable Authenticity or Contrived Post-Modernity." In *Changes in Tourism: People, Places, Processes*. Richard Butler and Douglas Pearce, eds. London: Routledge, 1995.

Cohen, Stanley. *States of Denial: Knowing About Atrocities and Suffering*. Cambridge: Polity Press, 2001.

Cohn, Bernard S. "Representing Authority in Victorian India." In *The Invention of Tradition*, Eric Hobsbawm and Terence Ranger, eds. Cambridge: Cambridge University Press, 1984. 165–209.

Cohn, Bernard S. and Nicholas B. Dirks. "Beyond the Fringe: The Nation State, Colonialism, and the Technologies of Power." *Journal of Historical Sociology* 1, 2 (June 1988): 224–9.

Cole, Donald and Soraya, Altorki. "Was Arabia Tribal? A Reinterpretation of the Pre-oil Society." *Journal of South Asian and Middle Eastern Studies* 15, 4 (1992): 71–87.

Comaroff, Jean and John L. Comaroff. "Policing the Occult in the Postcolony: Law and the Regulation of 'Dangerous' Cultural Practices, in South Africa and Elsewhere." Unpublished Paper, 1998.

——. "Occult Economies and the Violence of Abstraction: Notes from the South African Postcolony." *American Ethnologist* 26, 2 (May 1999).

——. "Naturing the Nation: Aliens, Apocalypse and the Postcolonial State." *HAGAR: International Social Science Review* 1, 1 (2000): 7–40.

——. "Policing Culture, Cultural Policing: Law and Social Order in Postcolonial South Africa." *Law and Social Inquiry* 29, 1 [forthcoming 2004].

Committee for Defence of Legitimate Rights in Saudi Arabia (CDLR) 1995. *diwan al-islah* (an anthology of reform poetry).

Cook, Michael. The Historians of Pre-Wahhabi Najd. *Studia Islamica* 76 (1992): 163–76.

——. "The Expansion of the First Saudi State: The Case of Washm." In *The Islamic World*. C.E. Bosworth, Charles Issawi, Roger Savory, and A.L. Udovitch, eds. Essays in Honor of Bernard Lewis. Princeton, NJ: Darwin Press, 1989.

Crawford, M.J. "Wahhabi 'Ulama and the Law 1745–1932 A.D." Unpublished M.A. Thesis, Oxford University, 1980.

——. "Civil War, Foreign Intervention, and the Question of Political Legitimacy: A Nineteenth-Century Sa`udi Qadi's Dilemma." *International Journal of Middle Eastern Studies* 14 (1982): 227–48.

Cronon, William, George Miles, and Jay Gitlin, eds. *Under an Open Sky: Rethinking America's Western Past.* New York: Norton, 1992.

Crystal, Jill. *Oil and Politics in the Gulf: Rulers and Merchants in Kuwait and Qatar.* Cambridge: Cambridge University Press, 1990.

Curtin, Philip D. *Cross-cultural Trade in World History.* Cambridge: Cambridge University Press, 1984.

al-Da`ajani, Ahmad ibn Zayd. *Al-Shaykh muhammad ibn ibrahim al-bawaridi.* Riyadh: al-`Ubaikan, 1419/1998.

Dakhil, Khalid S. "The Social Origins of Wahhabism." Ph.D. diss., University of California, Los Angeles, 1998.

Dakhlia, Jocelyne. "New Approaches in the History of Memory? A French Model." Paper delivered at the Marc Bloch Centre in Berlin, 1996.

Davis, Eric. "Theorizing Statecraft and Social Change in Arab Oil-Producing Countries." In *Statecraft in the Middle East: Oil, Historical Memory and Popular Culture.* Eric Davis and Nicolas Gavrieldes, eds. Miami: Florida International University Press, 1991.

Davis, Eric and Gavrielides, Nicolas, eds. *Statecraft in the Middle East: Oil, Historical Memory and Popular Culture.* Miami: Florida International University Press, 1991.

Davis, Uri. "Conceptions of Citizenship in the Middle East: State, Nation and People." In *Citizenship and the State in the Middle East.* Nils Butenschon, Uri Davis, and Manuel Hassassian, eds. New York: Syracuse University Press, 2000.

Detalle, Renaud. "The Yemeni elections up close." *Middle East Report* 185 (1993): 8–12.

——. Les élections legislatives du 27 Avril 1993. *Monde arabe Maghreb-Machrek* 141 (1993): 3–36.

——. "Esquisse d'une sociologie électorale in Sanaa." In *Sanaa hors les murs: une ville arabe contemporaine.* G. Grandguillaume et al., eds. Tours: URBAMA, Sanna: Centre Français d'Études Yéménites, 1995.

——. "Ajuster sans douleur? La méthode yéménite." In *Monde arabe Maghreb-Machrek,* 155, F. Mermier, ed. (1997): 20–36.

Dickson, Harold R.P. *The Arab of the Desert: A Glimpse into Badawin Life in Kuwait and Sa'udi Arabia.* London: George Allen & Unwin, 1951.

Dirks, Nicholas B. *Castes of Mind.* Princeton: Princeton University Press, 2001.

Doughty, Charles M. *Travels in Arabia Deserta.* 2 vols. Cambridge: Cambridge University Press, 1888.

Doumato, Eleanor Abdella. *Getting God's Ear: Women, Islam, and Healing in Saudi Arabia and the Gulf.* New York: Columbia University Press, 1999.

Dresch, Paul. "Tribal Relations and Political History in Upper Yemen." In *Contemporary Yemen.* B.R. Pridham, ed. London: Croom Helm, 1984.

——. "Keeping the Imam's Peace: A Response to Tribal Disorder in the late 1950's." *Peuples Mediterranéens* 46 (January–March 1989): 77–95.

——. "Guaranty of the Market at Huth," *Arabian Studies*. Vol. 8, R.B. Serjeant and R.L. Bidwell, eds. Cambridge: Cambridge University Press, 1990.

——. "Imams and Tribes: The Writing and Acting of History in Upper Yemen." In *Tribes and State Formation in the Middle East*. Philip S. Khoury and Joseph Kostiner, eds. London: I.B. Tauris, 1991.

——. *Tribes, Government, and History in Yemen*. Oxford: Clarendon Press, 1993.

——. *A History of Modern Yemen*. Cambridge: Cambridge University Press, 2000.

Duguid, Stephen. "A Biographical Approach to the Study of Social Change in the Middle East: Abdullah Altariki as a New Man." *International Journal of Middle Eastern Studies* 1, 3 (1970): 193–220.

al-Duraib, Sa'ud b. Sa'd. *Al-Malik `abd al-`aziz wa-wad qawa`id lil tanzim al-qada'i fi al-mamlaka*. Jidda: Dar al-Matbu'at al-Haditha, 1408/1988.

Eickleman, Dale F. "Musaylima: An Approach to the Social Anthropology of Seventh Century Arabia." *Journal of the Economic and Social History of the Orient* 10, 1 (1967): 17–56.

Elias, Norbert. *Power and Civility: The Civilizing Process*. Vol. 2. New York: Pantheon Books, 1982.

——. *Über den Prozeß der Zivilisation. Soziogenetische und psychogenetische Untersuchungen*. 2 vols. Frankfurt a. M.: Suhrkamp, 1993.

Evans, Richard J. "Epidemics and Revolutions: Cholera in Nineteenth-Century Europe." *Past and Present* 120 (1988): 123–46.

al-Fahd, Nasir ibn Hamad. *Mu`jam ansab al-usar al-mutahaddirah min `ashirat al-asa`idah*. Riyadh: Dar al-Bara, 2000.

Fandy, M. *Saudi Arabia and the Politics of Dissent*. Basingstoke: Macmillan, 1999.

Fanon, Frantz. *The Wretched of the Earth*. New York: Grove Press, [1961] 1963.

Farah, Caesar. *The Sultan's Yemen: Nineteenth-Century Challenges to Ottoman Rule*. London: I.B. Tauris, 2002.

Fattah, Hala. *The Politics of Regional Trade in Iraq, Arabia, and the Gulf, 1745–1900*. Albany: State University of New York Press, 1997.

Ferguson, James and Akhil Gupta. "Space, Identity, and the Politics of Difference." *Cultural Anthropology* 7, 1 (1989).

Field, Michael. *The Merchants: The Big Business Families of Saudi Arabia and the Gulf States*. Woodstock: Overlook Press, 1985.

Foucault, Michel. *Discipline and Punish: The Birth of the Prison*. New York: Vintage Books, 1979.

——. "On Governmentality." In *The Foucault Effect*. Graham Burchell, Colin Gordon, and Peter Miller, eds. Chicago: University of Chicago Press, 1991.

Gambetta, Diego. *The Sicilian Mafia: The Business of Private Protection*. Cambridge and London: Harvard, 1993.

Gavin, R.J. *Aden Under British Rule, 1839–1967*. London: C. Hurst & Company, 1975.

Gauss, Gregory Gause III. "The Idea of Yemeni Unity." *Journal of Arab Affairs* 6, 1 (1987): 55–81.

Geertz, Clifford. "Centers, Kings and Charisma: Reflections on the Symbolics of Power." In *Local Knowledge*. New York: Basic Books, 1983.

Gellner, Ernest. *Nations and Nationalism*. Oxford: Basil Blackwell, 1983.

General Staff, India. *Military Report on the Aden Protectorate* (Simla: Government Press, 1915). In *Military Handbooks of Arabia, 1913–1917*. Vol. 1. London: Archive Editions, 1988.

Getz, Donald. "Event Tourism and the Authenticity Dilemma." In *Global Tourism: The Next Decade*. William Theobald, ed. Oxford: Butterworth–Heinemann, 1996.

ibn Ghannam, Husayn. *Tarikh najd*. 2 vols. Cairo: Mustafa al-Babi al-Halabi, 1949.

Glosemeyer, Iris. "The First Yemeni Parliamentary Elections in 1993: Practising Democracy." *Orient* 34 (1993): 439–51.

Glubb, John B. *War in the Desert*. London: Hodder and Stoughton, 1960.

———. *Muthakkarat glubb pasha*. Trans. by S. Takriti. [A translation of Glubb's *The Changing Scenes of Life: An Autobiography*.] Baghdad: Al-fajr, 1988.

Goody, Jack. *The Domestication of the Savage Mind*. Cambridge: Cambridge University Press, 1977.

Gramsci, Antonio. *Selections from the Prison Notebooks*. Quintin Hoare and Geoffrey Nowell-Smith, eds. London: Lawrence and Wishart, 1971.

Gurung, Ghana, David Simmons, and Patrick Devlin. "The Evolving Role of Tourist Guides: The Nepali Experience." In *Tourism and Indigenous Peoples*. Thomas Hinch and Richard Butler, eds. London: International Thomson Business Press, 1996.

Habermas, Jurgen. *The Structural Transformation of the Public Sphere: An Inquiry into a Category of Bourgeois Society*. Cambridge, MA: MIT Press, [1962] 1996.

Habib, John S. *Ibn Sa'ud's Warriors of Islam: The Ikhwan of Najd and their Role in the Creation of the Sa'udi Kingdom, 1910–1930*. Leiden: E.J. Brill, 1978.

Hacking, Ian. "Memory Sciences, Memory Politics." In *Tense Past: Cultural Essays in Trauma and Memory*. Paul Antze and Michael Lambek, eds. London: Routledge. 1996.

al-Haddad, Yahya ibn `Ali ibn Naji. `Umdat al-qari' fi sirat imam zamanina sayf al-bari'. Western Library of the Great Mosque, San`a', Yemen. Tarikh: 2594.

Hajrah, Hassan Hamza. *Public Land Distribution in Saudi Arabia*. London: Longman, 1982.

Hall, Colin Michael. *Tourism and Politics: Policy, Power and Place*. Chichester: John Wiley and Sons, 1994.

Hall, Stuart. "Introduction: Who Needs Identity?" In *Questions of Cultural Identity*. Stuart Hall and Paul duGay, eds. London: Sage, 1996.

al-Hamad, Turki. "Tawhid al-jazira al-`arabiyya." *al-Mustaqbal al-`Arabi* 93 (1986): 27–40.

Hamilton, R.A.B. "The Social Organization of the Tribes of the Aden Protectorate." *Journal of the Royal Central Asian Society* 30 (1943).

Hamza, Fuad. *Al-Bilad al-arabiyya al-saudiyya* (Saudi Arabia). Riyadh: Maktabat al-Nasr al-Haditha, 1968.

"Handbook of Arabia (1916)." In *Military Handbooks of Arabia, 1913–1917*. Vol. 4. London: Archive Editions, 1988.

Handler, Richard. *Nationalism and the Politics of Culture in Quebec*. Madison and London: University of Wisconsin Press, 1988.

Harik, Iliya. "The Origins of the Arab State System." In *The Foundations of the Arab State*. Ghassan Salame, ed., London: Croom Helm, 1987.

Haykel, Bernard. "Al-Shawkani and the Jurisprudential Unity of Yemen." *Revue du Monde Musulman* 67 (Summer 1993): 53–65.

——. *Order and Righteousness: Muhammad `Ali al-Shawkani and the Nature of the Islamic State in Yemen*. Unpublished D.Phil. Thesis, Oxford, 1997.

Helms, Christine Moss. *The Cohesion of Saudi Arabia*. London: Croom Helm, 1981.

Hitchcock, Michael, Nick Stanley, and King Chung Siu. "The South-east Asian 'living museum' and its Antecedents." In *Tourists and Tourism: Identifying With People and Places*. Simone Abram, Jaqueline Waldren, and Donald McCleod, eds. Oxford: Berg, 1997.

Hobsbawm, Eric. *Nations and Nationalism since 1780*. Cambridge: Cambridge University Press, 1990.

Holden, David. *Farewell to Arabia*. London: Faber, 1966.

Humayd, Muhammad ibn `Abdallah. *Al-Suhub al-wabilah ala dara'h al-hanabilah*. Bakr abu Zayd and `Abd al-Rahman ibn `Uthaymin, eds. 3 vols. Beirut: Mu'assasat al-Risalah, 1996.

Hunter, F.M. *An Account of the British Settlement of Aden in Arabia*. 1877; reprint, London: Frank Cass and Company Limited, 1968.

Hunter, F.M and C.W.H. Sealy. *An Account of the Arab Tribes in the Vicinity of Aden*. Bombay: Government Central Press, 1886.

——. *The Arab Tribes in the Vicinity of Aden*. 1909; reprint, London: Darf Publishers, 1986.

Hutnyk, John. 1999. "Magical Mystery Tourism." In *Travel Worlds: Journeys in Contemporary Cultural Politics*. Raminder Kaur and John Hutnyk, eds. London: Zed Books, 1999.

Ibn Khaldun, A. *The Muqaddimah: An Introduction to History*. Trans. F. Rozenthal. London: Routledge and Kegan Paul, 1967.

Ibrahim, `Abd al-`Aziz `Abd al-Ghani. *Najdiyun wara'a lil hudud. al-`Uqailat wa-dawruhum fi `alaqat najd al-`askariyya wa al-iqtisadiyya bil `iraq wa al-sham wa-misr (m1750–m1950)*. London: al-Saqi, 1991.

Ingrams, Doreen and Leila Ingrams, eds. *Records of Yemen, 1798–1960*. 16 vols. London: Archive Editions, 1993.

Jackson, Robert H. *Quasi-States: Sovereignty, International Relations, and the Third World*. Cambridge: Cambridge University Press, 1990.

Jacob, Harold. *Kings of Arabia*. London: Mills & Boon Limited, 1923.

Jalal, Ayesha. "Conjuring Pakistan: History as Official Imagining." *International Journal of Middle East Studies* 27, 1 (1995): 73–89.

al-Jasir, Hamad. *Madinat al-riyadh `abr atwar al-tarikh*. Riyadh: Dar al-Yamama lil Tiba`a wa al-Nashr, A.H. 1386.

——. *Jamharat ansab al-usar al-mutahaddirah fi najd*. 2 vols. Riyadh: Dar al-Yamama lil Tiba`a wa al-Nashr, n.d.

al-Jirafi, `Abdalla ibn `Abd al-Karim. *Al-Muqtataf min tarikh al-yaman*. Beirut: Manshurat al-`Asr al-Hadith, [1951] 1987.

al-Juhany, Uwaida Metaireek. "The History of Najd Prior to the Wahhabis: A Study of Social, Political and Religious Conditions in Najd During Three Centuries Preceding the Wahhabi Reform Movement." Diss., Washington, 1983.

ibn Jurays, Rashid ibn `Ali. *Muthir al-wajd fi ansab muluk najd.* Muhammad ibn `Umar ibn Aqil, ed., Riyadh: Darart al-Malik `Abd al-`Aziz, 1999.

Kelly, J.B. *Eastern Arabian Frontiers.* London: Faber and Faber, 1964.

al-Khalil, S. *Republic of Fear: The Politics of Modern Iraq.* London: Hutchinson and Radius, 1989.

ibn Khamis, `Abd Allah ibn Muhmmad. *Mu`jam al-yamama.* 2 vols. Riyadh: Matab` al-Farazdaq, 1980.

———. *Tarikh al-yamama.* 7 vols. Riyadh: Matab` al-Farazdaq, 1987.

Kirmayer, Lawrence. "Landscapes of Memory: Trauma, Narrative, and Dissociation." In *Tense Past: Cultural Essays in Trauma and Memory.* Paul Antze and Michael Lambek, eds. London: Routledge. 1996.

Kostiner, Joseph. "On Instruments and Their Designers: The Ikhwan of Najd and the Emergence of the Saudi State." *Middle Eastern Studies* 21, 3 (1985): 298–323.

———. 1990. "Transforming Dualities: Tribe and State Formation in Saudi Arabia." In *Tribes and State Formation in the Middle East,* Philip S. Khoury and Joseph Kostiner, eds. Berkeley: University of California Press, 1990. 226–51.

———. *The Making of Saudi Arabia: 1916–1936.* Oxford: Oxford University Press, 1993.

Kour, Z.H. *The History of Aden, 1839–1872.* London: Frank Cass, 1981.

Lacey, R. *The Kingdom.* London: Hutchinson and Co., 1981.

Lackner, Helen. *A House Built on Sand: A Political Economy of Saudi Arabia.* London: Ithaca Press, 1978.

Laqueur, Thomas. "Introduction." *Representations* 69 (2000): 1–8. Special Issue: Grounds for Remembering.

Larson, Henrietta, Evelyn Knowlton, and Charles Popple. *New Horizons, 1927–1950: History of the Standard Oil Company (New Jersey).* Vol. 3. New York: Harper and Row, 1971.

Lash, S. and J. Urry. *Economies of Sign and Space.* London: Sage Publications, 1994.

Lauren, Paul Gordon. *Power and Prejudice: The Politics and Diplomacy of Racial Discrimination.* Second edition. Boulder: Westview, 1996.

Layoun, Mary. "A Guest at the Wedding." In *Between Woman and Nation.* Caren Kaplan, Norma Alarcon, and Minoo Moallem, eds. Durham: Duke University Press, 1999.

Lebkicker, Roy. *The Work and Life of Aramco Employees.* American Employees Handbook Series, Part II. New York: Aramco, 1950.

Lehmann, Hartmut. "Frömmigkeitsgeschichtliche Auswirkungen der 'Kleinen Eiszeit.' " In *Volksreligiosität in der modernen Sozialgeschichte* (= GG Sonderheft 11). Schieder, Wolfgang, ed. Göttingen: V&R, 1986. 31–50.

Lenczowski, George. *Oil and State in the Middle East.* Ithaca: Cornell University Press, 1960.

Leveau, Remy, Franck Mermier, and Udo Steinbach, eds. *Le Yémen contemporain.* Paris: Éditions Karthala, 1999.

Linz, Juan and Alfred Stepan. *Problems of Democratic Transition and Consolidation.* Baltimore and London: Johns Hopkins University Press, 1996.

Little, Douglas. "Pipeline Politics: American, Tapline, and the Arabs." *Business History Review* 64 (1990): 255–85.

Lloyd, David and Paul Thomas. *Culture and the State.* New York and London: Routledge, 1998.

Long, D. *The Kingdom of Saudi Arabia.* Gainsville: University of Florida Press, 1997.

Lorimer, J.G. *Gazetteer of the Persian Gulf, 'Oman, and Central Arabia.* Calcutta: Indian Government Press (Reprint Shannon/Westmeah: Irish University Press/Gregg International, 1970: 6 vols. in 2 Parts), 1915.

MacCannell, Dean. *The Tourist: A New Theory of the Leisure Class.* Berkeley: University of California Press, 1999.

Makdisi, Ussama. *The Culture of Sectarianism.* Berkeley: University of California Press, 2000.

Mamdani, Mahmood. *Citizen and Subject.* Princeton: Princeton University Press, 1996.

Markell, Patchen. "Making Affect Safe for Democracy? On 'Constitutional Patriotism.'" *Political Theory* 28, 1 (February 2000): 38–63.

McCartney, Laton. *Friends in High Places: The Bechtel Story: The Most Secret Corporation and How it Engineered the World.* New York: Simon and Schuster, 1988.

McLoughlin, L. *Ibn Saud: Founder of a Kingdom.* London: Macmillan, 1993.

Meissner, Jeffrey. "Tribes at the Core: Legitimacy, Structure and Power in Zaydi Yemen." Ph.D. diss., Columbia University, 1987.

Mermier, Franck. "Yemen: l'État face à la démocratie." *Monde arabe Maghreb-Machrek* 155 (1997): 3–5.

———. "L'islam politique au Yémen ou la 'Tradition' contre les traditions?" *Monde arabe Maghreb-Machrek* 155 (1997): 6–19.

Mermier, Franck. "Yémen, les héritages d'une histoire morcelée." In *Le Yémen contemporain.* Remy Leveau, Franck Mermier and Udo Steinbach, eds. Paris: Éditions Karthala, 1999.

Messick, Brinkley. *The Calligraphic State: Textual Domination and History in a Muslim Society.* Berkeley: University of California Press, 1993.

Metcalf, Barbara Daly. *Islamic Revival in British India: Deoband, 1860–1900.* Princeton: Princeton University Press, 1982.

Middleton, Karen. "Circumcision, Death, and Strangers." *Ancestors, Power, and History in Madagascar.* Karen Middleton, ed. Leiden: Brill, 1999.

Midhat Bey, Ali Haydar. *The Life of Midhat Pasha.* London: John Murray, 1903.

Migdal, Joel. *Strong Societies and Weak States: State–Society Relations and State Capabilities in the Third World.* Princeton, NJ: Princeton University Press, 1988.

Mitchell, Timothy. "The Limits of the State: Beyond Statist Approaches and Their Critics." *American Political Science Review* 85, 1 (March 1991): 77–96.

————. "Worlds Apart: An Egyptian Village and the International Tourism Industry." *Middle East Report* 25, 5 (September–October 1995): 8–11.

Moore, Barrington. *Moral Purity and Persecution in History*. Princeton: Princeton University Press, 2000.

Moraru, Christian. "We embraced each other by our names: Levinas, Derrida, and the Ethics of Naming." *Names* 48 (2000): 49–58.

Movement for Islamic Reform in Arabia (MIRA). Communiqué 147. London.

Murphy, Peter. "Tourism and Sustainable Development." In *Global Tourism: The Next Decade*. William Theobald, ed. Oxford: Butterworth–Heinemann, 1996. 274–90.

al-Murtada, Ahmad ibn Yahya. *al-Bahr al-zakhkhar*. 6 vols. San`a': Dar al-Hikmah al-Yamaniyya, 1988.

Musil, Alois. *Northern Najd, a Topographical Itinerary*. Published under the patronage of the Czech Academy of Sciences and Arts and of Charles R. Crane. New York: American Geographical Society, 1928.

al-Mutahhar, `Abd al-Karim ibn Ahmad. *Sirat al-imam yahya bin muhammad hamid al-din*. 2 vols. Muhammad `Isa al-Salihiyyah, ed. Amman: Dar al-Bashir, 1998.

al-Mutawakkil, Muhammad `Abd al Malik. "Al-Shar`iya al-mafquda wa al-shar`iya al-muhtamala." *al-Wahdawi* (October 5, 1999).

Muthana, Muslih Ahmad. "Hunak thalatha milayin marid bi fayrus al-kabid lan yusharik fi al-intikhabat." *al-Wahdawi* (September 21, 1999).

Nakhlah, Muhammad `Arabi. *Tarikh al-ihsa' al-siyasiyya*. Fat al-Salusil, n.d.

al-Naqeeb, Khaldoun Hasan. *Society and State in the Gulf and Arab Peninsula: A Different Perspective*. London: Routledge, 1990.

al-Nasiri, Ahmad ibn Khalid. *Al-`istiqsa lil akhbar dwal al-maghrib al-`aqsa*. 3 vols. Casablanca: Dar al-Kitab, 1997.

Nozick, Robert. *Anarchy, State, and Utopia*. Oxford: Basil Blackwell, 1974.

al-Nuaim, Mishary Abdalrahman. "State Building in a Non-Capitalist Social Formation: The Dialectics of Two Modes of Production and the Role of the Merchant Class, Saudi Arabia, 1902–1932." Ph.D. diss., UCLA, 1987.

Okruhlik, Gwenn. "Bringing the Peninsula in From the Periphery: From Imagined Scholarship to Gendered Discourse." *Middle East Report* 27, 204 (July–September 1997): 36–7.

————. "Image, Imagination and Place: The Political Economy of Tourism in Saudi Arabia." In *Iran, Iraq and the Gulf States*. Joseph Kechichian, ed. New York: St. Martin's Press, 2001. 191–226.

Ossman, Susan. "Boom Box in Ouarzazate: The Search for the Similarly Strange." *Middle East Report* 25, 5 (September–October 1995): 12–14.

Palgrave, William G. *Narrative of a Year's Journey through Central and Eastern Arabia (1862–63)*. 2 vols. London: Macmillan, 1865.

Parssinen, Jon, and Kaizir Talib, "A Traditional Community and Modernization: Saudi Camp, Dhahran." *Journal of Architectural Education* 35 (1982): 14–17.

Pearce, Philip L. *The Social Psychology of Tourist Behavior*. Oxford: Pergamon Press, 1982.

Peskes, Esther. *Muhammad ibn ʿAbdalwahhab (1703–92) im Widerstreit. Untersuchungen zuz Rekonstruktion der Frühgeschichte der Wahhabiya*. Beirut: Steiner, 1993.

Peters, F.E. *The Hajj. The Muslim Pilgrimage to Mecca and the Holy Places*. Princeton: Princeton University Press, 1994.

Peters, Rudolph. "*Idjtihad* and *Taqlid* in 18th and 19th Century Islam." *Welt des Islams*, 20, 3/4 (1980): 131–45.

Peterson, J.E. "The Arabian Peninsula in Modern Times: A Historiographical Survey." *American Historical Review* 96, 5 (1991): 1435–49.

Philby, Harry St. John. *Arabia of the Wahhabis*. London: Constable & Co., 1928.

———. *The Empty Quarter: Being a Description of the Great South Desert of Arabia Known as Rubʿ al Khali*. London: Constable & Co., 1933.

———. *Saudi Arabia*. London: Benn, 1955.

Phillips, Anne. *The Enigma of Colonialism: British Policy in West Africa*. London: James Currey, 1989.

Phillips, Wendell. *Qataban and Sheba*. New York: Harcourt Brace, 1955.

Pincus, Steven. "Nationalism, Universal Monarchy, and the Glorious Revolution." In *State/Culture: State-Formation after the Cultural Turn*. George Steinmetz, ed. Ithaca: Cornell University Press, 1999. 182–210.

Pratt, Mary Louise. *Imperial Eyes: Travel Writing and Transculturation*. New York: Routledge, 1992.

Przeworski, Adam. *Democracy and the Market: Political and Economic Reforms in Eastern Europe and Latin America*. Cambridge: Cambridge University Press, 1991.

al-Qadi, Muhammad ibn ʿUthman ibn Salih. *Rawdat al-nazirin ʿan maʾathirʿ ʿulamaʾ najd wa-hawadith al-sinin*. Vol. 1, Cairo: al-Halabi, 1403/1983. Vol. 2, Cairo: al-Halabi, 1400/1980.

ibn Qasim, al-ʿAsimi al-Qahtani al-Najdi. *al-Durar al-saniyya fi al-ajwiba al-najdiya*. 12 vols. Beirut: Matabiʿ al-Maktab al-Islami, 1385/1965.

ibn Qasim, ʿAbd al-Rahman ibn Muhammad, ed. *al-Durar al-saniyya fi al-ajwiba al-najdiyya*. 16 vols., n.p., 1996–99.

al-Rasheed, Madawi. *Politics in an Arabian Oasis: The Rashidi Tribal Dynasty*. London: I.B. Tauris. 1991.

———. "Durable and Non-Durable Dynasties." *British Society for Middle Eastern Studies Bulletin* 19, 2 (1992): 144–58.

al-Rasheed, Madawi. "God, the King and the Nation: Political Rhetoric in Saudi Arabia in the 1990s." *Middle East Journal* 50, 3 (1996): 359–71.

———. "Saudi Arabia's Islamic Opposition," *Current History* 95, 597 (1996): 16–22.

———. "Le couronne et le turban: l'etat saoudien a la rechereche d'une nouvelle legitimite." In *Les Etats arabes face a la contestation islamiste*. Kudmani-Darwish, B. and Chartouni-Dubarry, M. eds. Paris: Armand Colin, 1997.

———. "Political legitimacy and the Production of History: The Case of Saudi Arabia." In *New Frontiers in Middle East Security*. L. Martin, ed. New York: St. Martin's Press, 1999. 25–46.

———. "Political Legitimacy and the Production of History: The Case of Saudi Arabia." In *New Frontiers in Middle East Security*. L. Martin, ed. New York: St. Martin's Press, 1999.

————. *A History of Saudi Arabia*. Cambridge: Cambridge University Press, 2002.

al-Rashid, I. *The Struggle Between the Two Princes: The Kingdom of Saudi Arabia in the Final Days of Ibn Saud*. Salisbury, NC: Documentary Publications, 1985.

ibn Rashid, Dari ibn Fuhayd. *Nubtha tarikhiyya `an najd*. Hamad al-Jasir, ed. Riyadh: Dar al-Yamama lil Tiba`a wa al-Nashr, 1966.

Raunkiaer, Barclay. *Through Wahhabiland on Camelback*. New York: Frederick A. Praeger, 1969.

Rihani, Ameen. *Ibn Saud of Arabia*. London: Constable & Co., 1928.

————. *Najd al-hadith wa mulhaqatihi*. Beirut: Dar Rihani lil Tiba`a wa al-Nashr, 1954.

————. *Ibn Sa'oud of Arabia. His People and His Land*. Delmar, NY: Caravan (Original edition London: Constable & Co., 1928), 1983.

Rogan, Eugene. *Frontier of the State in the Ottoman Empire: Transjordan, 1850–1921*. Cambridge: Cambridge University Press, 1999.

Rosenfeld, Henry L. "A Military-Occupational Specialization of the Kin Among the Pastoral Bedouins: A Key to the Process of Caste Formation in the Arabian Desert." Ph.D. diss., Columbia University, 1951.

Rubin, Uri. "Muhammad's Curse of Mudar and the Blockade of Mecca." *Journal of the Economic and Social History of the Orient* 31, 3 (1988): 249–64.

Rumaihi, Mohamed G. "The Mode of Production in the Arab Gulf before the Discovery of Oil." In *Social and Economic Development in the Arab Gulf*. Niblock, Tim, ed. London: Croom Helm, 1980, 49–60.

Rustow, Dankwart A. "Transitions to Democracy: Toward a Dynamic Model." *Comparative Politics* 2, 3 (April 1970): 337–63.

Salame, Ghassan. " 'Strong' and 'Weak' States, a Qualified Return to the *Muqadimmah*." In *The Foundations of the Arab State*, Ghassan Salame, ed. London: Croom Helm, 1987, 205–40.

Salim, Sayyid Mustafa. *Watha'iq yamaniyya*. Cairo: al-Matba'a al-Fanniyya, 1985.

Salman, Muhammad ibn `Abd Allah. *Al-Ahwal al-siyasiyya fi al-qasim fi `ahd al-dawlah al-su`udiyya al-thaniya: 1238–1309/1823–1891*. N.p., 1999.

Salzman, Philip C. "Political Organization Among Nomadic People." *Proceeding of the American Philosophical Society* 3, 2 (1967): 115–31.

al-Saqqaf, Abu Bakr. *Wahdat al-yamaniyya: min al-indimaj al-fawri ila isti`mar al-dakhili*. London: Bareed al-Janub.

————. "The Yemeni Unity: Crisis in Integration." In *Le Yémen contemporain*. Remy Leveau, Franck Mermier, and Udo Steinbach, eds. Paris: Éditions Karthala, 1999. [Note: transliterated as Abou Bakr in this work.]

al-Saqqaf, Muhammad `Ali. "Al-Hanin ila shumuliyya." *al-Ayyam* (September 27, 1999).

Schulze, Reinhard. *Islamischer Internationalismus im 20. Jahrhundert: Untersuchungen zur Geschichte der Islamischen Weltliga*. Leiden: Brill, 1990.

Schwedler, Jillian. "Democratization in the Arab World? Yemen's Aborted Opening." *Journal of Democracy* 13, 4 (2002): 48–55.

Scott, David. "Colonial Governmentality," *Social Text* 43 (Fall 1995): 191–220.

Scott, James C. *Domination and the Arts of Resistance: Hidden Transcripts*. New Haven: Yale University Press, 1990.

Seccombe, Ian "A Disgrace to American Enterprise: Italian Labour and the Arabian American Oil Company in Saudi Arabia 1944–56." *Immigrants and Minorities* 5 (1986): 233–57.

Seccombe, Ian and Richard Lawless. *Work Camps and Company Towns: Settlement Patterns and the Gulf Oil Industry.* Durham: University of Durham, 1987.

Serjeant, Robert. "South Arabia," in *Commoners, Climbers and Notables.* C.A.O. van Nieuwenhuijze, ed. Leiden: Brill, 1977.

——. "The Yemeni Poet Al-Zubayri and his Polemic against the Zaydi Imams." *Arabian Studies* 5 (1979): 87–130.

Sewell, William H., Jr. "Three Temporalities: Toward an Eventful Sociology." In *The Historic Turn in the Human Sciences.* Terrence J. McDonald, ed. Ann Arbor: University of Michigan Press, 1997.

Shaafy, M.S. El-. The Military Organization of the First Saudi State. *Annal of Leeds University Oriental Society* 7 (1969–73): 61–74.

Shafir, Gershom. "Introduction: The Evolving Tradition of Citizenship." In *The Citizenship Debates: A Reader.* Minneapolis: University of Minnesota Press, 1998.

Sharara, Waddah. *Al-`ahl wa'l-ghanima.* Beirut: N.p., 1981.

al-Shawkani, Muhammad ibn `Ali. *Al-Sayl al-Jarrar.* Vol. 3. Muhammad Subhi ibn Hasan Hallaq, ed. Damascus: Dar Ibn al-Kathir, 2000.

al-Shaykh, `Abd al-Latif ibn `Abd al-Rahman. *Misbah al-zalam fi al-radd `ala man kathab `ala al-shaykh al-imam wa nasabahu ila takfir ahl al-iman w'l-islam.* Cairo: N.p., 1945.

——. *Minhaj al-ta'sis wa al-taqdis fi kashf shubuhat Dawud ibn Jarjis.* Riyadh: Dar al-Hidayah, 1987.

——. *Tuhfat al-talib wa al-jalis fi kashf shubah dawud ibn jarjis.* `Abd al-Salam Al `Abd al-Karim, ed. Riyadh: Dar al-`Asimah, 1990.

——. `*Uyun al-rasa'il wa al-ajwibah `ala al masa'il.* 2 vols. Husayn Muhammad Bawa, ed. Riyadh: Maktabat al-Rushd, 2000.

al-Shaykh, `Abd al-Rahman ibn `Abd al-Latif. *Mashahir `ulama najd wa ghayrihim.* Riyadh: Dar al-Yamama, 1974.

al-Shaykh, `Abd al-Rahman ibn Hasan. *Al-qawl al-fasl al-nafis fi al-radd `ala al-muftri dawud ibn jarjis.* Riyadh: Dar al-Hidayah, 1985.

——. *Al-matlab al-hamid fi biyan maqasid al-tawhid.* Riyadh: Dar al-Hidayah, 1991.

al-Shaykh, Ishaq ibn 'Abd al-Rahman. *Hukm takfir al-mu`ayyan wa al-farq bayna qiam al-hujjah wa fahm al-hujjah.* Riyadh: Dar al-Hidayah, 1988.

——. `*Idah al-mahajjah wa al-sabil wa `iqamat al-hujjah wa al-dalil `ala man ajaz al-`iqamah bayn ahl al-shirk wa al-t`atil.* Riyadh: Maktabat al-Hidayah, 1995.

al-Shaykh, Sulayman ibn `Abd Allah. *Majmu` al-rasa'il.* Al-Walid ibn Abd al-Rahman Al Furayyan, eds. Makkah: Dar `Alam al-Fawa'id, 2000.

Sihman, Sulayman ibn. *Irshad al-talib ila ahamm al-matalib.* Cairo: Mitba`at al-Manar, A.H. 1340.

——. *Minhaj ahl al-haqq wa al-`itidal fi mukhalaft ahl al-jahil wa al-ibtida`.* Cairo: Mitba`at al-Manar, A.H. 1340.

Simpson, Christopher. *The Splendid Blond Beast: Money, Law, and Genocide in the Twentieth Century.* New York: Grove Press, 1993.

Sinclair, Reginald W., ed. *Documents on the History of Southwest Arabia.* 2 vols. Salisbury, NC: Documentary Publications, 1976.

Sirriyeh, Elizabeth. "Wahhabis, Unbelievers and the Problem of Exclusivism." *British Society for Middle Eastern Studies Bulletin* 16, 2 (1989): 123–32.

Slyomovics, Susan. *The Object of Memory: Arab and Jew Narrate the Palestinian Village.* Philadelphia: University of Pennsylvania Press, 1998.

———. "Tourist Containment." *Middle East Report* 25, 5 (September–October 1995): 6.

Smith, Tony. *America's Mission: The United States and the Worldwide Struggle for Democracy in the Twentieth Century.* Princeton: Princeton University Press, 1994.

Snouck Hurgronje, C. *Mekka.* 2 vols. Haag: Martinus Nijhoff, 1888–89.

al-Sowayan, Saad Abdullah. *Nabati Poetry.* Berkeley: University of California Press, 1985.

———. *Al-shi`r al-nabati.* Beirut: Dar al-Saqi, 2000.

Stegner, Wallace. *Discovery! The Search for Arabian Oil.* Beirut: Middle East Export Press, 1971.

Steinberg, Guido. "Religion und Staat in Saudi-Arabien. Eine Sozialgeschichte der wahhabitischen Gelehrten 1912–1953." Unpublished Ph.D. diss., Free University of Berlin, 2000.

———. "Material Conditions, Knowledge and Trade in Central Arabia during the 19th and early 20th Centuries." Paper presented at the Second Mediterranean Social and Political Research Meeting, March 2001, European University Institute, Florence.

———. *Religion und Staat in Saudi-Arabien. Die wahhabitischen Gelehrten 1902–1953.* Würzburg: Ergon, 2002.

Stiftl, Ludwig. "Politischer Islam und Pluralismus: Theoretische und Empirische Studie am Beispiel des Jemen." Ph.D. diss., Free University of Berlin, 1998.

Stoler, Ann and Karen Strassler. "Castings for the Colonial: Memory Work in 'New Order' Java." *Comparative Study of Society and History* 42 (2000).

Stookey, Robert. *Yemen: The Politics of the Yemen Arab Republic.* Boulder: Westview Press, 1978.

al-Suwayda`,`Abd al-Rahman ibn Zayd. *Najd Fi al-ams al-qarib. Suwar wa malamih min utur al-hayat al-sa'ida qabla thalathina` amman.* Riyadh: Dar al-`Ulum, 1403/1983.

Swedenburg, Ted. *Memories of Revolt: The 1936–1939 Rebellion and the Palestinian National Past.* Minneapolis: University of Minnesota Press, 1995.

Sweet, L.E. "Camel Raiding of North Arabian Bedouin." *American Anthropologist* 67, 5 part 1 (1965): 1132–50.

Thatcher, Leland, Meyer Rubin, and Glen F. Brown. *Dating Desert Water Science* 134 (1961): 105–6.

Tilly, Charles. "War Making and State Making as Organized Crime." In *Bringing The State Back In.* Cambridge: Cambridge University Press, 1985.

Trench, Richard, ed. *Gazetteer of Arabian Tribes.* 18 vols. London: Archive Editions, 1996.

Troeller, Gary. *The Birth of Saudi Arabia: Britain and the Rise of the House of Saud*. London: Frank Cass, 1976.

Tucker, Hazel. "Tourism and the Ideal Village." In *Tourists and Tourism: Identifying With People and Places*. Simone Abram, Jaqueline Waldren, and Donald McCleod, eds. Oxford: Berg, 1997.

al-'Ubayyid, Muhammad 'Ali. *Al-najm al-lami` lil Nawadir jami`*. MS, n.p., n.d.

'Umari, Salih Al Muhammad. *`Ulama al-salim wa talamithatihim wa `ulama al-qasim*. n.p., 1985.

Urry, John. "The 'Consumption' of Tourism." *Sociology* 24, 1 (1990): 23–35.

———. *The Tourist Gaze: Leisure and Travel in Contemporary Societies*. London: Sage, 2001.

al-'Utaybi, Ibrahim ibn 'Awad al-Thi`li. *Tanzimat al-dawla fi `ahd al-malik `abd al-`aziz: 1343–1373/1924–1053*. al-Riyadh: Maktabat al-'Ubaykan, 1993.

al-'Uthaymin, 'Abd Allah al-Salih. *Buhuth wa ta`liqat fi tarikh al-mamlaka al-`arabiyya al-su`udiyya*. N.p., 1984.

———. *Nash'at imarat al-rashid*. N.p., 1991.

———. *Tarikh al-mamlaka al-arabiyya al-saudiyya* Riyadh: Wizarat al-Ma'arif, 1993.

———. *Tarikh al-mamlaka al-arabiyya al-saudiyya*. Vol. 2. Riyadh, Wizarat al-Ma'arif, 1995.

Vidal, Frederico S. *The Oasis of Al-Hasa*. New York: Aramco, 1955.

Vogel, Frank E. *Islamic Law and Legal System: Studies of Saudi Arabia* (Diss. Harvard 1993). Ann Arbor: University of Michigan Press, 1997.

———. *Islamic Law and Legal System: Studies of Saudi Arabia*. Leiden: Brill, 2000.

Von Eschen, Penny M. *Race Against Empire: Black Americans and Anticolonialism 1937–1957*. Ithaca: Cornell University Press, 1997.

Wahba, Hafiz. *Jazirat al-`arab Fi al-qarn al-`shirin*. N.P., 1935.

———. *Arabian Days*. London: Arthur Barker Ltd., 1964.

al-Wasi`i, 'Abd al-Wasi`. *Tarikh al-yaman*. San`a': Maktabat al-Yaman al-Kubra, 1990.

Waterfield, Gordon. *Sultans of Aden*. London: John Murray, 1968.

Wedeen, Lisa. *Ambiguities of Domination: Politics, Rhetoric, and Symbols in Contemporary Syria*. Chicago: University of Chicago Press, 1999.

Wenner, Manfred. *Modern Yemen, 1918–1966*. Baltimore: Johns Hopkins University Press, 1967.

West, Michael O. "The Tuskegee Model of Development in Africa: Another Dimension of the African/African-American Connection." *Diplomatic History* 16 (1992): 371–88.

Williamson, John Frederick. "A Political History of the Shammar Jarba Tribe of Al-Jazirah: 1800–1958." Ph.D. diss., Indiana University, 1975.

Winder, R. Bayly. *Saudi Arabia in the Nineteenth Century*. London: Macmillan/ St. Martin's Press, 1965.

Yoneyama, Lisa. *Hiroshima Traces: Time, Space, and the Dialectics of Memory*. Berkeley: University of California Press, 1999.

Za`arir, Muhammad. *Imarat al-rashid fi ha'il*. [Amman] Bisan lil Nashr wa al-Tawzi`, 1995.

al-Za'arir, Muhammad. *Imarat al rashid fi ha'il.* N.p.: Birsan, 1997.

al-Zabarah, Muhammad ibn Muhammd. *'A'immat al-yaman bil qarn al-rabi' 'ashr.* 2 vols. Cairo: al-Matba'ah al-Salafiyyah, 1955.

——. *Nuzhat al-nazr fi rijal al-qarn al-rabi' 'ashr.* San'a': Markaz al-Dirasat wa al-Abhath al-Yamaniyyah, 1979.

Zdanowski, Jerzy. "Military Organization of the Wahhabi Amirates (1750–1932)." *New Arabian Studies* 2 (1994): 130–9.

Zeghal, Malika. *Gardiens de l'Islam: Les oulémas d'al-Azhar dans l'Egypte contemporaine,* Paris: Presses de Sciences Po, 1996.

Zerubavel, Yael. "New Beginning, Old Past: The Collective Memory of Pioneering in Israeli Culture." In *New Perspectives on Israeli History: The Early Years of the State.* Laurence J. Silberstein, ed. New York: New York University Press, 1991.

al-Zirkili, K. *Shibh al-jazira fi ahd al-malik 'abd al-'aziz.* First edition, 4 vols. Beirut: Dar al-Qalam, 1970.

Saudi Official Publications

Saudi Arabia 1996. Ministry of Information. Foreign Information. *The Pictorial Book of King Abd al-Aziz.* Riyadh.

Saudi Arabia 1997. Ministry of Education. *Al-Masmak Museum.* Riyadh.

Saudi Arabia 1998. Ministry of Information. *A Brief Account of the Life of King Abd al-Aziz.* Riyadh.

Saudi Arabia 1999. *Directory of the Centennial Celebration.* Conference of Saudi Arabia in 100 Years.

Robert Vitalis
Department of Political Science
University of Pennsylvania

Archives and Special collections

Istanbul Turkey
  Basbakarlik Osmanli Arsivi Prime Ministers' Archives.
London, England
  British Library, India Office Records, Aden Residency Records, Public Records Office, Colonial Office Records.
Princeton, New Jersey
  Mudd Library, Princeton, University, William Alfred Eddy Papers.

Sana, Yemen
  National Center for Archives, Sayun Branch
  Western Library of the Great Mosque.
Washington, DC
  Georgetown University Library, Special Collections Division, William E. Mulligan Papers.
  National Archives and Record Administration, General Records of the Department of State, Record Group 59, 1945–49 and 1950–54.

Index